AMERICAN AUTHORS SERIES

GENERAL EDITOR

STANLEY T. WILLIAMS

THE HAFNER LIBRARY OF CLASSICS

[Number Twenty: COTTON MATHER]

SELECTIONS FROM

COTTON MATHER

EDITED WITH AN INTRODUCTION AND NOTES BY

KENNETH B. MURDOCK

HAFNER PRESS
NEW YORK

Reprinted by Arrangement

Published by
Hafner Press
A Division of Macmillan Publishing Co., Inc.
866 Third Avenue
New York, N.Y. 10022

Library of Congress Catalog Card Number:

60-11056

Printed in U.S.A. by
NOBLE OFFSET PRINTERS, INC.
New York, N.Y. 10003

AMERICAN AUTHORS SERIES

The chief purposes of the present series of volumes are two. The first is to provide for college students, teachers, and general readers authentic texts, with explanatory and critical commentary, of books in American literature unexploited but secure in reputation. Such a book is *Wieland*, by Charles Brockden Brown. The second purpose is to furnish complete texts of individual writers rather than selections from them. An illustration of this principle may be observed in *The Connecticut Wits*. It will not invariably be possible to include all the writing of an author, or even all of a particular book, but enough material will always be given to afford the reader an opportunity to know the writer thoroughly, rather than to encounter slight portions of his work.

Since the second aim of the series is, within given limits, completeness, the emphasis will be upon the text of a book rather than upon annotation or critical apparatus. Aside from footnotes essential to an understanding of the text, and a brief selected bibliography, editorial comment, for reasons of space, will be limited to a comprehensive introduction. Early texts will be reproduced, so far as practicable for their study in college classes, with the original spelling and punctuation.

The American Authors Series will also include texts of the standard writers of our literature.

S. T. W.

CONTENTS

Introduction:

    I. Cotton Mather.. ix

    II. The Scholar and the Man of Letters................. xxv

    III. The *Magnalia Christi Americana*................... xl

    IV. *The Christian Philosopher*........................ xlviii

    V. The *Political Fables*.............................. liv

    VI. *A Letter to Dr. Woodward*......................... lvi

Note on the Text.. lix

Selected Reading List................................... lxi

Magnalia Christi Americana

    A General Introduction............................... 1

    Book II: *Ecclesiarum Clypei*........................ 37

        I. *Galeacius Secundus.* The Life of William Bradford... 40

        II. Successors...................................... 51

        III. *Patres Conscripti;* or, Assistents............ 56

        IV. *Nehemias Americanus.* The Life of John Winthrop... 58

        V. Successors....................................... 84

        Pater Patriæ. The Life of Simon Bradstreet....... 97

        VI. *Viri Animati;* or, Assistants................. 103

        VII. *Publicola Christianus.* The Life of Edward Hopkins... 110

        VIII. Successors................................... 119

        IX. *Humilitas Honorata.* The Life of Theophilus Eaton... 120

        X. Successors....................................... 132

        XI. *Hermes Christianus.* The Life of John Winthrop... 135

        XII. Assistents..................................... 145

    The Life of Sir William Phips....................... 149

Selections from *The Christian Philosopher*............. 285

    The Introduction.................................... 286

    Essay XXIII. Of the Earth.......................... 293

    Essay XXIV. Of Magnetism........................... 302

    Essay XXV. Of Minerals............................. 317

Essay XXVI. Of the Vegetables........................ 324
Essay XXXII. Of Man............................. 349

Political Fables
    I. The New Settlement of the Birds in New England.... 363
    II. The Elephant's Case a Little Stated................ 365
    III. Mercury's Negotiation........................... 366
A Letter to Dr. Woodward............................... 373

INTRODUCTION

I

Cotton Mather

THE story of Cotton Mather's life has been often told. There are many brief sketches of his career, and two full-length biographies. One of these, Barrett Wendell's *Cotton Mather*, is so excellent a study of its difficult subject as to make quite superfluous any attempt to rewrite the tale. For this reason nothing more is needed here than a very short sketch of Mather's life and an indication of his chief traits, with the briefest of comments on those phases of his activity which are most often misunderstood and those which serve most definitely to shed light on his historical position in our literature.

Thus superficially considered, his life was not eventful. Born in Boston, March 12, 1663, he early showed himself precocious, and when he was twelve he could not only write and read Latin but speak it, had read most of the New Testament in Greek, and had made some progress in the study of Hebrew. With these attainments he was admitted to Harvard. There he suffered somewhat at the hands of certain fellow students who practiced what we should call "hazing," but in spite of such difficulties he was thoroughly at home wherever books were concerned and graduated triumphantly in 1678. In boyhood he stammered badly, and, feeling that this handicap unfitted him for the ministry, he planned

to train himself as a physician. He overcame, however, his defects in speech, and promptly aspired
again toward the pulpit. In 1680 he preached several
sermons, and, in the next year, he took his degree
of Master of Arts at Harvard. Thus at eighteen,
he stood forth as a full-fledged candidate for the
ministry. Young as he was, he was promptly offered
a pastorate in New Haven, but he preferred to continue as an assistant preacher at the Second Church
in Boston, where he had already served in this capacity for a year. Early in 1683 his congregation called
him to be regularly ordained as one of its two ministers. He hesitated in accepting, the offer was
repeated, and, finally, in May, 1685, he was formally
installed as his father's colleague at the Second Church.
There he remained until his death, February 13, 1728,
and the story of his professional career is simply
that of a devoted minister of one of the two or three
largest churches in the American colonies.

He was married, in 1686, to Abigail Phillips, the
daughter of a prominent citizen and politician of
Charlestown. She bore to him nine children, but
five of these died early. She herself lived only until
November, 1702, and in the next year Cotton Mather
married again. His second wife was Elizabeth Hubbard, a widow. By her he had six children, but only
two of them lived beyond childhood. Their mother
died in 1713, and in 1715 Mather married Lydia
George, widow of John George of Boston. With
her came tragedy, for she went insane, and to the
severe trials thus brought to her husband was added
the torment caused him by a scapegrace son. Lydia
Mather would not allow his favorite daughter to live
at home with him; three of his sisters were widowed

and often in need of his aid; he was burdened by financial worries; his father died in 1723, and when, in 1728, he himself gave up a life that had been for years sorely checkered by affliction, of all the fifteen children whom he had loved, there remained alive but two.

Yet, in spite of bereavements, and in spite of the duties of his pastorate, he studied and wrote constantly. Comment on the number of his writings, and on their nature, belongs elsewhere; it is sufficient to remember that he was throughout his life tireless as a man of letters. As a minister, too, he showed enormous energy. To think of him merely as a pastor in a colonial town, concerned simply with preaching and the routine duties of his office, is to misread the record. The ministry, as he conceived it, was a career of leadership. In it a man must not only toil to elevate his people spiritually but also strive to educate them otherwise, guide them in every detail of life, chasten them for their shortcomings, and inspire them to interest in all that might conduce to the service of God. His concrete achievements in organizing societies for various good purposes, and in countless other forms of public service, are too many to list here. Cotton Mather remains to-day, as he was in his own time, a marvel of industry, a man of endless vigor and extraordinarily varied interests and accomplishments. Whatever one may think of his character, or his deeds in this or that specific instance, his life as a whole was devoted to the pursuit of high ideals and to the doing of good works.

His family background and the environment of his life cannot be left out of consideration even in the most cursory study. He was the eldest child of Increase Mather, who was, until 1701, the foremost divine of New England, its most prolific and widely read man of letters, and for many years a power in affairs of state. He was President of Harvard College from 1685 until 1701. From 1688 to 1692 he served as the colonists' representative at the court of England. With the beginning of the new century, he retired in many ways from public affairs, except where the church was concerned, but until the day of his death in 1723 he was a recognized leader of his generation, and one whom even his erstwhile enemies came to respect. Throughout his life Cotton Mather was not only a devoted son to him but an ardent co-laborer in his church and in the other thronging interests of his busy years. Nor was he the only great figure whose achievements might nourish Cotton Mather's family pride. Increase Mather's father, and the grandfather of Cotton, was Richard Mather. Though he died in 1669, when his eldest grandson was but a child, his reputation, his books, and the results of his labors in establishing New England Congregationalism, lived after him. Cotton Mather's other grandfather, also, was renowned among the founders of New England. He was John Cotton, one of the most deservedly famous of the divines of early Boston. Few New Englanders could boast of such an ancestral tradition of godliness and service as that which Cotton Mather inherited, and few New Englanders accepted more proudly than he the task of keeping undimmed the brightness of a family name.

His relation to Richard Mather and John Cotton, and his devotion to his father, influenced him greatly.

His grandfathers had been pioneers in New England Puritanism, and, as a matter of course, he respected what they had worked to establish. His father, "the greatest native Puritan," carried on the tradition of those who had founded New England, inspired by the vision of making it a place where purity of worship and righteousness of life should be valued above all else. Moreover, because Increase Mather, in his own day and generation, forged head and shoulders above his contemporaries in almost everything he undertook, his son, working by his side, longed that he, too, might become great and win victories for the right. Quite naturally Cotton Mather, sure that his progenitors had been prophets and saints, dreamed that he, in turn might achieve sainthood and the dignities that were theirs. Who could have a better claim than he to be God's chosen champion in his generation? There was stimulus in such thoughts as these, and to them Cotton Mather undoubtedly owed much of his tireless zeal.

At the same time, his pride of birth could handicap as well as inspire. All too easily it led him to vanity, fostered by admiring friends who saw in his obvious talents proof that in him the virtues of his ancestors lived again. All too easily his close association with his father's successes made him ambitious for himself. If he was intemperate in his denunciation of his foes, if he was too eager for controversy with those who challenged his opinions, is it surprising? He believed that he, by right of birth and experience, could speak as one having authority. What wonder if he was often dictatorial? What wonder if his attitude toward others was too frequently one of jealous rivalry? A man temperamentally

more stable might have saved himself from such
shortcomings; but Cotton Mather was by nature
impulsive, nervously sensitive, and given to excessive introspection, and he was not able to keep a
due sense of proportion in matters which concerned
his pride.

His sense of the nobility of his name worked to
his disadvantage in still another way, for inevitably
he came to revere too emotionally all that his progenitors had revered. This would have been well
enough, had he lived in their times, but in his day
the first enthusiasm of Puritan New England was
waning fast. Men could not now recapture the full
zeal of their ancestors. Congregationalism still flourished, to be sure, but too often its ministers expounded
the letter rather than the spirit. The churches were
still crowded, but many who sat there each Sabbath-
day were far less concerned with worship than with
the week's successes in trade. But nothing save the
old ideal of religion as an all-embracing passion, nothing save the ardor of a John Cotton, could satisfy
Cotton Mather. Thus he was apart from his times,
not truly representative of them. His deep piety
expressed itself only too often, therefore, in querulous
denunciations of the age. His intense religious fervor
produced at times almost hysterical excesses of speech
and act. He knew how his forefathers had fasted
and prayed, and he strove to outdo them, in a rather
too conscious effort to prove that in him the fire burned
as brightly as in the saints of the past. And, like many
an admirer of bygone greatness, he suffered from the
short-sighted criticism of men who saw in him only a
striving to keep alive the ideas, manners, and thought
of an older time. Probably he realized all this but

he would not give up one iota of his faith, or fail
to fight for its public acceptance. So he became
more dogmatic; so bitterness more than once crept
into his words. Perhaps he should be blamed, but
there is real human tragedy in his case. He battled
valiantly for an ideal which was no less worthy because it could no longer command the colonists'
allegiance. He was defeated, not because he was
weak, but because his attempt to hold men fast to
the religious fervor of their fathers was by changing conditions foredoomed to fail.

Unfortunately later criticism of him has too often
exaggerated his shortcomings, and proved forgetful
of his virtues. For example, every one knows that
in popular tradition he appears as the bloodthirsty
persecutor responsible in large measure for the exe-
cutions of the New England witches. Yet in the
light of sober history, this is untrue. His writings
on witchcraft, and the contemporary records, prove
him to have been not less but more humane than
his contemporaries. Scholars have demonstrated
that his advice to the witch judges was always that
they should be more cautious in accepting evidence
against those who were haled before them. His
point of view was consistently that of a man as eager
to spare the innocent as to condemn the guilty. Longfellow makes him say:

> "Be careful. Carry the knife with such exactness,
> That on one side no innocent blood be shed
> By too excessive zeal, and, on the other
> No shelter given to any work of darkness."

Such lines create a truthful picture of his attitude.
The spectral Cotton Mather of the myth, thirsty

for blood and stirring up the people to deeds of violence, vanishes before the facts.

Indeed, the whole history of the Salem witch trials of 1692 is far less important in a study of Cotton Mather than most accounts of him lead one to suppose. To be sure, he was deeply interested in witchcraft, but this has no importance except as showing that he, like the vast majority of educated men of his day, physicians, scholars, divines, and scientists, believed that witches existed, and that it was the duty of the historian and the student to investigate and record their deeds. He wrote several books with this in mind, but they form only a tiny part of his whole literary production, and this subject was but one among the many he discussed in print. Often, however, one finds selections from the writings of Cotton Mather concerned wholly or in large part with his comments on witchcraft, and this has resulted in a belief that those comments are especially characteristic of him as a man and author. One needs no more than a glance at a bibliography of his publications to see how baseless is such a belief.

Nor is it true that Cotton Mather's interest in witchcraft was the cause of his declining popularity after 1692. He did suffer a loss of prestige in the last years of the seventeenth century, but the reasons for it were largely political. Later in this Introduction, in connection with Mather's "Life of Phips" and his *Political Fables*, there will be occasion to speak more fully of his activity in politics from 1688 to 1692, and all that is necessary at present is a bare outline of the case. By 1692 Increase Mather was a political force in the colony, an advocate of the new royal charter for Massachusetts which became operative in that year, and a trusted adviser of Sir William Phips, the new governor. Cotton Mather was, of course, allied with his father, and shared in his political influence. The new charter, however, was not universally popular, nor was Phips, and gradually there developed a party in Boston the members of which opposed the Mathers' political position, and inclined also to combat them in everything else. Within the church, too, there were disputes. Various Congregationalists who favored changes in ritual and church discipline gave expression to their ideas, and, eventually, set up a new meeting-house in which their theories could be put into practice. To Cotton Mather and his father such innovations were abhorrent, and neither hesitated to say so. But the combined influence of those who opposed them on political grounds and those whom they offended in ecclesiastical affairs, was too strong for them. By 1701 Increase Mather was forced by his enemies to resign the presidency of Harvard College. This did not mean that his wide influence was much impaired, but it demonstrated that he could no longer lead as of yore, and that those who were hostile to the Mathers were powerful in public affairs. For Increase Mather the defeat was not serious; for his son it was far more grave. He was still a young man, and he had no such career as his father's to look proudly back upon. For one so placed to realize suddenly that his policies were not always to prevail, was a sore blow. His comments on his adversaries and his replies to his critics express all too vigorously the depth of his feeling.

Abundant opportunities to continue his public-spirited endeavors in the ministry, and occasional chances to participate in politics, still remained, and there was no slackening of his activity after 1701. He schemed to have Joseph Dudley made governor, and, once Dudley was in office, and proving himself opposed to Mather's beliefs, he schemed to oust him again. He longed to be chosen President of Harvard, and was angry when the electors passed him by. No doubt this reveals ambition, but there is also no doubt that his desire was quite as much to keep the college orthodox in religion as to exalt himself. Unsuccessful, he turned to aid the founders of Yale, and throughout the early years of this college, worked hard to serve its interests. For this he has been called a traitor to his own Alma Mater, but it is well to remember that he must have believed good education was an ideal worth working for even at the expense of his personal affection for Harvard. It seemed to him that the new college was in the paths of truth and the old was not. Feeling thus he can have had no doubts as to which institution he must support. He continued to hope that Harvard might return to the strict religious principles of its founders, but in this, as in so much else, he was doomed to disappointment. Even Yale, by 1722, developed Episcopalian sentiment. Its rector, Timothy Cutler, resigned to join the Anglican church, and there is good evidence that Cotton Mather was invited to succeed him at New Haven.[1] He must have been sorely tempted to go. He felt that he had been badly treated in Boston, and that in another community

---

[1] A letter, now in my possession, contains this evidence. I hope to publish this letter with some investigation and comment in a forthcoming volume of the *Publications of the Colonial Society of Massachusetts*.

he might meet recognition of his deserts. But his father was old and feeble; his church in Boston was devoted to him and he to it, and, however reluctantly, he gave up the opportunity to preside over the destinies of Yale.

This refusal marks the passing of his last opportunity to take a high place in public affairs. His ambitions in regard to Harvard were not realized; his influence in affairs of state was important only so long as his father's political dominance was maintained. However much one may realize the tragic quality of his brave struggle against heavy odds, or however much one appreciates the heavy burdens of affliction that he bore through many years, it is hard to close one's eyes to his defects, and harder still to make his character seem appealing to men of to-day. But, whatever his shortcomings, no just estimate of him can leave out of account his good qualities and what he achieved. His energy and versatility were shown in his many humanitarian enterprises, in his success as a minister, in his services to Congregationalism, and in his labors as a man of letters. He was no mere creature of vanity, nor did his loyalty to many elements in the past imply hostility to the new. One needs only to study his life and his writings to discover how steadily he worked for progressive ideals, and to realize how marked was his intellectual preëminence among Americans of his time.

This is nowhere better displayed than in his work as a student and writer in the field of science. Puritan New England was not, probably, as indifferent to scientific matters or as ignorant of them as some historians would have us believe, but it is true that few of the colonists before Cotton Mather gave much thought to such topics. Increase Mather was, indeed, an exception to the rule. He bought and read scientific books, and more than once he showed a surprisingly up-to-date knowledge of the latest discoveries in English and European laboratories. Moreover, in his *Essay for the Recording of Illustrious Providences*, published in 1684, he used essentially the method of the scientist, and, although the purpose of the book was in the main theological, much of it deserves to be classified as popular science. In 1683, Increase Mather had organized in Boston a scientific society, comprising a small group of men who, like himself, desired to observe natural phenomena and to discuss the problems they suggested. Cotton Mather, fresh from college, was present at their meetings and seems to have been deeply interested. No doubt he read the scientific books in his father's library; probably he inherited his father's taste for the subjects with which they dealt. Certainly in many of his writings one finds much scientific information, and a definite leaning toward scientific themes.

It is in his later books that this is most evident, and the most important developments of his scientific bent appear in the last twenty years of his life. His labors did not go unnoticed. Dr. John Woodward of London, an eminent geologist, and physician, wrote to him, asking him for fossils, or any information he had acquired about them. This in itself testifies to the fact that Mather was known by reputation in England, and makes clear that he was not famous merely as a theologian. In answering Woodward he remarked that his "Infant Countrey" was "entirely destitute of Philosophers." He did much to disprove his own statement, however, for his letters

to his London correspondent were welcomed, and
the Royal Society, through its Secretary, urged him
to send over more of his "observations on Natural
subjects." Four days later, there was held a meeting of the Council of the Society, and in the minutes
one reads: "Mr. Cotton Mather was proposed, bal-
loted for, and approved to be a Member of the Society." His election could not be final until it had
been voted by the Society as a whole, but, early in
1714, he received word that this had been done.[1]
Thus his attainments were recognized by the one
learned scientific society of the English-speaking
world. No New England divine had achieved such
a distinction before, and, indeed, Mather was one
of the very few Americans elected by the Royal Society prior to 1750. No one of these few communicated
as much to the Society as he.

His letters on scientific subjects, and the books
in which similar matters are discussed, are too numerous to mention in detail. Nor is there space to consider all of the ways in which his "philosophical"
tastes manifested themselves. No account of him,
however, can be complete without some notice of
his courageous advocacy of inoculation against small-
pox. Making his views on this subject known in
1721, he was promptly denounced as a "credulous"
and "superstitious" champion of error. His en-

---

[1] The action of the Society, so far as its records are concerned,
was not taken actually until April 11, 1723, but the delay seems
to have been caused by some blunder. To all intents and purposes
Mather became a member in 1713, and he was so regarded by his
fellow members. For the whole story, see G. L. Kittredge, "Cotton
Mather's Election into the Royal Society," in *Publications of the
Colonial Society of Massachusetts*, xiv, 81–114. From this article are
taken the quotations in the text above.

lightenment was greater than the people's, greater even than that of most of the physicians, and therefore he was reviled. On one occasion, he tells us, a bomb was thrown through the window of his house, with a note reading: "Cotton Mather, you Dog; Dam you: I'l enoculate you with this, with a pox to you." But he could not be intimidated, and, supported by his fellow divines, he continued to write in favor of what he held to be a distinct advance in medicine. Nor was his belief in inoculation the result of a hasty infatuation with a new theory. He had read and studied the subject for years before 1721, and when he stood forth to combat the arguments of his opponents, he spoke from a thorough knowledge of the scientific problems involved. Had he revealed his intellectual eminence in no other way, his course in this affair would be enough to prove him to have been a man unusual in his era both for his learning and for his bravery in upholding the cause of progress against those to whose ignorance he appeared little better than a fool.

It has been said that in New England, for a full century after 1647, "the great importance attached to theology made real progress impossible. The period was sterile—glacial," and that, in this same period, the ascendancy of the clergy was undisputed, so that, for the community, "under the supreme rule of orthodoxy the result was not only benumbing and provincial, but produced a morbid general condition." [1] If this be true, it is the more surprising to find Cotton Mather, a divine, deep in the study of current science. It is startling to find that, far

[1] For the quoted passages, see W. C. Ford, "Preface" in *The Diary of Cotton Mather*, vol. i, p. xvii.

from being benumbed by his environment, he sought
to relieve its sterility, by bringing to it news of the
advanced thought of the outside world. Certainly
he was not "provincial," unless one means that he
never traveled far from Boston. To be awarded
an honorary degree from a Scottish university, to
maintain a correspondence with scholars, scientists,
and theologians in *"England, Scotland, Ireland, Holland, Germany,* and even the *Eastern* as well as
Western Indies,"[1] and to achieve celebrity for learning far beyond the boundaries of his own land—
these things are not what we expect from a "provincial" person. Nor can we suppose that the Royal
Society of London chose Mather to membership
without realizing what we are apt to ignore—that
this New England divine was in matters of scholarship truly a "citizen of the world."

Perhaps it is most important to appreciate, after this
hasty glimpse at his career, that he was in many ways,
as Mr. Robbins called him, a riddle to himself as well
as to us.[2] His life and character are nowhere more
striking than in their contrasts. Conservative in his
attitude toward Congregational orthodoxy, he is none
the less marked by his tolerance toward other sects.
In his relation to Harvard and Yale he seems to be more
wedded to the ideas of the past than to the changing demands of a new day. Yet in much of his writing
he was not only abreast of his contemporaries but
almost alone in his enthusiastic reception of new
ideas. If he was more interested in New England
and in Boston than in any other spot on the globe,

[1] Thomas Prince, quoted in J. L. Sibley, *Biographical Sketches*,
iii, 31.
[2] Quoted in J. L. Sibley, *op. cit.*, iii, 36.

he still found time to support a religious movement
in Bavaria, and he wrote books which had wide
and continued circulation far beyond the confines
of the New World. At times he was given to those
transports of religious feeling which have seemed
to some to be evidence of an unsound mental constitution, but he was still able on occasion to be highly
practical and to speak the right word at the right
time. If he was a hot-headed visionary, or a fanatic,
his sermons and books were often both timely and
constructively sane. If his character has its repellent
side, if even his personal conduct has been attacked
by rumor, in his own day he did not lack for friends.
Benjamin Colman, more than once an opponent of
Mather, said of him: "It was *Conversation* and Acquaintance with him, in his familiar and occasional
Discourses and private Communications, that dis-.
covered the vast compass of his Knowledge and the
Projections of his Piety; . . . . Here he excell'd; here
he shone; being exceeding communicative, and bringing
out of his *Treasury* things new and old, without measure. Here it was seen how his Wit, and Fancy, his
Invention, his Quickness of thought, and ready Apprehension were all consecrated to God, as well as his
Heart, Will and Affections; and out of his Abundance . . . . overflow'd, *dropt as the honey-comb, fed*
all that came near him, and were as the *choice silver*,
for richness and brightness, pleasure and profit." [1]
Colman did not deny Mather's faults, but he knew
that with the faults went virtues. To-day one still
finds Cotton Mather denounced as the persecutor
of witches, the colossal pedant, the epitome of the

[1] B. Colman, *The Holy Walk and Glorious Translation*, etc. (Boston, 1728), 23–24.

narrowness and bigotry of the Puritan, or, less often, defended as a walking type of righteousness, eulogized to the point of lifelessness and unreality. Neither view does him justice. Neither view lets the real fascination of his character appear. He was human in his shortcomings, deservedly famous for his good works, and to know him well is to understand a man whose nature abounds in baffling inconsistencies, and who is the more interesting because he defies reduction to the limits of a type. He is no pale historical abstraction, but an intensely active individual. He would be far less interesting if he were not so decidedly a complex creation of flesh and blood.

II

The Scholar and the Man of Letters

What is true of Mather's activity in the field of science applies also to his industry and attainments in other subjects. To comprehend why he was accepted as a scholar, it is necessary to read no further than the testimony of his contemporaries. Thomas Prince, himself a scholar and "the father of American bibliography," calls him "a Person of a wonderful *quick Apprehension*, tenacious Memory, lively Fancy, ready Invention, unwearied Industry: of vast Improvements in Knowledge," and adds: "He was a wonderfull *Improver of Time:* and 'tis almost amazing how much He had read & studied—How much He has wrote and published—How much He corresponded abroad . . . . How many languages, Histories, Arts and Sciences, both ancient and modern He was familiarly vers'd in—What a vast Amassment of *Learning* He had grasp'd in his Mind, from all sorts of

Writings . . . . His printed Writings so full of Piety and various Erudition, his vast Correspondence, and the continual Reports of Travellers who had conversed with Him, had spread his Reputation into other Countries: And when about *Fourteen* Years ago I travelled abroad, I cou'd not but admire to what Extent his Fame had reached." [1]

An unusual memory, and an unusual capacity for rapid reading, together with the ability to apply what he read, seem to have been among his most useful assets. Over the door of his study, "a large, yett a warm chamber, (the hangings whereof are boxes with . . . . Books in them,"[2] he had inscribed "Be Short." It was there that Benjamin Franklin, then a boy of eighteen, visited him and was impressed; it was there that his privileged friends sought him out. In spite of the warning legend above his door, when they penetrated to his library, they found him neither jealous of his time nor miserly in his discourse. "He would always entertain us with Ease & Pleasure, even in his Studying Hours, as long as we pleas'd or cou'd venture to hinder Him," says Prince, and he adds that Mather made use "of the most *unseasonable Visitants*, both to do more Good, and at the same time even advance Himself in learning; by the most artful Repetition of the more agreable Passages He had lately been reading, with his own Remarks or Improvements upon them; whereby He further digested them, and more perfectly made them his own."[3] The same writer gives us other

---

[1] T. Prince, *The Departure of Elijah Lamented* (Boston, 1728), 19, 20; and Preface to Samuel Mather's *Life of Cotton Mather* (Boston, 1729), 1.

[2] *Diary of Cotton Mather*, i, 447.   [3] T. Prince, *Departure*, 20, 21.

details as to Mather's method of work, saying "He cared not to trouble himself with any" books "but those that were likely to bring him something *New*, and so increase his Knowledge. In two or three Minutes turning thro' a Volumn, he cou'd easily tell whether it wou'd make Additions to the Store of his Ideas. If it cou'd not, He quickly laid it by: If otherwise, he read it . . . . perusing those Parts only that represented something *Novel*, which he Pencil'd as he went along, and at the End reduc'd the Substance to his *Common Places*, to be review'd at Leisure; and all this with wonderful Celerity . . . . As he increased in Years, the less Time he had occasion to expend in running thro' an Author; till at length there were but few Books published that would take him *much* to read."[1]

Cotton Mather was no mere bookworm, but one who impressed his visitors as "instructive, learned, pious and engaging . . . . in his *private Converse*— superior company for the greatest of Men" and "agreably temper'd with a various mixture of Wit and Chearfulness." Thus he easily aroused admiration for "the capacity of his mind; the readiness of his wit, the vastness of his reading; the strength of his memory . . . . the constant tenor of a most entertaining and profitable conversation."[2]

If Lord Chancellor King, protégé of John Locke and friend of Sir Isaac Newton, William Whiston, divine, philosopher, and savant, John Desaguliers, scientist and inventor and recipient of the Copley gold medal of the Royal Society, Sir Richard Blackmore,

[1] T. Prince, Preface in Samuel Mather's *Life of Cotton Mather*, 3, 4.
[2] T. Prince, *Departure*, 21; Joshua Gee, *Israel's Mourning* (Boston, 1728), 18.

a physician and poet, Dr. Woodward, and other Englishmen distinguished in the intellectual world all
took time to write to Mather, it was not because they
were obtuse, but because he was a scholar. So August
Hermann Francke, in Germany, found him worthy
of respect. His high standing in the learned world
of his day cannot be denied.

His library was famous for its size. We have no
complete catalogue of it, but from what we know
of his father's collection, half of which he inherited,
and from those volumes of his own which are still
preserved, we can be sure that John Dunton did
not exaggerate in calling "Mr. Mather's library
. . . . the Glory of New-England, if not of all America." [1] By 1700 Cotton Mather estimated that he had
between two and three thousand books, and we know
that the number grew larger every year.

Charles Chauncy remarked that "there were scarcely
any books written but" Mather "had somehow or
other got the sight of them." [2] Of course Mather
read, for the most part, theology; he owned more
books of this type than of any other. At the same
time he did not neglect the classics, and his knowledge of these would put to shame most "well-read"
men of the present. He was well acquainted with
the great histories of all ages, and if he unjustly dubbed
Clarendon's work a "*Romance* that goes under the
Title of, *The History of the Grand Rebellion*" and
said it should be treated "with the Disregard that
is proper for it," [3] he did read not only the histories
of antiquity but also those which in his era passed

[1] J. Dunton, *Letters from New-England* (1867), 75.
[2] *Massachusetts Historical Society Proceedings*, xxxvii, 70.
[3] C. Mather, *Manuductio ad Ministerium* (Boston, 1726), 63.

as current books. Nor did he overlook lighter forms
of literature. As he saw it, a scholar need not and
should not be "an Odd, Starv'd, Lank sort of a thing,
who had lived only on *Hebrew Roots* all his Days,"[1]
but one who could, if more serious concerns allowed,
enjoy music and poetry. In his *Manuductio ad Ministerium* he advises young men who would become
scholarly divines concerning the books they should
read and the studies they should pursue. He reveals
a surprising catholicity of taste. He extols science
and experimental philosophy. He recommends a
knowledge of French. "I cannot wish you a Soul
that shall be wholly *Unpoetical*,"[2] he declares. Although, in the *Manuductio*, he devotes most of his
praise of poetry to Homer and Virgil, we know that
he read *Paradise Lost*, that Chaucer was something
more than a name to him, and we even find him quoting Nahum Tate and lauding Blackmore to the skies.
As for the "stage-plays" which Mather held to be
unworthy of a scholar's attention, neither the drama
of the Restoration nor that of the early eighteenth
century is so obvious in its merits as to make it possible
to accuse Mather of narrowness simply because he
regarded the plays in question as less important for a
man of learning than such books as those of Sir Thomas
Browne, John Milton, and Thomas Fuller. In his
reading, as in his life, no undue reverence for the past
kept him from appreciation of the present. "Seldome
any *new Book* of Consequence finds the way from
beyond-Sea, to these parts of *America*, but I bestow
the Perusal upon it,"[3] he says. There is much illu-

---

[1] *Idem*, 30.
[2] *Idem*, 39.
[3] *Diary of Cotton Mather*, I, 548.

mination in Mather's note to Thomas Prince in 1718, "Favour me, by this Bearer, with the Book of Poetry, you bought the last week at your Booksellers." [1]

To-day we can easily find flaws in Mather's scholarship. He attempted to cover too large a field of knowledge, and many of his errors might have been avoided had he been content to limit the range of his studies. His methods are faulty. He accepted quotations and citations which he found in the authors he read, and used them himself without tracing them back to their sources. If he had a letter from a man whom he believed to be honest and wise, he was not apt to attempt verification. But, in general, his failure to measure up to present standards is due to the fact that our methods are not those of 1690 or 1720. We have resources which he had not, great libraries, and the accumulated experience of innumerable students. If to the Royal Society he seemed learned and scholarly, it is hardly fair to criticize him as "credulous" or "uncritical" simply because he did not know certain facts still unrevealed in his time. No other American of his generation could say with him: "I am able with little study to write in seven languages. I feast myself with the sweets of all sciences which the more polite part of mankind ordinarily pretend to. I am entertained with all kinds of histories, ancient and modern. I am no stranger to the curiosities which, by all sorts of learning, are brought to the curious. These intellectual pleasures are far beyond any sensual ones."[2]

Out of Mather's reading came his writing. His

---

[1] Quoted in *American Antiquarian Society Proceedings*, xx, 295.
[2] Quoted in H. E. Mather, *Lineage of Rev. Richard Mather* (Hartford, 1890), 81, 82.

"Common Places," his book of "Quotidiana" in which
he jotted down good things which he discovered
in other authors, he drew upon constantly as he
wrote. To some critics, therefore, he has presented
himself rather as an editor than as an author. But he
did write countless sermons, tracts, and records of his
own observations, in which the matter as well as the
manner is his own. He wrote with a scholar's point of
view—with a desire to make full use of his sources
—but even when this tendency is most marked he
still proves himself not only a man of letters but
in some measure an artist in his care for phrasing,
for the ways in which his stories were told and his
arguments developed, and for that element in writing which he called, as we should, "style."

Mather wrote in many forms. History, biography,
essays of a rudimentary sort, sermons, fables, books
of practical piety, and theological treatises are all
to be found among his works, and he tried his hand
at verse. *The Christian Philosopher* shows him dab-
bling in philosophy and science; his *Angel of Bethesda*
is a medical manual, while his *Biblia Americana*
is a great compilation of material designed to illus-
trate and interpret the Bible. The *Psalterium Americanum* is an entertaining experiment in translating
the Psalms and in adapting them for musical ren-
dering. Nor does this list by any means exhaust
all the various categories into which his writings fall.

His sermons outnumber any other class of his printed
works, chiefly because he was a divine and because the
notes for a pulpit discourse could easily be expanded
into a small book. These sermons are often interesting, but less so than his other work. They adhere
rigidly to the somewhat mechanical form in vogue

among most Puritan preachers of the period, and to us they seem overloaded with scriptural references and marred by a dogmatic manner. At the same time they are often admirably "practical" in their application of doctrine to life, and often splendidly emphatic in their exhortation. They should be read aloud; for their effectiveness was heightened by the timeliness of their subjects and by the dominant presence of the preacher.

Mather's discussions of purely theological topics have little interest except for special students. His scientific writing is exemplified in *The Christian Philosopher*, and, better still, in his communications to the Royal Society, in the *Angel of Bethesda*, and in parts of the *Biblia Americana*. These communications and the two last-named works have never been published completely—a fact which explains our forgetfulness concerning Mather the scientist. His scientific works reveal him perhaps better than his other productions as an expert manipulator of English prose. What seems to be an essay from his pen is found in what he calls his "digression" on style in the *Manuductio*.[1] His dexterity in the fable is shown in the *Political Fables* printed in this volume, and his verse is fairly represented by his elegy on Phips, also contained in these pages. The essay holds its own with many an English critical essay of Mather's time, even though it presents no startling excellence; the verse, though not "modern," is often technically deft, and, compared with similar poetry produced in England and her colonies in and before 1697, is creditable. Any one who looks through the pages of Quarles, Sylvester, Wither, Cowley—even Dryden at

---

[1] See quotation, pages xxxvi-xxxvii, below.

his least felicitous—will discover who were Mather's masters in verse and also that he sometimes wrote quite as well as did those masters on certain occasions. In poetry, as in some elements of his prose, Mather adopts a manner which was, by 1700, largely obsolete, but in that manner, he is skillful. However valid our later ideals for poetry may be, they are not fair criteria by which to judge a man who wrote his verse with reference to a definition of "fancy" and "wit" which is not acceptable to us.

As for "practical piety," two of Mather's books of this type show merit. The *Manuductio*, already referred to, is an exercise in unvarnished prose, and in respect to content is informed by an eminently sane understanding of the ideal of scholarship as it was understood when the book was written. Even Mr. Tyler, elsewhere so impressed by Mather's pedantry, finds this little volume one which is "written heartily, with real enthusiasm for the subject and with greater directness and simplicity of style than the author has shown in any other work."[1] Mather's *Bonifacius*, better known as *Essays to Do Good*, has the same good qualities and evokes from the same critic the comment that it is "quite remarkable for the clear ingenuity and the fascinating power with which it reduces charity to an exact science, and plans the systematic transaction of good deeds on business principles."[2] This is true. It is no less true that the prose is sound, the emphasis expertly maintained, while many passages are saved from dullness by an epigrammatic touch, revealing at once the writer's wit and his ready command of the technique of prose.

[1] M. C. Tyler, *History of American Literature*, ii, 85.
[2] *Idem.*, 84.

In biography, Mather wrote much. His son says, "by the Year 1718 the Doctor had published the lives of no less than *one hundred and fourteen* Men, and more than *twenty* Women, and since that Year, he has printed Accounts and Characters of many more."[1] No one will deny that these "Lives" often fall far short of our ideal for biography. They are all eulogistic, less concerned with the complete revelation of character than with the glorification of good deeds. Nevertheless, Mather loved anecdotes, and with them he lightened his pages. He gained vividness by directly quoted remarks, and where a straightforward narrative was called for he showed that he knew what a good story was and how it should be told. If Phips, or the earlier governors of Massachusetts, as portrayed in the *Magnalia*, or Increase Mather as depicted in his son's *Parentator*, lack some of the reality of life because they are too favorably displayed, it is still true that neither the *Parentator* nor the "Life of Phips," for example, need fear comparison with English work of the same type in the same period or earlier. And, as Barrett Wendell pointed out, the defects in Mather's biographies cannot prevent a careful reader "from recognizing the marked individuality of his separate portraits."[2]

The line between such works as the lives of the governors and historical writing in the strict sense, is hard to draw. There is likewise a great deal that may most safely be called history in Mather's books of "remarkable providences" or those on witchcraft. A "remarkable providence" was an event in which it seemed that God directly revealed His power on

[1] S. Mather, *op. cit.*, 70.
[2] B. Wendell, *Cotton Mather*, 161.

earth. Shipwrecks, deliverances from perils, great storms, calamities, and many other happenings of life were commonly regarded as such signs of God's power. Their significance was particularly urged by the Puritans, but a belief in them persisted among Christians of all sects well into the eighteenth century. To record such events had edificatory value, by turning men from their godless ways. At the same time, when one wrote of happenings actually observed by credible witnesses, one wrote what was, after all, history. So too, the events in question often presented scientific interest, and to collect records of them, based on observation, was to follow the method of the scientist. For a historian to leave untold, or a scientist to dismiss without investigation, the actions of the Devil's agents and their victims, would be quite as remiss as for a divine to fail to draw from the experiences of the "afflicted" and their diabolical tormentors a warning against Satan and his wiles. A little group of Mather's books, then, such as his *Memorable Providences* and *Wonders of the Invisible World*, should be classified as in part history, in part science, and in part works of admonition and edification.

As a historian pure and simple, Mather left merely fragments. The *Magnalia* sufficiently illustrates his deficiencies, but it is also true that Mather's theory of history was by no means wholly antiquated when he wrote, however misguided it seems to-day. Though not an accurate historian, he was not responsible for all the errors in his books. Nor should it be forgotten that some of his divagations are explained by the fact that our manifold historical resources were not his.

It would be stupid, of course, to deny that as a

writer he had grave faults. The minor accusations brought against him need not detain us. More serious and more fundamental are the charges that his style was above all pedantic, and that he was too much a disciple of the "fantastic school" of prose.

As to the latter point, it is true that Mather's style is often overloaded with strained metaphors, forced similes, and mannerisms familiar in much English prose and verse for generations before 1700. It is not true that his style was always thus fantastic. He could write without conceits or what one of his critics in his own day called "puns and jingles," and the selections in this volume show many pages of the most direct phrasing. He knew well in what passages he had nothing to lose and everything to gain by avoiding artificialities of prose. That he was "fantastic" at times is due undoubtedly to the influence of earlier English writers, together with his own tendency to think always in terms of analogies and images. Undoubtedly, also, "fantastic" prose was largely outlawed in England after 1700. Therefore we are prone to think of it as something inherently bad. Perhaps it was, but it remains true that not all of Cotton Mather's writing is bad and that on occasion his "fancy" and the "ornaments" of his prose are ingeniously employed.

The second charge against his writing is that of pedantry. In this connection it is perhaps just to hear Mather in his own defense:

"There has been a deal of ado about a STYLE; So much, that I must offer you my Sentiments upon it. There is a *Way of Writing*, wherein the Author endeavours, that the Reader may have *something to the Purpose* in every Paragraph. There is not only a *Vigour* sensible in every *Sentence*, but the Paragraph is embellished with *Profitable References*, even to something beyond what is *directly spoken*. Formal and Painful *Quotations* are not studied; yet all that could be learnt from them is insinuated. The Writer pretends not unto *Reading*, yet he could not have writ as he does if he had not *Read* very much in his Time; and his Composures are not only a *Cloth of Gold*, but also stuck with as many *Jewels*, as the Gown of a Russian Embassador. This *Way of Writing* has been decried by many, and is at this Day more than ever so, for the same Reason, that in the old Story, the *Grapes* were decried, *That they were not Ripe*. . . . . But, however *Fashion* and *Humour* may prevail, they must not think that the Club at their *Coffee-House* is, *All the World;* but there will always be those, who . . . . will think, that the real Excellency of a Book will never ly in *saying of little;* That the less one has for his Money in a Book, 'tis really the more Valuable for it; and that the less one is instructed in a Book, and the more of Superfluous *Margin*, and Superficial *Harangue*, and the less of *Substantial Matter* one has in it, the more tis to be accounted of. . . . . Nothing appears to me more Impertinent and Ridiculous than the *Modern Way*, [I cannot say, *Rule;* For they have *None!*] of *Criticising*. The Blades that set up for *Criticks*, I know not who constituted or commission'd 'em!—they appear to me, for the most part as *Contemptible*, as they are a *Supercilious* Generation. For indeed no Two of them have the same *Style;* and they are as intollerably Cross-grain'd and severe in their Censures upon one another, as they are upon the rest of Mankind. But while each of them, Conceitedly enough, sets up for the *Standard of Perfection*, we are entirely at a loss which *Fire* to follow. Nor can you easily find any one thing wherein they agree for their Style, except perhaps a perpetual care to give us Jejune and Empty Pages, without such *Touches of Erudition* . . . . as may make the Discourses less *Tedious*, and more *Enriching*, to the Mind of him that peruses them. . . . . After all, Every Man will have his own *Style*, which will distinguish him as much as his *Gate*:[1] And if you can attain to that which I have newly described, but always writing so as to give an *Easy Conveyance* unto your *Idea's*, I would not have you by any *Scourging* be driven out of your *Gate*."[2]

Mather, then, considered the chief function of good writing to be instruction. For him a good style

[1] *I.e.*, Gait.
[2] C. Mather, *Manuductio*, 44–46.

was one that conveyed ideas easily and emphatically, and the more information that was conveyed, the better the style. Moreover, he believed that style was an individual matter, and that a man should write as he thought. Thus he was "not driven out of his gait." He thought of his prose as a cloth of gold. So, no doubt, did the critics whom he denounced, think of theirs. But for him the golden threads and the jewels of style were the references and allusions which we call pedantic; while the critics wove their cloth of gold from simple English, adorned only with the jewels of graceful and urbane expression. The fundamental difference concerns the emphasis to be put upon style as opposed to content. We are not called upon to take Mather's view of the case, but we should recall that he wrote as he did because he knew his own "gait." He had courage to follow his own convictions in the face of the prevailing mode. His "pedantry" was no more universal in his writing than his "fantastic" prose. He could, when he wished, write as directly as Addison or Swift. The *Political Fables* prove this; so does that letter quoted by Barrett Wendell as showing that Mather might after all "have been no bad contributor to the 'Spectator': he was not insensible to the literary style of the new century."[1]

Whoever reads merely the selections from Cotton Mather in this volume, must feel that, in spite of his display of erudition, in spite of his "puns and jingles," there is a sure sense of prose rhythm, an ear for good phrasing, and a mastery of the means by which strength is woven into English prose. It is, I think, significant that Professor Kittredge and Professor Wen-

[1] B. Wendell, *op. cit.*, 250.

dell, the two literary scholars who have studied Mather's works most thoroughly, both have found good qualities in his style. The latter, writing of the *Magnalia*, said: "The style, in the first place, seems to me remarkably good . . . . [Mather] has two merits peculiarly his own: in the whole book I have not found a line that is not perfectly lucid, nor many paragraphs that, considering the frequent dulness of his subject, I could honestly call tiresome. In the second place . . . . I am inclined to think the veracity of spirit that pervades the book of very high order. Somehow, as no one else can, Cotton Mather makes you by and by feel what the Puritan ideal was: if he does not tell just what men were, he does tell just what they wanted to be, and what loyal posterity longed to believe them. . . . I have known the book for eleven years; and the better I know it, the more I value it. Whatever else Cotton Mather may have been, the 'Magnalia' alone, I think, proves him to have been a notable man of letters." [1]

Through his books one derives a knowledge of the spirit of his times, which can be secured in no other way. Benjamin Franklin was influenced throughout his life by one of Mather's books. Emerson was no stranger to them. Harrier Beecher Stowe in her girlhood delighted in the stories she found in the *Magnalia;* Lowell found much to read, if little to praise, in Mather's pages. Hawthorne, Longfellow, and Whittier pored over his histories of old New England. Even to-day we in America cannot wisely leave Cotton Mather quite unread.

Nor need one be interested only in national litera-

[1] *Idem*, 161, 162.

ture to fall under the spell of Mather.   Charles Lamb
rejoiced in reading Thomas Fuller; Dr. Johnson
rose early to read Burton's *Anatomy of Melancholy*,
though he declared he would leave his bed for no
other book.   Mather is less witty than Fuller, perhaps less fascinating in his erudition than Richard
Burton, but he will not lack for an audience so
long as there are men like Lamb and Johnson who
relish good writing, so long as there are readers fond
of the romance so richly harvested in the "Magnalia."
To them his pages offer entertainment; and, however
rarely, flashes of wit, gleams of inspiration—a breath
of the spirit that gives to every good book its right to
enduring life.

III

The Magnalia Christi Americana

Cotton Mather's *Magnalia* is his most celebrated
book.   In 1702, when it was published in London,
nothing else in print furnished a complete history of
New England.   Oldmixon and Neal, historians who
took exception to its faults, were obliged to draw
much of their material relating to Massachusetts
and the neighboring colonies from its pages.   To-
day, when many more of the early narratives have
been published, it offers illumination on many points.
   The book betrays Cotton Mather's deficiencies
as a writer of history.   There are seven books, the
first on the settlement of New England, the second
on the lives of the governors, the third devoted to
the biographies of ministers, the fourth telling the
story of Harvard College and sketching the lives
of some of its graduates, the fifth on the history of

the Congregational church in the colonies, the sixth on "remarkable providences," and the seventh on various disturbances in the churches, The *Magnalia* is rather a "historical collection" than a history. It reprinted many of Cotton Mather's books —sermons, biographies, historical narratives—whatever could be worked into the general scheme. The whole thus conveys an impression of formlessness, and there is justice in Whittier's speaking of its "strange and marvellous things, heaped up huge and undigested." At the same time it reveals Mather's skill in biography, it abounds in good narrative, and the individual books often have the unity which is lacking in the work as a whole. It should be remembered, too, that the book was designed as an "Ecclesiastical History," and that it was written to exalt the cause of godliness and to celebrate the triumphs of Christ in the New World. This explains many of its inclusions and omissions, and is a key to its historical point of view.

Its inaccuracy has been overemphasized. There are many errors of fact in its pages, there are slips in names and dates, and sometimes, it seems to us, misinterpretations of characters and events. These misinterpretations are probably due in many instances to Mather's proximity to the things under discussion, as well as to his desire to glorify righteousness. As to his other lapses, many are caused by carelessness, while a few come from untrustworthy sources, used because no others were available. Finally, the text of the *Magnalia*, as we have it, almost certainly does not represent the work precisely as he wrote it. The manuscript was sent to London in 1700; the book did not appear until 1702. A letter from John Quick, a London minister, and friend of Mather, written March 19, 1702, tells of the difficulties Quick had, as Mather's agent, with the publishers. Among the terms which Quick proposed to the printer were "Every sheet to be brought to Me hot from ye Presse to be revised & corrected . . . . Not one to be Sold off till all ye Books were first delivered to me," but he adds, "all these fair designes, hopes, & endeavors of mine for you are now vanished into smoak." In other words, his terms were refused, and the sheets were not corrected. He says, "And how to remedy any other miscarriages about ye Impression I am utterly at a losse."[1]

Neither Mather nor his agent, then, had a chance to read the proofs, or to rectify any misprints, while the *Magnalia* was in press. After it was completed, two pages of "Errata" were printed. Most of the copies of the *Magnalia* now extant, do not contain these pages, which makes it seem probable that many of the volumes sold were sent out without them. The result of the scarcity of complete copies has been that Mather's text has often been quoted without regard to the corrections made in the "Errata." Mather has thus been blamed for inaccuracies for which the printer was responsible. There are many mistakes not rectified in the printed corrections, but in respect to them, also, Mather is entitled to the benefit of the doubt. If Quick compiled the "Errata," Mather had nothing to do with them; if he compiled them himself he can have had no time to read over his work carefully enough to detect every slip, since the volume was ready for sale—

[1] Quick's letter is in the Library of the Massachusetts Historical Society.

was, indeed, probably already on sale in England. Thus to pass judgment on Mather's accuracy from the evidence of the printed text of the *Magnalia* is distinctly unfair.

The General Introduction is important because of its value as a piece of criticism, expressing Mather's views on the writing of history, and his conception of the purpose of the *Magnalia*. It is worth reading also because of its enthusiastic expression of Mather's ideal for his book. His paraphrase of the beginning of the *Æneid* in his first sentences, and his dedication of his work to the service of Christ, show how intensely he felt that he was writing a true epic and how passionately he longed to serve both the cause of literature and that of religion. The Second Book has more unity than some of the main divisions of the *Magnalia*, and it displays Mather the historian and biographer at his best. Detailed comment on it is not necessary, save for one or two points of interest.

The "Life of Bradford" shows two misprints at least, Ansterfield, for Austerfield and Grimsly for Grimsby. The former for some time baffled seekers for Bradford's birthplace, who failed to recognize in the form as printed the true name of the village. It is worth noting that, although neither of these errors is corrected in the "Errata," both are almost certainly printer's mistakes. To read "n" for "u," and "ly" for "by," still is a common error. Here is corroboration for the idea that not all of the inaccuracies in the *Magnalia* are fairly to be ascribed to its author.

The various lists of colonial officers printed in Book II show omissions and errors in names and dates. The omissions are doubtless to be accounted for by Mather's carelessness, for it must have been possible for him to secure complete lists; the errors in names and dates may quite as well represent mere misprints as slips on the part of the author.

The "Life of Dudley" was, as Mather said, an abridgment of a biography which he had written previously. Such a biography, written by him, has since been printed.[1] Comparison of it with the *Magnalia* version shows few significant differences, except that the statement of Dudley's dissent from the English church is more mildly expressed in the latter. It may be that Mather changed the phrasing himself, lest he offend his Anglican friends. There is, however, another possibility, for we know that the *Magnalia* biography of Dudley was, before it was printed, submitted to Joseph Dudley, who was, when the book appeared, Governor of New England. Quick writes "Governor Dudley desired that he might read over . . . . (wch he did in my Library) his ffather's Life, & altered one or two words, wch as as I remember were these; '*not a servant* but Uncle or Guardian to ye Earle of Lincolne.' He approved of ye performance."[2] Joseph Dudley was no hater of the English church, and he may well·have modified the statement of his father's nonconformity, as well as the passage noted by Quick. In any case, he found no other fault with Mather's biography, either as to facts or as to the presentation of them.

The "Life of Phips" deserves special comment. To understand it one should remember the chief his-

---

[1] See *The Life of Mr. Thomas Dudley*, ed. C. Deane, in *Massachusetts Historical Society Proceedings*, xi, 207–222, and, separately, Cambridge, 1870.

[2] Letter of March 19, 1702, cited above.

torical facts to which it refers. In 1683 a *quo warranto* was issued against the charter by which Massachusetts had hitherto been governed, and in 1684 the charter was revoked. This meant that the colonists were deprived of what they had believed to be their right to conduct a government virtually independent of England. In 1686 Sir Edmund Andros came to Boston as royal governor of New England, and he was promptly hailed as a "tyrant." He was accused of many crimes, sufficiently dilated upon by Cotton Mather, though Andros seems to have done no more than carry out his instructions from the king. As the colonists saw it, he attacked their titles to lands and homes, was in league with the French against the English, and had secret leanings toward Catholicism. He had, of course, supporters, but to most New Englanders he seems to have appeared as a creature of evil. By 1688 James II was convinced that it was to his interest to conciliate the nonconformists, and, in order to take advantage of this, Increase Mather was sent to England to enlist the sympathies of the king on behalf of the Puritan colonists against Andros, and, if possible, to procure the restoration of the old charter. He succeeded in getting fair promises from James, but the revolution of 1688 and the accession of William III made it necessary for him to begin a new campaign with the new king in order to secure the objects of his mission. Meanwhile, in Boston, there was a rebellion against Andros, who was captured and imprisoned, while the government of the colony was put into the hands of those who had held office under the old charter. In this rebellion Cotton Mather played a leading part, and it seems to have been he who wrote the official declaration justifying it. His father in England succeeded in making the revolt against Andros appear to William III as an uprising of the people opposed to James II and favorable to the new monarch. He was less successful in obtaining the restoration of the old charter. With him, as agents of the colony in England, were associated Sir Henry Ashurst, a London merchant, and two Bostonians, Thomas Oakes and Elisha Cooke. After long and somewhat tangled negotiations Mather became convinced that the old charter could not be obtained, and, on the advice of English lawyers and politicians, he and Ashurst accepted a new one. This deprived New England of many of her "privileges" and provided that she should be ruled by a governor, not chosen by representatives of the people, but appointed by the king. Probably the new charter was the best that could be obtained, but Cooke, and in some measure Oakes, opposed it. In general terms the issue was between those who, like Cooke and Oakes, were strict conservatives in their belief that no change in the old governmental scheme should be accepted, and the party of Mather and Ashurst, who realized that the colonists could not enforce their will on England, and that conciliation would be useful in gaining further favors. Certainly they were more immediately successful than Cooke, for to them was granted the chance to nominate the royal governor and other officers to be appointed under the new charter. It had been stipulated that the governor must be a military man. Sir William Phips was the one New Englander of any standing in English political circles, who could boast of any considerable experience in war, and

Mather and Ashurst nominated him as governor. There were, from Increase Mather's point of view, other reasons for this choice. Phips was an attendant at his church, sympathetic to Congregationalism, and, doubtless, largely influenced by him. Cotton Mather, in Boston, hearing the news of Phips's appointment, rejoiced that the new governor, as well as the other new officers, were his friends, and sympathetic to the policies he advocated. Cooke, however, was not without influence, and from 1692 he was the leader of the party opposed to the Mathers' views.

The "Life of Phips" came out first in 1697. Unquestionably Mather paints his subject in a highly favorable light, and quite as certainly Phips was, in reality, no paragon. He was hot-tempered, injudicious, without unusual statesmanship, and, however pious in his relation to the Second Church and the Mathers, by no means free from the vices of a badly educated, adventure-loving sea-dog. This side of Phips, Mather overlooks, and he emphasizes Phips, the "self-made man," raised to eminence by courage and industry, and Phips, the lover and servant of his country. There is an interesting problem—and an insoluble one—in deciding how far Mather's book was written to exalt himself and his father and to defend their political tenets, and how far it was designed as a tribute to Sir William Phips.

The work reveals Mather as a writer of narrative. The whole story is well told, concisely and with an eye to dramatic effect. The story of Phips's suppression of the projected mutiny, is distinguished by vividness of narration. Throughout, Mather gains life for his story by his use of colloquial terms. The "sows and pigs" of silver, the ship "careening," the boat "busking to and again," are all examples of his use of a vocabulary drawn from the speech of men like Phips himself. Thereby Mather gains the effect he doubtless sought—that of a story of real life told in the terms of real life, and bringing to its readers a sense of actual contact with the events described.

The "Life of Phips" also illustrates a point already noted—Mather's ability to follow sources and at the same time to adapt the words of his source to secure a literary effect. The same method will be observed if his "Life of Bradford," is compared with Bradford's *History* or the other early accounts of the Plymouth settlers, or if his "Life of Winthrop" is compared with Winthrop's *Journal*. In the case of the "Life of Phips" two contemporary accounts of the attempt on Quebec have been printed since Mather's day.[1] One of them, at least, he knew when he told the story of Phips's expedition to the St. Lawrence. To read his version in connection with the narratives from which he drew his facts is to see how he condensed and improved the style, with reference not only to the needs of truthful reproduction but also with a definite feeling for a graphic narrative.

IV

The Christian Philosopher

Cotton Mather's *Christian Philosopher* has a peculiar interest. In it, as in no other of his works,

[1] See *Two Accounts of the Expedition Against Quebec, A. D. 1690*, ed. S. A. Green (Cambridge, 1902).

are revealed certain fundamental traits in Mather as a man of letters. In the briefest comment the book should be considered from at least three aspects. First, it shows much concerning Cotton Mather's method of writing in a field where there were many authorities to consult; secondly, it is important as evidencing his advanced position in regard to certain lines of thought; and, finally, it makes plain how deeply æsthetic and purely literary considerations affected its author.

As for the first point, Cotton Mather in his Introduction gives the essential facts. He planned the *Christian Philosopher* as a sort of summary of scientific knowledge, and as an argument for religion based on the facts of science. He was not learned in all fields of science, and could not hope to become so. Therefore he turned to the writers of England, who had written on science and its relation to religion. Mr. Richard G. Wendell, working as a graduate student at Harvard, in 1924–25, made a careful investigation of the sources of Essay xxvi of the *Christian Philosopher*, and showed that Mather relied largely on a few English books, from which he took not only facts but quotations and citations of references. Mr. Wendell says: "I am now convinced that he has used comparatively few books as a background for his own. He mentions more than fifty writers in the chapter 'On Vegetables'; it is very doubtful if he was familiar with the works of ten. He has taken sentences and paragraphs from these works and incorporated them without change. . . . Sometimes he gives credit to his authority, but he is far more apt to report the original author, when he is mentioned in his source, while the intermediary writer from whom he obtained the material is slighted." Examination of the other sections of *The Christian Philosopher* here printed confirms this. Generally speaking, if one reads Mather's book with Ray's *Wisdom of God Manifested in the Works of the Creation*, and his *Physico-Theological Discourses*, William Derham's *Physico-Theology*, Dr. Cheyne's *Philosophical Principles of Religion*, and Grew's *Cosmologia Sacra*, open before him, he will discover that almost all that Mather says, almost all his quotations and references, are drawn from these books, or from a few others like them. At the same time, Mather rearranges what he thus extracts, condenses it, and in the process of his compilation shows once more his desire not only to take good material but to express it as well as may be. But the book is not merely a compilation, for often in discussing this or that topic he inserts observations of his own made in New England, or refers to a book recording original investigations in terms which show that he had a first-hand acquaintance with its contents.

More interesting than the light it sheds upon Mather as a writer of a compendium of science, is the *Christian Philosopher's* exposition of its author's advanced intellectual position. The book was an attempt to reconcile religion and science, and looks forward to Emerson's, "The Religion that is afraid of science dishonors God and commits suicide." It argues that the world is so wonderful and so beautiful a place that its very existence and nature are proof enough that an all-powerful and benevolent Creator exists, and scientific research is held up as the source of man's knowledge of its wonder and beauty. So admirable are the provisions of Nature that in them is an argument for the existence not only of God but of a forgiving

Christ. All this was not new in 1721, when the book appeared, though Cotton Mather's reasoning on some points was original. The English writers mentioned as his sources gave him the general argument. The intellectual significance of the book does not lie in its having originated the doctrine it contains, but in the fact that it was written in America, where such doctrine had not yet been expounded, and by Cotton Mather, a Calvinist, the devotee of the theology of the first American Puritans. To them God was a strict ruler, acting directly in earthly affairs, and much that later came to be regarded as simply the operation of natural law was held to be evidence of the power of the Lord manifested in the world. For them, too, man was vile, and only those divinely preordained were to be saved from Hell. Nature was rather awful than beautiful, a manifestation of God's dread power, rather than of his love for mankind. From Calvinism America reacted sharply to the deism of Thomas Paine, and Professor Riley shows that *The Christian Philosopher* is representative of the first stage in this reaction.[1] Its point of view is that the world is well planned and well ordered, that it is beautiful, that to study nature is to realize God's goodness, and, therefore, that man can appreciate God by the exercise of observation and reason. This is a far cry from Mather's own earlier position, and it is proof positive of his intellectual development. *The Christian Philosopher* is not gloomy in its point of view, but cheerful; it is not pessimistic but the reverse. It expresses as

[1] See the references to *The Christian Philosopher* in Woodbridge Riley, *American Thought* (New York, 1923), and the same author's *American Philosophy—The Early Schools* (New York, 1907).

no earlier American book had done the beginning
of the more liberal philosophy of the eighteenth
century, and that Mather wrote it, proves him to
have been far more "modern" than his times, so
far as New England was concerned, and the first
man in the Colonies to express in print the dawning
of the new ideas. This alone, had we no other evidence, would suffice to refute the theory that he
represented completely a day in which the Puritan
had ceased to develop intellectually and that "he
reflected the Puritan spirit as it had hardened" and
"become ossified." [1]

Last, and by no means least important, is the *Christian Philosopher's* revelation of Mather as a literary
artist. If the book is read with Mather's sources
its superiority as a piece of writing is at once apparent. To quote Mr. Richard Wendell again, "Like them
[the English writers] Mather tried to glorify God; unlike these English writers he succeeded in giving us,
not only a more or less heterogeneous compilation of
facts, but an interesting and readable volume."
Mather's whole attitude is one of enthusiasm, and
an enthusiasm with which we can sympathize.

Again and again Mather dilates on the beauty
of nature. This is a theme now familiar in our literature, but discussions of it are not frequent until the
late eighteenth century, and it is not easy to find
an American author prior to Mather giving much
attention to the beauty of his environment, But
The Christian Philosopher shows constantly not
only that Mather saw the wonders of nature with
the observant eye of the scientist, but also that his
feeling for them was akin to the poet's. The passage

[1] W. C. Ford, Preface in the *Diary of Cotton Mather*, i, p. xvii.

in which he writes of the moon is prosaic enough, perhaps, and certainly far removed from Henry Thoreau's passionate outburst of pagan adoration of the same "Luminary," but the next line, referring to what has gone before, reads, "These are some of the *Songs*, which God, the Maker of us both, has given me in the Night." [1] Mather's praise of God as revealed in the moon is a product of inspiration, of the mystic feeling that makes poets.

The passage beginning on page 330 of the selection must have been written with an interest in form, an ear for cadence and the sound of the individual word. The printing of most of the sentences and phrases as separate paragraphs indicates that Mather was concerned with the artistic effect of his lines. Many of Walt Whitman's poems made use of the method which Mather chose. To observe, to enumerate one's observations in long lines, without meter but with a certain cadence and a precise care for building up a structural effect in a long passage—these things were essential in Whitman, and they are also in *The Christian Philosopher*. Mather was content that his pages should pass as prose, but both men desired to find artistic means of revealing their emotions, and they hit upon similar methods.

Cotton Mather conceived of the "Anatomy of Plants" as a living testimony to the greatness of God, and his adoration for God was too great for ordinary prose.[2] To utter it he sought, consciously

[1] *The Christian Philosopher* (1721), p. 51.
[2] The passage in question is taken almost verbatim from William Derham's *Physico-Theology* (ed. London, 1714), Book X, but Mather's form is his own, Derham having written in flat prose.

liv INTRODUCTION

or unconsciously, a special form, and achieved a style
by no means unlike that adopted by a nineteenth
century American hailed as an original literary genius. I have no wish to draw a detailed parallel between
Whitman and Mather, but it is possible to maintain
that Cotton Mather was, at least in aspiration, a literary
artist. *The Christian Philosopher* shows him to have
been interested in skillful technique and in the power
of language and style.

Mather longed that this book might be put into
the hands of all students. No doubt this was largely
because of its lesson, its attempt to bring men to
understand and worship God. Even if this side
no longer interests, the book should not lose its appeal,
for we can realize that, as Professor Riley has said,
it anticipated by a hundred years the love of nature
for its own sake, characteristic of the American
transcendentalists, and that, in point of view and
style, it is marked by qualities rare in the early years
of our literary history.

V

The Political Fables

Cotton Mather's *Political Fables* were not printed
in Mather's time, but were circulated in manuscript,
presumably about 1692. Such fables were usual enough
in England, and cannot have been unfamiliar to the
colonists. Dryden's *Hind and the Panther* is but
one example of the use of such material, and when
Æsop was widely read, and the stories of Reynard
and his companions were well known, there was
nothing novel in pointing a political moral or telling a tale of current events through the medium

of the fable. It is true that Cotton Mather's *Po-litical Fables* seem to have no counterpart in earlier American literature, but their importance lies less in the novelty of their form than in their style. Here is Mather, the contemporary of Swift and Addison, not Mather the disciple of the "fantastic school"; here is Mather the writer of "modern" prose and the kinsman of the eighteenth century essayist, not Mather the pedant.

What has been said of the political background of the "Life of Phips" explains sufficiently the pur-port of the *Fables.* They were written, it appears, to defend Increase Mather's acceptance of the new charter against those who believed that he had wan-tonly sacrificed the old rights of New England.

In *The New Settlement of the Birds* the characters are:

The Birds	The New Englanders
Jupiter	The King of England
The Eagle	Increase Mather
The Goldfinch	Sir Henry Ashurst
The Harpies (or Locusts)	The foes of New England
The King's-fisher	Sir William Phips

The fable itself is simply a statement of the advan-tages of the new charter, and the reasons why the colonists should be grateful for it.

In *The Elephant's Case a little stated,* the new char-acters are:

The Elephant	Sir William Phips
Isgrim, or Bruin	Any governor not favorable to New England's best interests

The fable states Phips's defense of his position. In *Mercury's Negotiation* the new characters are:

Mercury	Increase Mather
The sheep	The New Englanders

The foxes	Their enemies
Janus	Some one of the English politicians instrumental in drawing the new charter.
Orpheus	Probably Cotton Mather himself.

"Eleven more of the celestial choristers" (page 370) seems to refer to eleven other ministers, and it is not clear who they were. When Increase Mather returned from England, thirteen English divines testified to his good work for the colony, and it may be that the reference is to them, with a change of thirteen to eleven.

In this fable Cotton Mather describes in some detail his father's services as agent for the colony, and discourses once more upon the merits of the new charter and the unreasonableness of protests against it.

In the last fable, the wolves are the French, and the dogs are the New Englanders. Its point is simply that in a time when there were enemies at her gates, New England could not safely allow herself to be weakened by political disputes at home.

How skillful the *Fables* are appears more clearly when one compares them with the history of the particular events and issues with which they dealt. In them Mather exemplified not only his ability as a writer but his grasp of at least one aspect of the tangled politics of the period.

VI

A Letter to Dr. Woodward

This letter is here printed as a sample of Cotton Mather's scientific communications to the Royal Society. These were many, and deserve study. They exist completely only in manuscript, but Professor

Kittredge has catalogued them, and given an outline of their contents.[1] He has said, referring to the
letter printed in this volume, "Mather's account
of the storm is a fine example of his style at its best."
He has also spoken a word of warning as to the way
in which all Mather's scientific communications
should be read, saying: "They should be judged,
not from the point of view of a modern specialist,
but from that of the eighteenth century *virtuosi* to
whom they were submitted. . . . The subjects that
Mather treats are highly miscellaneous, and some
of them seem to the casual reader more curious than
edifying. The documents, therefore, are likely to
be regarded as symptoms of a trivial and credulous
temper. Not at all! A sufficient corrective for this
notion is a cursory acquaintance with the writings
of Mather's European contemporaries, and in particular with their notes and essays in the scientific
journals of the day. . . . There is scarcely an item
in these letters that cannot be paralleled in the Philosophical Transactions, or in the Ephemerides of
what we now style the Leopoldina."[2]
The letter on "An horrid snow" has a special
interest because we can be sure just where Mather
got much of his material for it, and just how he treated
this material. On September 12, 1717, John Winthrop, grandson of the famous Governor John Winthrop of Massachusetts, wrote to Cotton Mather
from New London, acknowledging a letter in which
Mather had asked for his observations in regard

[1] G. L. Kittredge, "Cotton Mather's Scientific Communications
to the Royal Society," in *American Antiquarian Society Proceedings*
(1916), xxvi, 18–57.
[2] *Idem*, 18-19, 44.

to the great snowfall of the previous winter.[1]   He
tells the story of the wild animals coming down
to the seashore and terrifying the sheep, of the lambs
born "of Mounseir Reignards complexion & Couler,"
of the two sheep found alive after twenty-eight days'
burial in the snow, of the shells cast up by the sea,
and of the porpoises observed near the shore. Mather,
in writing to Woodward, follows Winthrop exactly,
for his data, but he condenses his informant's account, adds details from other sources, and puts the
whole into a style and form far better than that of
the original letter from Connecticut.   If a charge
of "credulity" is brought on the basis of Mather's
account of the storm, it should be made against Winthrop, not Mather.   The latter took his facts from
an excellent source—a letter from an honored magistrate of Connecticut, a "natural philosopher," and
the son of a Fellow of the Royal Society.   Moreover,
Winthrop was no superstitious believer in marvels,
but a scientist of parts.   He was later elected to the
Royal Society, and in the letter in which he writes
of the storm he thanks Mather for his good offices in
mentioning his name among the Fellows of that Society.

The letter to Woodward about the great storms
of 1717, brief as it is, serves to show Mather the
scientist, writing of matters about which he had trust-
worthy information, scrupulous in his treatment of
the evidence, and dextrous in the style in which he
wrote.   His scientific communications do not deserve
to be forgotten, for in them are made clear certain of
his best qualities as a student of science, a scholar, and
a man of letters.

[1] The letter is in the Library of the Massachusetts Historical
Society.

NOTE ON THE TEXT

IN accordance with the purpose of the Series of which this volume forms a part, comparatively full selections are printed here from the writings of Cotton Mather. The Second Book of the *Magnalia* given here is virtually a work complete in itself; the *Life of Phips* included in this Book was originally published separately. The *Political Fables*, never printed in Cotton Mather's lifetime, form a separate unit among his writings. The selections from *The Christian Philosopher* comprise a larger part of one of Mather's most interesting books than is elsewhere accessible. The *Letter to Dr. Woodward* is a sample of his scientific communications to the Royal Society, and has interest as representing this class of his writings.

The *Magnalia* does not exist in manuscript, nor does *The Christian Philosopher*, so that the present text reproduces the first printed edition of both of these works. The original punctuation, italicization, capitalization, and spelling have been preserved. The only changes have been the substitution of the modern *s* for the old long form of that letter, the representation by ordinary Roman capitals of words printed by Mather in antique capitals, and finally the substitution of modern Greek type for the archaic type used in the original edition. Cotton Mather's corrections given in the *Errata* to the printed editions are here made in the text as printed. The *Political Fables* follow the reprint in *The Andros Tracts* published by the Prince Society in 1869. The *Letter to Dr. Woodward* is printed from the manuscript owned by the Massachusetts Historical Society and reproduces it exactly, except that manuscript abbreviations of pronouns are given in their full form. For example, "ye" in the manuscript is printed "the," "yr" in the manuscript is printed "your," and so on.

I have made no effort to annotate Mather's text completely. I have given in footnotes the sense of the quotations in foreign languages, and I have commented briefly on most of the names and incidents alluded to in the text which seemed to need elucidation for modern readers. I have made no effort to identify Mather's biblical references or the sources of his quotations, except where to do so seemed valuable as an indication of the range of his information. Obviously it has been impossible to correct his errors or to add notes expanding and bringing up to date the historical and scientific data he gives. The notes are designed to meet the needs of students in colleges, and have been carefully selected from much possible annotation for reasons of space.

My gratitude for aid in the preparation of this book is due to many whom I should thank individually did space permit, and in particular to Professor George L. Kittredge of Harvard University.

K. B. M.

SELECTED READING LIST

I. WORKS OF COTTON MATHER

There is no complete bibliography of Cotton Mather's writings in print. The best bibliography available is in Sibley, J. L.: *Biographical Sketches of Graduates of Harvard University* (Cambridge, 1873–85), Vol. III, pp. 42–158. Only those works mentioned in the Introduction are listed here.

Angel of Bethesda, The. In manuscript, in the Library of the American Antiquarian Society.

Biblia Americana. In manuscript, in the Library of the Massachusetts Historical Society.

Bonifacius. An Essay Upon the Good, that is to be Devised and Designed, etc., Boston, 1710. Under the title of *Essays to do Good,* this was often republished, e. g. Boston, 1808; Johnstown, 1815; Edinburgh and London, 1825; Dover, 1826; London, 1842; Boston, 1845.

Christian Philosopher, The. London, 1721; Charlestown, 1815 (garbled).

Diary of Cotton Mather, The. Edited by W. C. Ford, in *Massachusetts Historical Society Collections,* Series 7, Vols. VII–VIII. Boston, 1911–12.

Letters to the Royal Society. See the list in G. L. Kittredge: *Cotton Mather's Scientific Communications,* mentioned in Section IV, below.

Magnalia Christi Americana: Or, the Ecclesiastical History of New England, etc. London, 1702; Hartford, 1820, 1853–55. The edition of 1853–55, though not satisfactory, is the best reprint of the work. A new reprint is now in preparation.

Manuductio ad Ministerium. Directions for a Candidate of the Ministry, etc., Boston, 1726, London, 1781, 1789.

Memorable Providences, Relating to Witchcrafts and Possessions, etc. Boston, 1689; Edinburgh, 1697.

Parentor. Memoirs of Remarkables in the Life and Death of Increase Mather. Boston, 1724.

Political Fables. First printed in *Massachusetts Historical Society Collections,* Third Series, Vol. I; reprinted in *The Andros Tracts* (Boston, 1868–74), Vol. II, pp. 325–32.

lxiiSELECTED READING LIST

Psalterium Americanum. The Book of Psalms, In a Translation Exactly conformed unto the Original; But all in Blank Verse, etc. Boston, 1718.

Wonders of the Invisible World, The. Observations As well Historical as Theological, upon the Nature, The Number, and the Operations of the Devils, etc. Boston, 1693; London, 1693, 1862.

II. BIOGRAPHIES

Marvin, A. P. *The Life and Times of Cotton Mather*. Boston and Chicago, 1892.

Wendell, Barrett. *Cotton Mather, the Puritan Priest*, New York, 1891, and Cambridge, 1926. The best biography of Mather.

III. BRIEF BIOGRAPHICAL ARTICLES

Robbins, C. *A History of the Second Church, or Old North, in Boston* (Boston, 1852), pp. 67–115.

Sibley, J. L. *Biographical Sketches* (see Section I, above), Vol. III, pp. 6–42.

IV. SPECIAL TOPICS

Deane, Charles. "The Light Shed upon Cotton Mather's 'Magnalia' by His Diary," *Massachusetts Historical Society Proceedings*, Vol. VI, pp. 404–414.

Francke, Kuno. "Cotton Mather and August Hermann Francke," *Harvard Studies in Philology and Literature*, Vol. V, pp. 57–67. "Further Documents Concerning Cotton Mather and August Hermann Francke," *Americana Germanica*, Vol. I, No. 4.

Holmes, T. J. "Cotton Mather and His Writings on Witchcraft," *Papers of the Bibliographical Society of America*, Vol. XVIII, pp. 30–59 (Chicago, 1925).

Kittredge, G. L. "Cotton Mather's Election into the Royal Society," *Publications of the Colonial Society of Massachusetts*, Vol. XIV, pp. 81–114. "Cotton Mather's Scientific Communications to the Royal Society," *American Antiquarian Society Proceedings*, Vol. XXVI, pp. 18–57 (Worcester, 1916). "Notes on Witchcraft," *American Antiquarian Society Proceedings*, Vol. XVIII, pp. 148–212 (Worcester, 1907). "Some Lost Works of Cotton Mather," *Massachusetts Historical Society Proceedings*, Vol. XLV, pp. 418–479 (Boston, 1912).

Murdock, K. B.   *Increase Mather* (Cambridge, 1925), Chaps. XIII–
   XV (on the relation of the Mathers to politics of the time),
   Chap. XVI (New England witchcraft).
Poole, W. F.   *Cotton Mather and Salem Witchcraft* (Boston, 1869).
   Also in *North American Review*, Vol. CVIII.
Tuttle, J. H.   "The Libraries of the Mathers," *American Antiquarian
   Society Proceedings*, Vol. XX, pp. 269–356 (Worcester, 1910).
Upham, C. W.   "Salem Witchcraft and Cotton Mather," *Historical
   Magazine*, September, 1869, and separately, Boston, 1869.
Walker, W.   "The Services of the Mathers in New England Religious
   Development," *Papers of the American Society of Church History*,
   Vol. V.

MAGNALIA CHRISTI AMERICANA

A GENERAL INTRODUCTION

Ἐρῶ δὲ τοῦτο, τῆς τῶν ἐντευξαμένων 'ωφελείας ἕνεκα.

Dicam hoc propter utilitatem eorum qui Lecturi sunt hoc opus. Theodorit.[1]

§ 1.   I WRITE the *Wonders* of the CHRISTIAN RELIGION, flying from the Depravations of *Europe*, to the *American Strand:* And, assisted by the Holy Author of that *Religion*, I do, with all Conscience of *Truth*, required therein by Him, who is the *Truth* it self, Report the *Wonderful Displays* of His Infinite Power, Wisdom, Goodness, and Faithfulness, wherewith His Divine Providence hath *Irradiated* an *Indian Wilderness*.

I Relate the *Considerable Matters*, that produced and attended the First Settlement of COLONIES, which have been Renowned for the Degree of REF–ORMATION, Professed and Attained by *Evangelical Churches*, erected in those *Ends of the Earth:* And a *Field* being thus prepared, I proceed unto a Relation of the *Considerable Matters* which have been acted thereupon.

I first introduce the *Actors*, that have, in a more exemplary manner served those *Colonies;* and give *Remarkable Occurrences*, in the exemplary LIVES of

[1] " I say this for the benefit of those who are readers of this book." Theodoret was one of the early fathers of the Church, c. 393–457.

many *Magistrates*, and of more *Ministers*, who so *Lived*, as to leave unto Posterity, *Examples* worthy of *Everlasting Remembrance*.

I add hereunto, the *Notables* of the only *Protestant University*, that ever *shone* in that Hemisphere of the *New World;* with particular Instances of *Criolians*,[1] in our *Biography*, provoking the *whole World*, with vertuous Objects of Emulation.

I introduce then, the *Actions* of a more Eminent Importance, that have signalized those *Colonies;* Whether the *Establishments*, directed by their *Synods;* with a Rich Variety of *Synodical* and *Ecclesiastical* Determinations; or, the *Disturbances*, with which they have been from all sorts of *Temptations* and *Enemies* Tempestuated; and the *Methods* by which they have still weathered out each *Horrible Tempest*.

And into the midst of these *Actions*, I interpose an entire *Book*, wherein there is, with all possible Veracity, a *Collection* made, of *Memorable Occurrences*, and amazing *Judgments* and *Mercies*, befalling many *particular Persons* among the People of *New-England*.

Let my Readers expect all that I have promised them, in this *Bill of Fare*; and it may be they will find themselves entertained with yet many other Passages, above and beyond their Expectation, deserving likewise a room in *History:* In all which, there will be nothing, but the *Author's* too mean way of preparing so great Entertainments, to Reproach the Invitation.

§ 2. The Reader will doubtless desire to know, what it was that

---

[1] Criolians or Creolians, an obsolete word for pérsons born or naturalized in America but of European race. *Cf.* modern "Creole," and see *New English Dictionary* for the history of the meanings of this word.

―――― *tot Volvere casus*
Insignes Pietate Viros, tot adire Labores,
Impulerit.[1]

And our *History* shall, on many fit Occasions which will
be therein offered, endeavour, with all *Historical*
Fidelity and Simplicity, and with as little Offence as
may be, to satisfy him. The Sum of the Matter is,
That from the very Beginning of the REFORMA-
TION in the *English Nation*, there hath always been
a Generation of *Godly Men*, desirous to pursue the
*Reformation of Religion, according to the Word of God,
and the Example of the best Reformed Churches*; and
answering the Character of *Good Men*, given by *Josephus*, in his Paraphrase on the words of *Samuel* to *Saul*,
μηδὲν ἄλλο πραχθήσεσθαι καλῶς ὑφ᾽ ἑαυτῶν νομίζοντες
ἢ ὅτι ἄν ποιήσωσι τοῦ θεοῦ κεκελευκότος. *They
think they do nothing Right in the Service of God, but
what they do according to the Command of God.* And
there hath been another Generation of Men, who have
still employed the *Power* which they have generally
still had in their Hands, not only to stop the Progress
of the Desired *Reformation*, but also, with Innumerable
Vexations, to Persecute those that most Heartily
wished well unto it. There were many of the *Reformers*,
who joyned with the Reverend *JOHN FOX*, in the
Complaints which he then entred in his *Martyrology*,[2]
about the *Baits of Popery* yet left in the Church; and

―――――

[1] "Drove men eminent in piety to endure so many calamities and
to undertake so many hardships." The quotation is slightly altered
from the *Æneid*, I, 9–11.

[2] John Fox, 1516–1587, whose famous *Acts and Monuments*, first
printed in 1563, and usually referred to as *Fox's Book of Martyrs*,
told the stories of many English Martyrs. It was a book popular
among American Puritans, and often cited by Cotton Mather.

in his *Wishes, God take them away, or ease us from them, for God knows, they be the Cause of much Blindness and Strife amongst Men!* They Zealously decried the *Policy* of complying always with the *Ignorance* and *Vanity* of the *People;* and cried out earnestly for *Purer Administrations* in the House of God, and more *Conformity* to the *Law of Christ,* and *Primitive Christianity:* While others would not hear of going any further than the *First Essay* of *Reformation.* 'Tis very certain, that the *First Reformers* never intended, that what *They* did, should be the *Absolute Boundary* of *Reformation,* so that it should be a Sin to proceed any further; as, by their own going beyond *Wicklift,* and *Changing* and *Growing* in their own *Models* also, and the Confessions of *Cranmer,* with the *Scripta Anglicana* of *Bucer,* and a thousand other things, was abundantly demonstrated. But after a Fruitless Expectation, wherein the truest Friends of the *Reformation* long waited, for to have that which *Heylin* himself [1] owns to have been the Design of the *First Reformers,* followed as it should have been, a Party very unjustly arrogating to themselves, the Venerable Name of, *The Church of* England, by Numberless Oppressions, grievously *Smote those their Fellow-Servants.* Then 'twas that, as our Great *OWEN* hath expressed it,[2] *Multitudes of Pious, Peaceable Protestants, were driven, by their Severities, to leave their Native Country, and seek a Refuge for their Lives and Liberties, with*

[1] Peter Heylyn, 1600–1662, an Anglican divine and historian, defended Bishop Laud, and wrote often against the Puritans. Naturally he was thoroughly disliked by men who thought as Cotton Mather did.

[2] John Owen, 1616–1683, usually called one of the three greatest English Puritans, was in high favor with American Puritans, and particularly with Cotton Mather. He wrote a preface for a book by Increase Mather.

Freedom, for the Worship of God, in a Wilderness, in the Ends of the Earth.

§ 3. It is the History of these PROTESTANTS, that is here attempted: PROTESTANTS that highly honoured and affected *The Church of* ENGLAND, and humbly Petition to be a *Part* of it: But by the Mistake of a few powerful *Brethren*, driven to seek a place for the Exercise of the *Protestant Religion*, according to the Light of their Consciences, in the Desarts of *America*. And in this Attempt I have proposed, not only to preserve and secure the Interest of *Religion*, in the Churches of that little Country *NEW-ENG-LAND*, so far as the Lord Jesus Christ may please to Bless it for that End, but also to offer unto the Churches of the *Reformation*, abroad in the World, some small *Memorials*, that may be serviceable unto the Designs of *Reformation*, whereto, I believe, they are quickly to be awakened. I am far from any such Boast, concerning these Churches, *That they have Need of Nothing*, I wish their *Works* were more *perfect before God*. Indeed, that which *Austin* called *The Perfection of Christians*, is like to be, until the Term for the *Antichristian Apostasie* be expired, *The Perfection of Churches* too; *Ut Agnoscant se nunquam esse perfectas*.[1] Nevertheless, I perswade my self, that *so far as they have attained*, they have given *Great Examples* of the *Methods* and *Measures*, wherein an *Evangelical Reformation* is to be prosecuted, and of the *Qualifications* requisite in the Instruments that are to prosecute it, and of the *Difficulties* which may be most likely to obstruct it, and the most likely *Directions* and *Remedies* for those

[1] "That they may acknowledge themselves to be by no means perfect."

Obstructions. It may be, 'tis not possible for me to do a greater Service unto the Churches on the *Best Island* of the Universe, than to give a distinct Relation of those *Great Examples* which have been occurring among Churches of *Exiles*, that were driven out of that *Island*, into an horrible *Wilderness*, meerly for their being Well-willers unto the *Reformation*. When that Blessed Martyr *Constantine* was carried, with other Martyrs, in a *Dung-Cart*, unto the place of Execution, he pleasantly said, *Well, yet we are a precious Odour to God in Christ*. Tho' the *Reformed Churches* in the *American Regions*, have, by very Injurious Representations of their Brethren (all which they desire to Forget and Forgive!) been many times thrown into a *Dung-Cart;* yet, as they have been a *precious Odour to God in Christ*, so, I hope, they will be a *precious Odour* unto *His People;* and not only *Precious*, but *Useful* also, when the *History* of them shall come to be considered. A *Reformation of the Church* is coming on, and I cannot but thereupon say, with the dying *Cyrus* to his Children in *Xenophon*, Ἐκ τῶν προγεγεννημένων μανθάνετε αὐτὴ γὰρ ἀρίστη διδασκαλία. *Learn from the things that have been done already, for this is the best way of Learning*. The Reader hath here an Account of *The Things that have been done already*. *Bernard* upon that Clause in the *Canticles*, [*O thou fairest among Women*] has this ingenious Gloss, *Pulchram, non omnimode quidem, sed pulchram inter mulieres eam docet, videlicet cum Distinctione, quatenus ex hoc amplius reprimatur, & sciat quid desit sibi*.[1] Thus I do not say, That the Churches of *New-England* are the most

---

[1] "He teaches that she is fair, not in a universal sense, but fair among women, plainly with a distinction, to which extent his praise is qualified, and she may know what is lacking to her."

Regular that can be; yet I do say, and am sure, That they are very like unto those that were in the *First Ages* of Christianity. And if I assert, That in the *Reformation* of the Church, the State of it in those *First Ages*, is to be not a little considered, the Great *Peter Ramus*,[1] among others, has emboldened me. For when the Cardinal of *Lorrain*, the *Mæcenas* of that Great Man, was offended at him, for turning *Protestant*, he replied, *Inter Opes illas, quibus me ditasti, has etiam in æternum recordabor, quod Beneficio, Poessiacæ Responsionis tuæ didici, de Quindecim a Christo sæculis, primum vere esse aureum, Reliqua, quo longius abscederent esse nequiora, atque deteriora: Tum igitur cum fieret optio, Aureum sæculum delegi.*[2] In short, The *First Age* was the *Golden Age:* To return unto *That*, will make a Man a *Protestant*, and I may add, a *Puritan*. 'Tis possible, That our Lord Jesus Christ carried some Thousands of *Reformers* into the Retirements of an *American Desert*, on purpose, that, with an opportunity granted unto many of his Faithful Servants, to enjoy the precious *Liberty* of their *M nistry*, tho' in the midst of many *Temptations* all their days, He might there, *To* them first, and then *By* them, give a *Specimen* of

---

[1] This opponent of Aristotelianism, and educational reformer, who lived 1515–1572, was much read by the Puritans. His books were favorites of Richard Mather, grandfather of Cotton, and when Increase Mather, Cotton's father, graduated from Harvard, his commencement thesis was so much influenced by Ramus's ideas as to arouse some criticism from the President of the College, who was a disciple of Aristotle's views.

[2] "Among those riches, with which you enriched me, this I was mindful of always, which I learned from your reply at Poissy—that of the fifteen centuries since Christ, the first is truly golden. The rest, the farther they are removed from the first, are the more worthless and degenerate. Therefore when choice was to be made, I chose the golden age."

many Good Things, which He would have His Churches elsewhere aspire and arise unto: And *This* being done, He knows whether there be not *All done*, that *New-England* was planted for; and whether the Plantation may not, soon after this, *Come to Nothing*. Upon that Expression in the Sacred Scripture, *Cast the unprofitable Servant into Outer Darkness*, it hath been imagined by some, That the *Regiones Exteræ* of *America*, are the *Tenebræ Exteriores*, which the *Unprofitable* are there condemned unto. No doubt, the Authors of those Ecclesiastical Impositions and Severities, which drove the English Christians into the *Dark Regions* of *America*, esteemed those *Christians* to be a very *unprofitable* sort of Creatures. But behold, ye *European* Churches, There are *Golden Candlesticks* [more than *twice Seven times Seven!*] in the midst of this *Outer Darkness;* Unto the *upright* Children of *Abraham*, here hath arisen *Light in Darkness*. And let us humbly speak it, it shall be *Profitable* for you to consider the *Light*, which from the midst of this *Outer Darkness*, is now to be Darted over unto the other side of the *Atlantick Ocean*. But we must therewithal ask your Prayers, that these *Golden Candlesticks* may not *quickly* be *Removed out of their place!*

§ 4. But whether *New-England* may *Live* any where else or no, it must *Live* in our *History!*

HISTORY, in general, hath had so many and mighty Commendations from the Pens of those Numberless Authors, who, from *Herodotus* to *Howel*,[1] have been the professed Writers of it, that a tenth part of them

---

[1]James Howell, 1594?–1666, famous for his familiar letters, the *Epistolæ Ho-Elianæ*, was somewhat of a historian. Cotton Mather, later in the "Introduction," attacks him for prejudice and bias,

Transcribed, would be a Furniture for a *Polyanthea in Folio*.[1] We, that have neither liberty, nor occasion, to quote those Commendations of *History*, will content our selves with the Opinion of one who was not much of a *profess'd Historian*, expressed in that passage, whereto all Mankind subscribe, *Historia est Testis temporum, Nuntia vetustatis, Lux veritatis, vita memoriæ, magistra vitæ*.[2] But of all *History* it must be confessed, that the *Palm* is to be given unto *Church History;* wherein the *Dignity*, the *Suavity*, and the *Utility* of the *Subject* is transcendent. I observe, that for the Description of the *whole World* in the Book of *Genesis*, that *First-born of all Historians*, the great *Moses*, employes but *one* or *two* Chapters, whereas he implies,[3] it may be *seven times* as many Chapters, in describing that one little *Pavilion, The Tabernacle*. And when I am thinking, what may be the Reason of this *Difference*, methinks it intimates unto us, That the *Church* wherein the Service of God is performed, is much more Precious than the *World*, which was indeed created for the Sake and Use of the *Church*. 'Tis very certain, that the greatest Entertainments must needs occur in the History of the *People*, whom the *Son* of God hath *Redeemed* and *Purified* unto himself, as a *Peculiar People*, and whom the *Spirit* of God, by *Supernatural Operations* upon their Minds, does cause to live like *Strangers* in *this World*, conforming themselves unto the *Truths* and *Rules* of his Holy Word, in Expectation

[1] *I.e.*, a large collection of select quotations, an anthology.

[2] "History is the witness of periods of time, the messenger of antiquity, the light of truth, the life of memory, the instructress of life." Cotton Mather here quotes Cicero (*De Oratore*, II, 9) but fails to preserve the original order. Probably he was relying on his memory of a familiar passage.

[3] Employes?

of a *Kingdom*, whereto they shall be in another and a better *World* advanced. Such a *People* our Lord Jesus Christ hath procured and preserved in all Ages *visible;* and the Dispensations of his *wonderous Providence* towards this People (for, *O Lord, thou do'st lift them up, and cast them down!*) their Calamities, their Deliverances, the Dispositions which they have still discovered, and the considerable *Persons* and *Actions* found among them, cannot but afford Matters of *Admiration* and *Admonition*, above what any other Story can pretend unto: 'Tis nothing but *Atheism* in the Hearts of Men, that can perswade them otherwise. Let any Person of good Sense peruse the History of *Herodotus*, which, like a River taking Rise, where the *Sacred Records* of the *Old Testament* leave off, runs along smoothly and sweetly, with Relations that sometimes perhaps want an *Apology*, down until the *Grecians* drive the *Persians* before them. Let him then peruse *Thucydides*, who from *Acting* betook himself to *Writing*, and carries the ancient State of the *Grecians*, down to the twenty first Year of the *Peloponnesian Wars* in a manner, which *Casaubon* judges to be *Mirandum potius quam imitandum.*[1] Let him next Revolve *Xenophon*, that *Bee* of *Athens*, who continues a Narrative of the *Greek Affairs*, from the *Peloponnesian Wars*, to the Battle of *Mantinea*, and gives us a *Cyrus* into the bargain, at such a rate, that *Lipsius* reckons the Character of a *Suavi, Fidus & Circumspectus Scriptor*,[2] to belong unto him. Let him from hence proceed unto *Diodorus Siculus*, who, besides a rich Treasure of *Egyptian*, *Assyrian*, *Lybian* and *Grecian*, and other

[1] "To be admired rather than imitated."
[2] "An agreeable, faithful and careful writer." Justus Lipsius, 1547–1606, was a learned critic, and editor of classical texts.

Antiquities, in a Phrase, which according to *Photius's*
Judgment, is ἱστορία μάλιστα πρεπούσῃ, *of all most
becoming an Historian*,[1] carries on the Thread begun
by his Predecessors, until the End of the Hundred
and nineteenth *Olympiad;* and where he is defective,
let it be supplied from *Arianus*, from *Justin*, and from
Curtius, who in the relish of *Colerus* is, *Quovis melle
dulcior*.[2] Let him hereupon consult *Polybius*, and
acquaint himself with the Birth and Growth of the
Roman Empire, as far as 'tis described, in *Five* of the
Forty Books composed by an Author, who with a
Learned *Professor of History* is, *Prudens Scriptor, si
quis alius*.[3] Let him now run over the Table of the
Roman Affairs, compendiously given by *Lucius Florus*,
and then let him consider the Transactions of above
three hundred Years reported by *Dionysius Halicar-
nassæus*, who, if the Censure of *Bodin* may be taken,
Græcos omnes & Latinos superasse videatur.[4] Let him
from hence pass to *Livy*, of whom the famous Critick
says, *Hoc solum ingenium (de Historicis Loquor) populus
Romanus par Imperio suo habuit*,[5] and supply those
of his *Decads* that are lost, from the best Fragments
of Antiquity, in others (and especially *Dion* and *Salust*)
that lead us on still further in our way. Let him then
proceed unto the Writers of the *Cesarean* times, and
first revolve *Suetonius*, then *Tacitus*, then *Herodian*,
then a whole Army more of *Historians*, which now

---

[1] Photius, patriarch of Constantinople in the second half of the
ninth century.

[2] "More sweet than honey." Colerus is probably Johann Coler,
a German theological writer of the sixteenth century.

[3] "A discreet writer, if there ever was one."

[4] "Seems to have surpassed all the Greeks and Latins."

[5] "As for historians, the Romans had this one genius worthy of
their empire."

crowd into our *Library;* and unto all the rest, let him
not fail of adding the Incomparable *Plutarch,* whose
Books they say, *Theodore Gaza* preferred above any
in the World, next unto the Inspired Oracles of the
Bible: But if the Number be still too little to satisfie
an *Historical Appetite,* let him add *Polyhistor* unto the
number, and all the *Chronicles* of the following Ages.
After all, he must sensibly acknowledge, that the two
short Books of *Ecclesiastical History,* written by the
Evangelist *Luke,* hath given us more *glorious Entertainments,* than all these voluminous Historians if they
were put all together. The *Atchievements* of one *Paul*
particularly, which that Evangelist hath *Emblazon'd,*
have more *True Glory* in them, than all the Acts of
those Execrable *Plunderers* and *Murderers,* and ir-
resistible *Banditti* of the World, which have been
dignified with the Name of *Conquerors. Tacitus* counted
*Ingentia bella, Expugnationes urbium, fusos captosque
Reges,*[1] the Ravages of *War,* and the glorious *Violences,*
whereof great Warriors make a wretched Ostentation,
to be the *Noblest Matter* for an *Historian.* But there
is a *Nobler,* I humbly conceive, in the planting and
forming of *Evangelical Churches,* and the *Temptations,*
the *Corruptions,* the *Afflictions,* which assault them,
and their *Salvations* from those Assaults, and the
Exemplary *Lives* of those that Heaven employs to be
Patterns of *Holiness* and *Usefulness* upon Earth: And
unto such it is, that I now invite my Readers; Things,
in comparison whereof, the Subjects of many other
Histories, are of as little weight, as the Questions about
Z, the last Letter of our Alphabet, and whether H is
to be pronounced with an Aspiration, where about
whole Volumes have been written, and of no more

[1] "Vast wars, captures of cities, kings captured or in flight."

Account, than the Composure of *Didymus*.[1] But for the *manner* of my treating this *Matter*, I must now give some account unto him.

§ 5. *Reader!* I have done the part of an *Impartial Historian*, albeit not without all occasion perhaps, for the Rule which a worthy Writer, in his *Historica*, gives to every Reader, *Historici Legantur cum Moderatione & venia, & cogitetur fieri non posse ut in omnibus circumstantiis sint Lyncei.*[2] *Polybius* complains of those *Historians*, who always made either the *Carthagenians* brave, and the *Romans* base, or è *contra*, in all their Actions, as their Affection for their own *Party* led them. I have endeavoured, with all *good Conscience*, to decline this writing meerly for a *Party*, or doing like the Dealer in History, whom *Lucian* derides, for always calling the Captain of his own Party an *Achilles*, but of the adverse Party a *Thersites:* Nor have I added unto the just Provocations for the Complaint made by the Baron *Maurier*,[3] That the *greatest part of Histories* are but so many *Panegyricks* composed by *Interested Hands*, which *elevate Iniquity to the Heavens, like Paterculus*, and like *Machiavel*, who propose *Tiberius Cesar*, and *Cesar Borgia*, as Examples fit for *Imitation*, whereas *True History* would have Exhibited them as Horrid *Monsters* as very *Devils*. 'Tis true, I am not of the Opinion, that one cannot merit the Name of an *Impartial*

[1] Alexandrian grammarian of the time of Cicero, sometimes accused of having written so much that in his later writing he contradicted statements he had made in earlier ones.

[2] "Historians are to be read with moderation and indulgence, and it is to be remembered that they cannot in everything be as keen-sighted as Lynceus."

[3] Probably Louis Aubery, Seigneur du Maury, d. 1687, writer of several historical works.

Historian, except he write bare *Matters of Fact,* without all *Reflection;* for I can tell where to find this given as the Definition of *History, Historia est rerum gestarum, cum laude aut vituperatione, Narratio:*[1] And if I am not altogether a *Tacitus,* when *Vertues* or *Vices* occur to be matters of *Reflection,* as well as of *Relation,* I will, for my Vindication, appeal to *Tacitus* himself, whom *Lipsius* calls one of the *Prudentest* (tho' *Tertullian,* long before, counts him the *Lyingest*) of them who have Inriched the World with *History:* He says, *Præcipuum munus Annalium reor, ne virtutes sileantur, utque pravis Dictis, Factisque ex posteritate & Infamia metus sit.*[2] I have not *Commended* any Person, but when I have really judg'd, not only *That* he *Deserved* it, but also that it would be a Benefit unto Posterity to know, Wherein he deserved it: And my Judgment of *Desert,* hath not been *Biassed,* by Persons being of my own particular Judgment in matters of *Disputation,* among the Churches of God. I have been as willing to wear the Name of *Simplicius Verinus,*[3] throughout my whole undertaking, as he that, before me, hath assumed it: Nor am I like Pope *Zachary,* impatient so much as to hear of any *Antipodes.*[4] The Spirit of a *Schlusselbergius,*[5] who falls foul with Fury and Reproach on all

[1] "History is the story of events, with praise or blame."

[2] "I regard it as history's highest function not to let virtues be uncelebrated, and to hold up as a terror the censure of posterity for bad words and deeds." (Tacitus, *Annals,* iii, 65.)

[3] Simplicius Verinus was the name assumed at times by Claude Saumaise (Salmasius), 1588–1653, a French classical scholar, famous for his controversy with Milton.

[4] Pope Zacharias, bishop of Rome from 741 to 752, directed that there be expelled from the church one Virgilius who held that there was another world below the earth.

[5] Konrad Schlüsselburg, 1543–1619, Lutheran writer and controversialist.

who differ from him; The Spirit of an *Heylin*, who seems to count no Obloquy too hard for a *Reformer;* and the Spirit of those (*Folio-writers* there are, some of them, in the English Nation!) whom a Noble Historian Stigmatizes, as, *Those Hot-headed, Passionate Bigots, from whom, 'tis enough, if you be of a Religion contrary unto theirs, to be defamed, condemned and pursued with a thousand Calumnies.* I thank Heaven I Hate it with all my Heart. But how can the *Lives* of the *Commendable* be written without *Commending* them? Or, is that Law of *History* given in one of the eminentest pieces of *Antiquity* we now have in our hands, wholly antiquated, *Maxime proprium est Historiæ, Laudem rerum egregie gestarum persequi?* [1] Nor have I, on the other side, forbore to mention many *Censurable* things, even in the Best of my Friends, when the things, in my opinion, were *not Good;* or so bore away for *Placentia,* in the course of our Story, as to pass by *Verona;*[2] but been mindful of the Direction which *Polybius* gives to the Historian, *It becomes him that writes an History, sometimes to extol Enemies in his Praises, when their praise-worthy Actions bespeak it, and at the same time to reprove the best Friends, when their Deeds appear worthy of a reproof; in-as much as History is good for nothing, if Truth (which is the very Eye of the Animal) be not in it.* Indeed I have thought it my duty upon all accounts, (and if it have proceeded unto the degree

---

[1] "It is in the highest degree the property of history to record praise of good deeds."

[2] Cotton Mather's phrasing here suggests that "to bear away for Placentia, and to miss Verona" was a proverbial expression, meaning about what our "to fail to see the woods for the trees" implies. Probably the reference is to Hasdrubal's entry into Italy, when his laying siege to Placentia delayed his entry into the heart of Italy. *Cf.* Livy, xxvii, 39, 43.

of a *Fault*, there is, it may be, something in my *Temper*
and *Nature*, that has betray'd me therein) to be more
sparing and easie, in thus mentioning of *Censurable*
things, than in my *other Liberty:* A writer of *Church-
History*, should, I know, be like the *builder of the Temple*,
one of the *Tribe of Naphthali;* and for this I will also
plead my *Polybius* in my Excuse; *It is not the Work of
an Historian, to commemorate the Vices and Villanies
of Men, so much as their just, their fair, their honest
Actions: And the Readers of History get more good by
the Objects of their Emulation, than of their Indignation.*
Nor do I deny, that tho' I cannot approve the Conduct
of *Josephus*, (whom *Jerom* not unjustly nor ineptly
calls, *The Greek Livy*) when he left out of his *Antiquities*,
the Story of the *Golden Calf*, and I don't wonder to
find *Chamier*, and *Rivet*,[1] and others, taxing him for
his *Partiality* towards his Country-men; yet I have left
unmentioned some *Censurable Occurrences* in the *Story*
of our *Colonies*, as things no less *Unuseful* than *Improper* to be raised out of the Grave, wherein *Oblivion*
hath now buried them; lest I should have incurred the
Pasquil bestowed upon Pope *Urban*, who employing
a *Committee* to Rip up the *Old Errors* of his Predecessors,
one clap'd a pair of Spurs upon the heels of the Statue
of *St. Peter;* and a Label from the Statue of St. *Paul*
opposite thereunto, upon the Bridge, ask'd him, *Whither
he was bound?* St. *Peter* answered, *I apprehend some
Danger in staying here; I fear they'll call me in Question
for denying my Master.* And St. *Paul* replied, *Nay,
then I had best be gone too, for they'll question me also,
for Persecuting the Christians before my Conversion.*
Briefly, My Pen shall Reproach none, that can give a

[1] Daniel Chamier, 1570?-1621, French Protestant writer, and
André Rivet, 1573-1651, French Calvinist theologian.

Good Word unto any Good Man that is not of their *own Faction*, and shall *Fall out* with none, but those that can *Agree* with no body else, except those of their own *Schism*. If I draw any sort of Men with *Charcoal*, it shall be, because I remember a notable passage of the *Best Queen* that ever was in the World, our late *Queen Mary*.[1] Monsieur *Jurieu*, that he might Justifie the Reformation in *Scotland*, made a very black Representation of their old Queen *Mary;* for which, a certain *Sycophant* would have incensed our Queen *Mary* against that Reverend Person, saying, *Is it not a Shame that this Man, without any Consideration for your Royal Person, should dare to throw such Infamous Calumnies upon a Queen, from whom your Royal Highness is descended?* But that Excellent Princess replied, *No, not at all; Is it not enough that by fulsome Praises great Persons be lull'd asleep all their Lives; But must Flattery accompany them to their very Graves? How should they fear the Judgment of Posterity, if Historians be not allowed to speak the Truth after their Death?* But whether I do my self *Commend*, or whether I give my Reader an opportunity to *Censure*, I am careful above all things to do it with *Truth;* and as I have considered the words of *Plato, Deum indigne & graviter ferre, cum quis ei similem hoc est, virtute præstantem, vituperet, aut laudet contrarium:*[2] So I have had the *Ninth Commandment* of a greater *Law-giver* than *Plato*, to preserve my care of *Truth* from first to last. If any Mistake have been any where committed, it will be found meerly *Circumstantial*, and wholly *Involuntary;* and let it be

[1] Queen Mary, wife of William III, died in 1694.
[2] "It is to act unworthily and offensively toward God, to abuse anyone who is like him excelling in virtue, or to praise the opposite of such a one."

remembred, that tho' no *Historian* ever merited better than the Incomparable *Thuanus*,[1] yet learned Men have said of *his* Work, what they never shall truly say of *ours*, that it contains *multa falsissima & indigna*.[2] I find *Erasmus* himself mistaking *One* Man for *Two*, when writing of the Ancients. And even our own English Writers too are often mistaken, and in Matters of a very late Importance, as *Baker*, and *Heylin*, and *Fuller*, (professed Historians) tell us, that *Richard Sutton*, a single Man, founded the *Charter-House;* whereas his Name was *Thomas*, and he was a married Man. I think I can Recite such Mistakes, it may be *Sans* Number occurring in the most credible Writers; yet I hope I shall *commit* none such. But altho' I thus challenge, as my due, the Character of an *Impartial*, I doubt I may not challenge *That* of an *Elegant Historian*. I cannot say, whether the *Style*, wherein this *Church-History* is written, will please the Modern *Criticks:* But if I seem to have used ἁπλουστάτῃ συντάξει γραφῆς,[3] a Simple, Submiss, Humble *Style*, 'tis the same that *Eusebius* affirms to have been used by *Hegesippus*, who, as far as we understand, was the first Author (after *Luke*) that ever composed an entire Body of *Ecclesiastical History*, which he divided into *Five Books*, and Entitled, ὑπομνήματα τῶν ἐκκλησιαστικῶν πράξεων.[4] Whereas *others*, it may be, will reckon the *Style* Embellished with too much of *Ornament*, by the multiplied References to other and former Concerns, closely couch'd, for the Observation of the *Attentive*, in almost every Paragraph; but I must

---

[1] Jacques Auguste de Thou, French historian and poet, 1553-1617.
[2] "Much that is most false and unworthy."
[3] "The most simple style of writing."
[4] "Memorials of ecclesiastical transactions."

confess, that I am of his mind who said, *Sicuti sal modice cibis aspersus Condit, & gratiam saporis addit, ita si paulum Antiquitatis admiscueris, Oratio fit venustior.*[1] And I have seldom seen that Way of Writing faulted, but by those, who, for a certain odd Reason, sometimes find fault, *That the Grapes are not ripe.* These *Embellishments* (of which yet I only—*Veniam pro laude peto*)[2] are not the puerile Spoils of *Polyanthea's;* but I should have asserted them to be as choice *Flowers* as most that occur in Ancient or Modern Writings, almost unavoidably putting themselves into the Authors Hand, while about his Work, if those words of *Ambrose* had not a little frightened me, as well•as they did *Baronius, Unumquemque Fallunt sua scripta.*[3] I observe that Learned Men have been so terrified by the Reproaches of *Pedantry*, which little Smatterers at Reading and Learning have, by their *Quoting Humours* brought upon themselves, that, for to avoid all Approaches towards that which those Feeble Creatures have gone to imitate, the best way of Writing has been most injuriously deserted. But what shall we say? The Best way of Writing, under Heaven, shall be the Worst, when *Erasmus* his Monosyllable Tyrant [4] will have it so! And if I should have resign'd my self wholly to the Judgment of *others*, What way of Writing

---

[1] "Just as salt discreetly spread on food seasons it, and increases its flavor, so to mix in a little of antiquity makes style more pleasing."

[2] "I ask pardon for this praise."

[3] "Everyone errs about his own writings."

[4] "Our speech at this day (for the most part) consisteth of words of one sillable. Which thing Erasmus observing, merily in his Ecclesiast, compareth the English toong to a Dogs barking, that soundeth nothing els, but Baw, waw, waw, in Monosillable." William Lambarde, *Perambulation of Kent*, p. 233 (ed. 1826). This was written in 1570.

to have taken, the Story of the two Statues made by *Policletus* tells me, what may have been the Issue:[1] He contrived one of them according to the Rules that best pleased himself, and the other according to the Fancy of every one that look'd upon his Work: The former was afterwards Applauded by all, and the latter Derided by those very Persons who had given their Directions for it. As for such *Unaccuracies* as the *Critical* may discover, *Opere in longo*,[2] I appeal to the *Courteous*, for a favourable Construction of them; and certainly they will be favourably Judged of, when there is considered the *Variety* of my *other Employments*, which have kept me in continual Hurries, I had almost said, like those of the *Ninth Sphere*,[3] for the few Months in which this Work has been *Digesting*. It was a thing well thought, by the wise Designers of *Chelsey-Colledge*, wherein able *Historians* were one sort of Persons to be maintained;[4] That the Romanists do in one Point condemn the Protestants; for among the Romanists, they don't burden their *Professors* with any *Parochial Incumbrances;* but among the *Protestants*, the very same *Individual* Man must *Preach*, *Catechize*, Administer the *Sacraments*, Visit the Afflicted, and manage all the parts of *Church-Discipline;* and if any *Books* for the Service of Religion, be written, Persons thus *extreamly incumbred* must be the Writers. Now, of all the Churches under Heaven, there are none that expect so much *Variety* of Service from their Pastors, as those of *New-England;* and of all the Churches

[1] The story which follows occurs in Ælian, and, doubtless, elsewhere.
[2] "In a long work."
[3] The ninth or "Crystalline Sphere" in the Ptolemaic svstem of astronomy.
[4] King James' College, Chelsea, founded 1609.

in *New-England*, there are none that require more, than those in *Boston*, the Metropolis of the English *America;* whereof *one* is, by the Lord Jesus Christ, committed unto the Care of the unworthy Hand, by which this *History* is compiled. Reader, Give me leave humbly to mention, with him in *Tully, Antequam de Re, Pauca de Me!* [1] Constant *Sermons*, usually more than once, and perhaps three or four times, in a Week, and all the other Duties of a *Pastoral Watchfulness*, a very *large Flock* has all this while demanded of me; wherein, if I had been furnished with as many *Heads* as a *Typheus*, as many *Eyes* as an *Argos*, and as many *Hands* as a *Briareus*, I might have had Work enough to have employ'd them all; nor hath my *Station* left me free from Obligations to spend very much time in the *Evangelical Service* of *others* also. It would have been a great *Sin* in me, to have *Omitted*, or *Abated*, my Just Cares, to *fulfil my Ministry in these things*, and in a manner *Give my self wholly to them*. All the time I have had for my *Church-History*, hath been perhaps only, or chiefly, that, which I might have taken else for less profitable Recreations; and it hath all been done by *Snatches*. My Reader will not find me the Person intended in his *Littany*, when he says, *Libera me ab homine unius Negotis:* [2] Nor have I spent *Thirty Years* in shaping this my *History*, as *Diodorus Siculus* did for his, [and yet both *Bodinus* and *Sigonius*[3] complain of the Σφαλματα [4] attending it.] But I wish I could have enjoy'd entirely for this Work, one quarter of the little more than

---

[1] "Before coming to the subject, a little about myself."

[2] "Deliver me from a man of but one interest."

[3] Charles Sigonius (Carlo Sigonio), 1524–1585, Italian writer and philologist.

[4] "Errors."

Two Years which have roll'd away since I began it; whereas I have been forced sometimes wholly to throw by the Work whole Months together, and then resume it, but by a stolen hour or two in a day, not without some hazard of incurring the *Title* which *Coryat* put upon his History of his Travels, *Crudities hastily gobbled up in five Months*. *Protogenes* being seven Years in drawing a Picture, *Apelles* upon the sight of it, said, *The Grace of the Work was much allay'd by the length of the Time*. Whatever else there may have been to take off the *Grace of the Work*, now in the Readers hands, (whereof the *Pictures* of Great and Good Men make a considerable part) I am sure there hath not been the *length of the Time* to do it. Our English Martyrologer, counted it a sufficient *Apology*, for what Meanness might be found in the first Edition of his *Acts and Monuments*, that it was *hastily rashed up in about fourteen Months:* And I may Apologize for this Collection of our *Acts and Monuments*, that I should have been glad, in the little more than *Two Years* which have ran out, since I enter'd upon it, if I could have had one half of *About fourteen Months* to have entirely devoted thereunto. But besides the *Time*, which the *Daily Services* of *my own* first, and then many *other* Churches, have necessarily call'd for, I have lost abundance of precious *Time*, thro' the feeble and broken State of my *Health*, which hath unfitted me for *Hard Study;* I can do nothing to purpose at *Lucubrations*. And yet, in this *Time* also of the two or three Years last past, I have not been excused from the further Diversion of *Publishing* (tho' not so many as they say *Mercurius Trismegistus* [1] did, yet) more than a *Score*

---

[1] The Latin name of the Egyptian God, Thoth, reputed author of many works on Egypt.

of other Books, upon a copious Variety of other Subjects, besides the composing of several more, that are not yet published. Nor is this neither all the *Task* that I have in this while had lying upon me; for (tho' I am very sensible of what *Jerom* said, *Non bene fit, quod occupato Animo fit;* [1] and of *Quintilian's* Remark, *Non simul in multa intendere Animus totum potest;*[2]) when I applied my mind unto this way of serving the Lord JESUS CHRIST in my Generation, I set upon another and a greater, which has had, I suppose, more of my *Thought* and *Hope* than this, and wherein there hath passed me, for the most part, *Nulla dies sine linea.*[3] I considered, That all sort of *Learning* might be made gloriously Subservient unto the *Illustration* of the *Sacred Scripture;* and that no *professed Commentaries* had hitherto given a thousandth part of so much *Illustration* unto it, as might be given. I considered, that Multitudes of *particular Texts*, had, especially of later Years, been more notably *Illustrated* in the *Scattered Books* of Learned Men, than in any of the *Ordinary Commentators*. And I consider'd, That the *Treasures* of *Illustration* for the Bible, dispersed in many hundred Volumes, might be fetch'd all together by a Labour that would resolve to *Conquer all things;* and that all the *Improvements* which the *Later-ages* have made in the *Sciences*, might be also, with an inexpressible Pleasure, call'd in, to Assist the *Illustration* of the *Holy Oracles*, at a Rate that hath not been attempted in the vulgar *Annotations;* and that a common degree of *Sense*, would help a Person, who should converse much with these things, to attempt sometimes also

---

[1] "What is done with an occupied mind, is not well done."
[2] "One cannot put his whole mind on many things at the same time."
[3] "No day without a line."

an *Illustration* of his own, which might expect some Attention. Certainly, it will not be ungrateful unto good Men, to have innumerable *Antiquities, Jewish, Chaldee, Arabian, Grecian* and *Roman,* brought home unto us, with a *Sweet Light* Reflected from them on the *Word,* which is our *Light:* Or, To have all the *Typical* Men and things in our *Book of Mysteries,* accommodated with their *Antitypes:* Or, To have many Hundreds of References to our dearest *Lord Messiah,* discovered in the Writings which *Testifie of Him,* oftner than the most of Mankind have hitherto imagined: Or, To have the *Histories* of all Ages, coming in with punctual and surprising *Fulfillments* of the Divine *Prophecies,* as far as they have been hitherto fulfilled; and not meer *Conjectures,* but even Mathematical and Incontestable *Demonstrations,* given of *Expositions* offered upon the *Prophecies,* that yet remain to be accomplished: Or, To have in *One Heap,* Thousands of those *Remarkable Discoveries of the deep things of the Spirit of God,* whereof *one* or *two,* or a few, sometimes, have been, with good Success accounted Materials enough to advance a Person into *Authorism;* or to have the delicious *Curiosities* of *Grotius,* and *Bochart,* and *Mede,* and *Lightfoot,* and *Selden,* and *Spencer* [1] (carefully selected and corrected) and many more Giants in Knowledge, all set upon one Table. Travellers tell us, That at *Florence* there is a rich Table, worth a thousand Crowns, made of Precious Stones neatly inlaid; a Table that was fifteen Years in making, with no less than thirty Men daily

[1] Grotius, 1583–1645, the great Dutch lawyer and theologian; Samuel Bochart, 1599–1667, French Protestant scholar; Joseph Mede, 1586–1638, English theologian; John Lightfoot, 1602–1675, learned English divine; John Selden, 1584–1654, statesman, political writer and archæologist; and John Spencer, 1630–1695, theologian and Hebraist, were all men whose works Cotton Mather knew well.

at work upon it; even such a Table could not afford so
rich Entertainments, as one that should have the
Soul-feasting Thoughts of those Learned Men together
set upon it. Only 'tis pitty, that instead of one poor
feeble *American*, overwhelm'd with a thousand other
Cares, and capable of touching this Work no otherwise
than in a Digression, there be not more than Thirty
Men daily employ'd about it. For, when the excellent
Mr. *Pool*[1] had finished his Laborious and Immortal
Task, it was noted by some considerable Persons,
That wanting Assistance to Collect for him many miscel-
laneous Criticisms, occasionally scattered in other Authors,
he left many better Things behind him than he found.
At more than all this, our *Essay* is levell'd, if it be not
anticipated with that Epitaph, *magnis tamen excidit*
ausis.[2] Designing accordingly, to give the Church of
God such displays of his blessed Word, as may be more
Entertaining for the Rarity and Novelty of them,
than any that have hitherto been seen together in any
Exposition; and yet such as may be acceptable unto
the most Judicious, for the Demonstrative Truth of
them, and unto the most Orthodox, for the regard
had unto the *Analogy of Faith* in all, I have now, in a
few Months, got ready an huge number of *Golden Keys*
to open the *Pandects* of Heaven, and some thousands
of charming and curious and singular Notes, by the
New Help whereof, the *Word of* CHRIST *may run and*
be glorified. If the *God of my Life*, will please to spare
my Life [my yet Sinful, and Slothful, and thereby
Fofeited Life!] as many years longer as the *Barren*
Fig-tree had in the Parable, I may make unto the

[1] Matthew Poole, 1624-1709, compiled a famous *Synopsis* of the
various biblical commentators.
[2] "Yet he fell short of what he had ventured to attenpt."

Church of God, an humble Tender of our BIBLIA AMERICANA,[1] a Volumn enrich'd with better things than all the Plate of the *Indies;* YET NOT I, BUT THE GRACE OF CHRIST WITH ME. My Reader sees, why I commit the Fault of a περιαυτία,[2] which appears in the mention of these Minute-passages; 'tis to excuse whatever other Fault of Inaccuracy, or Inadvertency, may be discovered in an History, which hath been a sort of Rapsody made up (like the Paper whereon 'tis written!) with many little Rags, torn from an Employment, multifarious enough to overwhelm one of my small Capacities.

Magna dabit, qui magna potest; mihi parva potenti, Parvaque poscenti, parva dedisse sat est.[3]

§ 6.   But shall I prognosticate thy Fate, now that,

Parve (sed invideo) ne me, Liber, ibis in Urbem.[4]

Luther, who was himself owner of such an Heart, advised every Historian to get the *Heart of a Lion;* and the more I consider of the Provocation, which this our *Church-History* must needs give to that Roaring Lion, who has, through all Ages hitherto, been tearing the Church to pieces, the more occasion I see to wish my self a *Cœur de Lion.* But had not my Heart been Trebly Oak'd and Brass'd for such Encounters as this our History may meet withal, I would have

[1] The MS of Cotton Mather's *Biblia Americana* is now owned by the Massachusetts Historical Society.

[2] "Discussion about myself."

[3] "He will give great things, who is able; for me, who am able to do little, and who ask for little, it is enough to have given a little."

[4] "O little book, though I envy, you, not I, shall go forth to the world."

worn the Silk-worms Motto, *Operitur dum Operatur*,[1]
and have chosen to have written *Anonymously;* or, as
Claudius Salmasius calls himself *Walo Messalinus*,
as *Ludovicus Molinæus* calls himself *Ludiomæus Col-
vinus*, as *Carolus Scribanius* calls himself *Clarus Bonar-
scius*, (and no less Men than *Peter du Moulin*, and Dr.
Henry More, stile themselves, the one *Hippolytus
Fronto*, the other *Franciscus Paleopolitanus*.)[2] Thus
I would have tried, whether I could not have Anagram-
matized my Name into some Concealment; or I would
have referr'd it to be found in the second Chapter of
the second Syntagm of *Selden de Diis Syris*.[3] Whereas
now I freely confess, 'tis COTTON MATHER that
has written all these things;

Me, me, ad sum qui scripsi; in me convertite Ferrum.[4]

I hope 'tis a right Work that I have done; but we are
not yet arrived unto the *Day, wherein God will bring
every Work into Judgment* (the Day of the *Kingdom*
that was promised unto *David*) and a Son of *David*
hath as Truly as Wisely told us, that until the arrival
of that Happy Day, this is one of the *Vanities* attendin;
Humane Affairs; *For a right Work a Man shall be
envied of his Neighbour*. It will not be so much a Surprise
unto me, if I should live to see our *Church-History*
vexed with *Anie-mad-versions* of Calumnious Writers,

[1] "It is hidden while it works."
[2] Louis Molinæus, or Moulin, was an English physician, born
about 1603; Charles Scribani, or Scribanius, was a Jesuit historian,
living 1561–1629; Peter du Moulin was an English theologian, and
Henry More was one of the English "Cambridge Platonists."
[3] The name Mather occurs in the book of John Selden referred to
(p. 165 of the London 1617 edition).
[4] "It is I who have written; turn the sword against me." This is an
alteration of the *Æneid*, ix, 427.

as it would have been unto *Virgil*, to read his *Bucolicks* reproached by the *Antibucolica* of a *Nameless Scribbler*, and his *Æneids* travestied by the *Æneidomastix* of *Carbilius:* Or *Herennius* taking pains to make a Collection of the *Faults*, and *Faustinus* of the *Thefts*, in his incomparable Composures: Yea, *Pliny*, and *Seneca* themselves, and our *Jerom*, reproaching him, as a Man of no Judgment, nor Skill in Sciences; while *Pædianus* affirms of him, that he was himself, *Usque adeo invidiæ Expers, ut si quid erudite dictum inspiceret alterius, non minus gauderet ac si suum esset.*[1] How should a Book, no better laboured than this of ours, escape *Zoilian*[2] Outrages, when in all Ages, the most exquisite Works have been as much vilified, as *Plato's* by *Scaliger*, and *Aristotle's* by *Lactantius?* .In the time of our K. *Edward* VI. there was an Order to bring in all the Teeth of St. *Apollonia*, which the People of his one Kingdom carried about them for the Cure of the *Tooth ach;* and they were so many, that they almost fill'd a Tun. Truly *Envy* hath as many *Teeth* as Madam *Apollonia* would have had, if all those pretended Reliques had been really hers. And must all these *Teeth* be fastned on thee, *O my Book?* It may be so! And yet the *Book*, when ground between these *Teeth*, will prove like *Ignatius* in the *Teeth* of the furious Tygers, *The whiter Manchet for the Churches of God.* The greatest and fiercest Rage of *Envy*, is that which I expect from those IDUMÆANS, whose Religion is all Ceremony, and whose Charity is more for them who deny

[1] "Ever so very free of envy, that when he examined anything learnedly written by another, he was not less delighted than as if it were his own."

[2] Zoilus, a fourth century Greek rhetorician, so severely criticized Homer as to be known as the "Scourge of Homer."

the most Essential things in the Articles and Homilies of the Church of *England*, than for the most Conscientious Men in the World, who manifest their being so, by their Dissent in some little Ceremony: Or those Persons whose Hearts are notably expressed in those words used by one of them ['tis *Howel* in his *Familiar Letters*, Vol. 1. Sect. 6. Lett. 32.] *I rather pitty, than hate, Turk or Infidel, for they are of the same Metal, and bear the same Stamp, as I do, tho' the Inscriptions differ; If I hate any, 'tis those Schismaticks that puzzle the sweet Peace of our Church; so that I could be content to see an Anabaptist go to Hell on a Brownists Back.*[1] The Writer whom I last quoted, hath given us a Story of a young Man in *High-Holbourn*, who being after his death Dissected, there was a Serpent with divers tails, found in the left Ventricle of his Heart. I make no question, that our Church-History will find some Reader disposed like that Writer, with an Heart as full of Serpent and Venom as ever it can hold: Nor indeed will they be able to hold, but the Tongues and Pens of those angry Folks, will scourge me as with Scorpions, and cause me to feel (if I will feel) as many Lashes as *Cornelius Agrippa* expected from their Brethren, for the Book in which he exposed their Vanities.[2] A Scholar of the great JUELS, made once about fourscore Verses, for which the Censor of *Corpus Christi* Colledge in the beginning of Queen *Maries* Reign, publickly and cruelly scourged him, with one Lash

[1] The Brownists were those who followed the beliefs of Robert Brown—in general, they were the more extreme Independents among the English Puritans. The Puritans in New England objected to being identified with the Brownists. (Cf. page 48 *post*).

[2] Heinrich Cornelius Agrippa, 1487–1535, published in 1531 his *De Vanitate et Incertitude Scientiarum*, which brought him into difficulties with the Inquisition.

for every Verse.[1] Now in those Verses, the young
Man's Prayers to the Lord JESUS CHRIST, have
this for part of the answer given to them.

> *Respondet Dominus, spectans de sedibus altis,*
> *Ne dubites recte credere, parve puer.*
> *Olim sum passus mortem, nunc occupo dextram*
> *Patris, nunc summi sunt mea regna poli.*
> *Sed tu, crede mihi, vires Scriptura resumet,*
> *Tolleturque suo tempore missa nequam.*

In English.

The Lord beholding from his Throne, reply'd,
Doubt not, *O Youth*, firmly in me confide.
I dy'd long since, now sit at the Right Hand
Of my bless'd Father, and the World command.
Believe me, *Scripture* shall regain her sway,
And wicked *Mass* in due time fade away.

Reader, I also expect nothing but *Scourges* from that
Generation, to whom the *Mass book* is dearer than the
Bible. But I have now likewise confessed another
Expectation, that shall be my Consolation under all.
They tell us, That on the highest of the *Caspian* Mountains in *Spain*, there is a Lake, whereinto if you throw
a Stone, there presently ascends a Smoke, which forms
a dense Cloud, from whence issues a Tempest of Rain,
Hail, and horrid Thunder-claps, for a good quarter
of an hour. Our Church-History will be like a Stone
cast into that Lake, for the furious Tempest which it
will raise among some, whose Ecclesiastical Dignities
have set them, as on the top of Spanish Mountains.

[1] Bishop John Jewel of Salisbury, 1522–1571. His scholar here
referred to was a certain Edward Year.

The Catholick Spirit of Communion wherewith 'tis written, and the Liberty which I have taken, to tax the Schismatical Impositions and Persecutions of a Party, who have always been as real Enemies to the English Nation, as to the Christian and Protestant Interest, will certainly bring upon the whole Composure, the quick Censures of that Party, at the first cast of their look upon it. In the Duke of *Alva's* Council of twelve Judges, there was one *Hessels* a *Flemming*, who slept always at the Trial of Criminals, and when they wak'd him to deliver his Opinion, he rub'd his Eyes, and cry'd between sleeping and waking, *Ad patibulum! ad Patibulum!* To the Gallows with 'em! [And, by the way, this Blade was himself, at the last, condemned unto the Gallows, without an Hearing!] As quick Censures must this our Labour expect from those who will not bestow waking thoughts upon the Representations of Christianity here made unto the World; but have a Sentence of Death always to pass, or at least, Wish, upon those Generous Principles, without which, 'tis impossible to maintain the Reformation: And I confess, I am very well content, that this our Labour takes the Fate of those Principles: Nor do I dissent from the words of the Excellent *Whitaker* upon *Luther, Fœlix ille, quem Dominus eo Honore dignatus est, ut Homines nequissimos suos haberet inimicos.*[1] But if the old Epigrammatist, when he saw Guilty Folks raving Mad at his Lines, could say——

Hoc volo; nunc nobis carmina nostra placent:[2]

[1] "Happy is he, whom God has deemed worthy of the honor that he may have the worst of men for his enemies."

[2] "This is what I wish; now my songs please me."

Certainly an Historian should not be displeased at it,
if the Enemies of Truth discover their Madness at the
true and free Communications of his History: and
therefore the more Stones they throw at this Book,
there will not only be the more Proofs, that it is a Tree
which hath good Fruits growing upon it, but I will
build my self a Monument with them, whereon shall
be inscribed, that Clause in the Epitaph of the Martyr
Stephen:

> *Excepit Lapides, cui petra Christus erat:* [1]

Albeit perhaps the *Epitaph*, which the old *Monks*
bestow'd upon *Wickliff*, will be rather endeavour'd
for me, (*If I am thought worth one!*)[2] by the Men, who
will, with all possible *Monkery*, strive to stave off the
approaching *Reformation*.

But since an Undertaking of this Nature, must
thus encounter so much Envy, from those who are
under the Power of the *Spirit that works in the Children
of Unperswadeableness*, methinks I might perswade
my self, that it will find another sort of Entertainment
from those Good Men who have a better Spirit in them:
For, as the Apostle *James* hath noted, (so with Monsieur
Claude I read it) *The Spirit that is in us, lusteth against
Envy;* and yet even in *us* also, there will be the *Flesh*,
among whose Works, one is *Envy*, which will be *Lusting*
against the *Spirit*. All Good Men will not be satisfied
with every thing that is here set before them. In my
own Country, besides a considerable number of loose

---

[1] Mr. Robinson, in the 1855 reprint of the *Magnalia*, translates
this, "He died by *stoning*, but his *Rock* was Christ."

[2] Wycliffe was reviled by many after his death, his books were
burned, and his body later exhumed. Speed's *History of Great Britaine*
(1611), p. 610, § 118, prints an epitaph bestowed on him by a monk.

and vain Inhabitants risen up, to whom the Congregational Church-Discipline, which cannot Live well, where the Power of Godliness dyes, is become distastful for the Purity of it; there is also a number of eminently Godly Persons, who are for a Larger way, and unto these my Church-History will give distast, by the things which it may happen to utter, in favour of that Church-Discipline on some few occasions; and the Discoveries which I may happen to make of my Apprehensions, that *Scripture*, and *Reason*, and *Antiquity* is for it; and that it is not far from a glorious Resurrection. But that, as the Famous Mr. *Baxter*, after Thirty or Forty Years hard Study, about the true Instituted Church-Discipline, at last, not only own'd, but also invincibly prov'd, That it is *The Congregational;* so, The further that the *Unprejudiced Studies* of Learned Men proceed in this Matter, the more generally the *Congregational Church-Discipline* will be pronounced for. On the other side, There are some among us, who very strictly profess the *Congregational Church-Discipline*, but at the same time they have an unhappy Narrowness of Soul, by which they confine their value and Kindness too much unto their own Party; and unto those my *Church History* will be offensive, because my Regard unto our own declared Principles, does not hinder me from giving the Right-hand of Fellowship unto the valuable Servants of the Lord Jesus Christ, who find not our Church-Discipline as yet agreeable unto their present Understandings and Illuminations. If it be thus in my own Country, it cannot be other wise in That whereto I send this account of my own. Briefly, as it hath been said, That if all *Episcopal* Men were like Archbishop *Usher*, and all *Presbyterians* like *Stephen Marshal*, and all *Independents* like *Jeremiah*

Burroughs, the Wounds of the Church would soon be healed;[1] my Essay to carry that Spirit through this whole Church-History, will bespeak Wounds for it, from those that are of another Spirit. And there will also be in every Country those Good Men, who yet have not had the Grace of Christ so far prevailing in them, as utterly to divest them of that piece of Ill Nature which the Comedian resents, *In homine Imperito, quo nil quicquam Injustius, quia nisi quod ipse facit, nil recte factum putat.*[2]

However, All these things, and an hundred more such things which I think of, are very small Discouragements for such a Service as I have here endeavoured. I foresee a Recompence, which will abundantly swallow up all Discouragements! It may be *Strato* the Philosopher counted himself well recompensed for his Labours, when *Ptolomy* bestow'd fourscore Talents on him. It may be *Archimelus* the Poet counted himself well recompensed, when *Hiero* sent him a thousand Bushels of Wheat for one little Epigram: And *Saleius* the Poet might count himself well recompensed, when *Vespasian* sent him twelve thousand and five hundred *Philippicks;* and *Oppian* the Poet might count himself well recompensed, when *Caracalla* sent him a piece of Gold for every Line that he had inscribed unto him. As I live in a Country where such Recompences never were in fashion; it hath no Preferments for me, and I shall count that I am well Rewarded in it, if I can escape without being heavily Reproached, Cen-

---

[1] James Ussher, Archbishop of Armagh, an Anglican, liberal toward Puritanism, 1581–1656; Marshall, 1594?–1655, and Burroughs, 1599–1646, were men of breadth of view and wide influence.

[2] "Nothing is more unjust than an inexperienced man, who thinks nothing is right except what he has done himself." (Terence, *Adelphi,* ll. 98–99.)

sured and Condemned, for what I have done: So I thank the Lord, I should exceedingly Scorn all such mean Considerations, I seek not out for Benefactors, to whom these Labours may be Dedicated: There is ONE to whom all is due! From Him I shall have a Recompence: And what Recompence? The Recompence, whereof I do, with inexpressible Joy, assure my self, is this, *That these my poor Labours will certainly serve the Churches and Interests of the Lord Jesus Christ.* And I think I may say, That I ask to live no longer, than I count a Service unto the Lord Jesus Christ, and his Churches, to be it self a glorious Recompence for the doing of it. When *David* was contriving to build the House of God, there was that order given from Heaven concerning him, *Go tell* David, *my Servant.* The adding of *that* more than *Royal Title* unto the Name of *David*, was a sufficient Recompence for all his Contrivance about the House of God. In our whole *Church-History*, we have been at work for the House of the Lord Jesus Christ, [Even that *Man* who is the *Lord God*, and whose *Form* seems on that occasion represented unto His *David*] And herein 'tis Recompence enough, that I have been a *Servant* unto that heavenly Lord. The greatest *Honour*, and the sweetest *Pleasure*, out of *Heaven*, is to Serve our Illustrious Lord JESUS CHRIST, who hath *loved us, and given himself for us;* and unto whom it is infinitely reasonable that we should *give our selves*, and all that we *have* and *Are:* And it may be the *Angels* in *Heaven* too, aspire not after an higher Felicity.

Unto thee, therefore, O thou Son of God, and King of Heaven, and Lord of all things, whom all the Glorious Angels of Light, unspeakably love to Glorifie; I humbly offer up a poor History of Churches, which own thee alone for their Head, and Prince, and Law-giver; Churches which thou hast purchas'd with thy own Blood, and with wonderful Dispensations of thy Providence hitherto protected and preserved; and of a People which thou didst Form for thy self, to shew forth thy Praises. I bless thy great Name, for thy inclining of me to, and carrying of me through, the Work of this History: I pray thee to sprinkle the Book of this History with thy Blood, and make it acceptable and profitable unto thy Churches, and serve thy Truths and Ways among thy People, by that which thou hast here prepared; for 'tis THOU *that hast prepar'd it for them.* Amen.

Quid sum? Nil. Quis sum? Nullus. Sed Gratia CHRISTI,
   Quod sum, quod Vivo, quodque Laboro, facit.[1]

   [1] "What am I? Nothing. Who am I? No one. But the Grace of Christ makes what I am, my life, and what I do."

MAGNALIA CHRISTI AMERICANA

BOOK II

ECCLESIARUM CLYPEI.[1]

The Second Book of the New English History Containing The Lives Of The Governours, and the Names of the Magistrates, that have been Shields unto the Churches of New-England, (until the Year 1686.) Perpetuated by the Essay of Cotton Mather.

INTRODUCTION

TWERE *to be wish'd that there might never be any* English Translation *of that* Wicked Position *in* Machiavel, Non requiri in Principe veram pietatem, sed sufficere illius quandam umbram, & simulationem Externam.[2] *It may be there never was any Region under Heaven happier than poor* New-England *hath been in* Magistrates, *whose* True Piety *was worthy to be made the* Example *of* After-Ages.

Happy hast thou been, O Land! *in* Magistrates, *whose Disposition to serve the Lord Jesus Christ, unto whom they still considered themselves accountable, answered the good Rule of* Agapetus,[3] Quo quis in Republica

[1] "Shields of the churches."

[2] "In a prince, true piety is not required; a certain shadow and external likeness of it suffices."

[3] "The higher rank one attains in the state, the more submissively one should live before God." Agapetus, a deacon of the church of Constantinople in the sixth century, wrote a letter to the Emperor Justinian on the duties of a prince.

Majorem Dignitatis gradum adeptus est, eo Deum Colat Submissius: Magistrates, *whose Disposition to serve the People that chose them to Rule over them, argued them sensible of that great Stroak in* Cicero, Nulla Re propius Homines ad Deum Accedunt, quam salute Hominibus danda:[1] Magistrates, *acted* [2] *in their Administrations by the Spirit of a* Joshua. *When the* Wise Man *observes unto us,* That Oppressions makes a Wise Man Mad, *it may be worth considering, whether the* Oppressor *is not intended rather than the* Oppressed *in the Observation.* 'Tis very certain that a Disposition to Oppress *other Men, does often make those that are otherwise very* Wise *Men, to forget the Rules of* Reason, *and commit most* Unreasonable *Exorbitancies.* Rehoboam *in some things* acted wisely; *but this Admonition of his Inspired Father could not restrain him from* acting madly, *when the Spirit of* Oppression *was upon him.* The Rulers *of* New-England *have been* Wise Men, *whom that* Spirit of Oppression *betray'd not into this* Madness.

The Father of Themistocles *disswading him from Government, show'd him the* Old Oars *which the Marriners had now thrown away upon the* Sea-shores *with Neglect and Contempt; and said,* That People would certainly treat their Old Rulers with the same Contempt. *But, Reader, let us now take up our* Old Oars *with all possible Respect, and see whether we can't still make use of them to serve our little Vessel. But this the rather, because we may with an easie turn change the Name into that of* Pilots.

The Word GOVERNMENT, *properly signifies the* Guidance of a Ship: Tully *uses it for that purpose; and in*

[1] "In nothing do men come nearer to God, than in giving safety to men."

[2] *I. e.,* actuated.

Plutarch, *the Art of* Steering a Ship, *is*, Τεχνη κυβερ-
vετικη. New-England *is a little* Ship, *which hath
Weathered many a Terrible* Storm; *and it is but reasonable
that they who have sat at the* Helm *of the* Ship, *should
be remembred in the* History *of its Deliverances.*

Prudentius [1] *calls* Judges, The Great Lights of the
Sphere; Symmachus [2] *calls* Judges, The better part of
Mankind. *Reader, Thou are now to be entertained with
the* Lives *of* Judges *which have deserved that Character.
And the* Lives *of those who have been called,* Speaking
Laws, *will excuse our History from coming under the
Observation made about the Works of* Homer, *That the
Word, LAW, is never so much as once occurring in them.
They are not written like the* Cyrus *of* Xenophon, *like
the* Alexander *of* Curtius, *like* Virgil's Æneas, *and like*
Pliny's Trajan: *But the Reader hath in every one of them
a Real and a Faithful History. And I please my self
with hopes, that there will yet be found among the Sons of*
New-England, *those Young Gentlemen by whom the
Copies given in this History will be written after; and
that saying of Old* Chaucer *be remembred,* To do the
Genteel Deeds, that makes the Gentleman. [3]

---

[1] Prudentius, the chief Christian poet of the early Church, lived
about 400 A. D.

[2] Quintus Aurelius Symmachus, Roman politician and orator,
lived about 400 A. D.

[3] A paraphrase of familiar lines in Chaucer's "Wife of Bath's Tale."

CHAP. I.

Galeacius Secundus.[1] *The LIFE of* WILLIAM BRAD-
FORD, *Esq; Governour of* PLYMOUTH *COLONY.*

*Omnium Somnos, illius vigilantia defendit, omnium
otium illius Labor, omnium Delitias illius Industria,
omnium vacationem illius occupatio.*[2]

§ 1. IT has been a Matter of some Observation, that
although *Yorkshire* be one of the largest Shires
in *England*, yet, for all the *Fires* of Martyrdom
which were kindled in the Days of Queen *Mary*, it
afforded no more *Fuel* than one poor *Leaf;* namely,
John Leaf, an Apprentice, who suffered for the *Doctrine* of the *Reformation* at the same Time and Stake
with the Famous *John Bradford*. But when the Reign
of Queen *Elizabeth* would not admit the *Reformation* of *Worship* to proceed unto those Degrees,
which were proposed and pursued by no small number of the Faithful in those Days, *Yorkshire* was
not the least of the Shires in *England* that afforded
Suffering *Witnesses* thereunto. The *Churches* there
gathered were quickly molested with such a raging
Persecution, that if the Spirit of *Separation* in them did
carry them unto a further *Extream* than it should have
done, one blameable Cause thereof will be found in the
Extremity of that *Persecution*. Their *Troubles* made
that *Cold* Country too *Hot* for them, so that they were
under a necessity to *seek* a Retreat in the *Low Countries;*
and yet the watchful Malice and Fury of their Ad-

---

[1] "The second helmet wearer."
[2] "His vigilance defends the sleep of all; his labor, their rest; his
industry, their pleasures; and his diligence, their leisure."

versaries rendred it almost impossible for them to *find* what they sought. For them to leave their *Native Soil*, their *Lands* and their *Friends*, and go into a *Strange Place*, where they must hear *Forreign Language*, and live *meanly* and *hardly*, and in other Imployments than that of *Husbandry*, wherein they had been Educated, *these* must needs have been such *Discouragements* as could have been Conquered by none, save those who *sought first the Kingdom of God, and the Righteousness thereof.* But that which would have made these Discouragements the more Unconquerable unto an ordinary Faith, was the terrible Zeal of their Enemies to Guard all *Ports*, and Search all *Ships*, that none of them should be carried off. I will not relate the *sad things* of this kind, then *seen* and *felt* by this People of God; but only exemplifie those *Trials* with one short Story. Divers of this People having Hired a *Dutchman* then lying at *Hull*, to carry them over to *Holland*, he promised faithfully to take them in between *Grimsly* and *Hull*;[1] but *they* coming to the Place a Day or Two too soon, the appearance of such a Multitude alarmed the *Officers* of the Town adjoining, who came with a great Body of *Soldiers* to seize upon them. Now it happened that one Boat full of *Men* had been carried Aboard, while the *Women* were yet in a *Bark* that lay Aground in a Creek at Low-Water. The *Dutchman* perceiving the *Storm* that was thus beginning *Ashore*, swore by the *Sacrament* that he would stay no longer for any of them; and so taking the Advantage of a Fair Wind then Blowing, he put out to *Sea* for *Zealand.* The Women thus left near *Grimsly-Common*, bereaved of their Husbands, who had been hurried from them, and forsaken of their Neighbours, of whom none durst

[1] *I.e.,* Grimsby.

in this Fright stay with them, were a very rueful Spectacle; some crying for *Fear*, some shaking for *Cold*, all dragg'd by Troops of *Armed* and *Angry* Men from one Justice to another, till not knowing what to do with them, they e'en dismiss'd them to shift as well as they could for themselves. But by their singular *Afflictions*, and by their Christian *Behaviours*, the *Cause* for which they exposed themselves did gain considerably. In the mean time, the Men at Sea found Reason to be glad that their Families were not with them, for they were surprized with an *horrible Tempest*, which held them for Fourteen Days together, in Seven whereof they saw not *Sun*, *Moon*, or *Star*, but were driven upon the Coast of *Norway*. The *Mariners* often despaired of Life, and once with doleful shrieks gave over all, as thinking the Vessel was Foundred: But the Vessel rose again, and when The *Mariners* with sunk Hearts often cried out, *We Sink! We Sink!* The Passengers without such Distraction of Mind, even while the Water was running into their Mouths and Ears, would chearfully Shout, *Yet Lord, thou canst save! Yet Lord, thou canst save!* And the Lord accordingly brought them at last safe unto their *Desired Haven:* And not long after helped their Distressed Relations thither after them, where indeed they found upon almost all Accounts *a new World*, but a World in which they found that they must live like *Strangers* and *Pilgrims*.

§ 2. Among those Devout People was our *William Bradford*, who was Born *Anno* 1588.[1] in an obscure Village call'd *Ansterfield*,[2] where the People were as unacquainted with the *Bible*, as the *Jews* do seem to

[1] March 19, 1588–89.
[2] Austerfield.

have been with *part* of it in the Days of *Josiah;* a most
Ignorant and Licentious *People*, and *like unto their
Priest.* Here, and in some other Places, he had a
Comfortable *Inheritance* left him of his Honest Parents,
who died while he was yet a Child, and cast him on the
Education, first of his *Grand Parents*, and then of his
Uncles, who devoted him, like his Ancestors, unto
the Affairs of *Husbandry.* Soon and long Sickness
kept him, as he would afterwards thankfully say,
from the *Vanities of Youth*, and made him the fitter
for what he was afterwards to undergo. When he was
about a Dozen Years Old, the Reading of the *Scriptures*
began to cause great Impressions upon him; and those
Impressions were much assisted and improved, when
he came to enjoy Mr. *Richard Clifton*'s [1] Illuminating
Ministry, not far from his Abode; he was then also
further befriended, by being brought into the Company
and Fellowship of such as were then called *Professors;*[2]
though the Young Man that brought him into it, did
after become a Prophane and Wicked *Apostate.* Nor
could the *Wrath* of his *Uncles*, nor the *Scoff* of his
Neighbours now turn'd upon him, as one of the *Puritans*,
divert him from his Pious Inclinations.

§ 3. At last beholding how fearfully the Evangelical
and Apostolical *Church-Form*, whereinto the Churches
of the *Primitive Times* were cast by the good Spirit of
God, had been *Deformed* by the *Apostacy* of the *Succeeding Times;* and what little Progress the *Reformation*
had yet made in many Parts of *Christendom* towards
its Recovery, he set himself by Reading, by Discourse,
by Prayer, to learn whether it was not his Duty to

[1] Richard Clifton, a Puritan, minister at Scrooby and later in
Amsterdam. He died in 1610.
[2] *I. e.*, those who professed to have religious faith.

withdraw from the Communion of the *Parish-Assemblies,* and *engage* with some *Society* of the Faithful, that should keep close unto the *Written Word* of God, as the *Rule* of their *Worship.* And after many Distresses of Mind concerning it, he took up a very Deliberate and Understanding *Resolution* of doing so; which *Resolution* he chearfully Prosecuted, although the provoked *Rage* of his Friends tried all the ways imaginable to reclaim him from it, unto all whom his Answer was, *Were I like to endanger my Life, or consume my Estate by any ungodly Courses, your Counsels to me were very seasonable: But you know that I have been Diligent and Provident in my Calling, and not only desirous to augment what I have, but also to enjoy it in your Company; to part from which will be as great a Cross as can befal me. Nevertheless, to keep a good Conscience, and walk in such a Way as God has prescribed in his Word, is a thing which I must prefer before you all, and above Life it self. Wherefore, since 'tis for a good Cause that I am like to suffer the Disasters which you lay before me, you have no Cause to be either angry with me, or sorry for me; yea, I am not only willing to part with every thing that is dear to me in this World for this Cause, but I am also thankful that God has given me an Heart so to do, and will accept me so to suffer for him.* Some lamented him, *some* derided him, *all* disswaded him: Nevertheless the more they did it, the more fixed he was in his Purpose to seek the Ordinances of the Gospel, where they should be dispensed with most of the *Commanded Purity;* and the *sudden Deaths* of the chief Relations which thus lay at him, quickly after convinced him what a Folly it had been to have quitted his *Profession,* in Expectation of any Satisfaction from them. So to *Holland* he attempted a removal.

§ 4. Having with a great Company of Christians Hired a Ship to Transport them for *Holland*, the Master perfidiously betrayed them into the Hands of those *Persecutors*, who Rifled and Ransack'd their Goods, and clapp'd their Persons into Prison at *Boston*, where they lay for a Month together. But Mr. *Bradford* being a Young Man of about *Eighteen*, was dismissed sooner than the rest, so that within a while he had Opportunity with some others to get over to *Zealand*, through *Perils* both by *Land* and *Sea* not inconsiderable; where he was not long Ashore e're a *Viper* seized on his Hand, that is, an Officer, who carried him unto the Magistrates, unto whom an envious Passenger had accused him as having *fled* out of *England*. When the Magistrates understood the True Cause of his coming thither, they were well satisfied with him; and so he repaired joyfully unto his Brethren at *Amsterdam*, where the Difficulties to which he afterwards stooped in Learning and Serving of a *Frenchman* at the Working of *Silks*, were abundantly Compensated by the *Delight* wherewith he sat under the *Shadow* of our Lord in his purely dispensed Ordinances.[1] At the end of Two Years, he did, being of Age to do it, convert his Estate in *England* into Money; but Setting up for himself, he found some of his Designs by the *Providence* of God frowned upon, which he judged a *Correction* bestowed by God upon him for certain Decays of *Internal Piety*, whereinto he had fallen; the *Consumption* of his *Estate* he thought came to prevent a *Consumption* in his *Virtue*. But after he had resided in *Holland* about half a Score Years, he was one of those who bore a part in

[1] W. C. Ford, in his edition of Bradford's *History* (Boston, 1912), i, 37n., says that the foregoing anecdote probably represents a tradition current in Mather's time.

that Hazardous and Generous Enterprize of removing into *New-England*, with part of the *English* Church at *Leyden*, where at their first Landing, his dearest Consort accidentally falling Overboard, was drowned in the *Harbour;* and the rest of his Days were spent in the Services, and the Temptations, of that *American Wilderness.*

§ 5. Here was Mr. *Bradford* in the Year 1621. Unanimously chosen the *Governour* of the Plantation: The Difficulties whereof were such, that if he had not been a Person of more than Ordinary Piety, Wisdom and Courage, he must have sunk under them. He had with a Laudable Industry been laying up a Treasure of *Experiences*, and he had now occasion to use it: Indeed nothing but an *Experienced* Man could have been suitable to the Necessities of the People. The Potent Nations of the *Indians*, into whose Country they were come, would have cut them off, if the Blessing of God upon *his* Conduct had not quell'd them; and if his Prudence, Justice and Moderation had not overruled them, they had been ruined by their own *Distempers*. One *Specimen* of his Demeanour is to this Day particularly spoken of. A Company of Young Fellows that were newly arrived, were very unwilling to comply with the Governour's Order for *Working* abroad on the Publick Account; and therefore on *Christmass-Day*, when he had called upon them, they excused themselves, with a pretence that it was against their *Conscience* to *Work* such a Day. The Governour gave them no Answer, only that he would spare them till they were better informed; but by and by he found them all at *Play* in the Street, sporting themselves with various Diversions; whereupon Commanding the Instruments of their Games to be taken from them, he effectually gave them to understand, *That it was against his Conscience that they should play whilst others were at Work; and that if they had any Devotion to the Day, they should show it at Home in the Exercises of Religion, and not in the Streets with Pastime and Frolicks;* and this gentle Reproof put a final stop to all such Disorders for the future.

§ 6. For Two Years together after the beginning of the Colony, whereof he was now Governour, the poor People had a great Experiment of *Man's not living by Bread alone;* for when they were left all together without one Morsel of *Bread* for many Months one after another, still the good Providence of God relieved them, and supplied them, and this for the most part out of the *Sea.* In this low Condition of Affairs, there was no little Exercise for the *Prudence* and *Patience* of the Governour, who chearfully bore his part in all: And that *Industry* might not flag, he quickly set himself to settle *Propriety*[1] among the New-Planters; foreseeing that while the whole Country labour'd upon a *Common Stock*, the *Husbandry* and *Business* of the Plantation could not *flourish*, as *Plato* and others long since dream'd that it would, if a *Community* were established. Certainly, if the Spirit which dwelt in the *Old Puritans*, had not inspired these *New-Planters*, they had sunk under the Burden of these Difficulties; but our *Bradford* had a *double Portion* of that Spirit.

§ 7. The Plantation was quickly thrown into a *Storm* that almost overwhelmed it, by the unhappy Actions of a Minister sent over from *England* by the *Adventurers* concerned for the Plantation; but by the Blessing of Heaven on the Conduct of the Governour, they Weathered out that *Storm.* Only the *Ad-*

[1] *I. e.*, property.

venturers hereupon breaking to pieces, threw up all their Concernments with the *Infant Colony;* whereof they gave this as one Reason, *That the Planters dissembled with His Majesty, and their Friends in their Petition, wherein they declared for a Church-Discipline, agreeing with the* French *and others of the Reforming Churches in* Europe. Whereas 'twas now urged, that they had admitted into their Communion a Person, who at his Admission utterly *renounced* the Churches of *England,* (which Person by the way, was *that* very Man who had made the Complaints against them) and therefore though they denied the *Name* of *Brownists* yet they were the *Thing.* In Answer hereunto, the very Words written by the Governour were these; *Whereas you Tax us with dissembling about the* French Discipline, *you do us wrong, for we both hold and practice the* Discipline *of the* French *and other* Reformed *Churches* (*as they have published the same in the* Harmony of Confessions) *according to our Means, in Effect and Substance. But whereas you would tie us up to the* French Discipline *in every Circumstance, you derogate from the* Liberty *we have in Christ Jesus. The Apostle* Paul *would have none to* follow him *in any thing, but wherein he* follows Christ; *much less ought any Christian or Church in the World to do it. The* French *may err, we may err, and other Churches may err, and doubtless do in many* Circumstances. *That Honour therefore belongs only to the* Infallible Word of God, *and* pure Testament of Christ, *to be propounded and followed as the only Rule and Pattern for Direction herein to all Churches and Christians. And it is too great Arrogancy for any Men or Church to think, that he or they have so sounded the Word of God unto the bottom, as precisely to set down the Churches Discipline without Error in Substance or*

Circumstance, that no other without blame may digress or differ in any thing from the same. And it is not difficult to shew that the Reformed Churches *differ in many* Circumstances *among themselves.* By which Words it appears how far he was free from that *Rigid Spirit* of *Separation,* which broke to pieces the *Separatists* themselves in the *Low Countries,* unto the great Scandal of the *Reforming Churches.* He was indeed a Person of a *well-temper'd Spirit,* or else it had been scarce possible for him to have kept the Affairs of *Plymouth* in so good a *Temper* for *Thirty Seven* Years together; in every one of which he was chosen their Governour, except the *Three Years,* wherein Mr. *Winslow,* and the *Two Years,* wherein Mr. *Prince,* at the choice of the People, took a *turn* with him.

§ 8. The *Leader* of a People in a *Wilderness* had need be a *Moses;* and if a *Moses* had not led the People of *Plymouth-Colony,* when this Worthy Person was their Governour, the People had never with so much Unanimity and Importunity still called *him* to lead them. Among many Instances thereof, let this one piece of *Self denial be told for a Memorial of him, wheresoever this History shall be considered.* The Patent of the Colony was taken in *his* Name, running in these Terms, *To* William Bradford, *his Heirs, Associates and Assigns:* But when the number of the *Freemen* was much Increased, and many New *Townships* Erected, the *General Court* there desired of Mr. *Bradford,* that he would make a Surrender of the same into *their Hands,* which *he* willingly and presently assented unto, and confirmed it according to their Desire by his *Hand* and *Seal,* reserving no more for himself than was his *Proportion,* with others, by *Agreement.* But as he found the Providence of Heaven many ways *Recompencing* his many Acts of *Self-denial,* so he gave this Testimony to the Faithfulness of the Divine Promises; *That he had forsaken Friends, Houses and Lands for the sake of the Gospel, and the Lord gave them him again.* *Here* he prospered in his *Estate;* and besides a Worthy *Son* which he had by a former Wife, he had also Two Sons and a Daughter by another, whom he Married in this Land.

§ 9. He was a Person for *Study* as well as *Action;* and hence, notwithstanding the Difficulties through which he passed in his Youth, he attained unto a notable Skill in *Languages;* the *Dutch* Tongue was become almost as Vernacular to him as the *English;* the *French* Tongue he could also manage; the *Latin* and the *Greek* he had Mastered; but the *Hebrew* he most of all studied, *Because,* he said, *he would see with his own Eyes the Ancient Oracles of God in their Native Beauty.* He was also well skill'd in *History,* in *Antiquity,* and in *Philosophy;* and for *Theology* he became so versed in it, that he was an *Irrefragable Disputant* against the *Errors,* especially those of *Anabaptism,* which with Trouble he saw rising in his Colony; wherefore he wrote some Significant things for the Confutation of those Errors. But the *Crown* of all was his Holy, Prayerful, Watchful and Fruitful *Walk with God,* wherein he was very Exemplary.

§ 10. At length he fell into an Indisposition of Body, which rendred him unhealthy for a whole *Winter;* and as the *Spring* advanced, his Health yet more declined; yet he felt himself not what he counted *Sick,* till one *Day;* in the *Night* after which, the God of Heaven so fill'd his Mind with *Ineffable Consolations,* that he seemed little short of *Paul,* rapt up unto the *Unutterable* Entertainments of *Paradise.* The next

Morning he told his Friends, *That the good Spirit of God had given him a Pledge of his Happiness in another World, and the First-fruits of his Eternal Glory:* And on the Day following he died, *May* 9. 1657. in the 69th Year of his Age. Lamented by all the Colonies of *New-England,* as a Common Blessing and Father to them all.

O mihi si Similis Contingat Clausula Vitæ![1]

Plato's brief Description of a *Governour,* is all that I will now leave as his Character, in an

EPITAPH.

Νομεὺς Τροφός ἀγέλης ἀνθρωπίνης.[2]

MEN are but FLOCKS: BRADFORD *beheld their Need, And long did them at once both* Rule *and* Feed.

CHAP. II.

SUCCESSORS.

Inter Omnia quæ Rempublicam, ejusq; fœlicitatem conservant, quid utilius, quid præstantius, quam Viros ad Magistratus gerendos Eligere, summa prudentia & Virtute preditos, quiq; ad Honores obtinendos, non Ambitione, non Largitionibus, sed Virtute & Modestia sibi parent adytum! [3]

[1] "Oh, may a similar ending of life come to me."
[2] "Shepherd and feeder of the human herd."
[3] "Among all the things which preserve the state, what is more useful or glorious, than to elect men to be magistrates who are equipped with the greatest prudence and virtue, and, in obtaining fame, prepare a shrine for themselves, not by ambition, nor by bribery, but by virtue and modesty."

§ 1. THE Merits of Mr. *Edward Winslow*, the
Son of *Edward Winslow*, Esq; of *Draught-
wich*,[1] in the Country of *Worcester*, obliged the Votes
of the *Plymouthean* Colony (whereto he arrived in the
Year 1624. after his Prudent and Faithful Dispatch
of an Agency in *England*, on the behalf of that Infant
Colony) to chuse him for many Years a Magistrate,
and for Two or Three their *Governour*. Travelling into
the *Low-Countries*, he fell into Acquaintance with the
English Church at *Leyden*, and joining himself to them,
he Shipped himself with that part of them which first
came over into *America;* from which time he was
continually engaged in such extraordinary Actions,
as the assistance of that People to encounter their
more than ordinary Difficulties, called for. But their
Publick Affairs then requiring an *Agency* of as wise a
Man as the Country could find at *Whitehall* for them,
he was again prevail'd withal in the Year 1635. to
appear for them at the *Council-board;* and his appearance there proved as *Effectual*, as it was very *Seasonable*, not only for the Colony of *Plymouth*, but for
the *Massachusets* also, on very important Accounts.
It was by the Blessing of God upon his wary and
proper Applications, that the Attempts of many Adversaries to overthrow the whole Settlement of *New-England*, were themselves wholly overthrown; and as a
small Acknowledgment for his great Service therein,
they did, upon his return again, chuse him their *Governour*. But in the Year 1646. the place of *Governour*
being reassumed by Mr. *Bradford*, the *Massachuset*-
Colony Addressed themselves unto Mr. *Winslow* to
take another Voyage for *England*, that he might there
procure their Deliverance from the Designs of many

[1] Droitwich.

Troublesome Adversaries that were Petitioning unto
the *Parliament* against them; and this *Hercules* having
been from his very early Days accustomed unto the
crussing[1] of that sort of *Serpents*, generously undertook
another *Agency*, wherein how many good Services he
did for *New-England*, and with what Fidelity, Discretion, Vigour and Success he pursued the Interests of
that Happy People, it would make a large History to
relate, an *History* that may not now be expected until
the *Resurrection of the Just*. After this he returned no
more unto *New-England;* but being in great Favour
with the greatest Persons then in the Nation, he fell
into those Imployments wherein the whole Nation
fared the better for him. At length he was imployed as
one of the *Grand Commissioners* in the Expedition
against *Hispaniola*, where a *Disease* (rendred yet
more *uneasie* by his Dissatisfaction at the strange
miscarriage of that Expedition) arresting him, he died
between *Domingo* and *Jamaica*, on *May* 8. 1655. in
the Sixty-first Year of his Life, and had his Body Honourably committed unto the *Sea*.

§ 2. Sometimes during the *Life*, but always after
the *Death* of Governour *Bradford*, even until his own,
Mr. *Thomas Prince* was chosen GOVERNOUR of
Plymouth. He was a Gentleman whose *Natural Parts*
exceeded his *Acquired;* but the want and worth of
Acquired Parts was a thing so sensible unto him, that
Plymouth perhaps never had a greater *Mecænas* of
Learning in it: It was he that in spite of much Contradiction, procured Revenues for the Support of *Gram-
mar-Schools* in that Colony. About the time of Governour *Bradford's* Death, *Religion* it self had like to have
died in that Colony, through a *Libertine* and *Brownistick*

[1] *I. e.*, crushing.

Spirit then prevailing among the People, and a strange
Disposition to Discountenance the *Gospel-Ministry,*
by setting up the *Gifts of Private Brethren* in Opposition
thereunto. The good People being in extream Distress
from the Prospect which this matter gave to them, saw
no way so likely and ready to save the Churches from
Ruin, as by the *Election* of Mr. *Prince* to the place of
Governour; and this Point being by the Gracious and
Marvellous Providence of the Lord Jesus Christ gained
at the next *Election;* the *Adverse Party* from that very
time sunk into Confusion. He had Sojourned for a
while at *Eastham,* where a Church was by his means
gathered; but after this time he returned unto his
former Scituation at *Plymouth,* where he resided until
he died, which was *March* 29. 1673. when he was about
Seventy-Three Years of Age: Among the many Excellent
Qualities which adorned him as *Governour* of the Colony,
there was much notice taken of that *Integrity,* wherewith indeed he was most *exemplarily* qualified: Whence
it was that as he ever would refuse any thing that
look'd like a *Bribe;* so if any Person having a Case to
be heard at Court, had sent a Present unto his Family
in his absence, he would presently send back the value
thereof in Money unto the Person. But had he been
only a private *Christian,* there would yet have been
seen upon him those Ornaments of *Prayerfulness,* and
Peaceableness, and profound Resignation to the Conduct
of the *Word* of God, and a strict *Walk* with God, which
might justly have been made an *Example* to a whole
Colony.

§ 3. Reader, If thou would'st have seen the true
Picture of *Wisdom, Courage* and *Generosity,* the Suc-
cessor of Mr. *Thomas Prince* in the Government of
Plymouth would have represented it. It was the truly

Honourable *Josiah Winslow*, Esq; the first Governour
that was Born in *New-England*, and one well worthy
to be an Example to all that should come after him:
A True *English Gentleman*, and (that I may say all
at once) the *True Son* of that Gentleman whom we
parted withal no more than Two Paragraphs ago.
His Education and his Disposition was that of a *Gentleman;* and his many Services to his Country in the
Field, as well as on the *Bench*, ought never to be
Buried in *Oblivion*. All that *Homer* desired in a *Ruler*,
was in the Life of this Gentleman expressed unto the
Life; to be, *Fortis in Hostes*, and, *Bonus in Cives*.
Though he hath left an *Off-spring*, yet I must ask for
One Daughter to be remembred above the rest. As
of Old, *Epaminondas* being upbraided with want of
Issue, boasted that he left behind him one Daughter,
namely, the Battel of *Leuctra* which would render him
Immortal; so our General *Winslow* hath left behind him
his Battel at the Fort of the *Narragansets*, to Immortalize him: *There* did he with his own *Sword* make and
shape a *Pen* to Write his History. But so large a
Field of Merit is now before me, that I dare not give
my self the liberty to Range in it lest I lose my self.
He died on *Dec*. 18. 1680.

Jam Cinis est, & de tam magno restat Achille,
Nescio quid; parvam quod non bene compleat Urnam.[1]

§ 4. And what *Successor* had *he?* Methinks of the
Two last Words in the wonderful Prediction of the
Succession, Oracled unto King *Henry* VII. *LEO,*
NULLUS, the First would have well suited the Valiant

[1] "Now he is ashes, and there remains of great Achilles I know
not what—something which does not completely fill a little urn."

Winslow of *Plymouth;* and the last were to have been wish'd for him that followed.

CHAP. III.

Patres Conscripti:[1] *Or, ASSISTENTS.*

THE GOVERNOURS of *New-England* have still had *Righteousness the Girdle of their Loins, and Faithfulness the Girdle of their Reins,* that is to say, *Righteous* and *Faithful* Men about them, in the *Assistance* of such *Magistrates* as were called by the *Votes* of the *Freemen* unto the Administration of the Government, (according to their *Charters*) and made the *Judges of the Land.* These Persons have been such *Members* of the *Churches,* and such *Patrons* to the *Churches,* and generally been such Examples of Courage, Wisdom, Justice, Goodness and Religion, that it is fit our *Church-History* should remember them. The Blessed *Apollonius,* who in a set Oration Generously and Eloquently Pleaded the Cause of *Christianity* before the *Roman Senate,* was not only a Learned Person, but also (if *Jerom* say right) a *Senator of* Rome. The *Senators* of *New-England* also have pleaded the Cause of *Christianity,* not so much by *Orations,* as by *Practising* of it, and by *Suffering* for it. Nevertheless, as the *Sicyonians* would have no other Epitaphs written on the Tombs of their *Kings,* but only their *Names,* that they might have no Honour, but what the Remembrance of their Actions and Merits in the Minds of the People should procure for them; so I shall content my self with only reciting the *Names* of these Worthy Persons, and the *Times* when I find them first chosen unto their Magistracy.

[1] "Senators."

MAGISTRATES in the Colony of New-Plymouth.

THE good People, soon after their first coming over, chose Mr. *William Bradford* for their Governour, and added Five *Assistents*, whose Names, I suppose, will be found in the Catalogue of them, whom I find sitting on the *Seat of Judgment* among them, in the Year 1633.

Edward Winslow, Gov.
William Bradford.
Miles Standish.
John Howland.
John Alden.
John Done.[1]
Stephen Hopkins.
William Gilson.

Afterwards at several times were added,

Thomas Prince.	1634.
William Collier.	1634.
Timothy Hatherly.	1636.
John Brown.	1636.
John Jenny.	1637.
John Atwood.	1638.
Edmund Freeman.	1640.
William Thomas.	1642.
Thomas Willet.	1651.
Thomas Southworth.	1652.
James Cudworth.	1656.
Josiah Winslow.	1657.
William Bradford. F.	1658.
Thomas Hinkley.	1658.

[1] Or Doane.

James Brown.   1665.
John Freeman.   1666.
Nathanael Bacon.   1667.

Thus far we find in a Book Entituled, *New-England's Memorial*, which was Published by Mr. *Nathanael Morton*, the Secretary of *Plymouth* Colony, in the Year 1669. Since then there have been added at several times,

Constant Southworth.   1670.
Daniel Smith.   1674.
Barnabas Lothrop.   1681.
John Thatcher.
John Walley.

CHAP. IV.

Nehemias Americanus.[1] *The LIFE of* JOHN WIN-THROP, *Esq; Governour of the* MASSACHUSET COLONY

Quicunq; Venti erunt, Ars nostra certe non aberit. Cicer.[2]

§ 1. L ET *Greece* boast of her patient *Lycurgus*, the *Lawgiver*, by whom *Diligence, Temperance, Fortitude* and *Wit* were made the *Fashions* of a therefore Long-lasting and Renowned Commonwealth: Let *Rome* tell of her Devout *Numa*, the *Lawgiver*, by whom the most Famous Commonwealth saw *Peace* Triumphing over extinguished *War*, and cruel *Plunders*, and *Murders* giving place to the more mollifying Exercises of his *Religion*. Our *New-England* shall tell and boast of her WINTHROP, a *Lawgiver*, as patient as *Lycurgus*,

[1] "The American Nehemiah."
[2] "Whatever winds shall blow, our art surely shall not die."

but not admitting any of *his* Criminal Disorders; as Devout as *Numa*, but not liable to any of *his* Heathenish Madnesses; a *Governour* in whom the Excellencies of *Christianity* made a most improving Addition unto the *Virtues*, wherein even without *those* he would have made a *Parallel* for the Great Men of *Greece*, or of *Rome*, which the Pen of a *Plutarch* has Eternized.

§ 2. A stock of *Heroes* by right should afford nothing but what is *Heroical;* and nothing but an extream Degeneracy would make any thing less to be expected from a Stock of *Winthrops.* Mr. *Adam Winthrop*, the Son of a Worthy Gentleman wearing the same Name, was himself a Worthy, a Discreet, and a Learned Gentleman, particularly Eminent for *Skill* in the *Law*, nor without Remark for *Love* to the *Gospel*, under the Reign of King *Henry* VIII. And Brother to a Memorable *Favourer* of the *Reformed Religion* in the Days of Queen *Mary*, into whose Hands the Famous Martyr *Philpot* committed his *Papers*, which afterwards made no Inconsiderable part of our *Martyr-Books.* This Mr. *Adam Winthrop* had a Son of the same Name also, and of the same Endowments and Imployments with his Father; and this Third *Adam Winthrop* was the Father of that Renowned *John Winthrop*, who was the Father of *New-England*, and the Founder *of a Colony*, which upon many Accounts, like *him* that Founded it, may challenge the *First Place* among the *English* Glories of *America*.[1] Our JOHN WINTHROP thus Born at the Mansion-House of his Ancestors, at *Groton* in *Suffolk*, on *June* 12. 1587.[2] enjoyed after-

---

[1] Mr. R. C. Winthrop in his *Life and Letters of John Winthrop* (2d ed.), i, 12, 13, calls attention to some possible errors in this paragraph.

[2] According to later biographers, January 12, 1587–88.

wards an agreeable Education.   But though he would
rather have Devoted himself unto the Study of Mr.
John Calvin, than of Sir *Edward Cook;* nevertheless,
the Accomplishments of a *Lawyer*, were those wherewith Heaven made his chief Opportunities to be
Serviceable.

§ 3. Being made, at the unusually early Age of
Eighteen, a *Justice of Peace*,[1] his Virtues began to fall
under a more general Observation; and he not only so
Bound himself to the Behaviour of a *Christian*, as to
become Exemplary for a Conformity to the *Laws* of
Christianity in his own Conversation, but also discovered a more than ordinary Measure of those Qualities,
which adorn an *Officer of Humane Society*.   His *Justice*
was Impartial, and used the *Ballance* to weigh not the
Cash, but the *Case* of those who were before him:
Prosopolatria, he reckoned as bad as *Idololatria:*[2] His
Wisdom did exquisitely Temper things according to
the *Art of Governing*, which is a Business of more Contrivance than the *Seven Arts* of the *Schools: Oyer* still
went before *Terminer* in all his Administrations:[3]
His *Courage* made him *Dare to do right*, and fitted him
to stand among the *Lions*, that have sometimes been
the *Supporters* of the Throne:[4] All which Virtues he
rendred the more Illustrious, by *Emblazoning* them with
the Constant *Liberality* and *Hospitality* of a *Gentleman*.
This made him the *Terror* of the Wicked, and the
Delight of the Sober, the *Envy* of the many, but the

---

[1] R. C. Winthrop, *op. cit.* i, 223.

[2] "Worship of persons" as bad as "worship of idols."

[3] "Hearing" before "judging."

[4] "Let judges also remember, that Solomon's throne was supported
by lions on both sides: let them be lions, but yet lions under the
throne."   Bacon, *Essay of Judicature*.

Hope of those who had any *Hopeful Design* in Hand
for the Common Good of the Nation, and the Interests
of Religion.

§ 4. Accordingly when the *Noble Design* of carrying
a Colony of *Chosen People* into an *American* Wilderness,
was by *some* Eminent Persons undertaken, *This* Eminent Person was, by the Consent of all, *Chosen* for the
Moses, who must be the Leader of so great an Undertaking: And indeed nothing but a *Mosaic Spirit* could
have carried him through the *Temptations*, to which
either his *Farewel* to his *own Land*, or his *Travel* in a
Strange Land, must needs expose a Gentleman of
his *Education*. Wherefore having Sold a fair Estate
of Six or Seven Hundred a Year, he Transported
himself with the Effects of it into *New-England* in the
Year 1630. where he spent it upon the Service of a
famous Plantation founded and formed for the Seat
of the most *Reformed Christianity:* And continued there,
conflicting with *Temptations* of all sorts, as many
Years as the *Nodes* of the *Moon* take to dispatch a
Revolution.[1] Those Persons were never concerned in
a *New-Plantation*, who know not that the unavoidable
Difficulties of such a thing, will call for all the *Prudence*
and *Patience* of a Mortal Man to Encounter therewithal; and they must be very insensible of the Influence, which the *Just Wrath* of Heaven has permitted
the *Devils* to have upon *this World*, if they do not
think that the Difficulties of a *New-Plantation*, devoted
unto the *Evangelical Worship* of our Lord Jesus Christ,
must be yet more than Ordinary. How *Prudently*,
how *Patiently*, and with how much Resignation to
our Lord Jesus Christ, our brave *Winthrop* waded

[1] The time required for a revolution of the nodes of the moon is
18.6 years.

through these *Difficulties*, let Posterity Consider with Admiration. And know, that as the *Picture* of this their *Governour*, was, after his *Death*, hung up with Honour in the *State-House* of his Country, so the *Wisdom*, *Courage*, and Holy *Zeal* of his *Life*, were an Example well-worthy to be Copied by all that shall succeed in *Government*.

§ 5. Were he now to be consider'd only as a *Christian*, we might therein propose him as greatly Imitable. He was a very *Religious* Man; and as he strictly kept his *Heart*, so he kept his *House*, under the Laws of *Piety; there* he was every Day constant in Holy Duties, both Morning and Evening, and on the *Lord's Days*, and *Lectures;* though he *wrote* not after the Preacher, yet such was his *Attention*, and such his *Retention* in *Hearing*, that he repeated unto his *Family* the *Sermons* which he had heard in the Congregation. But it is chiefly as a *Governour* that he is now to be consider'd. Being the *Governour* over the considerablest Part of *New-England*, he maintain'd the Figure and Honour of his Place with the Spirit of a true *Gentleman;* but yet with such obliging *Condescention* to the Circumstances of the Colony, that when a certain troublesome and malicious Calumniator, well known in those Times, printed his Libellous *Nick-Names* upon the chief Persons here, the worst *Nich-Name* [*sic*] he could find for the Governour, was *John Temper-well;* and when the Calumnies of that ill Man caused the Arch-Bishop to Summon one Mr. *Cleaves* before the King, in hopes to get some Accusation from him against the Country, Mr. *Cleaves* gave such an Account of the Governour's laudable Carriage in all Respects, and the serious Devotion wherewith Prayers were both publickly and privately made for His Majesty, that the King expressed himself most highly *Pleased* therewithal, only *Sorry* that so Worthy a Person should be no better Accommodated than with the Hardships of *America*. He was, indeed, a *Governour*, who had most exactly studied that Book, which pretending to Teach *Politicks*, did only contain *Three Leaves*, and but *One Word* in each of those Leaves, which Word was, MODERATION. Hence, though he were a Zealous Enemy to all *Vice*, yet his *Practice* was according to his *Judgment* thus expressed; *In the Infancy of Plantations, Justice should be administred with more Lenity than in a settled State; because People are more apt then to Transgress; partly out of Ignorance of new Laws and Orders, partly out of Oppression of Business, and other Straits.* [LENTO GRADU [1]] *was the old Rule; and if the Strings of a new Instrument be wound up unto their heighth, they will quickly crack.* But when some Leading and Learned Men took Offence at his Conduct in this Matter, and upon a *Conference* gave it in as their Opinion, *That a stricter Discipline was to be used in the beginning of a Plantation, than after its being with more Age established and confirmed,* the Governour being readier to see *his own* Errors than *other Mens*, professed his Purpose to endeavour their Satisfaction with less of *Lenity* in his Administrations. At that *Conference* there were drawn up several other *Articles* to be observed between the Governour and the rest of the Magistrates, which were of this Import: *That* the *Magistrates*, as far as might be, should aforehand ripen their *Consultations*, to produce that *Unanimity* in their *Publick Votes*, which might make them liker to the *Voice of God; that* if *Differences* fell out among them in their Publick Meetings, they should speak only to the *Case*, without any

[1] "By slow degrees."

Reflection, with all due *Modesty*, and but by way of *Question;* or Desire the deferring of the *Cause* to further time; and after *Sentence* to intimate privately no *Dislike; that* they should be more *Familiar*, Friendly and Open unto each other, and more frequent in their *Visitations*, and not any way expose each other's *Infirmities*, but seek the *Honour* of each other, and all the Court; *that* One Magistrate shall not *cross* the Proceedings of another, without first advising with him; and *that* they should in all their Appearances abroad, be so circumstanced as to prevent all Contempt of Authority; and *that* they should Support and Strengthen all *Under Officers*. All of which *Articles* were observed by no Man more than by the *Governour* himself.

§ 6. But whilst he thus did as our *New-English Nehemiah*, the part of a *Ruler* in Managing the Public Affairs of our *American Jerusalem*, when there were *Tobijahs* and *Sanballats* enough to vex him, and give him the Experiment of *Luther's* Observation, *Omnis qui regit, est tanquam signum, in quod omnia Jacula, Satan & Mundus dirigunt;* [1] he made himself still an exacter *Parallel* unto that Governour of *Israel*, by doing the part of a *Neighbour* among the distressed People of the *New-Plantation*. To teach them the *Frugality* necessary for those times, he abridged himself of a Thousand comfortable things, which he had allow'd himself elsewhere: His *Habit* was not that *soft Raiment*, which would have been disagreeable to a *Wilderness;* his *Table* was not covered with the *Superfluities* that would have invited unto *Sensualities:* *Water* was commonly his *own Drink*, though he gave

---

[1] "Everyone who rules is like a target against which Satan and the World aim all their darts."

Wine to *others*. But at the same time his *Liberality* unto the Needy was even beyond measure Generous; and therein he was continually causing *The Blessing of him that was ready to Perish to come upon him, and the Heart of the Widow and the Orphan to sing for Joy:* But none more than those of Deceas'd *Ministers*, whom he always treated with a very singular Compassion; among the Instances whereof we still enjoy with us the Worthy and now Aged Son of that Reverend *Higginson*, whose Death left his Family in a wide World soon after his arrival here, publickly acknowledging the Charitable *Winthrop* for his *Foster-Father*.[1] It was oftentimes no small Trial unto his *Faith*, to think, *How a Table for the People should be furnished when they first came into the Wilderness!* And for very many of the People, his *own good Works* were needful, and accordingly employed for the answering of his *Faith*. Indeed, for a while the Governour was the *Joseph*, unto whom the whole Body of the People repaired when their *Corn* failed them: And he continued Relieving of them with his *open-handed Bounties*, as long as he had any Stock to do it with; and a lively *Faith* to *see* the return of the *Bread after many Days*, and not *Starve* in the Days that were to pass till that *return* should be *seen*, carried him chearfully through those Expences. Once it was observable, that on *Feb.* 5. 1630. when he was distributing the last Handful of *the Meal in the Barrel* unto a Poor Man distressed by the Wolf *at the Door*, at that Instant they spied a Ship arrived at the Harbour's Mouth Laden with *Provisions* for them all. Yea, the Governour sometimes made his own *private Purse* to be the *Publick;*

---

[1] John, son of Francis Higginson. He wrote an "Attestation" prefixed to the *Magnalia*.

not by *sucking* into it, but by *squeezing* out of it; for when the *Publick Treasure* had nothing in it, he did himself defray the Charges of the *Publick*. And having learned that Lesson of our Lord, *That it is better to Give, than to Receive,* he did, at the General Court when he was a Third time chosen Governour, make a Speech unto this purpose, *That he had received Gratuties from divers Towns, which he accepted with much Comfort and Content; and he had likewise received Civilities from particular Persons, which he could not refuse without Incivility in himself: Nevertheless, he took them with a trembling Heart, in regard of God's Word, and the Conscience of his own Infirmities; and therefore he desired them that they would not hereafter take it Ill if he refused such Presents for the time to come.* 'Twas his Custom also to send some of his Family upon Errands, unto the Houses of the Poor about their *Mealtime,* on purpose to *spy* whether they *wanted;* and if it were found that they *wanted,* he would make *that* the Opportunity of sending Supplies unto them. And there was one Passage of his *Charity* that was perhaps a little *unusual:* In an hard and long Winter, when *Wood* was very scarce at *Boston,* a Man gave him a private *Information,* that a needy Person in the Neighbourhood stole *Wood* sometimes from *his* Pile; whereupon the Governour in a seeming Anger did reply, *Does he so? I'll take a Course with him; go, call that Man to me, I'll warrant you I'll cure him of Stealing!* When the Man came, the Governour considering that if he had *Stoln,* it was more out of *Necessity* than *Disposition,* said unto him, *Friend, It is a severe Winter, and I doubt you are but meanly provided for Wood; wherefore I would have you supply your self at my Wood-Pile till this cold Season be over.* And he then Merrily asked his Friends, *Whether he had not effectually cured this Man of Stealing his Wood?*

§ 7. One would have imagined that so *good* a Man could have had ṅo *Enemies;* if we had not had a daily and woful Experience to Convince us, that *Goodness* it self will *make* Enemies. It is a wonderful Speech of *Plato*, (in one of his Books, *De Republica*) *For the trial of true Vertue,* '*tis necessary that a good Man* μηδὲν αδικῶν, δόξαν ἔχει την μεγίϛην ἀδικιας. *Tho' he do no unjust thing, should suffer the Infamy of the greatest Injustice.* The Governour had by his unspotted *Integrity*, procured himself a great Repntation [*sic*] among the *People;* and then the Crime of *Popularity* was laid unto his Charge by such, who were willing to deliver him from the Danger of having *all Men speak well of him.* Yea, there were Persons eminent both for Figure and for Number, unto whom it was almost *Essential* to *dislike* every thing that came from *him;* and yet *he* always maintained an Amicable Correspondence with them; as believing that they acted according to their Judgment and Conscience, or that their Eyes were held by some *Temptation* in the worst of all their Oppositions. Indeed, his *right Works* were so many, that they exposed him unto the *Envy* of his Neighbours; and of such *Power* was that *Envy*, that sometimes he could not *stand before it;* but it was by *not standing* that he most effectually *withstood* it all. Great Attempts were sometimes made among the *Freemen*, to get him left out from his Place in the *Government* upon little Pretences, lest by the too *frequent Choice* of One Man, the *Government* should cease to be by *Choice;* and with a particular aim at *him*, Sermons were Preached at the Anniversary Court of *Election*, to disswade the *Freemen* from chusing *One Man* Twice together. This was the

Reward of his *extraordinary Serviceableness!* But when these Attempts *did* succeed, as they sometimes *did*, his Profound *Humility* appeared in that *Equality of Mind*, wherewith he applied himself cheerfully to serve the Country in whatever Station their *Votes* had allotted for him. And one Year when the *Votes* came to be Numbered, there were found Six less for Mr. *Winthrop*, than for another Gentleman who then stood in Competition: But several other Persons regularly Tendring their *Votes* before the *Election* was published, were, upon a very frivolous Objection, refused by some of the Magistrates, that were afraid lest the *Election* should at last fall upon Mr. *Winthrop:* Which though it was well perceived, yet such was the *Self-denial*, of this *Patriot*, that he would not permit any Notice to be taken of the Injury. But these *Trials* were nothing in Comparison of those harsher and harder *Treats*, which he sometimes had from the *Frowardness* of not a few in the Days of their *Paroxisms;* and from the *Faction* of some against him, not much unlike that of the *Piazzi* in *Florence* against the Family of the *Medices:* All of which he at last Conquered by Conforming to the Famous *Judges* Motto, *Prudens qui Patiens.*[1] The Oracles of God have said, *Envy is rottenness to the Bones;* and *Gulielmus Parisiensis*[2] applies it unto Rulers, who are as it were the *Bones* of the Societies which they belong unto: *Envy*, says he, *is often found among them, and it is rottenness unto them.* Our *Winthrop* Encountred this *Envy* from others, but Conquered it, by being free from it himself.

§ 8. Were it not for the sake of introducing the Exemplary Skill of this Wise Man, *at giving soft Answers,*

[1] "He is prudent who is patient."
[2] William, who became Bishop at Paris, in 1228.

one would not chuse to Relate those Instances of *Wrath*, which he had sometimes to Encounter with; but he was for his *Gentleness*, his *Forbearance*, and his *Longanimity*, a Pattern so worthy to be Written *after*, that something must here be Written *of* it. He seemed indeed never to speak any other Language than that of *Theodosius, If any Man speak evil of the Governour, if it be thro' Lightness, 'tis to be contemned; if it be thro' Madness, 'tis to be pitied; if it be thro' Injury, 'tis to be remitted.* Behold, Reader, the *Meekness of Wisdom* notably exemplified! There was a time when he received a very sharp Letter from a Gentleman, who was a Member of the Court, but he delivered back the Letter unto the Messengers that brought it with such a Christian Speech as this, *I am not willing to keep such a matter of Provocation by me!* Afterwards the same Gentleman was compelled by the scarcity of Provisions to send unto him that he would Sell him some of his Cattel; whereupon the Governour prayed him to accept what he had sent for as a *Token* of his Good Will; but the Gentleman returned him this Answer, *Sir, your overcoming of your self hath overcome me;* and afterwards gave Demonstration of it. The *French* have a saying, That *Un Honeste Homme, est un Homme mesle!* A *good* Man is a *mixt* Man; and there hardly ever was a more sensible *Mixture* of those Two things, *Resolution* and *Condescention*, than in this good Man. There was a time when the Court of *Election*, being for fear of Tumult, held at *Cambridge, May* 17. 1637. The Sectarian part of the Country, who had the Year before gotten a *Governour* more unto their Mind, had a Project now to have confounded the *Election*, by demanding that the *Court* would consider a *Petition* then tendered before their Proceeding thereunto. Mr.

Winthrop saw that this was only a Trick to throw all into Confusion, by putting off the *Choice* of the *Governour* and *Assistents* until the *Day* should be over; and therefore he did, with a strenuous *Resolution*, procure a disappointment unto that mischievous and ruinous Contrivance. Nevertheless, Mr. *Winthrop* himself being by the Voice of the Freemen in this Exigence chosen the *Governour*, and all of the other Party left out, that ill-affected Party discovered the *Dirt* and *Mire*, which remained with them, after the *Storm* was over; particularly the *Serjeants*, whose Office 'twas to attend the *Governour*, laid down their *Halberts;* but such was the *Condescention* of this Governour, as to take no present Notice of this Anger and Contempt, but only Order some of his own Servants to take the *Halberts*: And when the Country manifested their deep Resentments of the Affront thus offered him, *he* prayed them to *overlook* it. But it was not long before a Compensation was made for these things by the *doubled Respects* which were from all Parts paid unto him. Again, there was a time when the Suppression of an *Antinomian* and *Familistical* Faction, which extreamly threatned the Ruin of the Country, was generally thought much owing unto this Renowned Man; [1] and therefore when the Friends of that Faction could not wreak their Displeasure on him with any *Politick* Vexations, they set themselves to do it by *Ecclesistical* [2] ones. Accordingly when a Sentence of *Banishment* was passed on the Ringleaders of those Disturbances, who

---

[1] This refers to the "persecution" of Anne Hutchinson for her nonconformity to Puritan ideas—an incident celebrated in the early history of New England.

[2] Ecclesiastical.

—Maria & Terras, Cælumq; profundum,
Quippe ferant, Rapidi, secum, vertantq; per Auras; [1]

many at the Church of *Boston*, who were then that way
too much inclined, most earnestly solicited the Elders
of that Church, whereof the Governour was a *Member*,
to call him forth as an *Offender* for passing of that
Sentence. The *Elders* were unwilling to do any such
thing; but the Governour understanding the *Ferment*
among the *People*, took that occasion to make a Speech
in the Congregation to this Effect. '*Brethren*, Under-
'standing that some of you have desired that I should
'Answer for an *Offence* lately taken among you; had I
'been called upon so to do, I would, *First*, Have advised
'with the Ministers of the Country, whether the *Church*
'had Power to call in Question the *Civil Court;* and I
'would, *Secondly*, Have advised with the rest of the
'*Court*, whether I might discover their Counsels unto
'the *Church*. But though I know that the Reverend
'*Elders* of this Church, and some others, do very well
'apprehend that the *Church* cannot enquire into the
'Proceedings of the *Court;* yet for the Satisfaction of
'the weaker who do not apprehend it, I will declare
'my Mind concerning it. If the *Church* have any such
'Power, they have it from the Lord Jesus Christ; but
'the Lord Jesus Christ hath disclaimed it, not only
'by *Practice*, but also by *Precept*, which we have in
'his Gospel, *Mat.* 20. 25, 26. It is true indeed, that
'*Magistrates*, as they are *Church-Members*, are account-
'able unto the *Church* for their Failings; but that is
'when they are out of their Calling. When *Uzziah*
'would go offer Incense in the *Temple*, the Officers

---

[1] "Swift bear with them sea and earth and the lofty sky, and
drive them through the air."

'of the *Church* called him to an account, and withstood
'him; but when *Asa* put the Prophet in Prison, the
'Officers of the *Church* did not call *him* to an account
'for *that*. If the *Magistrate* shall in a *private way* wrong
'any Man, the *Church* may call him to an Account for
'it; but if he be in Pursuance of a Course of *Justice*,
'though the thing that he does be *unjust*, yet he is
'not accountable for it before the *Church*. As for my
'self I did nothing in the Causes of any of the *Brethren*,
'but by the Advice of the *Elders* of the *Church*. More-
'over, in the *Oath* which I have taken there is this
'Clause, *In all Causes wherein you are to give your Vote*,
'*you shall do as in your Judgment and Conscience you*
'*shall see to be Just, and for the publick Good*. And I am
'satisfied, it is most for the Glory of God, and the
'*publick Good*, that there has been such a *Sentence*
'passed; yea, those *Brethren* are so divided from the
'*rest* of the Country in their Opinions and Practices,
'that it cannot stand with the *publick Peace* for them
'to continue with us; *Abraham* saw that *Hagar* and
'*Ishmael* must be sent away. By such a Speech he
marvellously convinced, satisfied and mollified the
uneasie Brethren of the Church; *Sic cunctus Pelagi
cecidit Fragor—*.[1] And after a little patient waiting,
the *differences* all so wore away, that the Church,
meerly as a Token of Respect unto the Governour,
when he had newly met with some *Losses* in his Estate,
sent him a Present of several *Hundreds* of Pounds.
Once more there was a time, when some active Spirits
among the *Deputies* of the Colony, by their endeavours
not only to make themselves a *Court of Judicature*,
but also to take away the *Negative* by which the *Magistrates* might check their *Votes*, had like by over-driving

[1] "So all the din of the sea subsided."

to have run the whole Government into something too *Democratical.* And if there were a Town in *Spain* undermined by *Coneys,* another Town in *Thrace* destroyed by *Moles,* a Third in *Greece* ranversed by *Frogs,* a Fourth in *Germany* subverted by *Rats;* I must on this Occasion add, that there was a Country in *America* like to be confounded by a *Swine.* A certain *stray Sow* being found, was claimed by Two several Persons with a Claim so equally maintained on both sides, that after Six or Seven Years *Hunting* the Business, from one Court unto another, it was brought at last into the *General Court,* where the final Determination was, *that it was impossible to proceed unto any Judgment in the Case.* However in the debate of this Matter, the *Negative* of the *Upper-House* upon the *Lower* in that Court was brought upon the Stage; and agitated with so hot a Zeal, that a *little more and all had been in the Fire.* In these Agitations the Governour was informed that an offence had been taken by some eminent Persons, at certain Passages in a Discourse by him written thereabout; whereupon with his usual *Condescendency,* when he next came into the General Court, he made a Speech of this Import. 'I under-'stand, that some have *taken* Offence at something that 'I have lately written; which *Offence* I desire to remove 'now, and begin this Year in a reconciled State with 'you all. As for the *Matter* of my Writing, I had the 'Concurrence of my *Brethren;* it is a Point of *Judgment* 'which is not at my own disposing. I have examined 'it over and over again, by such *Light* as God has given 'me, from the Rules of *Religion, Reason,* and *Custom;* 'and I see no cause to Retract any thing of it: Where-'fore I must enjoy my *Liberty* in *that,* as *you* do your 'selves. But for the *Manner, this,* and all that was

'blame-worthy in it, was wholly *my own;* and whatso-
'ever I might alledge for my own Justification therein
'before *Men*, I wave it, as now setting my self before
'another *Judgment-Seat*.   However, what I wrote
'was upon *great Provocation*, and to vindicate my self
'and others from great Aspersion; yet that was no
'sufficient Warrant for me to allow any *Distemper of*
'*Spirit* in my self; and I doubt I have been too prodigal
'of my *Brethren's Reputation;* I might have maintained
'my Cause without casting any Blemish upon others,
'when I made that my Conclusion, *And now let Religion*
'*and sound Reason give Judgment in the Case;* it look'd
'as if I arrogated too much unto *my self*, and too little
'to *others*.   And when I made that Profession, *That*
'*I would maintain what I wrote before all the World*,
'though such Words might modestly be spoken, yet
'I perceive an unbeseeming *Pride* of my own Heart
'breathing in them.   For these Failings I ask Pardon
'both of God and Man.

Sic ait, & dicto citius Tumida Æquora placat,
Collectasq; fugat Nubes, Solemq; reducit.[1]

This *acknowledging Disposition* in the Governour,
made them all *acknowledge*, that he was truly *a Man*
of an excellent Spirit.   In fine, the *Victories* of an *Alex-*
ander, an *Hannibal*, or a *Cæsar* over *other Men*, were
not so Glorious, as the *Victories* of this great Man over
himself, which also at last prov'd *Victories* over *other*
Men.

§ 9.   But the stormiest of all the *Trials* that ever
befel this Gentleman, was in the Year 1645. when he
was in *Title* no more than *Deputy-Governour* of the

----

[1] "So he spoke, and thus quickly calmed the swelling sea, put to
rout the gathered clouds, and brought back the sun."

Colony. If the famous *Cato* were Forty-four times call'd into Judgment, but as often acquitted; let it not be wondred, and if our Famous *Winthrop* were one time so. There hapning certain Seditious and Mutinous Practices in the Town of *Hingham*, the *Deputy-Governour* as legally as prudently interposed his *Authority* for the checking of them: Whereupon there followed such an *Enchantment* upon the minds of the *Deputies* in the General Court, that upon a scandalous Petition of the Delinquents unto *them*, wherein a pretended Invasion made upon the *Liberties* of the *People* was complained of the *Deputy-Governour*, was most Irregularly call'd forth unto an Ignominous *Hearing* before them in a vast Assembly; whereto with a *Sagacious Humility* he *consented*, although he shew'd them how he might have *Refused* it. The result of that *Hearing* was, That notwithstanding the touchy *Jealousie* of the *People* about their *Liberties* lay at the bottom of all this Prosecution, yet Mr. *Winthrop* was publickly Acquitted, and the Offenders were severally Fined and Censured. But Mr. *Winthrop* then resuming the Place of *Deputy-Governour* on the Bench, saw cause to speak unto the *Root of the Matter* after this manner. 'I shall 'not now speak any thing about the past *Proceedings* 'of this Court, or the *Persons* therein concerned. Only 'I bless God that I see an Issue of this troublesome 'Affair. I am well satisfied that I was publickly *Accused*, 'and that I am now publickly *Acquitted*. But though 'I am justified before *Men*, yet it may be the *Lord* hath 'seen so much amiss in my Administrations, as calls 'me to be *humbled;* and indeed for me to have been 'thus charged by *Men*, is it self a Matter of *Humiliation*, 'whereof I desire to make a right use before the *Lord*. 'If *Miriam's* Father spit in her Face, she is to be *Ashamed*.

'But give me leave before you go, to say something
'that may rectifie the *Opinions* of many *People*, from
'whence the *Distempers* have risen that have lately
'prevailed upon the *Body* of *this* People. The Questions
'that have troubled the Country have been about the
'*Authority of the Magistracy*, and the *Liberty of the*
'*People*. It is *You* who have called *us* unto this Office;
'but being thus *called*, we have our *Authority* from *God;*
'it is the *Ordinance* of God, and it hath the *Image* of
'*God* stamped upon it; and the contempt of it has been
'vindicated by *God* with terrible Examples of his
'Vengeance. I intreat you to consider, That when
'you chuse *Magistrates*, you take them from among
'your selves, *Men subject unto like Passions with your*
'*selves*. If you see *our* Infirmities, reflect on *your own*,
'and you will not be so severe Censurers of *Ours*. We
'count him a *good Servant* who *breaks not his Covenant:*
'The *Covenant* between *Us* and *You*, is the *Oath* you
'have taken of *us*, which is to this Purpose, *That we*
'*shall govern you, and judge your Causes, according to*
'*God's Laws, and our own, according to our best Skill.*
'As for our *Skill*, you must run the hazard of it; and
'if there be an Error, not in the *Will*, but only in the
'*Skill*, it becomes *you* to bear it. Nor would I have
'you to. mistake in the Point of your own *Liberty*.
'There is a *Liberty* of corrupt Nature, which is affected
'both by *Men* and *Beasts*, to do what they list; and
'this *Liberty* is inconsistent with *Authority*, impatient
'of all Restraint; by this *Liberty*, *Sumus Omnes Deterio-*
'*res;* [1] 'Tis the Grand Enemy of *Truth* and *Peace*, and
'all the *Ordinances* of God are bent against it. But
'there is a Civil, a Moral, a Federal *Liberty*, which is
'the proper End and Object of *Authority;* it is a *Liberty*

[1] "We are all the worse."

'for that only which is *just* and *good;* for this *Liberty*
'you are to stand with the hazard of your very *Lives;*
'and whatsoever Crosses it, is not *Authority*, but a
'*Distemper* thereof: This *Liberty* is maintained in a
'way of *Subjection* to *Authority;* and the *Authority* set
'over you, will in all Administrations for your good
'be quietly submitted unto, by all but such as have a
'Disposition to *shake off the Yoke*, and lose their true
'*Liberty*, by their murmuring at the Honour and Power
'of *Authority*.[1]

The *Spell* that was upon the Eyes of the People
being thus dissolved, their *distorted* and *enraged* notions
of things all vanished; and the People would not afterwards entrust the Helm of the *Weather-beaten* Bark in
any other Hands, but Mr. *Winthrop's*, until he Died.

§ 10. Indeed such was the *Mixture* of *distant Qualities* in him, as to make a most admirable *Temper;* and
his having a certain *Greatness of Soul*, which rendered
him Grave, Generous, Courageous, Resolved, Well-
applied, and every way a *Gentleman* in his Deameanour,
did not hinder him from taking sometimes the old
Romans way to avoid Confusions, namely, *Cedendo;* [2]
or from discouraging some things which are agreeable
enough to most that wear the Name of *Gentlemen*.
Hereof I will give no Instances, but only *oppose* two
Passages of his Life.

In the Year 1632. the Governour, with his Pastor
Mr. *Wilson*, and some other Gentlemen, to settle a good
understanding between the Two Colonies, travelled
as far as *Plymouth*, more than Forty Miles, through

[1] De Tocqueville, *Democracy in America* (trans. Reeve, 4th ed.,
1864), i, 52, calls the speech of Winthrop here reported "a fine definition of liberty." It has become justly famous.
[2] "By yielding."

an Howling Wilderness, no better accommodated in those early Days, than the *Princes* that in *Solomon*'s time saw *Servants on Horseback*, or than *Genus* and *Species* in the old Epigram, *going on Foot*. The difficulty of the *Walk*, was abundantly compensated by the Honourable, *first* Reception, and *then* Dismission, which they found from the Rulers of *Plymouth;* and by the good Correspondence thus established between the New Colonies, who were like the floating Bottels wearing this Motto, *Si Collidimur, Frangimur*.[1] But there were at this time in *Plymouth* two Ministers, leavened so far with the Humours of the *Rigid Separation*, that they insisted vehemently upon the Unlawfulness of calling any *unregenerate* Man by the Name of *Good-man such an One*, until by their indiscreet urging of this Whimsey, the place began to be disquieted. The wiser People being troubled at these Trifles, they took the opportunity of Governour *Winthrop*'s being *there*, to have the thing publickly propounded in the Congregation; who in answer thereunto, distinguished between a *Theological* and a *Moral Goodness;* adding, that when *Juries* were first used in *England*, it was usual for the *Crier*, after the Names of Persons fit for that Service were called over, to bid them all, *Attend, Good Men, and True;* whence it grew to be a *Civil Custom* in the *English Nation*, for Neighbours living by one another, to call one another *Good-man such an One:* And it was pity now to make a stir about a *Civil Custom*, so innocently introduced. And that Speech of Mr. *Winthrop*'s put a lasting stop to the Little, Idle, Whimsical *Conceits*, then beginning to grow Obstreperous. Nevertheless there was one *Civil Custom* used *in* (and in few *but*) the *English Nation*, which this Gentleman

[1] "If we collide, we break."

did endeavour to abolish in *this Country*; and that was, *The usage of Drinking to one another*. For although by *Drinking to one another*, no more is meant than an act of *Courtesie*, when one going to *Drink*, does Invite another to do so too, for the same Ends with himself; nevertheless the Governour (not altogether unlike *to Cleomenes*, of whom 'tis reported by *Plutarch*, ἄηοντι οὐδεὶς ποτήριον προσέφερε, *Nolenti poculum nunquam præbuit*,[1]) considered the *Impertinency* and *Insignificancy* of this Usage, as to any of *those Ends* that are usually pretended for it; and that indeed it ordinarily served for *no Ends* at all, but only to provoke Persons unto *unseasonable*, and perhaps *unreasonable* Drinking, and at last produce that abominable *Health-Drinking*, which the *Fathers* of old so severely rebuked in the *Pagans*, and which the *Papists* themselves do Condemn, when their Casuists pronounce it, *Peccatum mortale, provocare ad Æquales Calices, & Nefas Respondere*.[2] Wherefore in his own most Hospitable House he left it off, not out of any silly or stingy *Fancy*, but meerly that by his *Example* a greater *Temperance*, with *Liberty* of *Drinking*, might be Recommended, and sundry *Inconveniences* in Drinking avoided; and his *Example* accordingly began to be much followed by the sober People in *this Country*, as it now also begins to be among Persons of the *Highest* Rank in the *English Nation* it self; until an *Order of Court* came to be made against that *Ceremony* in Drinking, and then the *old Wont* violently returned, with a *Nitimur in Vetitum*.[3]

§ 11. *Many were the Afflictions of this Righteous*

[1] "Never offered drink to one who was unwilling."
[2] "It is a mortal sin to challenge anyone to a drinking match, and wrong to accept such a challenge."
[3] "We strive for what is forbidden."

Man! He lost much of his Estate in a Ship, and in an *House*, quickly after his coming to *New-England*, besides the Prodigious Expence of it in the Difficulties of his first coming hither. Afterwards his assiduous Application unto the Publick *Affairs*, (wherein *Ipse se non habuit, postquam Respublica eum Gubernatorem habere capit*)[1] made him so much to neglect his own *private Interests*, that an *unjust Steward* ran him 2500 *l.* in Debt before he was aware; for the Payment whereof he was forced, many Years before his Decease, to sell the most of what he had left unto him in the Country. Albeit, by the observable Blessing of God upon the *Posterity* of this *Liberal Man*, his Children all of them came to fäir Estates, and lived in good Fashion and Credit. Moreover, he successively Buried Three *Wives;* the First of which was the Daughter and Heiress of Mr. *Forth*, of *Much Stambridge*[2] in *Essex*, by whom he had *Wisdom with an Inheritance;* and an excellent Son. The Second was the Daughter of Mr. *William Clopton*, of *London*,[3] who Died with her Child within a very little while. The Third was the Daughter of the truly Worshipful Sir *John Tyndal*,[4] who made it her whole Care to please, First *God*, and then her *Husband;* and by whom he had Four Sons, which Survived and Honoured their Father. And unto all these, the Addition of the *Distempers*, ever now and then raised in the *Country*, procured unto him a very singular share of Trouble; yea, so hard was the Measure

[1] "He did not possess himself after the state began to possess him as governor."

[2] Or Great Stambridge.

[3] R. C. Winthrop, *op. cit.*, says "of Castleins, a seat near Groton" (i, 75).

[4] *Cf. idem*, i, 123 ff.

which he found even among Pious Men, in the Temptations of a *Wilderness*, that when the *Thunder* and *Lightning* had smitten a *Wind-mill*, whereof he was Owner, some had *such things in their Heads*, as publickly to Reproach this *Charitablest* of Men, as if the *Voice of the Almighty* had rebuked, I know not what *Oppression*, which they *judged* him Guilty of: Which things I would not have mentioned, but that the Instances may fortifie the Expectations of my *best Readers* for such Afflictions.

§ 12. He that had been for his Attainments, as they said of the blessed *Macarius*, a Παιδαριογερων *An old Man, while a young One*, and that had in his *young Days* met with many of those *Ill Days*, whereof he could say, he had *little Pleasure in them;* now found *old Age* in its Infirmities advancing *Earlier* upon him, than it came upon his much longer lived Progenitors. While he was yet Seven Years off of that which we call *the grand Climacterical*,[1] he felt the Approaches of his *Dissolution;* and finding he could say,

Non Habitus, non ipse Color non Gressus Euntis,
Non Species Eadem, quæ fuit ante, manet.[2]

he then wrote this account of himself, *Age now comes upon me, and Infirmities therewithal, which makes me apprehend that the time of my departure out of this World is not far off. However our times are all in the Lord's Hand, so as we need not trouble our Thoughts how long or short they may be, but how we may be found Faithful when we are called for.* But at last when *that Year*

---

[1] The sixty-third year of life.
[2] "There remains not the appearance, not even the color, nor the way of life, and not the same aspect, of that which was before."

came, he took a *Cold* which turned into a *Feaver*, whereof he lay *Sick* about a Month, and in that *Sickness*,
as it hath been observed, that there was allowed unto
the *Serpent* the *bruising of the Heel;* and accordingly at
the *Heel* or the *Close* of our Lives the *old Serpent* will
be Nibbling more than ever in our Lives before; and
when the Devil sees that we shall shortly be, *where the
wicked cease from troubling*, that *wicked One* will *trouble*
us more than ever; so this eminent Saint now underwent
sharp Conflicts with the *Tempter*, whose *Wrath* grew
Great, as the *Time* to exert it grew *Short;* and he was
Buffetted with the Disconsolate Thoughts of Black
and Sore *Desertions*, wherein he could use that sad
Representation of his own Condition.

*Nuper Eram Judex; Jam Judicor; Ante Tribunat,
Subsistens paveo, Judicor ipse modo.*[1]

But it was not long before those *Clouds* were Dis-
pelled, and he enjoyed in his Holy Soul the *Great Consolations of God!* While he thus lay *Ripening* for
Heaven, he did out of Obedience unto the *Ordinance*
of our Lord, send for the *Elders of the Church* to *Pray*
with him; yea, they and the whole Church *Fasted* as
well as *Prayed* for him; and in that *Fast* the venerable
Cotton[2] Preached on *Psal.* 35. 13, 14. *When they were
Sick, I humbled my self with Fasting; I behaved my self
as though he had been my Friend or Brother; I bowed
down heavily, as one that Mourned for his Mother:* From
whence I find him raising that Observation, *The
Sickness of one that is to us as a Friend, a Brother, a*

---

[1] "Once I was a judge; now I am judged. I stand trembling before
the tribunal, now I myself am judged."

[2] Rev. John Cotton, grandfather of Cotton Mather.

*Mother, is a just occasion of deep humbling our Souls
with Fasting and Prayer;* and making this Application,
'Upon this Occasion we are now to attend this Duty for
'a *Governour,* who has been to us as a *Friend* in his
'*Counsel* for all things, and *Help* for our *Bodies* by
Physick, for our *Estates* by *Law,* and of whom there
'was no fear of his becoming an *Enemy,* like the *Friends*
'of *David:* A *Governour* who has been unto us as a
'*Brother;* not usurping *Authority* over the Church;
'often speaking his *Advice,* and often contradicted,
'even by Young Men, and some of low degree; yet not
'replying, but offering Satisfaction also when any
'supposed Offences have arisen; a *Governour* who has
'been unto us as a *Mother,* Parent-like distributing
'his *Goods* to Brethren and Neighbours at his first
'coming: and *gently* bearing our *Infirmities* without
'taking notice of them.

Such a *Governour* after he had been more than *Ten*
several times by the People chosen their *Governour,*
was *New-England* now to lose; who having, like *Jacob,*
first left his *Council* and *Blessing* with his Children
gathered about his Bed-side; and, like *David, served
his Generation by the Will of God,* he *gave up the Ghost*
and *fell asleep* on *March* 26. 1649. Having, like the
dying Emperour *Valentinian,* this above all his other
Victories for his Triumphs, *His overcoming of himself.*

The Words of *Josephus* about *Nehemiah,* the Governour of *Israel,* we will now use upon this Governour of
New-England, as his

EPITAPH.

Ἀνὴρ ἐγένετο χρηστὸς τὴν φύσιν, καὶ δίκαιος,
Καὶ περὶ τοὺς ὁμοεθνεῖς φιλοτιμότατος:

Μνημεῖον ἀιώνιον ἀυτω καταλιπὼν τὰ τῶν
'Ιεροσολύμων τείχη·[1]

VIR FUIT INDOLE BONUS, AC JUSTUS:
ET POPULARIUM GLORIÆ AMANTISSIMUS:
QUIBUS ETERNUM RELIQUIT MONUMENTUM,
Novanglorum MOENIA.

CHAP. V.

SUCCESSORS.

§ I. ONE as well acquainted with the Matter, as *Isocrates*, informs us, That among the *Judges* of *Areopagus* none were admitted, πλὴν οἱ καλῶς γέγονότες καὶ πολλὴν ἀρετὴν καὶ σωφροσύνην ἐν τῷ βίῳ ἐνδεδειγμένοι, *unless they were Nobly Born, and Eminently Exemplary for a Virtuous and a Sober Life.* The Report may be truly made concerning the *Judges* of *New-England,* tho' they were not *Nobly Born,* yet they were generally *Well Born;* and by being *Eminently Exemplary for a Virtuous and a Sober Life,* gave Demonstration that they were *New-Born.*[2] Some Account of them is now more particularly to be Endeavoured.

We read concerning *Saul,* [1 Sam. 15. 12.] *He set up himself a place.* The Hebrew Word, ד.י there used, signifies *A Monumental Pillar:* It is accordingly promised unto them who *please God,* [Isa. 56. 5.] *That they shall have a Place and a Name in the House of God;* that

---

[1] "He was a man by nature good and just, and most zealous for honor for his countrymen, leaving for them an eternal memorial— the walls of Jerusalem." The Latin paraphrase which follows substitutes New England for Jerusalem.

[2] *I. e.,* newborn religiously.

is to say, a *Pillar* Erected for *Fame* in the Church of
God. And it shall be fulfilled in what shall now be done
for our *Governours* in this our *Church-History*. Even
while the *Massachusettensians* had a *Winthrop* for their
Governour, they could not restrain the Channel of
their *Affections* from running towards another Gentleman in their *Elections* for the Year 1634. particularly,
when they chose unto the Place of *Governour Thomas
Dudley*, Esq; one whom after the Death of the Gentleman abovementioned, they again and again Voted
into the Chief Place of Government. He was Born at
the Town of *Northampton*, in the Year 1574.[1] the only
Son of Captain *Roger Dudley*, who being Slain in the
Wars, left this our *Thomas*, with his only Sister, for
the *Father of the Orphans*, to *take them up*. In the
Family of the Earl of *Northampton* he had opportunity
perfectly to learn the Points of *Good Behaviour;* and
here having fitted himself to do many other Benefits
unto the World, he next became a *Clerk* unto Judge
Nichols, who being his Kinsman by the Mother's Side,
therefore took the more special notice of him. From
his Relation to this *Judge*, he had and used an Advantage to attain such a Skill in the *Law*, as was of great
Advantage to him in the future changes of his Life;
and the *Judge* would have preferred him unto the
higher Imployments, whereto his prompt *Wit* not a
little recommended him, if he had not been by Death
prevented. But before he could appear to do much at
the *Pen*, for which he was very well Accomplished, he
was called upon to do something at the *Sword;* for being
a Young Gentlemen [*sic*] well-known for his Ingenuity,
Courage and Conduct, when there were Soldiers to be

[1] If Dudley's age at his death, as given by Mather, is correct, this
should be 1576, not 1574.

raised by Order from Queen *Elizabeth* for the *French*
Service, in the time of King *Henry* the Fourth, the
Young Sparks about *Northampton* were none of them
willing to enter into the Service, until a *Commission*
was given unto our Young *Dudley* to be their *Captain;*
and then presently there were *Fourscore* that Listed
under him. At the Head of these he went over into the
Low Countries, which was then an *Academy* of *Arms,*
as well as *Arts;* and thus he came to furnish himself
with Endowments for the *Field,* as well as for the
Bench. The Post assigned unto him with his Company,
was after at the Siege of *Amiens,* before which the
King himself was now Encamped; but the Providence
of God so Ordered it, that when both Parties were
drawn forth in Order to Battel, a Treaty of *Peace* was
vigorously set on Foot, which diverted the Battel that
was expected. Captain *Dudley* hereupon returned
into *England,* and settling himself about *Northampton,*
he Married a Gentlewoman whose Extract and Estate
were Considerable; and the Scituation of his Habitation
after this helped him to enjoy the Ministry of Mr.
Dod, Mr. *Cleaver,* Mr. *Winston,* and Mr. *Hildersham,*
all of them Excellent and Renowned Men; which
Puritan Ministry so seasoned his Heart with a Sense of
Religion, that he was a Devout and Serious Christian,
and a Follower of the Ministers that most effectually
Preached *Real Christianity* all the rest of his Days.
The Spirit of *Real Christianity* in him now also disposed
him unto *Sober Non-Conformity;* and from this time,
although none more hated the *Fanaticisms* and *En-
thusiasms* of Wild *Opinionists,* he became a *Judicious
Dissenter* from the *Unscriptural Ceremonies* retained
in the Church of *England.*[1]   It was not long after this

[1] *Cf.* p. xliv, *ante.*

that the Lord *Say*, the Lord *Compton*, and other Persons
of Quality, made such Observations of him, as to commend him unto the Service of the Earl of *Lincoln*,
who was then a Young Man, and newly come unto the
Possession of his *Earldom*, and of what belonged thereunto. The Grandfather of this Noble Person had left
his Heirs under vast Entanglements, out of which his
Father was never able to Extricate himself; so that the
Difficulties and Incumbrances were now devolved
upon this *Theophilus*,[1] which caused him to apply himself unto this our *Dudley* for his Assistances, who
proved so Able, and Careful, and Faithful a *Steward*
unto him, that within a little while the *Debts* of near
Twenty Thousand Pounds, whereinto the *Young
Earl* found himself desperately Ingulphed, were happily
waded through; and by his Means also a *Match* was
procured between the *Young Earl* and the Daughter
of the Lord *Say*, who proved a most Virtuous Lady,
and a great Blessing to the whole Family. But the
Earl finding Mr. *Dudley* to be a Person of more than
ordinary Discretion, he would rarely, if ever, do any
Matter of any Moment without his Advice; but some
into whose Hands there fell some of his Manuscripts
after his leaving of the Earl's Family, found a Passage
to this purpose. *The Estate of the Earl of* Lincoln,
*I found so, and so, much in Debt, which I have discharged,
and have raised the Rents unto so many Hundreds* Per
Annum; *God will, I trust, bless me and mine in such a
manner. I can, as sometimes* Nehemiah *did, appeal
unto God, who knows the Hearts of all Men, that I have
with Integrity discharged the Duty of my Place before him.*
    I had prepared and intended a more *particular Ac-*

[1] Theophilus Clinton, fourth Earl of Lincoln. *Cf.* Augustine Jones,
Life and Work of Thomas Dudley (Boston, 1899), ch. 4.

count of this Gentleman; but not having any opportunity to commit it unto the *Perusal* of any Descended from him, (unto whom I am told it will be unacceptable for me to Publish any thing of this kind, by *them* not *Perused*) I have laid it aside, and summed all up in this more *General Account.*[1]

It was about Nine or Ten Years, that Mr. *Dudley* continued a *Steward* unto the Earl of *Lincoln;* but then growing desirous of a more private Life, he retired unto *Boston,*[2] where the Acquaintance and Ministry of Mr. *Cotton* became no little Satisfaction unto him. Nevertheless the Earl of *Lincoln* found that he could be no more without Mr. *Dudley,* than *Pharaoh* without his *Joseph,* and prevailed with him to resume his former Employment, until the Storm of Persecution upon the *Non-Conformists* caused many Men of great Worth to Transport themselves into *New-England.* Mr. *Dudley* was not the least of the Worthy Men that bore a part in this Transportation, in hopes that in an *American* Wilderness they might peaceably attend and enjoy the pure Worship of the Lord Jesus Christ. When the first Undertakers for that Plantation came to know him, they soon saw *that* in him, that caused them to chuse him their *Deputy-Governour,* in which Capacity he arrived unto these Coasts in the Year 1630. and had no small share in the Distresses of that Young Plantation, whereof an account by him written to the Countess of *Lincoln* has been since Published unto the World.[3] Here his *Wisdom* in managing the most weighty and thorny Affairs was often signalized: His

[1] Cf. p. xliv *ante.*
[2] In Lincolnshire, England.
[3] This famous letter has been many times reprinted. *Cf.* A. Jones, *op. cit.*, 437, note, and 437–452.

Justice was a perpetual Terror to Evil Doers: His *Courage* procured his being the first *Major-General* of the Colony, when they began to put themselves into a *Military Figure*. His *Orthodox Piety* had no little Influence into the Deliverance of the Country, from the Contagion of the *Famalistical* [1] *Errors*, which had like to have overturned all. He dwelt first at *Cambridge;* but upon Mr. *Hooker's* removal to *Hartford*, he removed to *Ispwich;* nevertheless, upon the Importunity and Necessity of the Government for his coming to dwell nearer the Center of the whole, he fixed his Habitation at *Roxbury*, Two Miles out of *Boston*, where he was always at Hand upon the Publick Exigencies. Here he died, *July* 31. 1653. in the Seventy-Seventh Year of his Age; and there were found after his Death, in his Pocket, these Lines of his own Composing, which may serve to make up what may be wanting in the Character already given him.

Dim Eyes, Deaf Ears, Cold Stomach, shew
My Dissolution is in View.
Eleven times Seven near liv'd have I,
And now God calls, I willing Die.
My Shuttle's shot, my Race is run,
My Sun is set, my Day is done.
My Span is measur'd, Tale is told,
My Flower is faded, and grown old.
My Dream is vanish'd, Shadow's fled,
My Soul with Christ, my Body Dead.
Farewel Dear Wife, Children and Friends,
Hate Heresie, make Blessed Ends.
Bear Poverty, live with good Men;
So shall we live with Joy agen.

[1] Familistical. *Cf.* note 1, p. 70, *ante.*

Let Men of God in Courts and Churches watch
O're such as do a Toleration *hatch,*
Lest that Ill Egg bring forth a Cockatrice,
To poison all with Heresie and Vice.
If Men be left, and otherwise Combine,
My Epitaph's, I DY'D NO LIBERTINE.[1]

But when I mention the *Poetry* of this Gentleman as
one of his Accomplishments, I must not leave unmentioned the Fame with which the *Poems* of one
descended from him have been Celebrated in both
Englands. If the rare Learning of a *Daughter*, was not
the least of those bright things that adorn'd no less a
Judge of *England* than Sir *Thomas More;* it must now
be said, that a Judge of *New-England,* namely, *Thomas
Dudley*, Esq; had a *Daughter* (besides other Children)
to be a *Crown* unto him. Reader, *America* justly admires the Learned Women of the other *Hemisphere.*
She has heard of those that were *Tutoresses* to the
Old Professors of all Philosophy: She hath heard of
Hippatia, who formerly taught the Liberal Arts;
and of *Sarocchia,* who more lately was very often the
Moderatrix in the Disputations of the Learned Men
of *Rome:* She has been told of the Three *Corinnæ's*,
which equal'd, if not excell'd, the most Celebrated
Poet of their Time: She has been told of the Empress
Eudoxia, who Composed Poetical Paraphrases on
Divers Parts of the *Bible;* and of *Rosuida,* who wrote
the *Lives* of Holy Men; and of *Pamphilia,* who wrote

[1] In the MS. life of Dudley, by Cotton Mather, this poem is given
in a slightly different version. Apparently Mather revised it for in-
sertion in the *Magnalia.* The one important change is in the last
line, which reads in the MS.: "Mine epitaph's—I did no hurt to
thine."

other Histories unto the Life: The Writings of the most
Renowned *Anna Maria Schurman*, have come over
unto her. But she now prays, that into such Cata-
logues of *Authoresses*, as *Beverovicius*, *Hottinger*, and
Voetius, have given unto the World,[1] there may be a
room now given unto Madam ANN BRADSTREET,
the Daughter of our Governour *Dudley*, and the Consort
of our Governour *Bradstreet*, whose *Poems*, divers times
Printed, have afforded a grateful Entertainment unto
the Ingenious, and a Monument for her Memory
beyond the Stateliest *Marbles*. It was upon these
Poems that an Ingenious Person bestowed this *Epigram:*

Now I believe Tradition, *which doth call*
The Muses, Virtues, Graces, Females *all.*
Only they are not Nine, Eleven, *or* Three;
Our Auth'ress *proves them but an* Unity.
Mankind, *take up some Blushes on the score;*
Monopolize Perfection *hence no more.*
In your own Arts confess your selves outdone;
The Moon *hath totally Eclips'd the* Sun:
Not with her Sable Mantle muffling him,
But her bright Silver *makes his* Gold *look dim:*

[1] Hippatia is Hypatia, neo-Platonic philosopher of the end of the
fourth century; Sarocchia or Sarrochia was a Neapolitan poetess in the
beginning of the seventeenth century; Corinna was a Greek poetess
about the beginning of the fifth century B. C., and some writers
mention another Corinna of Thebes and one of Thespiæ; Eudoxia
was the Roman empress Eudocia, who lived about 393–460; Rosuida
(Hrotswitha, Hrosvitha, or Hrotsuit), c. 935–c. 1000, wrote poetical
chronicles and six Latin comedies; Pamphilia was Pamphila, a historian in the time of Nero, and Anna Maria von Schurmann, 1607–
1678, was a German artist and scholar. Beverovicius was Jan van
Beverwyck, Dutch physician, 1594–1647; John Henry Hottinger
was a Swiss theologian and historian, 1620–1667, and Gisbert Voet,
a Dutch theologian, lived 1589–1677.

Just as his Beams force our pale Lamps to wink,
And Earthly Fires *within their Ashes shrink.*[1]

What else might be said of Mr. *Dudley,* the Readers shall Construe from the Ensuing

EPITAPH.

Helluo Librorum, Lectorum Bibliotheca
  Communis, Sacræ Syllabus Historiæ.
Ad Mensam Comes, hinc facundus, Rostra disertus,
  (Non Cumulus verbis, pondus, Acumen erat,)
Morum acris Censor, validus Defensor amansq;
  Et Sanæ & Canæ Catholicæ fidei.
Angli-novi Columen, Summum Decus atq; Senatus;
  Thomas Dudleius, *conditur hoc Tumulo.*   E. R.[2]

§ 2.   In the Year 1635. at the Anniversary Election, the Freemen of the Colony testified their grateful Esteem of Mr. *John Haines,* a Worthy Gentleman, who had been very Serviceable to the Interests of the Colony, by chusing him their *Governour.*   Of him in an

---

[1] These lines appeared in the second edition of Anne Bradstreet's *Tenth Muse,* which came out in Boston in 1678, with the title *Several Poems, etc.* They are printed with the signature B. W., which probably represents Benjamin Woodbridge.   Cotton Mather, in reprinting the lines, has evidently tried his hand at editing them.   In line 3 he prints *or* for *nor,* line 4 *an* for *one,* and in line 6 he inserts *hence.*

[2] "Devourer of books; library of chosen things; compendium of sacred history; companion for the feast, hence eloquent; eloquent on the rostrum (he was weighty not with the heaping up of words, but with keenness); sharp censor of morals; stout defender and lover of a sane and ancient catholic faith; support of New England and the chief ornament of its councils; Thomas Dudley is embalmed in this tomb."   William Hubbard, in his *General History of New England,* finished about 1680, gives this epitaph with the signature N. R., instead of E. R.   The authorship seems to lie between Nathaniel and Ezekiel Rogers, both early New England divines.

Ancient Manuscript I find this Testimony given; *To him is* New-England *many ways beholden; had he done no more but stilled a Storm of Dissention, which broke forth in the beginning of his Government; he had done enough to Endear our Hearts unto him, and to account that Day happy when he took the Reins of Government into his Hands.* But this Pious, Humble, Well-bred Gentleman, removing afterwards into *Connecticut*, he took his turn with Mr. *Edward Hopkins*, in being every other Year the *Governour* of that Colony. And as he was a great Friend of *Peace* while he lived, so at his Death he entred into that *Peace* which attends the End of the *perfect* and *upright* Man, leaving behind him the Character sometimes given of a *Greater*, tho' not a *Better*, Man, [*Vespasian*] *Bonis Legibus multa correxit, sed exemplo probæ vitæ plus effecit apud populum.*[1]

§ 3. Near Twenty Ships from *Europe* visited *New-England* in the Year 1635. and in one of them was Mr. *Henry Vane*,[2] (afterward Sir *Henry Vane*) an Accomplished Young Gentleman, whose Father was much against his coming to *New-England;* but the King, upon Information of his Disposition, commanded him to allow his Son's Voyage hither, with a Consent for his continuing Three Years in this Part of the World. Although his Business had some Relation to the Plantation of *Connecticut*, yet in the Year 1636. the *Massachuset*-Colony chose him their *Governour*. And now, Reader, I am as much a *Seeker* for his *Character*,

---

[1] "He corrected many things by good laws, but accomplished more among the people by the example of a good life."

[2] For Vane, see, for example, J. K. Hosmer, *The Life of Young Sir Henry Vane* (Boston, 1888). Mather probably did not approve of Vane's views, and the account of him shows some adroitness in its avoidance of any definite expression of opinion.

as many have taken him to be a *Seeker* in *Religion*,[1]
while no less Persons than Dr. *Manton* have not been
to *seek* for the *Censure* of *A Wicked Book*, with which
they have noted the *Mystical Divinity*, in the Book of
this Knight, Entituled, *The Retired Man's Meditations*.[2]
There has been a strange variety of Translations bestowed upon the *Hebrew Names* of some *Animals*
mentioned in the *Bible: Kippod*, for Instance, which
we translate a *Bittern; R. Salomon* will have to be an
Owl, but *Luther* will have it be an *Eagle*, while *Paynin*
will have it be an *Hedg-hog*, but *R. Kimchi* will have it
a *Snail;* such a Variety of Opinions and Resentments
has the *Name* of this Gentleman fallen under; while
some have counted him an Eminent *Christian,* and
others have counted him almost an *Heretick;* some
have counted him a Renowned *Patriot,* and others
an Infamous *Traitor.* If *Barak* signifie both to *Bless*
and to *Curse;* and Ευλογειν[3] be of the same Significancy
with Βλασφημειν,[4] in such Philology as that of *Suidas*
and *Hesychius*,[5] the Usage which the *Memory* of this
Gentleman has met withal, seems to have been Accommodated unto that *Indifferency* of Signification in the
Terms for such an Usage.

On the one side, I find an Old *New-English* Manu-

[1] One not contented with any creed or sect, but seeking a more
perfect one.   Roger Williams, also, was regarded as a "seeker."
[2] This book of Vane's was published in 1655.   Vane's religious
views expressed here and elsewhere were freely attacked by the
divines of the time, who found them vague, and, apparently, dangerous, in their hostility to any organized church and their tolerant
tone toward all sects.   Dr. Manton was an eminent Presbyterian in
England, 1620–1677.
[3] "To praise."   [4] "To slander."
[5] Suidas, eleventh century Greek lexicographer, and Hesychius,
Alexandrine grammarian, c. 380.

script thus reflecting, *His Election will remain as a Blemish to their Judgments who did Elect him, while* New-England *remains a Nation; for he coming from* Old-England, *a Young Unexperienced Gentleman, (and as young in Judgment as he was in Years) by the Industry of some that could do much, and thought by him to play their own Game, was presently Elected Governour; and before he was scarce warm in his Seat, began to Broach New Tenets; and these were agitated with as much Violence, as if the Welfare of* New-England *must have been Sacrificed rather than these not take place. But the Wisdom of the State put a Period to his Government; necessity caused them to undo the Works of their own Hands, and leave us a Caveat, that all good Men are not fit for Government.* But on the other side, the Historian who has Printed *The Trial of Sir* Henry Vane, *Knt., at the* King's Bench, Westminster, June 2. *and* 6. 1662. *with other occasional Speeches; also his Speech and Prayer on the Scaffold,* has given us in him the Picture of nothing less than an *Heroe*.[1] He seems indeed by that Story to have suffered *Hardly* enough, but no Man can deny that he suffered *Bravely:* the *English* Nation has not often seen more of *Roman*, (and indeed more than *Roman*) Gallantry, out-facing *Death* in the most *pompous Terrors* of it. A great Royalist, present, at his Decollation, swore, *He died like a Prince:* He could say, *I bless the Lord I am so far from being affrighted at Death, that I find it rather shrink from me, than I from it!* He could say, *Ten Thousand Deaths rather than Defile my Conscience; the Chastity and Purity of which I value beyond all this World; I would not for Ten Thousand Worlds part with the Peace and Satisfaction I have in my own Heart.* When mention was

[1] The book referred to was published anonymously in 1662.

made of the Difficult Proceeding against him, all his reply was, *Alas, what a Do do they keep to make a poor Creature like his Saviour!* On the Scaffold they did, by the Blast of Trumpets in his Face, with much Incivility, hinder him from speaking what he intended; which Incivility he aforehand suspecting, committed a true Copy of it unto a Friend before his going thither; the last Words whereof were these, *As my last Words I leave this with you, That as the Present Storm we now lye under, and the dark Clouds that yet hang over the Reformed Churches of Christ, (which are coming thicker and thicker for a Season) were not unforeseen by me for many Years past; (as some Writings of mine declare) so the coming of Christ in these Clouds, in Order to a speedy and sudden revival of his Cause, and spreading his Kingdom over the Face of the whole Earth, is most clear to the Eye of my Faith, even that Faith in which I Die.* His Execution was *June* 14. 1662. about the Fiftieth Year of his Age.

§ 4. After the Death of Mr. *Dudley*, the Notice and Respect of the Colony fell chiefly on Mr. *John Endicot*, who after many Services done for the Colony, even before it was yet a *Colony*, as well as when he saw it grown into a *Populous Nation*, under his Prudent and Equal Government, expired in a good Old Age, and was Honourably Interr'd at *Boston, March* 23. 1665.

The Gentleman that succeeded Mr. *Endicot*, was Mr. *Richard Bellingham*, one who was bred a *Lawyer*, and one who lived beyond Eighty, well esteemed for his laudable Qualities; but as the *Thebans* made the Statues of their Magistrates *without Hands*, importing that they must be no *Takers;* in this fashion must be formed the *Statue* for this Gentleman; for among all his Virtues, he was noted for none more, than for his

notable and perpetual hatred of a *Bribe*, which gave
him, with his Country, the Reputation of Old Claimed
by *Pericles*, to be, φιλόπολίς τε καὶ χρημάτων κρείσσων·
Civitatis Amans, & ad pecunias Invictus.[1] And as he
never *took* any from any one *living;* so he neither could
nor would have *given* any to *Death;* but in the latter
end of the Year 1672. he had his *Soul gathered not with
Sinners, whose Right Hand is full of Bribes*, but with
such as *walk in their uprightness*.

The Gentleman that succeeded Mr. *Bellingham*,
was Mr. *John Leveret*, one to whom the Affections of
the Freemen were signalized, in his quick advances
through the lesser Stages of Office and Honour unto
the highest in the Country; and one whose *Courage* had
been as much Recommended by Martial Actions
abroad in his Younger Years, as his *Wisdom* and *Justice*
were now at Home in his Elder. The *Anniversary
Election* constantly kept him at the Helm from the
time of his first Sitting there, until *March* 16. 1678.
when *Mortality* having first put him on severe *Trials*
of his *Passive-Courage*, (much more difficult than the
Active) in pains of the *Stone*, released him.

Pater Patriæ:[2] *Or, The LIFE of* SIMON BRAD-
STREET, *Esq;*

——*Extinctus amabitur idem*.[3]

THE Gentleman that succeeded Mr. *Leveret*, was
Mr. *Simon Bradstreet*, the Son of a Minister in
Lincolnshire, who was always a *Non-Conformist*
at home, as well as when Preacher at *Middleburgh*
abroad. Him the *New-Englanders* in their Addresses full

[1] "A lover of the state, invincible by bribes."
[2] "Father of the country."
[3] "He shall be loved even when dead."

of profound Respects unto him, have with good reason called, *The venerable* Mordecai *of his Country.* He was born at *Horbling, March* 1603. His Father (who was the Son of a *Suffolk* Gentleman of a fine Estate) was one of the First Fellows in *Immanuel*-Colledge, under Dr. *Chaderton*, and one afterwards highly esteemed by Mr. *Cotton*, and by Dr. *Preston.* Our *Bradstreet* was brought up at the Grammar-School, until he was about Fourteen Years Old; and then the Death of his Father put a stop for the present unto the Designs of his further Education. But according to the *Faith* of his Dying Father, that *he should be well provided for*, he was within Two or Three Years after this taken into the Religious Family of the Earl of *Lincoln*, (the best Family of any Nobleman then in *England*,) where he spent about Eight Years under the Direction of Mr. *Thomas Dudley*, sustaining successively divers Offices. Dr. *Preston* then (who had been my Lord's Tutor) moved my Lord, that Mr. *Bradstreet* might have their permission to come unto *Immanuel* Colledge, in the Capacity of Governour to the Lord *Rich*, the Son of the Earl of *Warwick;* which they granting, he went with the Doctor to *Cambridge*, who provided a Chamber for him, with Advice that he should apply himself to Study until my Lord's Arrival. But he afterwards in a Writing of his, now in my Hands, made this humble Complaint; *I met with many Obstacles to my Study in* Cambridge; *the Earl of* Lincoln *had a Brother there, who often called me forth upon Pastimes. Divers Masters of Art, and other Scholars also, constantly met, where we spent most part of the Afternoons many times in Discourse to little purpose or profit; but that seemed an easie and pleasant Life then, which too late I repented.* My Lord *Rich* not coming to the University,

Mr. *Bradstreet* returned after a Year to the Earl of *Lincolns;* and Mr. *Dudley* then removing to *Boston,*[1] his Place of *Steward* unto the Earl was conferred on Mr. *Bradstreet.* Afterwards he with much ado obtained the Earl's leave to Answer the Desires of the Aged and Pious Countess of *Warwick*, that he would accept the *Stewardship* of her Noble Family, which as the former he discharged with an Exemplary Discretion and Fidelity. Here he Married the Daughter of Mr. *Dudley,*[2] by whose perswasion he came in Company with him to *New-England*, where he spent all the rest of his Days, Honourably serving his Generation. It was counted a singular Favour of Heaven unto *Richard Chamond*, Esq; one of *England*'s *Worthies*, that he was a *Justice of Peace* near Threescore Years;[3] but of *Simon Bradstreet*, Esq; one of *New-England's Worthies*, there can more than this be said; for he was chosen a *Magistrate* of *New-England* before *New-England* it self came into *New-England;* even in their first great Voyage thither *Anno* 1630. and so he continued annually chosen; sometimes also their *Secretary*, and at last their *Governour*, until the Colony had a share in the general Shipwrack of *Charters*, which the Reign of King *Charles* II. brought upon the whole *English* Nation.[4] Mr. *Joseph Dudley* was placed, *Anno* 1685. as *President* over the Territory for a few Months, when the *Judgment* that was entred against the *Charter* gave unto the late King *James* II. an opportunity to make what Alterations he pleased upon the Order of

---

[1] England.

[2] The poetess, Anne Dudley Bradstreet.

[3] Mather here draws on Thomas Fuller's Worthies of England. See i, 329 (ed. 1840).

[4] Cf. p. xlv, *ante.*

things, under which the Country had so long been Flourishing. But when the short *Presidentship* of that *New-English* and well Accomplished Gentleman, the Son of Mr. *Thomas Dudley* abovementioned, was expired, I am not in a Disposition here to relate what was the Condition of the Colony, until the *Revolution* whereto their Condition compell'd them. Only I have sometimes, not without Amazement, thought of the Representation which a Celebrated *Magician* made unto *Catherine de Medicis*, the *French* Queen, whose Impious Curiosity led her to desire of him a *Magical Exhibition* of all the Kings that had hitherto Reigned in *France*, and yet were to Reign. The Shapes of all the Kings, even unto the Husband of that Queen successively showed themselves, in the *Enchanted Circle*, in which that Conjurer had made his Invocations, and they took as many *Turns* as there had been Years in their Government. The Kings that were to come, did then in like manner sucessively come upon the Stage, namely, *Francis* II. *Charles* IX. *Henry* III. *Henry* IV. which being done, then Two Cardinals, *Richlieu* and *Mazarine*, in Red Hats, became visible in the Spectacle: But after those Cardinals, there entred WOLVES, BEARS, TYGERS, and LIONS, to consummate the Entertainment. If the People of *New-England* had not Imagined, that a Number of as *Rapacious Animals* were at last come into their Government, I suppose they would not have made such a *Revolution* as they did, on *April* 18. 1689. in conformity to the Pattern which the *English Nation* was then setting before them. Nevertheless, I have nothing in this Paragraph of our History to Report of it, but that Mr. *Bradstreet* was at this time alive; whose Paternal Compassions for a Country, thus remarkably *his own*, would not permit him to decline his Return unto his former *Seat* in the Government, upon the Unanimous Invitation of the People thereunto. It was a Remark then generally made upon him, *That though he were then well towards Ninety Years of Age, his intellectual force was hardly abated, but he retained a Vigour and Wisdom that would have recommended a younger Man to the Government of a greater Colony.* And the wonderful Difficulties, through which the Colony under his discreet Conduct waded, until the Arrival of his Excellency, Sir *William Phips,* with a Commission for the Government, and a *New Charter* in the Year 1692. gave a Remarkable *Demonstration* of it. Yea, this Honourable *Nestor* of *New-England,* in the Year 1696. was yet alive; and as *Georgius Leontinus,* who lived until he was an Hundred and Eight Years of Age, being asked by what means he attained unto such an Age, answered, *By my not Living Voluptuously;* thus this excellent Person attained his good old Age, in part, *By Living very Temperately.* And the *New-Englanders* would have counted it their Satisfaction, if like *Arganthonius,* who had been Fourscore Years the Governour of the *Tartessians,* he might have lived unto the Age of an Hundred and Twenty; or, even unto the Age of *Johannes de Temporibus,* who was Knighted by the Emperour *Charlemaign,* and yet was Living till the Emperour *Conrade,* and saw, they say, no fewer Years than *Three Hundred Threescore and One.* Though, *To be Dissolved and be with Christ,* was the Satisfaction which this our *Macrobius* himself was with a weary Soul now waiting and longing for; and Christ at length granted it unto him, on *March* 27. 1697. *Then* it was, that one of the oldest Servants that God and the King had upon Earth, drew his *Last,* in the very place where he drew his *First, American*

Breath.   He Died at *Salem,* in a Troublesome Time,
and entred into everlasting Peace.   And in Imitation
of what the Roman Orator said upon the Death of
Crassus, I will venture to say, *Fuit hoc, luctuosum suis,
Acerbum Patriæ, Grave Bonis Omnibus: Sed ii tamen
Rempublicam casus Secuti sunt, ut mihi non Erepta*
Bradstreeto *Vita, sed donata mors esse videatur.*[1]

The Epitaph on that famous Lawyer, *Simon Pistorius*
we will now Employ for this Eminently Prudent and
Upright Administrator of our *Laws.*

EPITAPH.

SIMON BRADSTREET.

*Quod Mortale fuit, Tellus tenet; Inclyta Fama
Nominis haud ullo stat violanda Die.*[2]

And Add,

*Extinctum luget quem tota Nov-Anglia Patrem,
O Quantum Claudit parvula Terra Virum!* [3]

[1] "This [death] was most lamentable for his family, bitter to the
fatherland, a woe to all good men; but yet such calamities have come
to the state since then, that it does not seem to me as though life were
snatched from Bradstreet, but as though death were given to him."
The quotation is from Cicero, altered.

[2] "Earth holds what was mortal; the glorious renown of his name
stands against the ravaging of time."   Simon Pistoris, or Pistorius,
1489–1562, was a famous German lawyer.

[3] "All New England mourns a dead father; how great a man a
little earth encloses."

CHAP. VI

בעלי נפש Id est, Viri Animati:[1] *Or, ASSISTANTS.*

THE Freemen of *New-England* had a great variety of Worthy Men, among whom they might pick and chuse a Number of MAGISTRATES to be the *Assistants* of their GOVERNOURS, both in directing the General Affairs of the Land, and in dispensing of Justice unto the People. But they wisely made few Alterations in their Annual *Elections;* and they thereby shew'd their Satisfaction in the wise and good Conduct of those whom they had *Elected.* If they called some few of their *Magistrates* from the *Plough* to the *Bench,* so the Old *Romans* did some of their *Dictators;* yea, the greatest Kings in the World once carried *Plough-shares* on the top of their *Scepters.* However, the Inhabitants of *New-England* never were so unhappy as the Inhabitants of *Norcia,* a Town scarce Ten Leagues from *Rome;* where they do at this Day chuse their own *Magistrates,* but use an exact Care, *That no Man who is able to Write, or to Read, shall be capable of any share in the Government.* The Magistrates of *New-England* have been of a better Education. Indeed, several deserving Persons, who were joined as *Associates* and *Commissioners* unto these, for the more effectual Execution of the Laws in some *Emergencies,* cannot be brought into our *Catalogue;* but the *Names* of all our *Magistrates,* with the *Times* when I find their first Advancement unto that Character, are these.

[1] "Living men."

MAGISTRATES of the *Massachuset*-Colony.

John Winthrop, Gov.	
Thomas Dudley, Deputy Gov.	
Matthew Cradock,	1629
Thomas Goff,	1629
Sir *Richard Saltonstal,*	1629
Isaac Johnson,	1629
Samuel Aldersley,	1629
John Venn,	1629
John Humfrey,	1629
Simon Whercomb,	1629
Increase Nowel,	1629
Richard Perry,	1629
Nathanael Wright,	1629
Samuel Vassal,	1629
Theophilus Eaton,	1629
Thomas Adams,	1629
Thomas Hutchins,	1629
George Foxcroft,	1629
William Vassal,	1629
William Pinchon,	1629
John Pocock,	1629
Christopher Cowlson,	1629
William Coddington,	1629
Simon Bradstreet,	1629
Thomas Sharp,	1629
Roger Ludlow,	1630
Edward Rossiter,	1630
John Endicot,	1630
John Winthrop, Jun.	1632
John Haines,	1634
Richard Billingham,[1]	1635

[1] Bellingham.

Atterton[1] *Hough,*	1635
Richard Dummer,	1635
Henry Vane,	1636
Roger Hartackenden,[2]	1636
Israel Stoughton,	1637
Richard Saltonstal,	1637
Thomas Flint,	1643
Samuel Symons,	1643
William Hibbons,	1643
William Tynge,	1643
Herbert Pelham,	1645
Robert Bridges,	1647
Francis Willoughby,	1650
Thomas Wiggan,	1650
Edward Gibbons,	1650
John Glover,	1652
Daniel Gookin,	1652
Daniel Denison,	1654
Simon Willard,	1654
Humphrey Atherton,	1654
Richard Russel,	1659
Thomas Danforth,	1659
William Hawthorn,	1662
Eleazer Lusher,	1662
John Leveret,	1665
John Pinchon,	1665
Edward Tyng,	1668
William Stoughton,	1671
Thomas Clark,	1673
Joseph Dudley,	1676
Peter Bulkley,	1677
Nathanael Saltonstal,	1679

[1] Atherton.
[2] Harlakenden.

Humphrey Davy,	1679
James Russel,	1680
Samuel Nowel,	1680
Peter Tilton,	1680
John Richards,	1680
John Hull,	1680
Bartholomew Gidney,	1680
Thomas Savage,	1680
William Brown,	1680
Samuel Appleton,	1681
Robert Pike,	1682
Daniel Fisher,	1683
John Woodbridge,	1683
Elisha Cook,	1684
William Johnson,	1684
John Hawthorn,	1684
Elisha Hutchinson,	1684
Samuel Sewal,	1684
Isaac Addington,	1686
John Smith,	1686

Major-Generals of the Military Forces in the Colony, successively chosen.

Thomas Dudley.
John Endicot.
Edward Gibbons.
Robert Sedgwick.
Humfry Atherton.
Daniel Denison.
John Leveret.
Daniel Gookin.

Secretaries of the Colony, successively chosen.

William Burgis.
Simon Bradstreet.
Increase Nowel.
Edward Rawson.

That these *Names* are proper and worthy to be found in our *Church-History*, will be acknowledged, when it is considered, not only that they were the *Members of Congregational Churches*, and by the *Members* of the *Churches* chosen to be the *Rulers* of the *Commonwealth;* and that their exemplary Behaviour in their *Magistracy* was generally such as to *adorn the Doctrine of God our Saviour*, and according to the Old *Jewish* Wishes, *prohibitum est Homini, instar principis Dominari super populum, & cum elatione Spiritus, sed,* בצבעה ויראה *cum mansuetudine ac Timore:*[1] But also that their Love to, and Zeal for, and Care of these *Churches*, was not the least part of their Character.

The Instances of their Concern for the Welfare of the *Churches* were innumerable. I will single out but one from the rest, because of some Singular Subserviency to the Designs of our *Church-History*, therein to be propos'd. I'll do it only by Transcribing an Instrument, published *Anno* 1668. in such Terms as these.

[1] "It is forbidden for a man to rule over a people like a prince, and with exaltation of spirit, but [he should rule] with mildness and fear."

To the Elders and Ministers of every Town within the Jurisdiction of the Massachusets *in* New-England, *the Governour and Council sendeth Greeting.*

Reverend and Beloved in the Lord,

WE find in the Examples of Holy Scripture, 'that *Magistrates* have not only excited and 'commanded all the People under their 'Government, *to seek the Lord God of their Fathers,* 'and do the Law and Commandment, (2. Chron. 14. 2, '3, 4. Ezra 7. 25, 26, 27.) but also stirred up and sent 'forth the *Levites,* accompanied with other Principal 'Men, *to Teach the good Knowledge of the Lord through-* 'out all the Cities, (2. Chron. 17. 6, 7, 8, 9.) which En- 'deavours have been Crowned with the Blessing of 'God.

'Also we find that our Brethren of the *Congregational* 'Perswasion in *England,* have made a good Profession 'in their Book, Entituled, *A Declaration of their Faith* 'and Order, (Page 59. Sect. 14.) where they say, *That* 'altho' *Pastors and Teachers stand especially related* 'unto their particular Churches, yet they ought not to 'neglect others Living within their Parochial Bounds; but 'besides their constant publick Preaching to them, they 'ought to enquire after their profiting by the Word, In- 'structing them in, and Pressing upon them, (whether 'Young or Old) the great Doctrines of the Gospel, even 'personally and particularly, so far as their Strength and 'Time will permit.

'We hope that sundry of you need not a *Spur* in 'these things, but are consciexiously careful to do 'your Duty. Yet, forasmuch as we have cause to 'fear that there is too much Neglect in many places, 'notwithstanding the *Laws* long since provided therein,

'we do therefore think it our Duty to emit this *Dec-*
'*laration* unto you, earnestly Desiring, and, in the Bowels
'of our Lord Jesus, requiring you to be very Diligent
'and Careful to *Catechise* and Instruct all People
'(especially the *Youth*) under your Charge, in the sound
'Principles of Christian Religion; and that not only
'in *Publick*, but privately *from House to House*, as Blessed
'*Paul* did; (*Act.* 20. 20.) or at least, Three, Four, or
'more Families meeting together, as Time and Strength
'may permit; taking to your Assistance such godly
'and grave Persons as to you may seem most expedient:
'And also that you Labour to Inform your selves (as
'much as may be meet) how your Hearers do profit
'by the Word of God, and how their Conversations
'do agree therewith; and whether the Youth are Taught
'to Read the *English* Tongue: Taking all occasions
'to apply suitable *Exhortations* particularly unto them,
'for *the Rebuke of those that do evil, and the Encouragement*
'*of them that do well.*

'The effectual and constant Prosecution hereof,
'we hope will have a Tendency to promote the *Salvation*
'*of Souls;* to suppress the Growth of *Sin* and Profane-
'ness; to beget more Love and *Unity* among the People,
'and more *Reverence* and Esteem of the *Ministry:* And
'it will assuredly be to the enlargement of your *Crown*,
'and Recompence in *Eternal Glory.*

Given at Boston, *the* 10*th of* March, 1668. *by the Gover-*
nour and Council, and by them Ordered to be Printed,
and sent accordingly.

Edward Rawson, *Secret.*

CHAP. VII.

Publicola Christianus.[1] *The LIFE of* EDWARD
HOPKINS, *Esq; Governour of* CONNECTICUT–
COLONY.

Superiores sint, qui superiores esse sciunt.[2]

§ 1. WHEN the Great God of Heaven had carried his *Peculiar People* into a *Wilderness,* the *Theocracy,* wherein he became
(as he was for *that Reason* stiled) *The Lord of Hosts,*
unto them and the *Four* Squadrons of their *Army,* was
most eminently display'd in *his* Enacting of their *Laws,
his* Directing of their *Wars,* and his Electing and Inspir-
ing of their *Judges.* In some resemblance hereunto,
when *Four* Colonies of Christians had marched like so
many *Hosts* under the Conduct of the good Spirit of our
Lord Jesus Christ into an *American* Wilderness, there
were several Instances wherein that *Army* of *Confessors*
was under a *Theocracy:* For their *Laws* were still
Enacted, and their *Wars* were still Directed by the
Voice of God, as far as they understood it, speaking
from the *Oracle* of the *Scriptures;* and though their
Judges were still *Elected* by themselves, and not *Inspired*
with such extraordinary Influences as *carried* them of
Old, yet *these* also being singularly furnished and
offered by the special Providence of God unto the Government of his *New-English* People, were so eminently
acted [3] by *His Graces,* and *His Precepts,* in the Discharge
of their Government, that the Blessed People were
still sensibly *Governed by the Lord of All.* Now among

[1] "Christian patriot."
[2] "They may be superiors, who know how to be superiors."
[3] *I. e.,* actuated.

the First *Judges* of *New-England,* was EDWARD
HOPKINS, Esq; in whose time the *Colony* of *Connecticut* was favoured with *Judges as at the first;* and put
under the Power of those with whom it was a Maxim,
Gratius est pietatis Nomen, quam potestatis.[1]

§ 2. The Descent and Breeding of Mr. EDWARD
HOPKINS, (who was Born, I think, near *Shrowsbury,*
about the Year 1600.) first fitted him for the Condition
of a *Turky-Merchant,* in *London;* where he lived several
Years in good Fashion and Esteem, until a powerful
Party in the Church of *England,* then resolving not
only to *separate* from the Communion of all the *Faithful*
that were Averse to certain confessedly *unscriptural*
and *uninstituted* Rites in the Worship of God, but also
to *Persecute* with destroying Severities those that were
Non-Conformists thereunto, compelled a considerable
Number of good Men to seek a shelter among the
Salvages of *America.* Among these, and with his
Excellent Father-in-Law, Mr. *Theophilus Eaton,* he
came to *New-England;* where then removing from the
*Massachuset-*Bay unto *Hartford* upon *Connecticut-*
River, he became a *Ruler* and *Pillar* of that Colony,
during the time of his Abode in the Country.

§ 3. In his Government he acquitted himself as
the *Solomon* of his Colony, to whom *God gave Wisdom
and Knowledge, that he might go out and come in before
the People;* and as he was the *Head,* so he was the *Heart*
of the People, for the Resolution *to do Well,* which he
maintained among them. An *unjust Judge* is, as one
says, *A cold Fire, a dark Sun, a dry Sea, an ungood
God, a* contradictio in Adjecto [2] Far from such was our
Hopkins; no, he was, δίκαιον ἔμψυχον, a meer piece

[1] "A reputation for piety is dearer than a reputation for power."
[2] "A paradox."

of *Living Justice*. And as he had no *separate Interests* of his own, so he pursued their *Interests* with such an unspotted and successful Fidelity, that they might call him as the Tribe of *Benjamin* did their Leader in the Wilderness, *Abidan*, that is to say, *Our Father is Judge*. *New-England* saw little *Dawnings*, and *Emblems*, and *Earnests* of the Day, *That the greatness of the Kingdom under the whole Heaven shall be given unto the People of the Saints of the most High*, when such a *Saint* as our HOPKINS was one of its Governours. And the Felicity which a Great Man has Prognosticated for *Europe*, *That God will stir up some happy Governour in some Country in Christendom, indued with Wisdom and Consideration, who shall discern the true Nature of Godliness and Christianity, and the Necessity and Excellency of serious Religion, and shall place his Honour and Felicity in pleasing God, and doing Good, and attaining Everlasting Happiness, and shall subject all Worldly Respects unto these High and Glorious Ends:* This was now Exemplified in *America*.

§ 4. Most Exemplary was his *Piety* and his *Charity;* and while he governed *others* by the *Laws* of God, he did *himself* yield a profound Subjection unto those *Laws*. He was exemplarily watchful over his own Behaviour, and made a continual *Contemplation* of, and *Preparation* for *Death*, to be the Character of his *Life*. It was his manner to *Rise early*, even before Day, to enjoy the Devotions of his *Closet:* after which he spent a considerable time in Reading, and Opening, and Applying the *Word* of God unto his *Family*, and then *Praying* with them: And he had one particular way to cause Attention in the People of his Family, which was to ask any Person that seemed Careless in the midst of his Discourse, *What was it that I Read or*

Spoke last? Whereby he Habituated them unto such Attention, that they were still usually able to give a ready Account. But as for his *Prayers*, they were not only *frequent*, but so *fervent* also, that he frequently fell a *Bleeding* at the Nose through the *Agony* of Spirit with which he labour'd in them. And, especially when imploring such *Spiritual Blessings*, as, *That God would grant in the End of our Lives, the End of our Hopes, even the Salvation of our Souls*, he would be so Transported, that the Observing and Judicious Hearers would say sometimes upon it, *Surely this Man can't be long out of Heaven.* Moreover, in his Neighbourhood he not only set himself to Encourage and Countenance real *Godliness*, but also would himself kindly visit the *Meetings* that the Religious Neighbours privately kept for the Exercises of it; and where the least Occasion for *Contention* was offered, he would, with a prudent and speedy Endeavour, Extinguish it. But the *Poor* he so considerered, that besides the *Daily Reliefs* which with his own Hands he dispenced unto them, he would put considerable Sums of Money into the Hands of his Friends, to be by them employed as they saw *Opportunity to do good unto all, especially the Houshold of Faith.* In this thing he was like that Noble and Worthy *English* General, of whom 'tis noted, *He never thought he had any thing but what he gave away;* and yet after all, with much humility he would profess, as one of the most Liberal Men that ever was in the World often would, *I have often turned over my Books of Accounts, but I could never find the Great God charged a Debtor there.*

§ 5. But *Suffering* as well as *Doing* belongs to the Compleat Character of a *Christian;* and there were several *Trials* wherein our Lord called this Eminently Patient Servant of his to *Suffer the Will of God.* He

Conflicted with *Bodily Infirmities*, but especially with a Wasting and a Bloody *Cough*, which held him for Thirty Years together. He had been by *Persecutions* driven to cross an *Ocean*, to which he had in his Nature an *Antipathy;* and then a *Wilderness* full of such Crosses as attend the *beginning of a Plantation*, exercised him. Nevertheless there was one Affliction which *continually dropt* upon him above all the rest, and that was this, He Married a Daughter which the Second Wife of Mr. *Eaton* had by a former Husband; one that from a Child had been Observable for Desirable Qualities. But some time after she was Married she fell into a Distempered *Melancholly*, which at last Issued in an Incurable *Distraction*, with such Illshaped *Ideas* in her Brain, as use to be formed when the *Animal Spirits* are *fired* by Irregular Particles, fixed with Acid, Bilious, Venemous Ferments in the Blood. Very Grievous was this Affliction unto this her worthy Consort, who was by temper a very Affectionate Person: And who now left no part of a tender Husband undone, to *Ease*, and, if it were possible, to *Cure* the Lamentable Desolation thus come upon, *The Desire of his Eyes;* but when the Physician gave him to understand, that no means would be likely to *Restore* her *Sense*, but such as would be also likely to *Hazard* her *Life*, he Replied with Tears, *I had rather bear my Cross unto the End that the Lord shall give!* But upon this Occasion he said unto *her* Sister, who, with all the rest related unto *her*, were as dear unto him as *his own; I have often thought, what should be the meaning of the Lord, in chastising of me with so sharp a Rod, and with so long a Stroke!* Whereto, when she Reply'd, *Sir, nothing singular has, in this Case, befallen you; God hath afflicted others in the like way; and we must be content with our Portion:* He

Answered, *Sister, This is among the Lord's Rarities.*
For my part I cannot tell what Sore to lay my Hand upon:
However, in General, my Sovereign Lord is Just, and I
will justifie him for ever: But in Particular, I have
thought the matter might lye here: I promised my self
too much Content in this Relation and Enjoyment; and
the Lord will make me to know that this World shall not
afford it me. So he wisely, meekly, fruitfully bore this
heavy *Affliction* unto his *Dying Day;* having been
taught by the Affliction to *Die Daily,* as long as he
Lived.

§ 6. About Governour *Eaton,* his Father-in-Law,
he saw cause to say unto a *Sister-in-Law,* whom he
much valued; *I have often wondred at my Father and*
your Father; I have heard him say, That he never had a
Repenting, or a Repining Thought, about his coming to
New-England: *Surely, in this Matter he hath a Grace*
far out-shining Mine. But he is our Father! I cannot
say, as he can, I have had hard work with my own Heart
about it. But upon the Death of his Elder Brother,
who was *Warden of the Fleet,*[1] it was necessary for him
to Return into *England,* that he might look after the
Estate which then fell unto him; and accordingly, after
a Tempestuous and a Terrible Voyage, wherein they
were eminently endangered by *Fire,* accidentally
enkindled on the Ship, as well as by *Water,* which tore
it so to Pieces, that it was Towed in by another Ship,
he at length,

Per Varios Casus; per tot Discrimina Rerum,[2]

arrived there. *There* a great Notice was quickly
taken of him: He was made *Warden of the Fleet,* Com-

---

[1] Warden of Fleet Prison.
[2] "Through varied misfortunes, through so many dangers."

missioner of the Admiralty, and the Navy-Office, a Parliament-Man; and he was placed in some other considerable Stations: In all which he more than answered the Expectations of those who took him to be a Person *Eminently Qualified for Publick Service.* By these Employments, his design of Returning to *New-England,* with which he left it, was diverted so far, that he sent for his Family; and about the time that he looked for them, he being advantaged by his great Places to employ certain Frigots for their safety on the Coast, by that means had them safely brought unto him. When they were with him in *London,* one of them told him how much his Friends in *New-England* Wish'd and Pray'd for his Return: And how that Passage had been used in our Publick Supplications for that Mercy, *Lord, If we may win him in Heaven, we shall yet have him on Earth:* But he Reply'd, *I have had many Thoughts about my Return, and my Affections have been bent very strongly that way; and tho' I have now, blessed be God, received my Family here, yet that shall be no hindrance to my Return. I will tell you, though I am little worth, yet I have that Love which will dispose me to serve the Lord, and that People of his. But as to that matter, I incline to think they will not win it in Heaven; and I know not whether the Terrors of my dreadful Voyage hither might not be ordered by the Divine Providence, to Stake me in this Land, being in my Spirit sufficiently loth to run the hazard of such another. I must also say to you, I mourn exceedingly, and* I fear, I fear, *the Sins of* New-England *will e're long be read in its Punishments. The Lord has planted that Land with a* Noble Vine; *and* Blessed hast thou been, O Land, in thy Rulers! *But, alas! for the generality they have not considered how they were to Honour the* Rules *of* God,

in Honouring of those whom God made Rulers *over them;
and I fear they will come to smart by having them set over
them, that it will be an* hard Work to Honour, *and that
will hardly be capable to manage their Affairs.*

§ 7. Accordingly he continued in *England* the rest
of his Days, in several places of Great *Honour* and
Burden faithfully serving the Nation; but in the midst
of his *Publick* Employments most exactly maintaining
the *Zeal* and *Watch* of his own private *Walk with God.*
His *Mind* kept continually Mellowing and Ripening
for *Heaven;* and one Expression of his *Heavenly Mind,*
among many others, a little before his End, was, *How
often have I pleased my self with thoughts of a joyful
Meeting with my Father* Eaton! *I remember with what
pleasure he would come down the Street, that he might
meet me when I came from* Hartford *unto* New-Haven:
*But with how much greater Pleasure shall we shortly meet
one another in Heaven!* But as an *Heavenly Mind* is
oftentimes a *Presaging Mind,* so he would sometimes
utter this *Presage* unto some that were Near and Dear
unto him; *God will shortly take the* Protector[1] *away, and
soon after that you will see great Changes overturning the
present Constitution, and sore Troubles come upon those
that now promise better things unto themselves.* However,
he did not Live to see the Fulfilment of this *Prediction.*

§ 8. For the *time now drew near that this Israelite
was to Die!* He had been in his Life troubled with many
Fears of Death; and after he fell Sick, even when he
drew very near his Death, he said with Tears, *Oh!
Pray for me, for I am in extream Darkness!* But at
length, on a Lord's Day, about the very time when Mr.
Caryl was publickly praying for him, his Darkness all
vanished, and he broke forth into these Expressions,

[1] Cromwell.

*Oh! Lord, thou hast kept the best Wine until the last!
Oh! Friends, could you believe this? I shall be blessed
for ever, I shall quickly be in Eternal Glory. Now let the
whole World count me Vile, and call me an Hypocrite,
or what they will, I matter it not; I shall be blessed; there
is reserved for me a Crown of Glory. Oh! Blessed be God
for Jesus Christ! I have heretofore thought it an hard
thing to die, but now I find that it is not so. If I might
have my choice, I would now chuse to die; Oh! my Lord,
I pray thee send me not back again into this Evil World,
I have enough of it; no, Lord, now take me to Glory, and
the Kingdom that is prepared for me!* Yea, the standers
by thought it not possible for them to utter exactly
after him, the *Heavenly Words* which now proceeded
from him; and when one of them said, *Sir, The Lord
hath enlarged your Faith;* he replied, *Friend, this is Sense;
the Lord hath even satisfied my Sense; I am sensibly satisfied of Everlasting Glory!* Two or Three Days he now
spent in *Prayers* and *Praises*, and in Inexpressible
Joys: In which time, when some Eminent Persons of
a very Publick Station and Imployment came to
Visit him, unto *them*, he said, *Sirs, Take heed of your
Hearts while you are in your Work for God, that there be
no root of bitterness within you. It may be pretended
your Desires are to serve God, but if there are in you secret
Aims at advancing of your selves, and your own Estates
and Interests, the Lord will not accept your Services as
pure before him.*

But at length in the Month of *March*, 1657. at
London he expired; when being opened, it was found
that his *Heart* had been unaccountably, as it were,
Boiled and Wasted in Water, until it was become a
little brittle Skin, which being touch'd, presently dropp'd
in pieces. He had often wished, upon some great

Accounts, that he might live till the beginning of this Year; and now when he lay a dying, he said, *Lord! Thou hast fulfilled my Desires according to thy Word, that thou wilt fulfil the Desires of them that fear thee.*

Now from the Tombstone of another Eminent Person, we will fetch what shall here be a proper

EPITAPH.

Part of *EDWARD HOPKINS*, Esq;[1]

But Heaven, *not brooking that the* Earth *should share*
In the least Atom *of a Piece so rare,*
Intends to Sue out, by a New Revise,
His Habeas Corpus *at the* Grand Assize.

CHAP. VIII.

SUCCESSORS.

§ 1. ALternately, for the most part every other Year, Mr. *Hains*, whom we have already mentioned elsewhere, took a turn with Mr. *Hopkins* in the Chief place of Government. And besides these (Reader, the *Oracle* that once Predicted Government unto a Θ, would now and here Predict it unto a W.[2]) there were Mr. *Willis*, Mr. *Wells*, and Mr. *Webster*, all of whom also had Oppor-

[1] Probably this line and the one preceding should be transposed to read "proper Part of Edward Hopkins, Esq., Epitaph."

[2] Ammianus Marcellinus (xxix, ch. 1, §§ 28–32) tells of a reputed oracle which prophesied by means of a ring hung on a thread, over a plate on the rim of which were marked the letters of the alphabet. Asked who would be the next emperor, the ring touched the letters ΘΕΟ, and this was believed to indicate that Theodorus would reign. The same story is in Sozomen's *Ecclesiatical History*, vi, ch. 35.

tunity to express their Liberal and Generous Dispositions, and the *Governing Virtues* of Wisdom, Justice
and Courage, by the Election of the Freemen in the
Colony before its being United with *Newhaven*. Had
the Surviving Relations of these Worthy Men sent in
unto me a Tenth Part of the *Considerable* and *Imitable*
Things which occurr'd in their *Lives*, they might have
made more of a Figure in this our *History;* whereas I
must now Sum up all, with assuring my Reader, that
it is the want of *Knowledge* in *Me*, and not of *Desert* in
Them, that has confined us unto this Brevity.

§ 2.   After the Union of *Connecticut* with *Newhaven*,
there were in Chief Government Mr. *Leet*, whom we
have already paid our Dues unto; and Mr. *Treat*, who
is yet living, a Pious and a Valiant Man, and (if even[1]
Annosa Quercus [2] be an Honourable thing!) worthy to
be Honoured for *An Hoary Head found in the Way of
Righteousness:* Besides, Mr. *Winthrop*, of whom anon,
Reader, expect a Compleater History.

CHAP. IX.

Humilitas Honorata.[3]   *The LIFE of* THEOPHILUS
EATON, *Esq; Governour of* NEW–HAVEN *COLONY.*

> *Justitiæ Cultor, Rigidi Servator Honesti,*
> *In Commune Bonum.* [4]

§ 1. IT has been enquired, why the Evangelist
Luke in the *First* Sacred History which he
Addressed unto his Fellow-Citizen, gave him
the Title of *The most Excellent Theophilus*, but in the
next he used no higher a Stile than plain *Theophilus?*

---

[1] Ever.   [2] "an aged oak."   [3] "Honored humility."
[4] "A cultivator of justice, a servant of inflexible honesty, for the
common good."

And though several other Answers might be given to that Enquiry, 'tis enough to say, That neither the *Civility* of *Luke*, nor *Nobility* of *Theophilus*, were by Age abated; but *Luke* herein considered the Disposition of *Theophilus*, as well as his own, with whom a reduced Age had render'd all *Titles of Honour* more *Disagreeable Superfluities*. Indeed nothing would have been more Unacceptable to the Governour of our *New-Haven Colony* all the time of his being so, than to have been Advanced and Applauded above the rest of Mankind; yet it must be *now* Published unto the Knowledge of Mankind, that *New-England* could not of his Quality show a *More Excellent Person*, and this was *Theophilus Eaton*, Esq; the first Governour of that Colony. *Humility* is a Virtue whereof *Amyraldus* [1] observes, *There is not so much as a Shadow of Commendation in all the Pagan Writers*. But the Reader is now concerned with Writings which will *Commend* a Person for *Humility;* and therefore our *EATON*, in whom the shine of every Virtue was particularly set off with a more than ordinary Degree of *Humility*, must now be propos'd as *Commendable*.

§ 2. 'Tis *Reported*, that the Earth taken from the Banks of *Nilus*, will very strangely Sympathize with the place from whence it was taken, and grow moist or dry according to the Increase and the Decrease of the River. And in spite of that *Popish Lie* which pretends to observe the contrary, this thing has been signally *Moraliz'd* in the daily Observation, that the *Sons of Ministers*, though betaking themselves to other Imployments, do ordinarily carry about with them an Holy and Happy Savour of their *Ministerial Education*.

[1] Amyraldus, Moses Amyraut, 1596–1664, French Protestant divine.

'Twas remarkably Exemplified in our *Theophilus Eaton*, who was Born at *Stony-Stratford*, in *Oxfordshire*,[1] the Eldest Son to the Faithful and Famous *Minister* of the place.   But the Words of Old used by *Philostratus* concerning the Son of the Great Man, *As for his Son I have nothing else to say, but that he was his Son;* they could not be used concerning our *Theophilus*, who having received a good Education from his *Pious Parents*, did live many Years to Answer that Education in his own *Piety* and *Usefulness*.

§ 3.   His Father being removed unto *Coventry*, he there at School fell into the Intimate Acquaintance of that Worthy *John Davenport*,[2] with whom the Providence of God many Years after united him in the great Undertaking of settling a Colony of Christian and Reformed Churches on the *American Strand.* Here his Ingenuity and Proficiency render'd him notable; and so vast was his *Memory*, that although he wrote not at the Church, yet when he came home, he would, at his Father's Call, *repeat* unto those that met in his Father's House, the *Sermons* which had been publickly Preached by others, as well as his own Father, with such exactness, as astonished all the Neighbourhood.   But in their after Improvements, the *Hands* of Divine Providence were laid *across* upon the Heads of *Theophilus Eaton* and *John Davenport;* for *Davenport*, whose Father was the *Mayor* of *Coventry*, became a *Minister;* and *Eaton*, whose Father was *Minister* of *Coventry*, contrary to his Intentions, became a *Merchant.* His Parents were very loth to have complied with his

---

[1] Buckinghamshire.

[2] John Davenport, one of the greatest of the early New England divines, was for years a friend of Increase Mather. Cotton Mather wrote Davenport's life in the *Magnalia*, Book III, Part I, ch. iv.

Inclinations; but their Compliance therewithal did at
last appear to have been directed by a special Favour
of Heaven unto the Family, when after the Death of his
Father, he, by this means, became the *Joseph*, by whom
his *Mother* was maintained until she died, and his Orphan
Brethren and *Sisters* had no small part of their Subsistence.

§ 4. During the time of his hard Apprenticeship
he *behaved himself wisely;* and his *Wisdom*, with God's
Favour, particularly appeared in his chaste Escape
from the *Snares* of a Young Woman in the House where
he lived, who would fain have taken him in the *Pits*
by the *Wise Man* cautioned against, and who was
herself so taken *only* with his most Comely Person,
that she dy'd for the *Love* of him, when she saw him
gone too far to be obtained: Whereas, by the like
Snares, the Apprentice that next succeeded him was
undone for ever. But being a Person herewithal most
signally *Diligent in his Business*, it was not long before
the *Maxim* of the *Wise Man* was most literally accomplished in his coming to *Stand before Princes;*[1] for being
made a *Freeman* of *London*, he applied himself unto
the *East-Country* Trade, and was publickly chosen the
Deputy-Governour of the Company, wherein he so
acquitted himself as to become considerable. And
afterwards going himself into the *East-Country*, he not
only became so well Acquainted with the Affairs of the
Baltick-Sea, but also became so well Improved in the
Accomplishments of a *Man of Business*, that the King
of *England* imploy'd him as an *Agent* unto the King
of *Denmark*. The Concerns of his *Agency* he so discreetly managed, that as he much obliged and engaged

[1] For the references to "the Wise Man" in this paragraph, *cf.*
Proverbs xxii, 14, 29.

the *East-Land* Company, (who in Token thereof presented his Wife with a Bason and Ewer double gilt, and curiously wrought with Gold, and weighing above Sixty Pound,) so he found much Acceptance with the King of *Denmark*, and was afterwards used by that Prince to do him no little Services. Nevertheless he kept his Integrity amongst the Temptations of that Court, whereat he was now a *Resident*; and not seldom had he most Eminent Cause to acknowledge the *Benignity* and *Interposal* of Heaven for his Preservations; once particularly, when the King of *Denmark* was beginning the King of *England's* Health, while Mr. *Eaton*, who disliked such *Health-Drinking*, was in his Presence; the King fell down in a sort of a Fit, with the Cup in his Hand, whereat all the Nobles and Courtiers wholly applied themselves to convey the King into his Chamber, and there was no notice taken who was to Pledge his Health; whereby Mr. *Eaton* was the more easily deliver'd from any share in the Debauch.

§ 5.   Having arrived unto a fair Estate, (which he was *first* willing to do,[1] he Married a most Virtuous Gentlewoman, to whom he had first Espoused himself after he had spent Three Years in an Absence from her in the *East-Country*. But this dearest and greatest of his *Temporal* Enjoyments proved but a *Temporal* one; for living no longer with him than to render him the Father of Two Children, she almost *killed him* with her own *Death;* and yet at her Death she expressed herself wondrous willing *to be Dissolved, and to be with Christ, from whom* (she said) *I would not be detained one Hour for all the Enjoyments upon Earth.* He afterwards Married a Prudent and Pious Widow, the Daughter of the Bishop of *Chester;* unto the Three former *Chil-*

[1])

dren of whic [1] Widow, he became a most Exemplary
Loving and Faithful *Father*, as well as a most Worthy
Husband unto herself, by whom *he* afterwards had
Five Children, *Two* Sons and *Three* Daughters. But
the Second of his Children by his latter Wife dying
some while before, it was not long before his Two
Children by his former Wife were smitten with the
Plague, whereof the Elder died, and his House there-
upon shut up with a, *Lord have Mercy!* However the
Lord had this *Mercy* on the Family, to let the Distemper
spread no further; and so Mr. *Eaton* spent many Years
a Merchant of great Credit and Fashion in the City of
London.

§ 6. At length Conformity to *Ceremonies* Humanely
Invented and Imposed in the Worship of God, was
urged in the Church of *England* with so much Rigour,
that Mr. *Davenport* was thereby driven to seek *a
Refuge from the Storm* in the Cold and Rude Corners of
America. Mr. *Eaton* had already assisted the New
Massachuset-Colony, as being one of the *Patentees* for
it; but had no purpose of removing thither himself,
until Mr. *Davenport*, under whose Excellent Ministry
he lived, was compelled unto a share in this Removal.
However, being fully satisfied in his own Conscience,
that *Unlawful things* were now violently demanded of
him, he was willing to accompany his *Persecuted Pastor*
in the Retreat from Violence now Endeavoured, and
many Eminent *Londoners* chearfully engaged with him
in this Undertaking. Unto *New-England* this Company
of good Men came in the Year 1637. where chusing to
be a distinct Colony by themselves, more Accommodated
unto the Designs of *Merchandize* than of *Husbandry*,
they sought and bought a large Territory in the

[1] Which.

Southern Parts of the Country for their Habitations. In the Prosecution hereof, the Chief Care was devolved upon Mr. *Eaton*, who with an Unexempled Patience took many tedious and hazardous Journies through a Desolate Wilderness full of Barbarous *Indians*, until upon Mature Deliberation he pitched upon a place now called *New-Haven*, where they soon formed a very regular Town; and a number of other Towns along the Sea side were quickly added thereunto. But by the Difficulties attending these Journies, Mr. *Eaton* brought himself into an extream Sickness; from which he recovered not without a *Fistula* in his Breast, whereby he underwent much Affliction. When the *Chirurgeon* came to Inspect the Sore, he told him, *Sir, I know not how to go about what is necessary for your Cure;* but Mr. *Eaton* answered him, *God calls you to do, and me to suffer!* And God accordingly strengthened him to bear miserable Cuttings and Launcings of his Flesh with a most Invincible Patience. The *Chirurgeon* indeed *made* so many Wounds, that he was not able to *Cure* what he had made; another, and a better, Hand was necessarily imployed for it; but in the mean while great were the *Trials* with which the God of Heaven exercised the Faith of this his Holy Servant.

§ 7.   Mr. *Eaton* and Mr. *Davenport* were the *Moses* and *Aaron* of the Christian Colony now Erected in the South-West Parts of *New-England;* and Mr. *Eaton* being *yearly* and *ever* chosen their Governour, it was the Admiration of all Spectators to behold the *Discretion*, the *Gravity*, the *Equity* with which he still managed all their Publick Affairs. He carried in his very Countenance a *Majesty* which cannot be described; and in his Dispensations of *Justice* he was a *Mirrour* for the most Imitable *Impartiality*, but Ungainsayable

Authority of his Proceedings, being awfully sensible
of the Obligations which the *Oath* of a *Judge* lays upon
him. *Ils sont plus tenus de raison de garder Leur Ser-
ment, doubter mort, ou aucutie forfeiture:*[1] And hence he,
who would most patiently bear *hard things* offered unto
his *Person* in *private* Cases, yet would never pass by
any *Publick* Affronts, or Neglects offered when he
appeared under the Character of a *Magistrate*. But
he still was the Guide of the *Blind,* the Staff of the
Lame, the Helper of the *Widow* and the *Orphan,* and
all the Distressed; none that had a *Good Cause* was
afraid of coming before him: On the one side, *In his
Days did the Righteous flourish;* on the other side, *He
was the Terror of Evil Doers*. As in his Government of
the *Commonwealth,* so in the Government of his *Family,*
he was Prudent, Serious, Happy to a Wonder; and
albeit he sometimes had a large *Family,* consisting of
no less than *Thirty Persons,* yet he managed them with
such an *Even Temper,* that Observers have affirmed,
They never saw an House ordered with more Wisdom!
He kept an Honourable and Hospitable *Table;* but
one thing that still made the Entertainment thereof
the better, was the continual Presence of his Aged
Mother, by feeding of whom with an Exemplary *Piety*
till *she died,* he ensured his own *Prosperity* as long as
he lived. His *Children* and *Servants* he would mightily
Encourage unto the Study of the *Scriptures,* and Countenance their Addresses unto himself with any of their
Enquiries; but when he discerned any of them sinfully
negligent about the Concerns either of their General
or Particular *Callings,* he would admonish them with
such a Penetrating Efficacy, that they could scarce

[1] "They are more bound to keep their oath [than] to fear death or
any forfeiture"; *aucutie* is probably for *aucune*.

forbear falling down at his Feet with Tears. A *Word* of his was enough to steer them!

§ 8. So *Exemplary* was he for a *Christian*, that one who had been a *Servant* unto him, could many Years after say, *Whatever Difficulty in my daily Walk I now meet withal, still something that I either saw or heard in my Blessed Master* Eaton's *Conversation, helps me through it all; I have Reason to bless God that ever I knew him!* It was his Custom when he first rose in a *Morning*, to repair unto his *Study;* a Study well Perfumed with the *Meditations* and *Supplications* of an Holy Soul. After this, calling his *Family* together, he would then read a Portion of the *Scripture* among them, and after some Devout and Useful *Reflections* upon it, he would make a Prayer not long, but Extraordinary Pertinent and Reverent; and in the *Evening* some of the same Exercises were again attended. On the *Saturday* Morning he would still take notice of the Approaching *Sabbath* in his *Prayer*, and ask the Grace to be *Remembring* of it, and *Preparing* for it; and when the Evening arrived, he, besides this, not only *Repeated* a Sermon, but also *Instructed* his People, with putting of *Questions* referring to the Points of Religion, which would oblige them to Study for an *Answer;* and if their Answer were at any time insufficient, he would wisely and gently Enlighten their Understandings; all which he concluded with *Singing of a Psalm*. When the *Lord's Day* came, he called his *Family* together at the time for the Ringing of the First Bell, and *repeated* a Sermon, whereunto he added a Fervent *Prayer*, especially tending unto the Sanctification of the *Day*. At *Noon* he sang a *Psalm*, and at *Night* he retired an Hour into his Closet; advising those in his House to improve the same time for the good of their own Souls. He then called his *Family* together again, and in an obliging manner conferred with them about the things with which they had been Entertained in the House of God, shutting up all with a *Prayer* for the Blessing of God upon them all. For Solemn Days of *Humiliation*, or of *Thanksgiving*, he took the same Course, and Endeavoured still to make those that belonged unto him, understand the meaning of the Services before them. He seldom used any *Recreations*, but being a great *Reader*, all the time he could spare from Company and Business, he commonly spent in his Beloved *Study;* so that he merited the Name which was once given to a *Learned Ruler* of the *English Nation*, the Name of *Beauclerk:* [1] In Conversing with his Friends, he was Affable, Courteous, and generally *Pleasant*, but *Grave* perpetually; and so Cautelous and Circumspect in his Discourses, and so Modest in his Expressions, that it became a Proverb for Incontestable Truth, *Governour* Eaton *said it.*

But after all, his *Humility* appeared in his having always but *Low Expectations*, looking for little Regard and Reward from any Men, after he had merited as highly as was possible by his *Universal Serviceableness.*

§ 9. His Eldest Son he maintained at the *Colledge* until he proceeded *Master of Arts;* and he was indeed the Son of his *Vows*, and a Son of great *Hopes*. But a severe *Catarrh* diverted this Young Gentleman from the Work of the Ministry whereto his Father had once devoted him; and a Malignant Fever then raging in those Parts of the Country, carried off him with his Wife within Two or Three Days of one another. This was counted the sorest of all the Trials that ever befel

[1] Henry I.

his *Father* in the *Days of the Years of his Pilgrimage;* but he bore it with a Patience and Composure of Spirit which was truly admirable. His dying Son look'd earnestly on him, and said, *Sir, What shall we do!* Whereto, with a well-ordered Countenance, he replied, *Look up to God!* And when he passed by his Daughter drowned in Tears on this Occasion, to her he said, *Remember the Sixth Commandment, Hurt not your self with Immoderate Grief; Remember* Job, *who said,* The Lord hath given, and the Lord hath taken away, Blessed be the Name of the Lord! *You may mark what a Note the Spirit of God put upon it;* in all this *Job* sinned not, nor charged God foolishly: *God accounts it a charging of him foolishly, when we don't submit unto his Will patiently.* Accordingly he now governed himself as one that had attained unto the Rule of *Weeping as if we wept not;* for it being the *Lord's Day,* he repaired unto the Church in the *Afternoon,* as he had been there in the *Forenoon,* though he was never like to see his Dearest Son alive any more in this World. And though before the First Prayer began, a Messenger came to prevent Mr. *Davenport's* praying for the *Sick* Person, who was now *Dead,* yet his Affectionate Father alter'd not his Course, but *Wrote* after the Preacher as formerly;[1] and when he came Home he held on his former Methods of Divine Worship in his Family, not for the Excuse of *Aaron,* omitting any thing in the Service of God. In like sort, when the People had been at the Solemn Interment of this his Worthy Son, he did with a very Unpassionate Aspect and Carriage then say, *Friends, I thank you all for your Love and*

---

[1] "Writing after the preacher"—*i. e.* taking notes on the sermon— was a common practice, and many early notebooks kept in this way, are preserved.

Help, and for this Testimony of Respect unto me and mine: The Lord hath given, and the Lord hath taken; blessed be the Name of the Lord! Nevertheless, retiring here-upon into the Chamber where his Daughter then lay Sick, some Tears were observed falling from him while he uttered these Words, *There is a difference between a sullen Silence or a stupid Senslesness under the Hand of God, and a Child-like Submission thereunto.*

§ 10. Thus continually he, for about a Score of Years, was the *Glory* and *Pillar* of *New-Haven* Colony. He would often say, *Some count it a great matter to* Die *well, but I am sure 'tis a great matter to* Live *well. All our Care should be while we have our* Life *to use it well, and so when Death puts an end unto that, it will put an end unto all our Cares.* But having Excellently managed his *Care* to *Live well,* God would have him to *Die well,* without any room or time then given to take any *Care* at all; for he enjoyed a Death *sudden* to every one but himself! Having Worshipped God with his Family after his usual manner, and upon some Occasion with much Solemnity charged all the Family to carry it well unto their Mistress who was now confined by Sickness, he Supp'd, and then took a turn or two abroad for his Meditations. After that he came in to bid his Wife *Good-night,* before he left her with her *Watchers;* which when he did, she said, *Methinks you look sad!* Whereto he reply'd, *The Differences risen in the Church* of Hartford *make me so;* she then added, *Let us e'en go back to our Native Country again;* to which he an-swered, *You may,* [and so she did] *but I shall Die here.* This was the last Word that ever she heard him speak; for now retiring unto his Lodging in another Chamber, he was overheard about midnight fetching a *Groan;* and unto one, sent in presently to enquire how he did, he answered the Enquiry with only saying, *Very Ill!* And without saying any more, he fell *asleep in Jesus:* In the Year 1657. *loosing Anchor* from *New-Haven* for the better.

————————————*Sedes, ubi Fata, Quietas Ostendunt.*[1]

Now let his *Gravestone* wear at least the following

EPITAPH.

NEW-ENGLAND'*s* Glory, *full of* Warmth *and* Light, Stole away (*and* said nothing) *in the Night.*

CHAP. X.

SUCCESSORS.

§ 1.   WHEN the Day arrived in the *Anniversary Course* for the Freemen of the Colony to Elect another Governour in the place of the Deceased *Eaton,* Mr. *Davenport* Preached on that Passage of the Divine Oracle, in *Josh.* 1. 1, 2. *Now after the Death of* Moses, *the Servant of the Lord, it came to pass that the Lord spake unto* Joshua, *the Son of* Nun, Moses *Minister, saying, Now arise thou and all this People.* The Colony was abundantly sensible that their EATON had been a Man of a *Mosaic* Spirit; and that while they chose him, as they did every Year of his Life among them to be their Governour, they could

---

[1] "Places where the Fates promise peace." From the point of view of sense, the period after "better" just before the Latin quotation, should be removed.

not chuse a better. But they now considered that Mr. *Francis Newman*, who had been for many Years the Secretary of the Colony, was there a *Minister* to their *Moses*, as he had been otherwise his intimate Friend, Neighbour, Companion and Counsellor. For this Cause the Unanimous *Choice* of the Freemen fell upon this Gentleman to succeed in the Government. And I shall have given a sufficient History of his Government; which *through Death was not suffered to continue* above Three or Four Years, by only saying, *That he walk'd exactly in the Steps of his Predecessor.*

§ 2. Upon the setting of Mr. *Francis Newman*, there arose Mr. *William Leet*, of whom let not the Reader be displeased at this brief Account. This Gentleman was by his *Education* a *Lawyer*, and by his Imployment a Register[1] in the *Bishop's Court*. In that Station, at *Cambridge*, he observed that there were Summoned before the Court certain Persons to answer for the *Crime* of going to *hear Sermons abroad*, when there were *none* to be heard in their own Parish Churches at home; and that when any were brought before them for *Fornication* or *Adultery*, the Court only made themselves merry with their *Peccadillo's;* and that these latter Transgressors were as favourably dealt withal, as ever the *Wolf* was when he came with an *Auricular Confession* of his Murders to his Brother *Fox* for *Absolution;* but the former found as hard measure as ever the poor *Ass*, that had only taken a *Straw* by mistake out of a Pilgrim's Pad, and yet upon *Confession*, was by Chancellour *Fox* pronounced *Unpardonable.* This Observation extreamly scandalized Mr. *Leet*, who always thought, that *Hearing a good Sermon* had been a lesser Fault than *Lying with*

[1] Registrar.

one's Neighbour's Wife: And had the same Resentments that *Austin* sometimes had of the Iniquity which made *the Transgression of a Ceremony more severely reprehended than a Transgression of the Law of God;* but it made an Everlasting Impression upon his Heart, when the Judge of the Court furiously demanded of one then to be censured, *How he durst be so bold as to break the Laws of the Church, in going from his own Parish to hear Sermons abroad?* And the Honest Man answered, *Sir, How should I get Faith else? For the Apostle saith, Faith comes by Hearing the Word Preached; which Faith is necessary to Salvation; and Hearing the Word is the Means appointed by God for the obtaining and encreasing of it: And these Means I must use, whatever I suffer for it in this World.* These Words of that Honest Man were Blessed by God with such an Effect upon the Mind of Mr. *Leet,* that he presently left his *Office* in the Bishop's Court, and forsaking that *Untoward Generation* of Men, he associated himself with such as would go *Hear the Word, that they might get Faith;* and in *Hearing* he did happily get the *Like precious Faith.* On this, and *for* this, he was exposed unto the *Persecution,* which caused him to retire into *New-England* with many Worthy Ministers and other Christians in the Year 1639. In that Country he settled himself under the Ministry of the Excellent Mr. *Whitfield* at *Gilford,* where being also chosen a *Magistrate,* and then *Governour* of the *Colony;* and being so at the Juncture of time, when the *Royal Charter* did join *Connecticut* and *New-Haven,* he became next unto Governour *Winthrop,* the *Deputy-Governour* of the whole; and after the Death of Mr. *Winthrop,* even until his own Death, the *Annual Election* for about a *Decad* of Years together still made him *Governour.* But in his whole Government he gave continual Demonstrations of an *Excellent Spirit,* especially in that part of it where the *Reconciliation* and the *Coalition* of the Spirits of the People under it was to be accomplished. Mr. *Robert Treat* is the Follower of his *Example,* as well as the Successor in his *Government.*

CHAP. XI.

Hermes Christianus.[1] *The LIFE of* JOHN WIN-THROP, *Esq; Governour of* CONNECTICUT *and* NEW-HAVEN *United.*

> ——*Et Nos aliquod Nomenq; Decusq; Gessimus.*——[2]

§ 1. IF the Historian could give that Character of of the best *Roman Emperor,* that he was *Bonus a Bono, Pius a Pio,*[3] the *Son* of a *Father* like himself, our History may affirm concerning a very good *New-English Governour* also, that he was the *Father* of a *Son* like himself. The Proverb of the *Jews* which doth observe, *That Vinegar is the Son of Wine;* and the Proverb of the *Greeks,* which doth observe, *That the Sons of Heroes are Trespassers,* has been more than once contradicted in the happy Experience of the *New-Englanders:* But none of the least remarkable Contradictions given to it has been in the Honourable Family of our WINTHROPS.

§ 2. The Eldest Son of JOHN WINTHROP, Esq;

---

[1] "The Christian Mercury."
[2] "And we bore some fame and glory."
[3] "A good son of a good father, and a pious son of a pious father."

the Governour of one Colony, was JOHN WINTHROP, Esq; the Governour of another, in, therefore happy, *New-England*, born *Feb.* 12. 1605. at *Groton* in *England*. His *Glad Father* bestowed on him a liberal Education at the University, first of *Cambridge* in *England*, and then of *Dublin* in *Ireland;* and because *Travel* has been esteemed no little Accomplisher of a *Young Gentleman*, he then Accomplished himself by Travelling into *France, Holland, Flanders, Italy, Germany*, and as far as *Turky* it self; in which places he so improved his Opportunity of Conversing with all sorts of Learned Men, that he returned home equally a Subject of much *Experience*, and of great *Expectation*.

§ 3.   The Son of *Scipio Africanus* proving a degenerate Person, the *People* forced him to pluck off a Signet-Ring, which he wore with his *Father's Face* engraven on it.   But the Son of our Celebrated Governour *Winthrop*, was on the other side so like unto his Excellent Father for early Wisdom and Virtue, that arriving at *New-England* with his Father's Family, *Nov.* 4. 1631. he was, though not above Twenty Three Years of Age,[1] by the Unanimous Choice of the People, chosen a *Magistrate* of the Colony, whereof his Father was the *Governour*.   For this Colony he afterwards did many Services, yea, and he did them *Abroad* as well as *at Home;* very particularly in the Year 1634. when returning for *England*, he was by bad Weather forced into *Ireland*, where being invited unto the House of Sir *John Clotworthy*, he met with many Considerable Persons, by conferring with whom, the Affairs of *New-England* were not a little promoted; but it was another *Colony* for which the Providence of Heaven intended

---

[1] If he was born in 1605, as Mather says, this should be twenty-six, not twenty-three.

him to be such another *Father*, as his own Honourable
Father had been to *this*.

§ 4. In the Year 1635. Mr. *Winthrop* returned unto
New-England, with Powers from the Lord *Say* and the
Lord *Brook*, to settle a Plantation upon the *Long River*
of *Connecticut*, and a Commission to be himself the
Governour of that Plantation. But inasmuch as many
good People of the *Massachuset*-Colony had just before
this taken Possession of Land for a *New-Colony* there-
abouts, this Courteous and Peaceable Gentleman gave
them no Molestation; but having wisely Accommodated
the Matter with them, he sent a convenient number of
Men, with all Necessaries, to Erect a Fortification at
the Mouth of the River, where a *Town*, with a *Fort*,
is now distinguished by the Name of *Say-Brook;* by
which happy Action, the *Planters* further up the River
had no small Kindness done unto them; and the *Indians*,
which might else have been more Troublesome, were
kept in Awe.

§ 5. The Self-denying Gentleman, who had imployed his *Commission* of *Governour* so little to the
Disadvantage of the Infant-Colony at *Connecticut*,
was himself, e're long, by *Election* made *Governour*
of that Colony. And upon the *Restoration* of King
Charles II. he willingly undertook another Voyage to
England, on the behalf of the People under his Government, whose Affairs he managed with such a Successful
Prudence, that he obtained a *Royal Charter* for them,
which Incorporated the Colony of *New-Haven* with
them, and Invested both Colonies, now happily United,
with a firm Grant of *Priviledges*, beyond those of the
Plantations which had been settled before them. I
have been informed, that while he was engaged in this
Negotiation, being admitted unto a private Conference

with the King, he presented His Majesty with a Ring,
which King *Charles* I. had upon some Occasion given
to his Grandfather; and the King not only accepted
his Present, but also declared, that he accounted it
one of his *Richest Jewels;* which indeed was the Opinion
that *New-England* had of the Hand that carried it.
But having thus laid his Colony under Everlasting
Obligations of Gratitude, they did, after his return to
New-England, express of their Gratitude, by saying to
him as the *Israelites* did unto *Gideon, Rule thou over us,
for thou hast delivered us;* chusing *him* for their *Governour*
twice Seven Years together.

§ 6. When the Governour of *Athens* was a *Philosopher*, namely *Demetrius*, the Commonwealth so flourished, that no less than Three Hundred Brazen Statues
were afterward by the Thankful People Erected unto
his Memory. And a *Blessed Land* was *New-England*,
when there was over part of it a Governour, who was
not only a *Christian* and a *Gentleman*, but also an Eminent *Philosopher;* for indeed the Government of the
State is then most successfully managed, when the
measures of it are, by a *Wise Observer*, taken from the
Government of the *World;* and very unreasonable is
the *Jewish* Proverb,
Ne Habites in urbe ubi caput urbis est Medicus:[1] But
highly reasonable the Sentence of *Aristotle, Ubi præses
fuerit Philosophus, ibi Civitas erit Fœlix;*[2] and this
the rather for what is truly noted by *Thucydides,
Magistratus est Civitatis Medicus.*[3] Such an one was
our WINTHROP, whose Genius and Faculty for
Experimental Philosophy, was advanced in his *Travels*

[1] "Dwell not in the city where the chief is a physician."
[2] "Where the leader is a philosopher, there the state will be happy."
[3] "The magistrate is the physician of the state."

abroad, by his Acquaintance with many Learned *Virtuosi*. One Effect of this Disposition in him, was his being furnished with *Noble Medicines*, which he most Charitably and Generously gave away upon all Occasions; insomuch that where-ever he came, still the Diseased flocked about him, as if the Healing Angel of *Bethesda* had appeared in the place; and so many were the *Cures* which he wrought, and the *Lives* that he saved, that if *Scanderbeg*[1] might boast of his having slain in his Time Two Thousand Men with his own Hands, this Worthy Person might have made a far more desirable *Boast* of his having in his Time *Healed* more than so many Thousands; in which Beneficence to Mankind, there are of his Worthy Children, who to this Day do follow his Direction and Example. But it was not unto *New-England* alone that the Respects of this Accomplished *Philosopher* were confined. For, whereas in pursuance of the Methods begun by that Immortally Famous *Advancer of Learning*, the most Illustrious Lord Chancellor *Bacon*, a Select Company of Eminent Persons, using to meet in the Lodgings of Dr. *Wilkins* of *Wadham* Colledge in *Oxford*, had laid the Foundation of a Celebrated *Society*, which by the Year 1663. being Incorporated with a *Royal Charter*, hath since been among the Glories of *England*, yea, and of *Mankind;* and their Design was to make Faithful Records of all the Works of *Nature* or of *Art*, which might come under their Observation, and Correct what had been *False*, Restore what should be *True*, Preserve what should be *Rare*, and Render the Knowledge of the World, as well more *Perfect* as more *Useful;* and by multiplied Experiments both of *Light* and *Fruit*, advance the *Empire* of Man over the whole

---

[1] Scanderbeg is George Castriota, an Albanian hero, c. 1450.

visible Creation; it was the Honour of Mr. *Winthrop* to be a Member of this *Royal Society*. And accordingly among the *Philosophical Transactions* Published by Mr. *Oldenburgh*, there are some notable Communications from this Inquisitive and Intelligent Person, whose Insight into many Parts of the *Creation*, but especially of the *Mineral Kingdom*, was beyond what had been attained by the most in many Parts of *America*.[1]

§ 7. If one would therefore desire an exact Picture of this Worthy Man, the Description which the most Sober and Solid Writers of the Great *Philosophick Work* do give of those Persons, who alone are qualified for the Smiles of Heaven upon their Enterprizes, would have exactly fitted him. He was a *Studious, Humble, Patient, Reserved* and *Mortified* Person, and one in whom the Love of *God* was Fervent, the Love of *Man* sincere: And he had herewithal a certain *Extension of Soul*, which disposed him to a *Generous Behaviour* towards those, who by Learning, Breeding and Virtue, deserve Respects, though of a Perswasion and Profession in Religion very different from *his own;* which was *that* of a Reformed *Protestant*, and a *New-English Puritan*. In sum, he was not more an *Adeptist*[2] in those Noble and Secret *Medicines*, which would reach the *Roots* of the Distempers that annoy Humane Bodies, and procure an *Universal Rest* unto the *Archæus*[3] on all Occasions of Disturbance, than he was in those *Christian Qualities*, which appear upon the Cure of the Distempers in the Minds of Men, by the Effectual *Grace* of our Lord Jesus Christ.

[1] Mather here refers to the Royal Society of London.

[2] *I. e.*, an adept.

[3] The Archæus—an old medical term for the essential vital principle in the body.

§ 8. In the Year 1643. after divers *Essays* made in some former Years, the several Colonies of *New-England* became in *Fact*, as well as *Name*, UNITED COLONIES. And an Instrument was formed, wherein having declared, *That we all came into these parts of* America *with the same End and Aim, namely, to advance the Glory of our Lord Jesus Christ, and enjoy the Liberties of the Gospel with Purity and Peace*, it was firmly agreed between the several Jurisdictions, that there should yearly be chosen *Two Commissioners* out of each, who should meet at fit Places appointed for that purpose, with full Powers from the *General Courts* in each, to Concert and Conclude Matters of General Concernment for *Peace* or *War* of the several Colonies thus *Confederated*. In pursuance of this Laudable *Confederacy*, this most Meritorious *Governour* of *Connecticut* Colony accepted the Trouble of appearing as a *Commissioner* for that Colony, with the rest met at *Boston*, in the Year 1676. when the Calamities of the *Indian-War* [1] were distressing the whole Country: But *here* falling Sick of a Fever, he dy'd on *April* 5. of that Year, and was Honourably Interred in the same Tomb with his Honourable Father.

§ 9. His Father, as long ago as the Year 1643. had seen Cause to Write unto him an Excellent Letter, wherein there were these among other Passages.

'You are the Chief of *Two* Families; I had by your 'Mother *Three Sons* and *Three Daughters*, and I had 'with her a *Large Portion* of outward Estate. These 'now are all *gone;* Mother *gone;* Brethren and Sisters '*gone;* you only are left to see the Vanity of these '*Temporal things*, and learn *Wisdom* thereby, which 'may be of more use to you, through the Lord's Blessing,

[1] King Philip's War.

'than all that *Inheritance* which might have befallen
'you: And for which this may stay and quiet your
'Heart, *That God is able to give you more than this:*
'and that it being spent in the furtherance of *his Work,*
'which hath here prospered so well, through his Power
'hitherto, you and yours may *certainly expect a liberal*
'*Portion in the Prosperity and Blessing thereof hereafter;*
'and the rather, because it was not *forced* from you
'by a Father's Power, but freely *resigned* by your
'self, out of a Loving and Filial Respect unto me, and
'your own readiness unto the Work it self. From
'whence, as I do often take Occasion to Bless the
'Lord for you, so do I also Commend you and yours to
'his *Fatherly Blessing,* for a plentiful Reward to be
'rendred unto you. And doubt not, my Dear Son,
'but let your *Faith* be built upon his Promise and
'Faithfulness, that as he hath carried you hitherto
'through many Perils, and provided liberally for you,
'so he will do for the time to come, and will *never fail*
'*you, nor forsake you.* ———— *My Son,* the Lord knows
'how Dear thou art to me, and that my Care has been
'more for thee than for my self. But I *know* thy Pros-
'perity depends not on my Care, nor on *thine own,*
'but upon the Blessing of our *Heavenly Father;* neither
'doth it on the things of this World, but on the *Light*
'*of God's Countenance,* through the Merit and Media-
'tion of our Lord Jesus Christ. It is *that* only which
'can give us *Peace of Conscience* with *Contentation;*
'which can as well make our Lives Happy and Com-
'fortable in a *mean* Estate, as in a *great* Abundance.
'But if you weigh things aright, and sum up all the
'Turnings of Divine Providence together, you shall
'find great Advantage.—The Lord hath brought us
'to a *Good Land;* a Land, where we enjoy outward

'*Peace* and *Liberty*, and above all, the *Blessings of the*
'*Gospel*, without the Burden of *Impositions* in Matters
'of *Religion*. Many Thousands there are who would
'give *Great Estates* to enjoy our Condition. Labour
'therefore, my good Son, to increase our *Thankfulness*
'to God for all his Mercies to thee, especially for that
'he hath revealed his *Everlasting Good-will* to thee in
'Jesus Christ, and joined thee to the visible Body of
'his *Church*, in the Fellowship of his People, and hath
'saved thee in all thy *Travails* abroad, from being
'Infected with the *Vices* of these Countries where thou
'hast been, (a Mercy vouchsafed but unto few Young
Gentlemen *Travellers*.) Let *him* have the Honour of
'it who kept thee. *He* it was who gave thee Favour
'in the Eyes of all with whom thou hadst to do, both
'by Sea and Land; *He* it was who saved thee in all
'Perils; and *He* it is who hath given thee a Gift in
'Understanding and Art; and he it is who hath pro-
'vided thee a Blessing in Marriage, a Comfortable
'Help, and many Sweet Children; and hath hitherto
'provided liberally for you all: And therefore I would
'have you to *Love* him again, and *Serve* him, and *Trust*
'him for the time to come. Love and Prize that *Word*
'*of Truth*, which only makes known to you the Precious
'and Eternal Thoughts and Councils of the *Light*
'*Inaccessible*. Deny your *own Wisdom*, that you may
'find his; and esteem it the greatest Honour to lye under
'the Simplicity of the Gospel of *Christ Crucified*, with-
'out which you can never enter into the *Secrets of his*
'*Tabernacle*, nor enjoy those sweet things which *Eye*
'*hath not seen, nor Ear heard, nor can the Heart of*
'*Man conceive;* but God hath granted unto some few
'to know them even in this Life. Study well, my Son,
'the saying of the Apostle, *Knowledge puffeth up*. It

'is a *good Gift* of God, but when it lifts up the Mind
'above the *Cross of Christ*, it is the *Pride of Life*, and
'the High-way to *Apostacy*, wherein many Men of
'great Learning and Hopes have perished.—In all the
'Exercise of your *Gifts*, and Improvement of your
'*Talents*, have an Eye to your *Master's End*, more than
'your *own;* and to the *Day of your Account*, that you
'may then have your *Quietus est*, even, *Well done,*
'*Good and Faithful Servant!* But my last and chief
'Request to you, is, that you be careful to have your
'*Children* brought up in the Knowledge and Fear of
'God, and in the Faith of our Lord Jesus Christ. *This*
'will give you the best *Comfort* of them, and keep them
'sure from any *Want* or *Miscarriage:* And when you
'part from them, it will be no small joy to your Soul,
'that you *shall meet them again in Heaven!*

Doubtless, the Reader considers the *Historical*
Passages in this Extract of the Letter thus Recited.
Now, but by making this Reflection upon the Rest,
that as the *Prophetical Part* of it was notably fulfilled
in the Estate, whereto the good Providence of God
Recovered this Worthy Gentleman and his Family,
so the *Monitory Part* of it was most Exemplarily attended in his Holy and Useful Conversation. I shall
therein briefly sum up the *Life* of a Person whom we
shall call a *Second* unto none of our *Worthies*, but as
we call him our *Second Winthrop*.

EPITAPHIUM.

Abi Viator;
Et Luge plures Magistratus in Uno periisse.
Redi Viator.
Non Periit, *sed ad Cœlestem Societatem*

Regia Magis Regiam,
Vere Adeptus,
Abiit:
WINTHROPUS, *Non minor magnis Majoribus.*[1]

CHAP. XII.

ASSISTENTS.

MAGISTRATES of *Connecticut*-Colony, before *New-Haven* Colony was actually annexed unto it, were, (besides the two Alternately, for the most Part, Elected Governours, *HOPKINS*, and *HAINS*.)

Roger Ludlow,	1636
John Steel,	1636
William Phelps,	1636
William Westwood,	1636
Andrew Ward,	1636
Thomas Wells,	1637
William Swayn,	1637
Matthew Mitchel,	1637
George Hull,	1637
William Whiting,	1637
John Mason,	1637
George Willis,	1639
John Webster,	1639
William Ludlow,	1640

[1] "Epitaph. Go, wayfarer, and bewail many magistrates who have died in this one. Return, traveler. He has not died, but, one who has truly succeeded, has gone to a heavenly society more royal than the Royal Society: Winthrop, not inferior to the great elders of his name."

William Hopkins,	1642
Henry Woolcot,	1643
George Fenwick,	1644
Cosmore,	1647
John Howel,	1647
John Cullick,	1648
Henry Clark,	1650
John Winthrop,	1651
Thomas Topping,	1651
John Talcot,	1654
John Ogden,	1656
Nathan Gold,	1657
Matthew Allyn,	1658
Richard Treat,	1658
Thomas Baker,	1658
Mulford,	1658
Alexander Knowles,	1658
John Wells,	1658
Robert Band,	1659
Rayner,	1661
John Allyn,	1662
Daniel Clark,	1662
Samuel Sherman,	1662
John Young,	1664

MAGISTRATES of *New-Haven* Colony, before *Connecticut*-Colony could accomplish its Coalition therewith, were, (besides the Governours elsewhere mentioned)

Stephen Goodyear,	1637
Thomas Grigson,	1637
Richard Malbon,	1637
William Leet,	1637

John Desborough,	1637
Tapp,	1637
William Fowler,	1637
Francis Newman,	1653
Astwood,	1653
Samuel Eaton,	1654
Benjamin Fen,	1654
Matthew Gilbert,	1658
Jasper Crane,	1658
Robert Treat,	1659
William Jones,	1662

MAGISTRATES after the Two Colonies were content, according to their Charter, to become ONE, were,

John Winthrop, Gov.	1665
John Mason,	1665
Matthew Allyn,	1665
Samuel Willys,	1665
Nathan Gold,	1665
John Talcot	1665
Henry Woolcot,	1665
John Allyn,	1665
Samuel Sherman,	1665
James Richards,	1665
William Leet,	1665
William Jones,	1665
Benjamin Fen,	1665
Jasper Crane,	1665
Daniel Clark,	1666
Alexander Bryans,	1668
James Bishop,	1668
Anthony Howkins,	1668
Thomas Wells,	1668

John Nash,	1672
Robert Treat,	1673
Thomas Topping,	1674
Matthew Gilbert,	1677
Andrew Leet,	1678
John Wadsworth,	1679
Robert Chapman,	1681
James Fitch,	1681
Samuel Mason,	1683
Benjamin Newberry,	1685
Samuel Talcot,	1685
Giles Hamlin,	1685

While the Colonies were Clusters of *Rich Grapes,* which had a *Blessing* in them.[1] Such *Leaves* as these (which is in the *Proverbs* of the Jewish Nation, a Name for *Magistrates*) happily defended them from the *Storms* that molest the World.

Those of the least Character among them, yet came up to what the *Roman* Commonwealth required in their *Magistrates.*

Populus Romanus delegit Magistratus, quasi Reipublicæ Villicos, in quibus, si qua præterea est Ars, facile patitur; sin minus, virtute eorum & Innocentia Contentus est.[2] Cic. Orat. Pro Plan.

[1] The sense seems to require a comma, not a period, here.

[2] "The Roman people chose magistrates as if they were stewards of the state, in whom any other ability is welcomed, but if no such other ability exists, they were content with the virtue and honesty of those they chose." The quotation is from Cicero.

Pietas in Patriam:[1]

THE
LIFE
OF HIS
EXCELLENCY
Sir WILLIAM PHIPPS, Knt.

Late Captain General, and Governour in Chief of the
Province of the *Massachuset*-Bay,

NEW-ENGLAND.

Containing the Memorable *Changes* Undergone, and
Actions Performed by Him.

Written by one intimately acquainted with Him.

Discite Virtutem ex Hoc, verumque Laborem.[2]

[1] "Love to one's country."
[2] "Learn virtue and true labor from him."

THE Author of the following Narrative, is a Person of such well known Integrity, Prudence and Veracity, that there is not any cause to Question the Truth of what he here Relates. And moreover, this Writing of his is adorned with a very grateful Variety of Learning, and doth contain such surprizing workings of Providence, as do well deserve due Notice and Observation. On all which accounts, it is with just Confidence recommended to the Publick by

April 27.
1697.

Nath. Mather,
John Howe,
Matth. Mead.[1]

[1] Nathaniel Mather was Cotton Mather's uncle, at this time in England. When the *Magnalia* came out he was dead, the certificate above being simply reprinted from the first edition of the Life of Phips. John Howe and Matthew Mead were two leading English Puritan divines, both friends of Cotton Mather's father and uncle.

To his Excellency the Earl of Bellomont, *Baron of* Coloony *in* Ireland, *General Governour of the Province of* Massachusets *in* New-England, *and the Provinces annexed.*

May it please your Excellency,

THE Station in which the Hand of the God of Heaven hath disposed His Majesties Heart to place your Honour, doth so manifestly entitle your Lordship to this ensuing Narrative, that its being thus Presented to your Excellencies Hand, is thereby both Apologized for and Justified. I believe, had the Writer of it, when he Penned it, had any Knowledge of your Excellency, he would himself have done it, and withal, would have amply and publickly Congratulated the People of *New-England*, on account of their having such a Governour, and your Excellency, on account of your being made Governour over them. For though as to some other thiugs[1] it may possibly be a place to some Persons not so desirable; yet I believe this Character may be justly given of them, that they are the best People under Heaven; there being among them, not only less of open Profaneness, and less of Lewdness, but also more of the serious Profession, Practice, and Power of Christianity, in proportion to their number, than is among any other People upon the Face of the whole Earth. Not but I doubt, there are many bad Persons among them, and too many distemper'd Humours, perhaps even among those who are truly good. It would be a wonder if it should be otherwise; for it hath of late Years, on various accounts,

[1] Things.

151

and some very singular and unusual ones, been a Day of sore Temptation with that whole People. Nevertheless, as I look upon it as a Favour from God to those Plantations, that he hath set your Excellency over them, so I do account it a Favour from God to your Excellency, that he hath committed and trusted in your Hand so great a part of his peculiar Treasure and precious Jewels, as are among that People. Besides, that on other accounts the Lord Jesus hath more of a visible Interest in *New-England*, than in any of the Outgoings of the *English* Nation in *America*. They have at their own Charge not only set up Schools of lower Learning up and down the Country; but have also erected an University, which hath been the happy Nursery of many Useful, Learned, and excellently Accomplished Persons. And moreover, from them hath the blessed Gospel been Preached to the Poor, Barbarous, Savage *Heathen* there; and it hath taken such Root among them, that there were lately four and twenty Assemblies in which the Name of the Lord Jesus was constantly called on, and celebrated in their own Language. In these things *New-England* outshineth all the Colonies of the *English* in those goings down of the Sun. I know your Excellency will Favour and Countenance their University, and also the Propagating of the Gospel among the Natives; for the Interest of Christ in that Part of the Earth is much concerned in them. That the God of the Spirits of all Flesh would abundantly replenish your Excellency with a suitable Spirit for the Service to which he hath called your Lordship, that he would give your Honour a prosperous Voyage thither, and when there, make your Excellency a rich Blessing to that People, and them a rejoicing to your Excellency, is the Prayer of,

April 27.   *My Lord,*
  1697.

                              Your Excellencies most

                                Humble Servant,

                            Nath. Mather.

THE
LIFE
Of His EXCELLENCY
Sir *WILLIAM PHIPS*, Knt.
LATE
GOVERNOUR
OF
NEW-ENGLAND.

§ 1. **I**F such a Renowned Chymist, as *Quercetanus*, with a whole Tribe of *Labourers in the Fire*, since that Learned Man, find it no easie thing to make the common part of Mankind believe, That they can take a *Plant* in its more vigorous Consistence, and after a due *Maceration, Fermentation* and *Separation*, extract the *Salt* of that *Plant*, which, as it were, in a *Chaos*, invisibly reserves the *Form* of the whole, with its vital Principle; and, that keeping the *Salt* in a *Glass* Hermetically sealed, they can, by applying a *Soft Fire* to the *Glass*, make the *Vegetable* rise by little and little out of its *Ashes*, to surprize the Spectators with a notable Illustration of that *Resurrection*, in the Faith whereof the *Jews* returning from the Graves of their Friends, pluck up the *Grass* from the Earth, using those Words of the Scripture thereupon, *Your Bones shall flourish like an Herb:* 'Tis likely, that all the Observations of such Writers, as the Incomparable *Borellus*, will find it hard enough to produce our Belief, that the *Essential Salts* of *Animals* may be so Prepared and Preserved, that an Ingenious Man may have the whole *Ark* of *Noah* in his own Study, and raise the fine *Shape* of an *Animal* out of its Ashes at his Pleasure: And, that by the like Method from the

Essential Salts of Humane Dust, a Philosopher may, without any Criminal *Necromancy,* call up the *Shape* of any *Dead* Ancestor from the Dust whereinto his Body has been Incinerated.[1] The *Resurrection of the Dead,* will be as Just, as Great an Article of our *Creed,* although the *Relations* of these Learned Men should pass for *Incredible Romances:* But yet there is an *Anticipation* of that Blessed *Resurrection,* carrying in it some Resemblance of these *Curiosities,* which is performed, when we do in a *Book,* as in a *Glass,* reserve the History of our Departed *Friends;* and by bringing our *Warm Affections* unto such an History, we revive, as it were, out of their *Ashes,* the true *Shape* of those Friends, and bring to a fresh View, what was *Memorable* and *Imitable* in them.   Now, in as much as *Mortality* has done its part upon a Considerable Person, with whom I had the Honour to be well acquainted, and a Person as *Memorable* for the Wonderful *Changes* which befel him, as *Imitable* for his *Virtues* and *Actions* under those *Changes;* I shall endeavour, with the *Chymistry* of an Impartial *Historian,* to *raise* my Friend so far out of his *Ashes,* as to shew him again unto the World; and if the Character of *Heroick Virtue* be for a Man to *deserve well of Mankind, and be great in the Purpose and Success of Essays to do so,* I may venture to promise my Reader such Example of *Heroick Virtue,* in the Story whereto I Invite him, that he shall say, it would have been little short of a *Vice* in *me,* to have withheld it from him.   Nor is it any *Partiality* for the Memory of my Deceased Friend, or any other Sinister Design whatsoever, that has Invited me to this Undertaking;

---

[1] Quercetanus is Joseph du Chesne, a French medical writer, who died in 1609. Borellus is Giovanni Alfonso Borelli, 1608–1679, author of *De Motu Animalium.*

but I have undertaken this Matter from a sincere
Desire, that the Ever-Glorious Lord *JESUS CHRIST*
may have the Glory of his *Power* and *Goodness*, and of
his *Providence*, in what he did for such a Person, and
in what he disposed and assisted that Person to do for
him.   Now, *May he assist my Writing, even he that
prepared the Subject, whereof I am to Write!*
   § 2.   So *obscure* was the *Original* of that Memorable
Person, whose *Actions* I am going to relate, that I
must, in a way of Writing, like that of *Plutarch*, prepare
my Reader for the intended Relation, by first searching
the *Archives* of Antiquity for a *Parallel*.   Now, because
we will not *Parallel* him with *Eumenes*, who, though he
were the Son of a Poor Carrier, became a Governour
of Mighty Provinces; nor with *Marius*, whose mean
Parentage did not hinder his becoming a Glorious
Defender of his Country, and Seven times the Chief
Magistrate of the Chiefest City in the Universe: Nor
with *Iphicrates*, who became a Successful and Renowned
General of a Great People, though his Father were a
Cobler: Nor with *Dioclesian*, the Son of a poor *Scrive-
ner*: Nor with *Bonosus*, the Son of a poor *School-
Master*, who yet came to sway the Scepter of the *Roman*
Empire: Nor, lastly, will I compare him to the more
late Example of the Celebrated *Mazarini*, who though
no Gentleman by his Extraction, and one so sorrily
Educated, that he might have wrote *Man*, before he
could write at all; [1] yet ascended unto that Grandeur,
in the Memory of many yet living, as to Umpire the
most Important Affairs of *Christendom:* We will decline
looking any further in that *Hemisphere* of the World,
and make the *Hue and Cry* throughout the Regions of
America, the *New World*, which *He*, that is becoming

[1] *I. e.*, was a man grown before he learned to write.

the Subject of our History, by his *Nativity*, belong'd unto. And in *America*, the first that meets me, is *Francisco Pizarro*, who, though a *Spurious Offspring*, exposed when a *Babe* in a Church-Porch, at a sorry Village of *Navarre*, and afterwards employ'd while he was a *Boy*, in keeping of Cattel, yet, at length, stealing into *America*, he so thrived upon his Adventures there, that upon some Discoveries, which with an handful of Men he had in a desperate Expedition made of *Peru*, he obtain'd the King of *Spain*'s Commission for the Conquest of it, and at last so incredibly enrich'd himself by the Conquest, that he was made the first Vice-Roy of *Peru*, and created Marquess of *Anatilla*.

To the Latter and Highest Part of that Story, if any thing hindred His Excellency Sir *WILLIAM PHIPS*, from affording of a *Parallel*, it was not the want either of *Design*, or of *Courage*, or of *Conduct* in himself, but it was the Fate of a *Premature Mortality*. For my Reader now being satisfied, that a Person's being *Obscure* in his *Original*, is not always a Just Prejudice to an Expectation of *Considerable Matters* from him; I shall now inform him, that this our *PHIPS* was Born *Feb.* 2. *A. Dom.* 1650. at a despicable Plantation on the River of *Kennebeck*, and almost the furthest Village of the Eastern Settlement of *New-England*. And as the *Father* of that Man, which was as great a Blessing as *England* had in the Age of that Man, was a *Smith*,[1] so a *Gun-Smith*, namely, *James Phips*, once of *Bristol*, had the Honour of being the *Father* to him, whom we shall presently see, made by the God of Heaven as great a Blessing to *New-Eng-*

[1] Mather refers to Thomas Cromwell.

land, as that Country could have had, if they themselves had pleased. His fruitful *Mother*, yet living, had no less than *Twenty-Six* Children, whereof *Twenty-One* were Sons; but Equivalent to them all was *WILLIAM*, one of the youngest, whom his *Father* dying, left young with his *Mother*, and with her he lived, *keeping of Sheep in the Wilderness*, until he was Eighteen Years Old; at which time he began to feel some further Disposi-tions of Mind from that *Providence* of God which *took him from the Sheepfolds, from following the Ewes great with young, and brought him to feed his People.* Reader, enquire no further who was his *Father?* Thou shalt anon see, that he was, as the *Italians* express it, *A Son to his own Labours!*

§ 3. His Friends earnestly solicited him to settle among them in a Plantation of the *East;* but he had an Unaccountable *Impulse* upon his Mind, perswading him, as he would privately hint unto some of them, *That he was Born to greater Matters.* To come at those *greater Matters*, his first Contrivance was to bind him-self an Apprentice unto a *Ship-Carpenter* for Four Years; in which time he became a Master of the *Trade*, that once in a Vessel of more than *Forty Thousand Tuns*, repaired the Ruins of the Earth; *Noah's*, I mean; he then betook himself an Hundred and Fifty Miles further a Field, even to *Boston*, the Chief Town of *New-England;* which being a Place of the most Business and Resort in those Parts of the World, he expected there more Commodiously to pursue the *Spes Majorum & Meliorum*,[1] *Hopes* which had inspir'd him. At *Boston*, where it was that he now learn'd, first of all, to *Read* and *Write*, he followed his Trade for about a Year; and by a laudable Deportment, so recom-

[1] "Hopes of greater and better things."

mended himself, that he Married a Young Gentlewoman of good Repute, who was the Widow of one
Mr. *John Hull*, a well-bred Merchant, but the Daughter
of one Captain *Roger Spencer*, a Person of good Fashion,
who having suffer'd much damage in his Estate, by
some unkind and unjust Actions, which he bore with
such Patience, that for fear of thereby injuring the
Publick, he would not seek Satisfaction, *Posterity* might
afterward see the Reward of his *Patience*, in what
Providence hath now done for one of his own *Posterity*.
Within a little while after his Marriage, he indented
with several Persons in *Boston*, to Build them a Ship at
Sheeps-coat [1] River, Two or Three Leagues Eastward
of *Kennebeck;* where having Lanched the Ship, he also
provided a *Lading* of Lumber to bring with him, which
would have been to the Advantage of all Concern'd.
But just as the Ship was hardly finished, the Barbarous
Indians on that River, broke forth into an Open and
Cruel War upon the *English;* and the miserable People,
surprized by so sudden a storm of Blood, had no Refuge
from the Infidels, but the *Ship* now finishing in the
Harbour.   Whereupon he left his intended *Lading* behind him, and instead thereof, carried with him his
old Neighbours and their Families, free of all Charges,
to *Boston;* so the *first Action* that he did, after he was
his own Man, was to *save his Father's House*, with the
rest of the Neighbourhood, from Ruin; but the Disappointment which befel him from the Loss of his
other *Lading*, plunged his Affairs into greater Embaras-
ments with such as had employ'd him.

§ 4.   But he was hitherto no more than beginning
to make *Scaffolds* for further and higher *Actions!*
He would frequently tell the Gentlewoman his Wife,

---

[1] Sheepscot.

That he should yet be *Captain of a King's Ship;* That he should come to have the *Command of better Men* than he was now accounted himself; and, That he should be Owner of a *Fair Brick-House* in the *Green-Lane* of *North-Boston;* and, That, it may be, this would not be all that the Providence of God would bring him to. She entertained these Passages with a sufficient Incredulity; but he had so *serious* and *positive* an Expectation of them, that it is not easie to say, what was the *Original* thereof. He was of an Enterprizing *Genius,* and naturally disdained *Littleness:* But his Disposition for *Business* was of the *Dutch* Mould, where, with a little shew of *Wit,* there is as much *Wisdom* demonstrated, as can be shewn by any Nation. His Talent lay not in the *Airs* that serve chiefly for the pleasant and sudden Turns of *Conversation;* but he might say, as *Themistocles, Though he could not play upon a Fiddle, yet he knew how to make a little City become a Great One.* He would *prudently* contrive a weighty Undertaking, and then patiently pursue it unto the End. He was of an Inclination, cutting rather like a *Hatchet,* than like a *Razor;* he would propose very Considerable Matters to himself, and then so *cut through* them, that no Difficulties could put by the *Edge* of his Resolutions. Being thus of the *True Temper,* for doing of *Great Things,* he betakes himself to the *Sea,* the Right *Scene* for such Things; and upon Advice of a *Spanish Wreck* about the *Bahama*'s, he took a Voyage thither; but with little more success, than what just served him a little to furnish him for a Voyage to *England;* whither he went in a Vessel, not much unlike that which the *Dutchmen* stamped on their *First Coin,* with these Words about it, *Incertum quo Fata ferant.*[1] Having first informed

[1] "It is uncertain where the Fates will carry me."

himself that there was another *Spanish Wreck*, wherein
was lost a mighty Treasure, hitherto undiscovered,
he had a strong Impression upon his Mind that *He*
must be the Discoverer; and he made such Representations of his Design at *White-Hall*, that by the Year
1683. he became the Captain of *a King's Ship*, and
arrived at *New-England* Commander of the *Algier-
Rose*, a Frigot of Eighteen Guns, and Ninety-Five
Men.

§ 5. To Relate all the *Dangers* through which he
passed, both by Sea and Land, and all the Tiresome
Trials of his *Patience*, as well as of his *Courage*, while
Year after Year the most vexing Accidents imaginable
delay'd the Success of his Design, it would even Tire
the patience of the Reader: For very great was the
Experiment that Captain *Phips* made of the *Italian*
Observation, *He that cann't suffer both Good and Evil,
will never come to any great Preferment.* Wherefore I
shall supersede all *Journal* of his Voyages to and fro,
with reciting one Instance of his Conduct, that show'd
him to be a Person of no contemptible Capacity.
While he was Captain of the *Algier-Rose*, his Men growing weary of their unsuccessful Enterprize, made a
Mutiny, wherein they approach'd him on the Quarter-
Deck, with Drawn Swords in their Hands, and required
him to join with them in Running away with the Ship,
to drive a Trade of Piracy on the *South Seas*. Captain
Phips, though he had not so much of a Weapon as an
Ox-Goad, or a *Jaw-bone* in his Hands, yet like another
Shamgar or *Samson*, with a most undaunted Fortitude,
he rush'd in upon them, and with the Blows of his bare
Hands, *Fell'd* many of them, and *Quell'd* all the Rest.
But this is not the Instance which I intended: That
which I intend is, That (as it has been related unto me)

One Day while his Frigot lay *Careening*,[1] at a desolate *Spanish* Island, by the side of a Rock, from whence they had laid a Bridge to the Shoar, the Men, whereof he had about an *Hundred*, went all, but about Eight or Ten, to divert themselves, as they pretended, in the *Woods:* Where they all entred into an *Agreement*, which they Sign'd in a Ring, That about seven a Clock that Evening they would seize the Captain, and those Eight or Ten, which they knew to be True unto him, and leave them to perish on this Island, and so be gone away unto the *South Sea* to *seek their Fortune*. Will the Reader now imagine, that Captain *Phips* having Advice of this Plot but about an Hour and half before it was to be put in Execution, yet within *Two Hours* brought all these Rogues down upon their Knees to beg for their Lives? But so it was! For these Knaves considering that they should want a *Carpenter* with them in their *Villanous Expedition*, sent a Messenger to fetch unto them the *Carpenter*, who was then at Work upon the Vessel: and unto him they shew'd their *Articles;* telling him what he must look for if he did not *subscribe* among them. The *Carpenter* being an honest Fellow, did with much importunity prevail for one half hours Time to consider of the Matter; and returning to Work upon the Vessel, with a *Spy* by them set upon him, he feigned himself taken with a Fit of the *Cholick*, for the Relief whereof he suddenly run unto the Captain in the Great Cabbin for a *Dram*; where, when he came, his business was only in brief, to tell the Captain of the horrible Distress which he was fallen into; but the Captain bid him as briefly return to the Rogues in the *Woods*, and Sign

[1] *I. e.*, lay on her side, so that the bottom might be cleaned and calked.

their *Articles*, and leave *him* to provide for the Rest. The *Carpenter* was no sooner gone, but Captain *Phips* calling together the few Friends (it may be seven or eight) that were left him aboard, whereof the Gunner was one, demanded of them, whether they would stand by him in the Extremity, which he informed them was now come upon him; whereto they reply'd, *They would stand by him, if he could save them;* and he Answer'd, *By the help of God he did not fear it.* All their Provisions had been carried Ashoar to a Tent, made for that purpose there; about which they had placed several Great Guns to defend it, in case of any *Assault* from *Spaniards*, that might happen to come that way. Wherefore Captain *Phips* immediately ordered those Guns to be silently Drawn'd[1] and Turn'd; and so pulling up the Bridge, he charged his Great Guns aboard, and brought them to Bear on every side of the Tent. By this Time the *Army of Rebels* comes out of the Woods; but as they drew near to the Tent of Provisions, they saw such a change of Circumstances, that they cried out, *We are Betray'd!* And they were soon confirm'd in it, when they heard the Captain with a stern Fury call to them, *Stand off, ye Wretches, at your Peril!* He quickly saw them cast into a more than ordinary Confusion, when they saw *Him* ready to Fire his Great Guns upon them, if they offered one Step further than he permitted them: And when he had signified unto them his *Resolve* to abandon them unto all the Desolation which they had purposed for *him*, he caused the *Bridge* to be again laid, and his Men begun to take the Provisions abroad. When the Wretches beheld what was coming upon them, they fell to very humble Entreaties; and at last fell down upon their Knees,

[1] Drawn.

protesting, *That they never had any thing against him, except only his unwillingness to go away with the King's Ship upon the* South-Sea *Design: But upon all other Accounts, they would chuse rather to Live and Die with him, than with any Man in the World; however, since they saw how much he was dissatisfied at it, they would insist upon it no more, and humbly begg'd his Pardon.* And when he judg'd that he had kept them on their *Knees* long enough, he having first secur'd their *Arms,* received them aboard; but he immediately weighed Anchor, and arriving at *Jamaica,* he Turn'd them off. Now with a small Company of other Men he sailed from thence to *Hispaniola,* where by the Policy of his Address, he fished out of a very old *Spaniard,* (or *Portuguese*) a little Advice about the true Spot where lay the *Wreck* which he had been hitherto seeking, as unprosperously, as the *Chymists* have their *Aurisick Stone:* [1] That it was upon a *Reef of Shoals,* a few Leagues to the Northward of *Port de la Plata,* upon *Hispaniola,* [2] a Port so call'd, it seems, from the Landing of some of the *Shipwreck'd* Company, with a Boat full of Plate, saved out of their Sinking Frigot: Nevertheless, when he had searched very narrowly the Spot, whereof the old *Spaniard* had advised him, he had not hitherto exactly lit upon it. Such *Thorns* did vex his Affairs while he was in the *Rose-Frigot;* but none of all these things could retund the Edge of his Expectations to find the *Wreck*; with such Expectations he return'd then into *England,* that he might there better furnish himself to Prosecute a *New Discovery;* for though he judged he might, by proceeding a little further, have

[1] Probably a misprint for Aurific Stone—*i. e.,* "gold-producing" stone, the "philosopher's stone."
[2] Haiti.

come at the right *Spot*, yet he found his present Company too ill a Crew to be confided in.

§ 6. So *proper* was his Behaviour, that the best Noble Men in the Kingdom now admitted him into their Conversation; but yet he was opposed by powerful Enemies, that Clogg'd his Affairs with such Demurrages, and such *Disappointments*, as would have wholly Discouraged his Designs, if his Patience had not been *Invincible. He who can wait, hath what he desireth.* This his Indefatigable *Patience*, with a proportionable *Diligence*, at length overcame the Difficulties that had been thrown in his way; and prevailing with the Duke of *Albemarle*, and some other Persons of Quality, to fit him out, he set Sail for the *Fishing-Ground*, which had been so well *baited* half an Hundred Years before: And as he had already discovered his *Capacity for Business* in many considerable Actions, he now added unto those Discoveries, by not only *providing* all, but also by *inventing* many of the Instruments necessary to the prosecution of his intended *Fishery.* Captain *Phips* arriving with a Ship and a *Tender* at *Port de la Plata*, made a stout *Canoo* of a stately *Cotton-Tree*, so large as to carry Eight or Ten Oars, for the making of which *Periaga* (as they call it) he did, with the same industry that he did every thing else, employ his own *Hand* and *Adse*, and endure no little hardship, lying abroad in the Woods many Nights together. This *Periaga*, with the *Tender*, being Anchored at a place Convenient, the *Periaga* kept Busking to and again,[1] but could only discover a *Reef of Rising Shoals* there-

[1] Periaga is for piragua, a long narrow canoe, made of the hollowed trunk of a tree. "To busk to and again" meant, in nautical parlance, "to cruise about."

abouts, called, *The Boilers*, which Rising to be within
Two or Three Foot of the Surface of the Sea, were yet
so steep, that a Ship striking on them, would immediately sink down, who could say, *how many Fathom*
into the Ocean? Here they could get no other Pay
for their long *peeping* among the *Boilers*, but only such
as caused them to think upon returning to their Captain
with the *bad News* of their total Disappointment.
Nevertheless, as they were upon the Return, one of
the Men looking over the side of the *Periaga*, into the
calm Water, he spied a *Sea Feather*,[1] growing, as he
judged, out of a Rock; whereupon they had one of their
Indians to Dive and fetch this *Feather*, that they might
however carry home *something* with them, and make,
at least, as fair a *Triumph* as *Caligula*'s. The *Diver*
bringing up the *Feather*, brought therewithal a surprizing Story, That he perceived a Number of *Great Guns*
in the *Watry World* where he had found his *Feather;*
the *Report* of which *Great Guns* exceedingly astonished
the whole Company; and at once turned their *Despon-
dencies* for their ill success into *Assurances*, that they
had now lit upon the *true Spot* of Ground which they
had been looking for; and they were further confirmed
in these *Assurances*, when upon further Diving, the
Indian fetcht up a *Sow*, as they stil'd it, or a Lump
of Silver, worth perhaps Two or Three Hundred Pounds.
Upon this they prudently *Buoy'd* the place, that they
might readily find it again; and they went back unto
their Captain whom for some while they distressed
with nothing but such *Bad News*, as they formerly
thought they must have carried him: Nevertheless,
they so slipt in the Sow of Silver on one side under the
Table, where they were now sitting with the Captain,

[1] A kind of coral or polyp.

and hearing him express his Resolutions to wait still patiently upon the Providence of God under these Disappointments, that when he should look on one side he might see that *Odd Thing* before him. At last he *saw* it; seeing it, he cried out with some Agony, *Why? What is this? Whence comes this?* And then, with changed Countenances, they told him *how*, and *where* they got it: *Then, said he, Thanks be to God! We are made;* and so away they went, all hands to Work; wherein they had this one further piece of Remarkable Prosperity, that whereas if they had first fallen upon that part of the *Spanish Wreck*, where the Pieces of Eight had been stowed in Bags among the Ballast, they had seen a more laborious, and less enriching time of it: Now, most happily, they first fell upon that Room in the *Wreck* where the *Bullion* had been stored up; and they so prospered in this *New Fishery*, that in a little while they had, without the loss of any Man's Life, brought up *Thirty Two Tuns* of Silver; for it was now come to measuring of Silver by *Tuns*.[1] Besides which, one *Adderly* of *Providence*, who had formerly been very helpful to Captain *Phips* in the Search of this *Wreck*, did upon former Agreement meet him now with a little Vessel here; and *he*, with his few hands, took up about *Six Tuns* of Silver; whereof nevertheless he made so little use, that in a Year or Two he Died at *Bermudas*, and as I have heard, he ran *Distracted* some while before he Died. Thus did there once again come into the Light of the Sun, a Treasure which had been half an Hundred Years *groaning under the Waters:* And in this time there was grown upon the Plate a Crust

---

[1] "Tun" as a measure of gold meant 100,000 guilders, florins, etc. Whether Mather uses it in this sense here, or simply as equivalent to "ton," is not clear.

like *Limestone*, to the thickness of several Inches; which Crust being broken open by Irons contrived for that purpose, they knockt out whole Bushels of rusty Pieces of Eight which were grown thereinto. Besides that incredible Treasure of Plate in various Forms, thus fetch'd up, from Seven or Eight Fathom under Water, there were vast Riches of *Gold*, and *Pearls*, and *Jewels*, which they also lit upon; and indeed, for a more Comprehensive *Invoice*, I must but summarily say, *All that a* Spanish *Frigot uses to be enricht withal*. Thus did they continue *Fishing* till their Provisions failing them, 'twas time to be gone; but before they went, Captain *Phips* caused *Adderly* and his Folk to swear, That they would none of them Discover the Place of the *Wreck*, or come to the Place any more till the next Year, when he expected again to be there himself. And it was also Remarkable, that though the Sows came up still so fast, that on the very last Day of their being there, they took up *Twenty*, yet it was afterwards found, that they had in a manner wholly cleared that Room of the Ship where those *Massy things* were Stowed.

But there was one extraordinary Distress which Captain *Phips* now found himself plunged into: For his Men were come out with him upon Seamens Wages, at so much *per* Month; and when they saw such vast Litters of Silver *Sows* and *Pigs*, as they call them, come on Board them at the Captain's Call, they knew not how to bear it, that they should not *share* all among themselves, and be gone to lead *a short Life and a merry*, in a Climate where the Arrest of those that had hired them should not reach them. In this terrible Distress he made his Vows unto Almighty God, that if the Lord would carry him safe home to *England* with what *he* had now given him, *to suck of the Abundance of the Seas, and of the Treasures hid in the Sands*, he would for ever Devote himself unto the Interests of the Lord *Jesus Christ*, and of his People, especially in the *Country* which he did himself Originally belong unto. And he then used all the obliging *Arts* imaginable to make his Men true unto him, especially by assuring them, that besides their *Wages*, they should have ample *Requitals* made unto them; which if the rest of his Employers would not agree unto, he would himself distribute his *own share* among them. Relying upon the Word of One whom they had ever found worthy of their *Love*, and of their *Trust*, they declared themselves *Content:* But still keeping a most careful Eye upon them, he hastned back for *England* with as much *Money* as he thought he could then safely *Trust* his Vessel withal; not counting it safe to supply himself with necessary Provisions at any nearer Port, and so return unto the *Wreck*, by which delays he wisely feared lest all might be lost, more ways than one. Though he also left so much behind him, that many from divers Parts made very considerable Voyages of *Gleanings* after his *Harvest:* Which came to pass by certain *Bermudians*, compelling of *Adderly's* Boy, whom they *spirited* away with them, to tell them the exact place where the *Wreck* was to be found. Captain *Phips* now coming up to *London* in the Year 1687. with near *Three Hundred Thousand Pounds Sterling* aboard him, did acquit himself with such an Exemplary Honesty, that partly by his fulfilling his Assurances to the Seamen, and partly by his exact and punctual Care to have his Employers defrauded of nothing that might conscienciously belong unto them, he had less than *Sixteen Thousand Pounds* left unto himself: As an acknowledgment of which

Honesty in him, the Duke of *Albemarle* made unto his Wife, whom he never saw, a Present of a *Golden Cup*, near a Thousand Pound in value. The Character of an *Honest Man* he had so merited in the whole Course of his Life, and especially in this last act of it, that this, in Conjunction with his other serviceable Qualities, procured him the Favours of the Greatest Persons in the Nation; and *he that had been so diligent in his Business, must now stand before Kings, and not stand before mean Men.* There were indeed certain *mean Men*, if base, little, dirty Tricks, will entitle Men to Meanness, who urged the King to seize his *whole Cargo*, instead of the Tenths, upon his first Arrival; on this pretence, that he had not been rightly inform'd of the *True state of the Case*, when he Granted the *Patent*, under the Protection whereof these *particular Men* had made themselves Masters of all this Mighty Treasure; but the King replied, That he had been *rightly informed* by Captain *Phips* of the whole Matter, as it now proved; and that it was the Slanders of one then present, which had, unto his Damnage, hindred him from hearkning to the Information: Wherefore he would give them, he said, no Disturbance; they might keep what they had got; but Captain *Phips*, he saw, was a Person of that Honesty, Fidelity and Ability, that he should not want his Countenance. Accordingly the King, in Consideration of the Service done by him, in bringing such a Treasure into the Nation, conferr'd upon him the Honour of *Knighthood;* and if we now reckon him, *A Knight of the Golden Fleece*, the Stile[1] might pretend unto some Circumstances that would justifie it. Or call him, if you please, *The Knight of Honesty;* for it was *Honesty* with *Industry* that raised him; and he

---

[1] *I. e.*, "title."

became a Mighty River, without the running in of Muddy Water to make him so. Reader, now make a Pause, and behold *One Raised by God!*

§ 7. I am willing to Employ the Testimonies of others, as much as may be, to support the Credit of my History: And therefore, as I have hitherto related no more than what there are others *Others* [*sic*] enough to avouch; thus I shall chuse the Words of an Ingenious Person Printed at *London* some Years ago, to express the Sum of what remains, whose Words are these; 'It has always been Sir *William Phips*'s Disposition 'to seek the *Wealth* of his People with as great Zeal 'and Unweariedness, as our *Publicans* use to seek their '*Loss* and *Ruin*. At first it seems they were in hopes 'to gain this Gentleman to their Party, as thinking 'him *Good Natur'd*, and easie to be flattered out of 'his Understanding; and the more, because they had 'the advantage of some, no very good, Treatment that 'Sir *William* had formerly met with from the People 'and Government of *New-England*. But Sir *William* 'soon shewed them, that what they expected would 'be his *Temptation* to lead them into their *little Tricks*, 'he embraced as a Glorious Opportunity to shew his '*Generosity* and *Greatness of Mind;* for, in Imitation of 'the Greatest Worthies that have ever been, he rather 'chose to join in the Defence of his Country, with 'some Persons who formerly were none of his Friends, 'than become the Head of a *Faction*, to its Ruin and 'Desolation. It seems this Noble Disposition of Sir '*William*, joined with that Capacity and good Success 'wherewith he hath been attended, in Raising himself 'by such an Occasion, as it may be, all things considered, 'has *never happened to any before him*, makes these 'Men apprehensive;——And it must needs heighten 'their trouble to see, that he neither hath, nor doth 'spare himself, nor any thing that is near and dear 'unto him, in promoting the Good of his Native Country.

When Sir *William Phips* was *per ardua & aspera*,[1] thus raised into an *Higher Orb*, it might easily be thought that he could not be without Charming Temptations to take the *way on the left hand*. But as the Grace of God kept him in the midst of none of the strictest Company, unto which his Affairs daily led him, from abandoning himself to the lewd Vices of *Gaming*, *Drinking*, *Swearing* and *Whoring*, which the Men *that made* England *to Sin*, debauch'd so many of the Gentry into, and he deserved the Salutations of the *Roman* Poet:

Cum Tu, inter scabiem tantam, & Contagia Lucri,
Nil parvum sapias, & adhuc Sublimia cures:[2]

Thus he was worthy to pass among the Instances of *Heroick Vertue* for that *Humility* that still Adorned him: He was *Raised*, and though he prudently accommodated himself to the *Quality* whereto he was now *Raised*, yet none could perceive him to be *Lifted up*. Or, if this were not *Heroick*, yet I will Relate one Thing more of him that must certainly be accounted so. He had in his own Country of *New-England* met with *Provocations* that were enough to have Alienated any Man Living, that had no more than *Flesh and Blood* in him, from the Service of it; and some that were Enemies to that Country, now lay hard at him to join

[1] "Through difficulties and hardships."
[2] "You, amid so great a leprosy and contagion of avarice, are wise, and seek higher things."

with them in their Endeavours to Ravish away their
Ancient Liberties.   But this *Gentleman* had studied
another way to *Revenge* himself upon his Country, and
that was to serve it in all *its* Interests, with all of *his*, even
with his *Estate*, his *Time*, his *Care*, his *Friends*, and his
very *Life!* The old *Heathen* Virtue of PIETAS IN
PATRIAM, or *LOVE TO ONES COUNTRY*, he
turned into *Christian;* and so notably exemplified it,
in all the Rest of his *Life*, that it will be an Essential
Thread which is to be now interwoven into all that
remains of his *History*, and his *Character*.   Accordingly
though he had the Offers of a very Gainful Place among
the *Commissioners of the Navy*, with many other Invita-
tions to settle himself in *England*, nothing but a Return
to *New-England* would content him.   And whereas the
Charters of *New-England* being taken away, there was
a Governour Imposed upon the Territories with as
Arbitrary and as *Treasonable* a *Commission*, perhaps,
as ever was heard of; a *Commission*, by which the
Governour, with Three or Four more, none of whom
were chosen by the People, had Power to make what
Laws they would, and Levy *Taxes*, according to their
own Humours, upon the People; and he himself had
Power to send the best Men in the Land more than
Ten Thousand Miles out of it, as he pleased: And in
the Execution of his Power, the Country was every Day
suffering Intollerable *Invasions* upon their *Proprieties*,
yea, and the Lives of the best Men in the Territory
began to be practised upon: Sir *William Phips* applied
himself to Consider what was the most significant
Thing that could be done by him for that poor People
in their present Circumstances.   Indeed, when King
James offered, as he did, unto Sir *William Phips* an
Opportunity to Ask what he pleased of him, Sir *William*

Generously prayed for nothing but *this*, *That* New-England *might have its lost Priviledges Restored*. The King then Replied, *Any Thing but that!* Whereupon he set himself to Consider what was the *next Thing* that he might ask for the Service, not of himself, but of his *Country*. The Result of his Consideration was, That by Petition to the King, he Obtained, with expence of some Hundreds of *Guinea's*, a *Patent*, which constituted him *The High Sheriff of that Country;*[1] hoping, by his Deputies in that Office, to supply the Country still with Consciencious Juries, which was the only Method that the *New-Englanders* had left them to secure any thing that was Dear unto them. Furnished with this *Patent*, after he had, in Company with Sir *John Narborough*, made a Second Visit unto the *Wreck*, (not so advantageous as the former for a Reason already mentioned) in his way he Returned unto *New-England*, in the Summer of the Year 1688. able, after Five Years Absence, to Entertain his Lady with some Accomplishment of his Predictions; and then Built himself a *Fair Brick House* in the very *place* which we foretold, the Reader can tell how many *Sections* ago. But the *Infamous Government* then Rampant there, found a way wholly to put by the Execution of this *Patent;* yea, he was like to have had his *Person* Assassinated in the Face of the Sun, before his own Door, which with some further Designs then in his Mind, caused him within a few Weeks to take another Voyage for *England*.

§ 8. It would require a long Summers-Day to Relate the Miseries which were come, and coming in upon poor *New-England*, by reason of the *Arbitrary Government* then imposed on them; a *Government* wherein, as old *Wendover* says of the Time, when *Stran-*

[1] Provost Marshal-general of New England.

gers were domineering over *Subjects* in *England, Judicia committebantur Injustis, Leges Exlegibus, Pax Discordantibus, Justitia Injuriosis;*[1] and *Foxes* were made the Administrators of Justice to the *Poultrey;* yet some *Abridgment* of them is necessary for the better understanding of the Matters yet before us. Now to make this *Abridgment* Impartial, I shall only have Recourse unto a little Book, Printed at *London,* under the Title of *The Revolution of* New-England *Justified;* wherein we have a *Narrative of the Grievances* under the Male Administrations of that Government, written and signed by the chief Gentlemen of the *Governour's Council;* together with the *Sworn Testimonies* of many good Men, to prove the several Articles of the *Declaration,* which the *New-Englanders* published against their Oppressors. It is in that Book demonstrated.[2]

That the Governour neglecting the greater Number of his *Council,* did Adhere principally to the Advice of a *few Strangers,* who were Persons without any *Interest* in the Country, but of declared *Prejudice* against it, and had plainly laid their *Designs* to make an Unreasonable *Profit* of the poor People: And *four* or *five* Persons had the absolute Rule *over a Territory, the most Considerable of any belonging to the Crown.*

That when *Laws* were proposed in the *Council,* tho' the *Major* part at any time Dissented from them, yet if the Governour were positive, there was no fair *Counting* the Number of *Councellors* Consenting, or Dissenting, but the Laws were immediately *Engrossed, Published* and *Executed.*

---

[1] "Judgments were entrusted to the unjust, laws to outlaws, peace to quarrelers, and justice to wrongdoers." Wendover was Roger de Wendover, historian, who died in 1236.

[2] A colon instead of a period here makes the sense clear.

That this *Junto* made a *Law*, which prohibited the Inhabitants of any *Town* to meet about their *Town-Affairs* above *once* in a Year; for fear, you must Note, of their having any opportunity to Complain of *Grievances*.

That they made another *Law*, requiring all Masters of *Vessels*, even *Shallops* and *Woodboats*,[1] to give *Security*, that no Man should be Transported in them, except his Name had been so many Days posted up: Whereby the Pockets of a few *Leeches* had been filled with *Fees*, but the whole Trade of the Country destroyed; and all Attempts to obtain a *Redress* of these Things obstructed; and when this *Act* had been strenuously opposed in Council at *Boston*, they carried it as far as *New-York*, where a Crew of them enacted it.

That without any *Assembly*, they Levied on the People a *Penny* in the Pound of all their *Estates*, and Twenty-pence *per* Head, as *Poll-money*, with a Penny in the Pound for *Goods* Imported, besides a Vast *Excise* on Wine; Rum; and other *Liquors*.

That when among the Inhabitants of *Ispwich*, some of the Principal Persons modestly gave Reasons why they could not chuse a *Commissioner* to *Tax* the Town, until the King should first be Petitioned for the Liberty of an *Assembly*, they were committed unto *Goal* for it, as an *High Misdemeanour*, and were denied an *Habeas Corpus*, and were dragg'd many Miles out of their own County to answer it at a Court in *Boston;* where *Jurors* were pickt for the Turn, that were not *Freeholders*, nay, that were meer *Sojourners;* and when the Prisoners pleaded the Priviledges of *English-men, That they should not be Taxed without their own consent;* they were told, *That those things would not follow them*

---

[1] Small boats used for transporting wood.

to the ends of the Earth: As it had been before told them in *open Council,* no one in the Council contradicting it, *You have no more Priviledges left you, but this, that you are not bought and sold for Slaves:* And in fine, they were all *Fined* severely, and laid under great *Bonds* for their good Behaviour; besides all which, the *hungry Officers* extorted *Fees* from them that amounted unto an Hundred and Threescore Pounds; whereas in *England,* upon the like Prosecution, the *Fees* would not have been Ten Pounds in all. After which fashion the *Townsmen* of many other Places were also served.

That these Men giving out, That the *Charters* being lost, all the Title that the People had unto their Lands was lost with them; they began to *compel* the People everywhere to take *Patents* for their Lands: And accordingly *Writs of Intrusion* were issued out against the chief Gentlemen in the Territory, by the Terror whereof, many were actually driven to Petition for *Patents,* that they might quietly enjoy the Lands that had been Fifty or Sixty Years in their Possession; but for these *Patents* there were such exorbitant Prices demanded, that Fifty Pounds could not purchase for its Owner an Estate not worth *Two Hundred,* nor could all the Money and Moveables in the Territory have defrayed the Charges of *Patenting* the Lands at the Hands of these *Crocodiles:* Besides the considerable *Quit-Rents* for the King. Yea, the Governour caused the Lands of *particular Persons* to be measured out, and given to his Creatures: And some of his Council Petitioned for the *Commons* belonging to several Towns; and the *Agents* of the Towns going to get a *voluntary Subscription* of the Inhabitants to maintain their Title at Law, they have been dragg'd Forty or Fifty Miles to answer as Criminals at the next Assizes;

the Officers in the mean time extorting Three Pounds *per* Man for fetching 'them.

That if these *Harpies*, at any time, were a little *out of Money*, they found ways to Imprison the *best Men* in the Country; and there appeared not the least *Information* of any Crime exhibited against them, yet they were put unto Intollerable Expences by these Greedy Oppressors, and the Benefit of an *Habeas Corpus* not allowed unto them.

That packt and pickt *Juries* were commonly made use of, when under a pretended *Form of Law*, the Trouble of some Honest and Worthy Men was aimed at; and these also were hurried out of their own Counties to be tried, when *Juries* for the Turn were not like to be found there. The *Greatest Rigour* being used still towards the *soberest sort* of People, whilst in the mean time the most horrid Enormities in the World, committed by Others, were overlook'd.

That the publick Ministry of the Gospel, and all *Schools of Learning*, were discountenanced unto the Utmost.

And several more such abominable things, too notorious to be denied, even by a *Randolphian*[1] Impudence it self, are in that Book proved against that *unhappy Government*. Nor did that most Ancient Set of the *Phœnician Shepherds*, who scrued the Government of *Egypt* into their Hands, as old *Manethon*[2] tells us, by their *Villanies*, during the Reigns of those Tyrants, make a *Shepherd* more of an *Abomination* to the *Egyptians* in all after Ages, than these *Wolves* under the Name of *Shepherds* have made the Remem-

[1] Edward Randolph, an English official in the colonies at the time, was cordially hated by Mather and by many of the New Englanders.
[2] Egyptian historian, third century B. C.

brance of their *French Government* [1] an *Abomination* to all Posterity among the *New-Englanders:* A *Government*, for which, now, Reader, as fast as thou wilt, get ready this Epitaph:

Nulla quæsita Scelere Potentia diuturna. [2]

It was under the Resentments of these Things that Sir *William Phips* returned into *England* in the Year 1688. In which *Twice-Wonderful-Year* such a *Revolution* was wonderfully accomplished upon the whole Government of the *English* Nation, that *New-England*, which had been a *Specimen* of what the whole Nation was to look for, might justly hope for a share in the General Deliverance. Upon this Occasion Sir *William* offered his best Assistances unto that Eminent Person, who a little before this Revolution betook himself unto *White-Hall*, that he might there lay hold on all Opportunities to procure some Relief unto the Oppressions of that afflicted Country. But seeing the *New-English* Affairs in so able an Hand, he thought the best Stage of *Action* for him would now be *New-England* it self; and so with certain Instructions from none of the least considerable Persons at *White-Hall*, what Service to do for his Country, in the Spring of the Year 1689. he hastened back unto it. Before he left *London*, a Messenger from the Abdicated King tender'd him the Government of *New-England*, if he would accept it: But as that excellent Attorney General, Sir *William Jones*, when it was proposed that the *Plantations* might be Governed without *Assemblies*, told the King, *That*

---

[1] The colonists fondly believed that Andros and his followers were secretly in league with the French against England.

[2] "No power achieved by wrongdoing is lasting."

*he could no more Grant a Commission to levy Money on
his Subjects there, without their consent by an Assembly,
than they could Discharge themselves from their Allegiance
to the* English *Crown.* So Sir *William Phips* thought it
his Duty to refuse a *Government without an Assembly,*
as a thing that was Treason in the very *Essence* of it;
and instead of Petitioning the succeeding Princes, that
his *Patent* for *High Sheriff* might be rendred Effectual,
he joined in Petitions, that *New-England* might have
its own old *Patent* so Restored, as to render ineffectual
that, and all other Grants that might cut short any of
its Ancient Priviledges. But when Sir *William* arrived
at *New-England,* he found a new Face of things; for
about an Hundred Indians in the *Eastern Parts* of the
Country, had unaccountably begun a War upon the
English in *July,* 1688. and though the Governour then
in the *Western Parts* had immediate Advice of it, yet
he not only delayed and neglected all that was necessary
for the *Publick Defence,* but also when he at last returned, he manifested a most Furious Displeasure
against those of the Council, and all others that had
forwarded any one thing for the security of the Inhabitants; while at the same time he dispatched some
of his Creatures upon secret Errands unto *Canada,*
and set at Liberty some of the most Murderous *Indians*
which the *English* had seized upon.

This Conduct of the Governour, which is in a *Printed*
Remonstrance of some of the best Gentlemen in the
Council complained of, did extreamly dissatisfie the
Suspicious People: Who were doubtless more extream
in some of their *Suspicions,* than there was any *real
Occasion* for: But the Governour at length raised an
Army of a *Thousand English* to Conquer this *Hundred
Indians;* and this Army, whereof some of the chief

Commanders were *Papists*, underwent the Fatigues
of a long and a cold Winter, in the most *Caucasæan*
Regions of the Territory, till, without the killing of
One Indian, there were more of the poor People killed,
than they had Enemies there alive! This added not
a little to the Dissatisfaction of the People, and it
would much more have done so, if they had seen what
the World had not *yet* seen of the *Suggestions* made
by the *Irish Catholicks* unto the Late King, published
in the Year 1691. in the *Account of the State of the
Protestants in* Ireland, Licensed by the Earl of *Nottingham*, whereof one Article runs in these Express Terms,
That if any of the Irish *cannot have their Lands in Specie,
but Money in Lieu, some of them may Transport themselves into* America, *possibly near* New-England, *to
check the growing* Independants *of that Country:* Or if
they had seen what was afterwards seen in a Letter
from K. *James* to His *Holiness*, (as they stile his *Foolish-
ness*) the Pope of *Rome;* that it was his full Purpose
to have set up *Roman-Catholick* Religion in the *English*
Plantations of *America:* Tho' after all, there is Cause
to think that there was more made of the *Suspicions*
then flying like Wild-Fire about the Country, than
a strong *Charity* would have Countenanced. When
the People were under these *Frights*, they had got by
the Edges a little Intimation of the then Prince of
Orange's glorious Undertaking to deliver *England* from
the *Feared* Evils, which were already *felt* by *New-England;* but when the Person who brought over a Copy of
the Prince's *Declaration* was Imprisoned for bringing
into the Country a *Treasonable Paper*, and the Govern-
nour, by his Proclamation, required all Persons to
use their *utmost Endeavours to hinder* the *Landing* of
any whom the Prince might send thither, *this* put

them almost out of Patience. And one thing that plunged the more Considerate Persons in the Territory into uneasie thoughts, was the *Faulty Action* of some Soldiers, who upon the Common *Suspicions*, deserted their *Stations* in the Army, and caused their Friends to gather together here and there in little Bodies, to protect from the Demands of the Governour their poor Children and Brethren, whom they thought bound for a *Bloody Sacrifice*: And there were also belonging to the *Rose-Frigot* some that buzz'd surprizing Stories about *Boston*, of many Mischiefs to be thence expected. Wherefore, some of the Principal Gentlemen in *Boston* consulting what was to be done in this Extraordinary Juncture, They all agreed that they would, if it were possible, extinguish all Essays in the People towards an *Insurrection*, in daily Hopes of Orders from *England* for their Safety: But that if the Country People by any violent Motions push'd the Matter on so far, as to make a *Revolution* unavoidable, then to prevent the shedding of *Blood* by an ungoverned *Mobile*, some of the Gentlemen present should appear at the Head of the *Action* with a *Declaration* accordingly prepared. By the *Eighteenth* of *April*, 1689. Things were pushed on so far by the People, that certain Persons first Seized the Captain of the *Frigot*, and the Rumor thereof running like Lightning through *Boston*, the whole Town was immediately in Arms, with the most *Unanimous Resolution* perhaps that ever was known to have Inspir'd any People. They then seized those Wretched Men, who by their innumerable *Extortions* and *Abuses* had made themselves the Objects of *Universal Hatred;* not giving over till the *Governour* himself was become their *Prisoner:* The whole *Action* being managed without the least *Bloodshed* or *Plunder,* and with as much *Order* as ever attended any *Tumult,* it may be, in the World. Thus did the *New-Englanders* assert their Title to the Common Rights of *Englishmen;* and except the Plantations are willing to Degenerate from the Temper of True *Englishmen,* or except the *Revolution* of the whole *English* Nation be condemned, their *Action* must so far be justified. On their late *Oppressors,* now under just Confinement, they took no other Satisfaction, but sent them over unto *White-Hall* for the Justice of the King and Parliament. And when the Day for the *Anniversary Election,* by their vacated *Charter,* drew near, they had many Debates into what Form they should cast the Government, which was till then Administred by a *Committee for the Conservation of the Peace,* composed of Gentlemen whose *Hap* it was to appear in the Head of the late *Action;* but their Debates Issued in this Conclusion; That the *Governour* and *Magistrates,* which were in power before the late *Usurpation,* should Resume their Places, and apply themselves unto the *Conservation of the Peace,* and put forth what *Acts of Government* the Emergencies might make needful for them, and thus to wait for further Directions from the Authority of *England.* So was there Accomplished a *Revolution* which delivered *New-England* from grievous Oppressions, and which was most graciously Accepted by the *King* and *Queen,* when it was Reported unto their Majesties. But there were new Matters for Sir *William Phips,* in a little while, now to think upon.

§ 9. Behold the great things which were done by the Sovereign God, for a Person once as little in his *own Eyes* as in *other Mens.* All the Returns which he had hitherto made unto the *God of his Mercies,* were but Preliminaries to what remain to be related. It has been the Custom in the Churches of *New-England*, still to expect from such Persons as they admitted unto constant Communion with them, that they do not only Publickly and Solemnly *Declare* their *Consent* unto the *Covenant of Grace*, and particularly to those Duties of it, wherein a *Particular Church-State* is more immediately concerned, but also first relate unto the *Pastors*, and by them unto the *Brethren*, the special Impressions which the *Grace* of God has made upon their Souls in bringing them to this *Consent*. By this *Custom* and *Caution*, though they cannot keep *Hypocrites* from their Sacred Fellowship, yet they go as far as they can, to render and preserve themselves *Churches of Saints*, and they do further very much *Edifie one another*. When Sir *William Phips* was now returned unto his *own House*, be began to bethink himself, like *David*, concerning the *House* of the *God* who had surrounded him with so many Favours in *his own;* and accordingly he applied himself unto the *North Church* in *Boston*,[1] that with his open Profession of his Hearty Subjection to the *Gospel* of the Lord Jesus Christ, he might have the *Ordinances* and the *Priviledges* of the *Gospel* added unto his other Enjoyments. One thing that quickned his Resolution to do what might be in this Matter expected from him, was a Passage which he heard from a Minister Preaching on the Title of the *Fifty-First* Psalm: *To make a publick and an open Profession of Repentance, is a thing not misbecoming the greatest Man alive. It is an Honour to be found among the Repenting People of God, though they be in Circumstances never so full of Suffering. A Famous Knight going with other Christians to be Crowned with Martyr-*

---

[1] The Second Church of Boston, of which Cotton and Increase Mather were ministers.

dom, observed, That his Fellow-Sufferers were in Chains, from which the Sacrificers had, because of his Quality, excus'd him; whereupon he demanded, that he might wear Chains as well as they. For, *said he,* I would be a Knight of that Order too; *There is among our selves a Repenting People of God, who by their Confessions at their Admissions to his Table, do signalize their being so; and thanks be to God that we have so little of Suffering in our Circumstances. But if any Man count himself grown too big to be a* Knight of that Order, *the Lord Jesus Christ himself will one Day be ashamed of that Man!* Upon this Excitation, Sir *William Phips* made his Address unto a *Congregational-Church,* and he had therein one thing to propound unto himself, which few Persons of his Age, so well satisfied in *Infant-Baptism* as he was, have then to ask for. Indeed, in the Primitive Times, although the *Lawfulness* of *Infant-Baptism,* or the Precept and Pattern of *Scripture* for it, was never so much as once made a Question, yet we find *Baptism* was frequently delayed by Persons upon several superstitious and unreasonable Accounts, against which we have such Fathers as *Gregory Nazianzen, Gregory Nyssen, Basil, Chrysostom, Ambrose,* and others, employing a variety of Argument. But Sir *William Phips* had hitherto delayed his *Baptism,* because the Years of his Childhood were spent where there was no settled Minister, and therefore he was now not only willing to attain a good Satisfaction of his own Internal and Practical *Christianity,* before his receiving that *Mark* thereof, but he was also willing to receive it among those *Christians* that seemed most sensible of the *Bonds* which it laid them under. Offering himself therefore, first unto the *Baptism,* and then unto the *Supper* of the Lord, he presented unto the

Pastor of the Church, with his own *Hand-Writing*, the following *Instrument;* which because of the Exemplary *Devotion* therein expressed, and the Remarkable *History* which it gives of several Occurrences in his Life, I will here faithfully Transcribe it, without adding so much as one Word unto it.

'The first of God's making me sensible of my *Sins,*
'was in the Year 1674. by hearing your Father Preach
'concerning, *The Day of Trouble near.*[1] It pleased
'Almighty God to smite me with a deep Sence of my
'miserable Condition, who had lived until then in the
'World, and had *done nothing for God.* I did then
'begin to think *what I should do to be saved?* And did
'bewail my *Youthful Days,* which I had spent *in vain:*
'I did think that I would begin to mind the *things of*
'*God.* Being then some time under your Father's
'Ministry, much troubled with my *Burden,* but think-
'ing on that Scripture, *Come unto me, you that are*
'*weary and heavy Laden, and I will give you Rest;* I
'had some thoughts of drawing as near to the Com-
'munion of the Lord *Jesus* as I could; but the Ruins
'which the *Indian Wars* brought on my Affairs, and
'the Entanglements which my following the *Sea* laid
'upon me, hindred my pursuing the Welfare of my own
'Soul as I ought to have done. At length God was
'pleased to smile upon my *Outward Concerns.* The
'various *Providences,* both Merciful and Afflictive,
'which attended me in my Travels, were sanctified unto
'me, to make me *Acknowledge God in all my Ways.*
'I have divers Times been in danger of my *Life,* and
'I have been brought to see that I owe my *Life* to him
'that has given a *Life* so often to me: I thank God,
'he hath brought me to see my self altogether unhappy,

[1] Increase Mather preached, and later printed, this sermon.

'without an Interest in the Lord Jesus Christ, and to
'close heartily with him, desiring him to Execute *All*
'*his Offices* on my Behalf. I have now, for some time,
'been under serious *Resolutions*, that I would avoid
'whatever I should know to be Displeasing unto God,
'and that I would *Serve him all the Days of my Life.*
'I believe *no Man will Repent the Service of such a*
'*Master.* I find my self *unable* to keep such *Resolutions*,
'but my serious *Prayers* are to the Most High, that
'*he* would *enable* me. God hath done so much for me,
'that I am sensible I owe my self to him; *To him would*
'*I give my self, and all that he has given to me.* I can't
'express his Mercies to me. But as soon as ever God
'had smiled upon me with a Turn of my Affairs, I had
'laid my self under the VOWS of the Lord, *That I*
'*would set my self to serve his People, and Churches here,*
'*unto the utmost of my Capacity.* I have had great
'Offers made me in *England;* but the Churches of *New-*
'*England* were those which my Heart was most set
'upon. I knew, *That if God had a People any where, it*
'*was here:* And I *Resolved to rise and fall with them;*
'neglecting very great Advantages for my Worldly
'Interest, that I might come and enjoy the Ordinances
'of the Lord Jesus here. It has been my Trouble, that
'since I came Home I have made no more haste to get
'into the *House of God*, where *I desire to be:* Especially
'having heard so much about the *Evil* of that Omission.
'I can do little for God, but I desire to wait upon him
'in his Ordinances, and to live to his Honour and Glory.
'My being Born in a part of the Country, where I
'had not in my *Infancy* enjoyed the *First Sacrament*
'of the *New-Testament*, has been something of a *Stum-*
'*bling-Block* unto me. But though I have had Profers
'of *Baptism* elsewhere made unto me, I resolved rather

'to defer it, until I might enjoy it in the Communion
'of these Churches; and I have had awful Impressions
'from those Words of the Lord Jesus in *Matth*. 8. 38.
'*Whosoever shall be ashamed of me, and of my Words,*
'*of him also shall the Son of Man be ashamed.* When
'God had blessed me with something of the World, I
'had no Trouble so great as this, *Lest it should not be*
'*in Mercy;* and I trembled at nothing more than being
'*put off with a Portion here.* That I may make sure
'of *better things,* I now offer my self unto the Communion
'of this Church of the Lord JESUS.

Accordingly on *March* 23. 1690.[1] after he had in
the Congregation of *North-Boston* given himself up,
first unto the Lord, and then unto his People, he was
Baptized, and so received into the *Communion* of the
Faithful there.

§ 10. Several times, about, before and after *this
time,* did I hear him express himself unto this purpose:
*I have no need at all to look after any further Advantages
for my self in this World; I may sit still at Home, if I
will, and enjoy my Ease for the rest of my Life; but I
believe that I should offend God in my doing so: For I am
now in the Prime of my Age and Strength, and, I
thank God, I can undergo Hardship: He only knows
how long I have to live; but I think 'tis my Duty to venture
my Life in doing of good, before an useless Old Age
comes upon me: Wherefore I will now expose my self
while I am able, and as far as I am able, for the Service
of my Country: I was Born for others, as well as my self.*
I say, many a time have I heard him so express himself: And agreeable to this Generous *Disposition* and
Resolution was all the rest of his Life. About this time

[1] The Church Records, as copied by Mr. Robbins in his *History
of the Second Church,* say March 8, 1690.

New-England was miserably *Briar'd* in the Perplexities of an *Indian War;* and the Salvages, in the *East* part of the Country, issuing out from their inaccessible *Swamps*, had for many Months made their Cruel Depredations upon the poor *English* Planters, and surprized many of the Plantations on the Frontiers, into Ruin. The *New-Englanders* found, that while they continued only on the *Defensive* part, their *People* were thinned, and their *Treasures* wasted, without any hopes of seeing a Period put unto the *Indian Tragedies;* nor could an Army greater than *Xerxes*'s have easily come at the seemingly contemptible handful of *Tawnies*[1] which made all this Disturbance; or, *Tamerlain*, the greatest Conqueror that ever the World saw, have made it a Business of no *Trouble* to have *Conquered* them: They found, that they were like to make no Weapons reach their Enswamped Adversaries, except Mr. *Milton* could have shown them how

> *To have pluckt up the Hills with all their Load,*
> *Rocks, Waters, Woods, and by their shaggy tops,*
> *Up-lifting, bore them in their Hands, therewith*
> *The Rebel Host to've over-whelm'd——*[2]

So it was thought that the *English* Subjects, in these Regions of *America*, might very properly take this occasion to make an attempt upon the *French*, and by reducing them under the *English* Government, put an Eternal Period at once unto all their Troubles from the *Frenchified Pagans*. This was a Motion urged by Sir *William Phips* unto the General Court of the *Massachuset-Colony;* and he then made unto the Court

[1] A name for the Indians, because of their "tawny" skins.
[2] Paraphrased from *Paradise Lost*, vi, 643–47.

a brave *Offer* of his own Person and Estate, for the Service of the Publick in their present Extremity, as far as they should see Cause to make use thereof. Whereupon they made a *First Essay* against the *French*, by sending a Naval Force, with about Seven Hundred Men, under the Conduct of Sir *William Phips*, against *L'Acady*[1] and *Nova Scotia;* of which Action we shall give only this General and Summary Account; that Sir *William Phips* set Sail from *Nantascot, April* 28. 1690. Arriving at *Port-Royal, May* 11. and had the Fort quickly Surrender'd into his Hands by the *French* Enemy, who despaired of holding out against him. He then took Possession of that Province for the *English* Crown, and having Demolished the Fort, and sent away the Garrison, Administred unto the Planters an *Oath of Allegiance* to King *William* and Queen *Mary*, he left what Order he thought convenient for the Government of the Place, until further Order should be taken by the Governour and Council of the *Massachuset*-Colony, unto whom he returned *May* 30. with an acceptable Account of his Expedition, and accepted a Place among the *Magistrates* of that Colony, to which the *Free-Men* had chosen him at their *Anniversary Election* Two Days before.

Thus the Country, once given by King *James* the First unto Sir *William Alexander*, was now by another Sir *William* recovered out of the Hands of the *French*, who had afterwards got the Possession of it; and there was added unto the *English Empire*, a Territory, whereof no Man can Read Monsieur *Denys*'s *Description Geographique & Historique des Costes de l'Amerique Septentrionale*,[2] but he must reckon the

---

[1] Acadie or L'Acadie.

[2] This book by Nicolas Denys, 1598–1688, was published in 1672.

Conquest of a Region so Improvable, for *Lumber*, for *Fishing*, for *Mines*, and for *Furrs*, a very considerable *Service.*, But if a smaller *Service* has, e'er now, ever merited a *Knighthood*, Sir *William* was willing to Repeat his Merits by Actions of the greatest *Service* possible:

Nil Actum credens, si quid superesset agendum.[1]

§ 11. The Addition of this *French* Colony to the *English* Dominion, was no more than a *little step* towards a *greater Action*, which was first in the Design of Sir *William Phips*, and which was, indeed, the *greatest Action* that ever the *New-Englanders* Attempted. There was a time when the *Philistines* had made some Inroads and Assaults from the *Northward*, upon the Skirts of *Goshen*, where the *Israelites* had a Residence, before their coming out of *Egypt*. The *Israelites*, and especially that Active Colony of the *Ephraimites*, were willing to Revenge these Injuries upon their wicked Neighbours; they presumed themselves Powerful and Numerous enough to Encounter the *Canaanites*, even in their own Country; and they formed a brisk *Expedition*, but came off unhappy Losers in it; the *Jewish Rabbins* tell us, they lost no less than *Eight Thousand* Men. The *Time* was not yet come; there was more *Haste* than good *Speed* in the Attempt; they were not enough concerned for the *Counsel* and *Presence* of God in the Undertaking; they mainly propounded the *Plunder* to be got among a People, whose Trade was that wherewith *Beasts* enriched them; so the business miscarried. This History the Psalmist going to recite, says, *I will utter dark Sayings of old.* Now that what befel Sir *William Phips*, with his whole

[1] "Thinking nothing done, if anything remained to be done."

Country of *New-England*, may not be almost forgotten among *the dark Sayings of old*, I will here give the true Report of a very memorable Matter.

It was *Canada* that was the chief Source of *New-England*'s Miseries. *There* was the main Strength of the *French; there* the *Indians* were mostly supplied with Ammunition; *thence* Issued Parties of Men, who uniting with the Salvages, barbarously murdered many Innocent *New-Englanders*, without any Provocation on the *New-English* part, except this, that *New-England* had Proclaimed King *William* and Q. *Mary*, which they said were *Usurpers;* and as *Cato* could make no Speech in the Senate without that Conclusion, *Delenda est Carthago;*[1] so it was the general Conclusion of all that Argued sensibly about the safety of that Country, *Canada must be Reduced.* It then became the con-curring Resolution of all *New-England*, with *New-York*, to make a Vigorous Attack upon *Canada* at once, both by Sea and Land.

And a Fleet was accordingly fitted out from *Boston*, under the Command of Sir *William Phips*, to fall upon *Quebeque*, the chief City of *Canada*. They waited until *August* for some Stores of War from *England*, whither they had sent for that purpose early in the Spring; but none at last arriving, and the Season of the Year being so far spent, Sir *William* could not, without many Discouragements upon his Mind, proceed in a Voyage, for which he found himself so poorly provided. How-ever, the Ships being taken up, and the Men on Board, his usual Courage would not permit him to Desist from the Enterprize; but he set Sail from *Hull* near *Boston*, *August* 9. 1690. with a Fleet of *Thirty Two* Ships and Tenders; whereof one, called *the Six Friends*, carrying

[1] "Carthage must be destroyed."

Forty Four great Guns, and Two Hundred Men, was *Admiral.* Sir *William* dividing the Fleet into several Squadrons, whereof there was *the Six Friends,* Captain *Gregory Sugars* Commander, with Eleven more of the Admiral's Squadron, of which one was also a Capital Ship, namely, *The John and Thomas,* Captain *Thomas Carter* Commander; of the *Vice-Admirals,* the *Swan,* Captain *Thomas Gilbert* Commander, with Nine more; of the *Rear Admirals,* the *America-Merchant,* Captain *Joseph Eldridge* Commander, with Nine more, and above Twenty Hundred Men on Board the whole Fleet: He so happily managed his Charge, that they every one of them Arrived safe at Anchor before *Quebeck,* although they had as dangerous, and almost untrodden a *Path,* to take *Un-Piloted,* for the whole Voyage, as ever any Voyage was undertaken with. Some small *French Prizes* he took by the way, and set up *English* Colours upon the Coast, here and there, as he went along; and before the Month of *August* was out, he had spent several Days as far onward of his Voyage, as between the Island of *Antecosta,* and the *Main.*[1] But when they entred the mighty River of *Canada,* such adverse Winds encountred the Fleet, that they were *Three Weeks* dispatching the way, which might otherwise have been gone in *Three Days,* and it was the Fifth of *October,* when a fresh Breeze coming up at *East,* carried them along by the *North* Shore, up to the Isle of *Orleans;* and then haling *Southerly,* they passed by the *East* end of that *Island,* with the whole Fleet approaching the City of *Quebeck.* This loss of Time, which made it so late before the Fleet could get into the Country, where a cold and fierce *Winter* was already very far advanced, gave no

[1] Between Anticosti and the mainland.

very *good* Prospect of Success to the Expedition; but that which gave a much *worse*, was a most horrid *Mismanagement*, which had, the mean while, happened in the *West*. For a Thousand *English* from *New-York*, and *Albany*, and *Connecticut*, with Fifteen Hundred *Indians*, were to have gone over-land in the *West*, and fallen upon *Mount-Royal*, while the Fleet was to Visit *Quebeck* in the *East;* and no Expedition could have been better laid than *This*, which was thus contrived. But those *English* Companies in the *West*, marching as far as the great Lake that was to be passed, found their *Canoos* not provided, according to Expectation; and the *Indians* also were [*How?* God knows, and will one Day Judge[1] Dissuaded from Joining with the *English;* and the Army met with such Discouragements, that they returned.

Had this *Western Army* done but so much as continued at the *Lake*, the Diversion thereby given to the *French* Quartered at *Mount-Royal*, would have rendered the Conquest of *Quebeck* easie and certain; but the Governour of *Canada* being Informed of the Retreat made by the *Western*-Army, had opportunity, by the cross Winds that kept back the Fleet, unhappily to get the whole Strength of all the Country into the City, before the Fleet could come up unto it. However, none of these Difficulties hindred Sir *William Phips* from sending on Shoar the following Summons, on *Monday* the Sixth of *October*.

Sir *William Phips*, Knight, General and Commander in Chief, in and over Their Majesties Forces of *New-England*, by Sea and Land;

[1].

To Count *Frontenac*, Lieutenant-General and Gover-
nour for the *French* King at *Canada;* or in his
Absence, to his Deputy, or Him, or Them, in Chief
Command at *Quebeck*.

THE War between the Two Crowns of England
and France, *doth not only sufficiently* Warrant;
but the Destruction made by the French *and*
Indians, *under your Command and Encouragement, upon
the Persons and Estates of Their Majesties Subjects
of* New-England, *without Provocation on their part,
hath put them under the* Necessity *of this Expedition,
for their own Security and Satisfaction. And although
the Cruelties and Barbarities used against them, by the*
French *and* Indians, *might, upon the present Opportunity,
prompt unto a severe* Revenge, *yet being desirous to
avoid all Inhumane and Unchristian-like Actions, and
to prevent shedding of Blood as much as may be;*
I the aforesaid Sir William Phips, *Knight, do hereby,
in the Name, and in the Behalf of Their Most Excellent
Majesties,* William *and* Mary, *King and Queen of*
England, Scotland, France *and* Ireland, *Defenders of
the Faith, and by Order of Their said Majesties Government of the* Massachuset-*Colony in* . New-England,
*Demand a present Surrender of your Forts and Castles,
undemolished, and the King's and other Stores, unim-
bezzelled, with a seasonable Delivery of all Captives;
together with a Surrender of all your Persons and Estates
to my Dispose: Upon the doing whereof you may expect
Mercy from me, as a* Christian, *according to what shall
be found for Their Majesties Service, and the Subjects
Security. Which if you Refuse forthwith to do, I am come
Provided, and am Resolved, by the help of God, in whom
I trust, by Force of Arms, to Revenge all Wrongs and*

Injuries offered, and bring you under Subjection to the Crown of England; *and when too late, make you wish you had accepted of the Favour tendered.*

Your Answer Positive in an Hour, returned by your own Trumpet, with the Return of mine, is Required, upon the Peril that will ensue.

The Summons being Delivered unto Count *Frontenac,* his Answer was;

That Sir William Phips, *and those with him, were* Hereticks *and* Traitors *to their King, and had taken up with that* Usurper, *the Prince of* Orange, *and had made a* Revolution, *which if it had not been made,* New-England *and the* French *had been* all One; *and that no other Answer was to be expected from him, but what should be from the Mouth of his* Cannon.

General *Phips* now saw that it must cost him *Dry Blows,*[1] and that he must Roar his Perswasions out of the Mouths of *Great Guns,* to make himself Master of a City which had certainly Surrender'd it self unto him, if he had arrived but a little sooner, and Summon'd it before the coming down of Count *Frontenac* with all his Forces, to Command the oppressed People there, who would have been, many of them, glader of coming under the *English* Government. Wherefore on the Seventh of *October,* the *English,* that were for the Land-Service, went on Board their lesser Vessels, in order to Land; among which there was a Bark, wherein was Captain *Ephraim Savage,* with sixty Men, that ran a-ground upon the *North*-Shoar, near two

[1] Strictly "dry blows" means "blows not involving bloodshed," but the phrase was at times loosely used for "hard" or "severe blows."

Miles from *Quebeck*, and could not get off, but lay in
the same Distress that *Scæva* did, when the *Britains*
poured in their Numbers upon the *Bark*, wherein he,
with a few more Soldiers of *Cæsar*'s Army, were, by
the disadvantage of the *Tide*, left Ashoar: The *French*,
with *Indians*, that saw them lye there, came near,
and Fired thick upon them, and were bravely Answered;
and when two or Three Hundred of the Enemy, at
last planted a Field-Piece against the *Bark*, while the
Wind blew so hard, that no help could be sent unto
his Men, the General advanced so far, as to Level
Two or Three great Guns, conveniently enough to
make the Assailants Fly; and when the Flood came,
the Bark happily got off, without the hurt of one Man
aboard.   But so violent was the Storm of Wind all
this Day, that it was not possible for them to Land
until the Eighth of *October;* when the *English* counting
every *Hour* to be a *Week* until they were come to
Battel, vigorously got Ashoar, designing to enter the
East-end of the City. The *Small-Pox* had got into
the Fleet, by which Distemper prevailing, the number
of Effective Men which now went Ashoar, under the
Command of Lieutenant General *Walley*, did not
amount unto more than Fourteen Hundred; but Four
Companies of these were drawn out as *Forlorns*,[1] whom,
on every side, the Enemy fired at; nevertheless, the
English Rushing with a shout, at once upon them
caused them to Run as fast as Legs could carry them:
So that the whole *English* Army, expressing as much
Resolution as was in *Cæsar*'s Army, when they first
landed on *Britain*, in spight of all opposition from the
Inhabitants, marched on until it was dark, having
first killed many of the *French*, with the loss of but

[1] *I. e.*, bodies of troops dispatched to the front, vanguards.

Four Men of their own; and frighted about Seven or
Eight Hundred more of the *French* from an Ambuscado,
where they lay ready to fall upon them. But some
thought, that by *staying in the Valley*, they took the
way *never to get over the Hill:*[1] And yet for them to
stay where they were, till the smaller Vessels came up
the River before them, so far as by their Guns to
secure the Passage of the Army in their *getting over*,
was what the Council of War had ordered. But the
Violence of the *Weather*, with the General's being
sooner plunged into the heat of Action than was intended, hindred the smaller Vessels from attending
that Order. And this Evening a *French* Deserter
coming to them, assured them, that Nine Hundred
Men were on their March from *Quebeck* to meet them,
already passed a little Rivulet that lay at the end of
the City, but seeing them Land so suddenly, and so
valiantly run down those that first Encounted them,
they had Retreated: Nevertheless, That Count *Frontenac* was come down to *Quebeck* with no fewer than
Thirty Hundred Men to defend the City, having left
but *Fifty* Souldiers to defend *Mount Real*, because
they had understood, that the *English* Army on that
side, were gone back to *Albany*. Notwithstanding
this dis-spiriting Information, the common Souldiers
did with much vehemency Beg and Pray, that they
might be led on; professing, that they had rather lose
their Lives on the Spot, than fail of taking the City;
but the more wary Commanders considered how rash
a thing it would be, for about Fourteen Hundred Raw
Men, tired with a long Voyage, to assault more than
Twice as many Expert Souldiers, who were *Galli in*

[1] There is a proverb, "He that stays in the valley shall never get
over the hill."

suo sterquilinio,[1] or *Cocks Crowing on their own Dunghil.*
They were, in truth, now gotten into the grievous
Case which *Livy* describes, when he says, *Ibi grave est
Bellum gerere, ubi non consistendi aut procedendi locus;
quocunque aspexeris Hostilia sunt omnia;*[2] look on one
side or t'other, all was full of *Hostile Difficulties.* And
indeed, whatever Popular Clamour has been made
against any of the Commanders, it is apparent that
they acted considerately, in making a *Pause* upon
what was before them; and they did a greater kindness
to their Souldiers than they have since been thanked
for. But in this time, General *Phips* and his Men of
War, with their *Canvas Wings,* flew close up unto the
West-end of the City, and there he behaved himself
with the greatest Bravery imaginable; nor did the
other Men of War forbear to follow his brave Example:
Who never discovered himself more in his Element,
than when (as the Poet expresseth it,)

*The Slaughter-Breathing Brass grew hot, and spoke
In Flames of Lightning, and in Clouds of Smoke:*

He lay within *Pistol-shot* of the Enemies Cannon,
and beat them from thence, and very much batter'd
the Town, having his own Ship shot through in almost
an Hundred Places with *Four and Twenty Pounders,*
and yet but one Man was killed, and only Two Mortally
Wounded Aboard him, in this hot Engagement, which
continued the greatest part of that Night, and several
Hours of the Day ensuing. But wondring that he
saw no *Signal* of any Effective Action Ashoar at the

[1] Cotton Mather puns here on the meaning of "gallus,"cock, and
"gallus," Frenchman, Gaul.
[2] "It is difficult to wage war, when there is no chance to halt or
to proceed, and, wherever one looks, everything is hostile."

East-end of the City, he sent that he might know the Condition of the Army there; and received Answer, That several of the Men were so frozen in their Hands and Feet, as to be disabled from Service, and others were apace falling sick of the *Small-Pox*. Whereupon he order'd them on Board immediately to refresh themselves, and he intended then to have renew'd his Attack upon the City, in the Method of Landing his Men in the Face of it, under the shelter of his great Guns; having to that purpose provided also a considerable number of well-shaped *Wheel-Barrows*, each of them carrying Two *Petarraro's*[1] apiece, to March before the Men, and make the Enemy Fly, with as much Contempt as overwhelmed the *Philistines*, when undone by *Foxes* with *Torches* in their Tails; (remembred in an Anniversary Diversion every *April* among the Ancient *Romans*, taught by the *Phenicians*.)

While the Measures to be further taken were debating, there was made an Exchange of Prisoners, the *English* having taken several of the *French* in divers Actions, and the *French* having in their Hands divers of the *English*, whom the *Indians* had brought Captives unto them. The Army now on Board continued still Resolute and Courageous, and on fire for the Conquest of *Quebeck;* or if they had missed of doing it by Storm, they knew that they might, by possessing themselves of the Isle of *Orleans*, in a little while have starved them out. Incredible Damage they might indeed have done to the Enemy before they Embarked, but they were willing to preserve the more undefensible Parts of the Country in such a Condition, as might more sensibly

[1] Petarraro probably means "peterero," or "pedrero," an old name for a very short piece of chambered ordnance—a small gun or cannon.

Encourage the Submission of the Inhabitants unto the Crown of *England*, whose Protection was desired by so many of them. And still they were loth to play for any lesser Game than the immediate Surrender of *Quebeck* it self. But e're a full *Council of War* could conclude the next Steps to be taken, a violent *Storm* arose that separated the Fleet, and the Snow and the Cold became so extream, that they could not continue in those Quarters any longer.

Thus, by an evident *Hand of Heaven*, sending one unavoidable Disaster after another, as well-formed an Enterprize, as perhaps was ever made by the *New-Englanders*, most unhappily miscarried; and General *Phips* underwent a very mortifying Disappointment of a Design, which his Mind was, as much as ever any, set upon. He arrived *Nov.* 19. at *Boston*, where, although he found himself, as well as the Publick, thrown into very *uneasie* Circumstances, yet he had this to Comfort him, that neither his Courage nor his Conduct could reasonably have been Taxed; nor could it be said that any Man could have done more than he did, under so many *Embarassments of his Business*, as he was to Fight withal. He also relieved the uneasiness of his Mind, by considering, that his Voyage to *Canada*, diverted from his Country an *Horrible Tempest* from an Army of *Boss-Lopers*,[1] which had prepar'd themselves, as 'tis affirmed, that Winter, to fall upon the

---

[1] This word seems to be a Dutch form, translating "coureurs de bois," which probably was used by the settlers in New York and from them came into speech elsewhere in the colonies. In a contemporary account of Phips's expedition against Quebec (S. A. Green, *Two Narratives of the Expedition Against Quebec*, Cambridge, 1902, 39n.) we read "Bosslopers (or mongrel french begat on Indian women)," but, however the word came to be understood, it quite clearly originally was simply a translation of "coureurs de bois."

New-English Colonies, and by falling on them, would probably have laid no little part of the Country desolate. And he further considered, that in this Matter, like *Israel* engaging against *Benjamin*, it may be, we saw yet but the *beginning* of the matter: And that the way to *Canada* now being learnt, the Foundation of a Victory over it might be laid in what had been already done. Unto this purpose likewise, he was heard sometimes applying the Remarkable Story reported by *Bradwardine*.

'There was an *Hermit*, who being vexed with Blas-'phemous Injections about the Justice and Wisdom of 'Divine *Providence*, an Angel in Humane Shape in-'vited him to Travel with him, *That he might see the* '*hidden Judgments of God.* Lodging all Night at the 'House of a Man who kindly entertain'd them, the 'Angel took away a valuable Cup from their Host, 'at their going away in the Morning, and bestowed 'this Cup upon a very *wicked Man*, with whom they 'lodged the Night ensuing. The Third Night they 'were most lovingly Treated at the House of a very 'Godly Man, from whom, when they went in the 'Morning, the Angel meeting a Servant of his, threw 'him over the Bridge into the Water, where he was 'drowned. And the Fourth, being in like manner most 'courteously Treated at the House of a very Godly 'Man, the Angel before Morning did unaccountably 'kill his only *Child.* The Companion of the Journey 'being wonderfully offended at these things, would 'have left his *Guardian:* But the Angel then thus 'Addressed him, *Understand now the Secret Judgments* '*of God! The first Man that entertained us, did inordi-*'*nately affect that* Cup *which I took from him; twas for* '*the Advantage of his Interiour that I took it away, and*

'*I gave it unto the impious Man, as the present Reward*
'*of his good Works, which is all the Reward that he is*
'*like to have. As for our* Third Host, *the Servant which*
'*I slew had formed a bloody Design to have slain his*
'*Master, but now, you see, I have saved the Life of the*
'*Master, and prevented something of growth unto the*
'*Eternal Punishment of the Murderer. As for our*
'Fourth *Host, before his* Child *was Born unto him, he*
'*was a very liberal and bountiful Person, and he did*
'*abundance of good with his Estate; but when he saw he*
'*was like to leave such an Heir, he grew Covetous; where-*
'*fore the Soul of the Infant is Translated into Paradise,*
'*but the occasion of Sin is, you see, mercifully taken*
'*away from the Parent.*

Thus General *Phips*, though he had been used unto
Diving in his time, would say, *That the things which had
befallen him in this Expedition, were too deep to be* Dived
into!

§ 12. From the time that General *Pen* made his
Attempt upon *Hispaniola*, with an Army that, like
the *New-English* Forces against *Canada*, miscarried
after an Expectation of having little to do but to
Possess and Plunder; even to this Day, the general
Disaster which hath attended almost every Attempt
of the *European* Colonies in *America*, to make any
considerable Encroachments upon their Neighbours,
is a Matter of some close Reflection. But of the Disaster which now befel poor *New-England* in particular,
every one will easily conclude none of the least Consequences to have been the *Extream Debts* which that
Country was now plunged into; there being *Forty
Thousand* Pounds, more or less, now to be paid, and
not a Penny in the Treasury to pay it withal. In this
Extremity they presently found out an *Expedient*,

which may serve as an *Example* for any People in other Parts of the World, whose Distresses may call for a sudden supply of *Money* to carry them through any Important *Expedition.* The *General Assembly* first pass'd *an Act* for the Levying of such a Sum of *Money* as was wanted, within such a Term of time as was judged convenient; and this *Act* was a *Fund*, on which the *Credit* of such a Sum should be rendered *passable* among the People. Hereupon there was appointed an able and faithful *Committee* of Gentlemen, who Printed, from *Copper-Plates*, a just Number of *Bills*, and Florished, Indented, and Contrived them in such a manner, as to make it impossible to Counterfeit any of them, without a speedy Discovery of the *Counterfeit:* Besides which, they were all Signed by the Hands of *Three* belonging to that *Committee.* These *Bills* being of several Sums, from *Two Shillings*, to *Ten Pounds*, did confess the *Massachuset-Colony* to be *Endebted* unto the Person, in whose Hands they were, the Sums therein expressed; and Provision was made, that if any *Particular Bills* were Irrecoverable Lost, or Torn, or Worn by the Owners, they might be Recruited without any Damage to the *whole in general.* The *Publick Debts* to the *Sailors* and *Soldiers*, now upon the point of Mutiny, (for, *Arma Tenenti, Omnia dat, qui Justa negat!*[1]) were in these *Bills* paid immediately: But that further *Credit* might be given thereunto, it was Ordered that they should be accepted by the Treasurer, and all Officers that were Subordinate unto him, in all *Publick Payments*, at Five *per Cent.* more than the Value expressed in them. The People knowing that the *Tax-Act* would, in the space of Two Years at least, fetch into the Treasury as much as all the

[1] "He who denies what is just, gives all to one who bears arms."

Bills of Credit, thence emitted, would amount unto, were willing to be furnished with Bills, wherein 'twas their Advantage to pay their *Taxes*, rather than in any other *Specie;* and so the *Sailors* and *Soldiers* put off their *Bills*, instead of *Money*, to those with whom they had any Dealings, and they *Circulated* through all the Hands in the Colony pretty Comfortably. Had the *Government* been so settled, that there had not been any doubt of any Obstruction, or Diversion to be given to the Prosecution of the *Tax-Act*, by a *Total Change* of their Affairs then depending at *Whitehall*, 'tis very certain, that the *Bills of Credit* had been better than so much ready *Silver;* yea, the *Invention* had been of more use to the *New-Englanders*, than if all their *Copper Mines* had been opened, or the Mountains of *Peru* had been removed into these Parts of *America.* The *Massachuset Bills of Credit* had been like the *Bank Bills* of *Venice*, where though there were not, perhaps, a *Ducat* of Money in the *Bank*, yet the *Bills* were esteemed more than Twenty *per Cent.* better than Money, among the Body of the People, in all their Dealings. But many People being afraid, that the Government would in half a Year be so overturned, as to Convert their *Bills of Credit* altogether into *Wast Paper*, the *Credit* of them was thereby very much impaired; and they, who first received them, could make them yield little more than *Fourteen* or *Sixteen* Shillings in the Pound; from whence there arose those Idle *Suspicions* in the Heads of many more Ignorant and Unthinking Folks concerning the use thereof, which, to the Incredible Detriment of the Province, are not wholly laid aside unto this Day. However, this Method of paying the *Publick Debts*, did no less than save the Publick from a perfect Ruin: And e're many Months were expired, the Governour and Council had the Pleasure of seeing the *Treasurer* burn before their Eyes many a Thousand Pounds Worth of the *Bills*, which had passed about until they were again returned unto the Treasury; but before their being returned, had happily and honestly, without a Farthing of *Silver Coin*, discharged the *Debts*, for which they were intended. But that which helped these *Bills* unto much of their *Credit*, was the Generous Offer of many Worthy Men in *Boston*, to run the Risque of selling their *Goods* reasonably for them: And of these, I think I may say, that General *Phips* was in some sort the *Leader;* who at the very beginning, meerly to Recommend the *Credit* of the *Bills* unto other Persons, chearfully laid down a considerable quantity of *ready Money* for an equivalent parcel of them. And thus in a little time the Country waded through the Terrible *Debts* which it was fallen into: In this, though unhappy enough, yet not so unhappy as in the *Loss of Men*, by which the Country was at the same time consumed. 'Tis true, there was very *little Blood* spilt in the Attack made upon *Quebeck;* and there was a *Great Hand* of Heaven seen in it. The Churches, upon the Call of the Government, not only observed a General *Fast* through the Colony, for the Welfare of the Army sent unto *Quebeck*, but also kept the *Wheel of Prayer* in a *Continual Motion*, by Repeated and Successive Agreements, for Days of *Prayer* with *Fasting*, in their several Vicinities. On these Days the Ferventest Prayers were sent up to the *God of Armies*, for the Safety and Success of the *New-English* Army gone to *Canada;* and though I never understood that any of the Faithful did in their *Prayers* arise to any assurance that the Expedition should *prosper in all respects*, yet they sometimes in their Devotions on these Occasions, uttered their Perswasion, that Almighty God had heard them in *this* thing, *that the* English *Army should not fall by the Hands of the* French *Enemy*. Now they were marvellously delivered from doing so; though the Enemy had such unexpected Advantages over them, yea, and though the horrid *Winter* was come on so far, that it is a Wonder the *English* Fleet, then Riding in the River of *Canada*, fared any better than the Army which a while since besieged *Poland*, wherein, of *Seventy Thousand* Invaders, no less than *Forty Thousand* suddenly perished by the severity of the *Cold*, albeit it were but the Month of *November* with them. Nevertheless, a kind of *Camp-Fever*, as well as the *Small-Pox*, got into the Fleet, whereby some Hundreds came short of Home. And besides this Calamity, it was also to be lamented, that although the most of the Fleet arrived safe at *New-England*, whereof some Vessels indeed were driven off by Cross-Winds as far as the *West-Indies*, before such Arrival; yet there were Three or Four Vessels which totally miscarried: *One* was never heard of, a *Second* was Wreck'd, but most of the Men were saved by another in Company; a *third* was Wreck'd so, that all the Men were either starv'd, or drown'd, or slain by the *Indians*, except *one*, which a long while after was by means of the *French* restored: And a *fourth* met with Accidents, which, it may be, my Reader will by and by pronounce not unworthy to have been Related.

A *Brigantine*, whereof Captain *John Rainsford* was Commander, having about Threescore Men aboard, was in a very stormy Night, *Octob.* 28. 1690. stranded upon the desolate and hideous Island of *Antecosta*, an Island in the mouth of the Mighty River of *Canada;*

but through the singular Mercy of God unto them, the Vessel did not, immediately, stave to pieces, which if it had happened, they must have, one way or another, quickly perished. There they lay for divers Days, under abundance of bitter Weather, trying and hoping to get off their Vessel; and they solemnly set apart one Day for *Prayer* with *Fasting*, to obtain the Smiles of Heaven upon them in the midst of their Distresses; and this especially, That if they must go Ashoar, they might not, by any stress of Storm, lose the *Provisions* which they were to carry with them. They were at last convinced, that they must continue no longer on Board, and therefore, by the Seventh of *November*, they applied themselves, all Hands, to get their *Provisions* Ashoar upon the dismal *Island*, where they had nothing but a sad and cold Winter before them; which being accomplished, their Vessel *overset* so, as to take away from them all expectation of getting off the Island in it. Here they now built themselves Nine small *Chimney-less things* that they called *Houses;* to this purpose employing such *Boards* and *Planks* as they could get from their shattered Vessel, with the help of *Trees*, whereof that squalid Wilderness had enough to serve them; and they built a particular *Store-House*, wherein they carefully Lodg'd and Lock'd the poor quantity of *Provisions*, which though scarce enough to serve a very abstemious Company for *one Month*, must now be so stinted, as to hold out *Six* or *Seven;* and the Allowance agreed among them could be no better than for One Man, *Two Biskets, half a pound of Pork, half a pound of Flower, one Pint and a quarter of Pease, and two Salt Fishes* per *Week*. This little Handful of Men were now a sort of *Commonwealth*, extraordinarily and miserably separated from all the rest of Mankind; (but I believe, they thought little enough of an *Utopia:* Wherefore they consulted and concluded such *Laws* among themselves, as they judged necessary to their subsistence, in the doleful Condition whereinto the *Providence* of God had cast them; now

———Penitus toto divisos Orbe.[1]

They set up *Good Orders,* as well as they could, among themselves; and besides their daily Devotions, they Observed the *Lord's Days,* with more solemn Exercises of Religion.

But it was not long before they began to feel the more mortal effects of the Straits whereinto they had been Reduced: Their *short* Commons, their Drink of *Snow-Water,* their Hard, and Wet, and Smoaky *Lodgings,* and their Grievous *Despair of Mind,* overwhelmed some of them at such a rate, and so *ham-string'd* them, that sooner than be at the pains to go abroad, and cut their one Fuel, they would lye after a Sottish manner in the Cold; these things quickly brought *Sicknesses* among them. The first of their Number who Died was their *Doctor,* on the 20*th* of *December;* and then they dropt away, one after another, till between *Thirty* and *Forty* of the *Sixty* were buried by their disconsolate Friends, whereof every one look'd still to be the next that should lay his Bones in that Forsaken Region. These poor Men did therefore, on *Monday* the Twenty Seventh of *January,* keep a *Sacred Fast* (as they did, in some sort, a *Civil* one, every Day, all this while) to beseech of Almighty God, that his *Anger* might be turned from them, that he would not go on to cut them off in his *Anger,* that the Extremity of the

[1] "Utterly separated from all the world."

Season might be mitigated, and that they might be prospered in some Essay to get Relief as the *Spring* should Advance upon them; and they took *Notice* that God gave them a Gracious Answer to every one of these Petitions.

But while the *Hand of God* was killing *so many* of this little *Nation* (and yet uncapable to become a *Nation*, for it was, *Res unius Ætatis, populus virorum!*[1]) they apprehended, that they must have been under a most uncomfortable Necessity to *kill* One of their Company.

Whatever *Penalties* they Enacted for other Crimes, there was One, for which, like that of *Parricide* among the Antients, they would have promised themselves, that there should not have been Occasion for any *Punishments;* and that was, the Crime of *Stealing* from the Common-Stock of their Provisions. Nevertheless they found their *Store-House* divers times broken open, and their *Provisions* therefrom *Stolen* by divers unnatural *Children* of the *Leviathan*,[2] while it was not possible for them to preserve their feeble Store-House from the *Stone-Wall-breaking* Madness of these unreasonable Creatures. This Trade of *Stealing*, if it had not been stopp'd by some *exemplary Severity*, they must in a little while, by *Lot* or *Force*, have come to have *Canibally* devoured one another; for there was nothing to be done, either at *Fishing*, or *Fowling*, or *Hunting*, upon that Rueful Island, in the depth of a Frozen Winter; and though they sent as far as they could upon Discovery, they could not find on the Island any *Living thing* in the World, besides themselves. Wherefore, though by an *Act* they made *Stealing* to

[1] "A republic of one age and of men."
[2] The Leviathan, in obsolete usage, meant Satan.

be so *Criminal*, that several did Run the *Gantlet* for
it, yet they were not far from being driven, after all,
to make one Degree and Instance of it *Capital*. There
was a wicked *Irishman* among them, who had such a
Voracious Devil in him, that after divers *Burglaries*
upon the *Store-House*, committed by him, at last he
Stole, and *Eat* with such a *Pamphagous*[1] *Fury*, as to
Cram himself with no less than *Eighteen Biskets* at one
Stolen Meal, and he was fain to have his Belly strok'd
and bath'd before the Fire, lest he should otherwise
have burst. This Amazing, and indeed Murderous
Villany of the *Irishman*, brought them all to their
Wits Ends, how to defend themselves from the Ruin
therein threatned unto them; and whatever *Methods*
were proposed, it was feared that there could be no
stop given to his *Furacious* Exorbitancies any way
but *One;* he could not be past *Stealing*, unless he were
past *Eating* too. Some think therefore they might
have Sentenced the Wretch to Die, and after they had
been at pains, upon Christian and Spiritual Accounts,
to prepare him for it, have Executed the Sentence, by
Shooting him to Death: Concluding Matters come to
that pass, that if *they* had not Shot him, he must have
Starved them unavoidably. Such an Action, if it were
done, will doubtless meet with no harder a Censure,
than that of the Seven *Englishmen*, who being in a
Boat carried off to Sea from St. *Christopher*'s, with
but *one* Days Provision aboard for *Seventeen*, Singled
out some of their Number by Lot, and Slew them, and
Eat them; for which, when they were afterwards
accused of *Murder*, the Court, in consideration of
the *inevitable Necessity*, acquitted them. Truly the
inevitable Necessity of *Starving*, without such an Action,

[1] *I. e.*, all-devouring.

sufficiently grievous to them all, will very much plead for what was done (whatever it were!) by these poor *Antecostians*. And *Starved* indeed they must have been, for all this, if they had not Contrived and Performed a very desperate Adventure, which now remains to be Related. There was a very diminutive kind of Boat belonging to their *Brigantine*, which they recovered out of the Wreck, and cutting this Boat in Two, they made a shift, with certain odd Materials preserved among them, to lengthen it so far, that they could therein form a *little Cuddy*, where Two or Three Men might be stowed, and they set up a *little Mast*, whereto they fastened a little Sail, and accommodated it with some other *little Circumstances*, according to their present poor Capacity.

On the Twenty Fifth of *March*, Five of the Company Shipped themselves upon this Doughty *Fly-Boat*, intending, if it were possible, to carry unto *Boston* the Tidings of their woful Plight upon *Antecosta*, and by help from their Friends there, to return with seasonable Succours for the rest. They had not Sail'd long before they were Hemm'd in by prodigious Cakes of Ice, whereby their Boat sometimes was horribly wounded, and it was a Miracle that it was not Crush'd into a *Thousand Pieces*, if indeed a *Thousand Pieces* could have been Splintred out of so minute a *Cock-Boat*. They kept labouring, and fearfully Weather-beaten, among enormous Rands[1] of Ice, which would ever now and then rub formidably upon them, and were enough to have broken the Ribs of the strongest Frigot that ever cut the Seas; and yet the signal Hand of Heaven so preserved this petty Boat, that by the Eleventh of *April* they had got a quarter of their way, and came to

[1] Pieces.

an Anchor under Cape St. *Lawrence*, having seen
Land but *once* before, and that about seven Leagues
off, ever since their first setting out; and yet having
seen the *open* and *Ocean Sea not so much as once* in all
this while, for the Ice that still encompassed them.
For their support in this Time, the little Provisions
they brought with them would not have kept them
alive; only they killed *Seale* upon the Ice, and they
melted the upper part of the Ice for Drink; but fierce,
wild, ugly *Sea-Horses*,[1] would often so approach them
upon the Ice, that the fear of being devoured by them
was not the least of their Exercises. The Day following
they weig hed [2] Anchor betimes in the Morning but the
Norwest Winds persecuted them, with the raised and
raging Waves of the Sea, which almost continually
poured into them; and Monstrous Islands of Ice, that
seemed almost as big as *Antecosta* it self, would ever
now and then come athwart them. In such a Sea
they lived by the special assistance of God, until, by
the Thirteenth of *April*, they got into an Island of
Land, where they made a Fire, and killed some Fowl,
and some *Seale*, and found some *Goose-Eggs*, and supplied themselves with what Billets of Wood were necessary and carriageable for them; and there they stayed
until the Seventeenth. Here their Boat lying near a
Rock, a great Sea hove it upon the Rock, so that it
was upon the very point of *oversetting*, which if it had,
she had been utterly disabled for any further Service,
and they must have called that Harbour by the Name,
which, I think, one a little more *Northward* bears,
The Cape *without Hope*. There they must have ended
their weary Days! But here the good Hand of God

[1] Walruses.
[2] Weighed.

again interposed for them; they got her off; and though they lost their *Compass* in this Hurry, they sufficiently Repaired another defective one that they had aboard. Sailing from thence, by the Twenty-fourth of *April*, they made Cape *Brittoon;*[1] when a thick Fog threw them into a new Perplexity, until they were safely gotten into the Bay of *Islands*,[2] where they again wooded, and watred, and killed a few Fowl, and catched some Fish, and began to reckon themselves as good as *half way home*. They reached *Cape Sables*[3] by the Third of *May*, but by the Fifth all their Provision was again spent, and they were out of sight of Land; nor had they any prospect of catching any thing that lives in the *Atlantick:* which while they were lamenting one unto another, a stout *Halibut* comes up to the top of the Water, by their side; whereupon they threw out the Fishing-Line, and the Fish took the Hook; but he proved so heavy, that it required the help of several Hands to hale him in, and a *thankful Supper* they made on't. By the Seventh of *May* seeing no Land, but having once more spent all their Provision, they were grown almost wholly hopeless of Deliverance, but then a Fishing Shallop of Cape *Ann* came up with them, Fifteen Leagues to the Eastward of that Cape. And yet before they got in, they had so Tempestuous a Night, that they much feared perishing upon the Rocks after all: But God carried them into *Boston* Harbour the Ninth of *May*, unto the great surprize of their Friends that were in Mourning for them: And there furnishing themselves with a Vessel fit for their Undertaking, they took a Course in a few Weeks more to

[1] Breton.
[2] Newfoundland.
[3] Cape Sable.

fetch home their Brethren that they left behind them
at *Antecosta.*

But it is now time for us to return unto Sir *William!*

§ 13. All this while *CANADA* was as much written
upon Sir *William's* Heart, as *CALLICE,*[1] they said
once, was upon Queen *Mary's.*[2] He needed not one to
have been his daily Monitor about *Canada:* It lay down
with him, it rose up with him, it engrossed almost all
his thoughts; he thought the subduing of *Canada* to
be the greatest Service that could be done for *New-
England,* or for the Crown of *England,* in *America.*
In pursuance whereof, after he had been but a few
Weeks at Home, he took another Voyage for *England,*
in the very depth of Winter, *when Sailing was now
dangerous;* conflicting with all the Difficulties of a
tedious and a terrible Passage, in a very little Vessel,
which indeed was like enough to have perished, if it
had not been for the help of his generous Hand aboard,
and *his Fortunes in the bottom.*

Arriving —— *per tot Discrimina,*[3] at *Bristol,* he
hastned up to *London;* and made his Applications to
their Majesties, and the Principal Ministers of State,
for assistance to renew an Expedition against *Canada,*
concluding his Representation to the King with such
Words as these:

'If Your Majesty shall graciously please to Com-
'mission and Assist me, I am ready to venture my Life
'again in your Service. And I doubt not, but by the
'Blessing of God, *Canada* may be added unto the rest
'of your Dominions, which will (all Circumstances
'considered) be of more Advantage to the Crown of
'*England,* than all the Territories in the *West-Indies* are.

[1] Calais.   [2] Mary I of England.
[3] "Through so many dangers."

The Reasons *here subjoined, are humbly Offered unto*
Your Majesties Consideration.

'*First*, The Success of this Design will greatly add
'to the Glory and Interest of the *English* Crown and
'Nation; by the Addition of the *Bever-Trade*, and
'Securing the *Hudson's Bay* Company, some of whose
'*Factories* have lately fallen into the Hands of the
'*French;* and increase of *English* Shipping and Seamen,
'by gaining the Fishery of *Newfoundland;* and by
'consequence diminish the number of *French* Seamen,
'and cut off a great Revenue from the *French* Crown.

'*Secondly*, The Cause of the *English* in *New-England*,
'their failing in the late Attempt upon *Canada*, was
'their waiting for a Supply of *Ammunition* from *Eng-*
'*land* until *August;* their long Passage up that River;
'the *Cold Season* coming on, and the *Small-Pox* and
'*Fevers* being in the Army and Fleet, so that they could
'not stay Fourteen Days longer; in which time probably
'they might have taken *Quebeck;* yet, if a few Frigots
'be speedily sent, they doubt not of an happy Success;
'the Strength of the *French* being small, and the *Planters*
'desirous to be under the *English* Government.

'*Thirdly*, The *Jesuites* endeavour to seduce the
'*Maqua's*, and other *Indians* (as is by them affirmed)
'suggesting the Greatness of King *Lewis*, and the
'Inability of King *William*, to do any thing against
'the *French* in those Parts, thereby to engage them in
'their Interests: In which, if they should succeed, not
'only *New-England*, but all our *American* Plantations,
'would be endangered by the great increase of Shipping,
'for the *French* (built in *New-England* at easie rates)
'to the Infinite Dishonour and Prejudice of the *English*
'Nation.

But now, for the Success of these Applications, I must entreat the Patience of my Reader to wait until we have gone through a little more of our History.

§ 14. The Reverend *INCREASE MATHER* beholding his Country of *New-England* in a very Deplorable Condition, under a *Governour* that acted by an Illegal, Arbitrary, Treasonable Commission, and Invaded *Liberty* and *Property* after such a manner, as that no Man could say any thing was *his own*, he did, with the Encouragement of the Principal Gentlemen in the Country, but not without much Trouble and Hazard unto his own Person, go over to *Whitehall* in the Summer of the Year 1688. and wait upon King *James*, with a full *Representation* of their Miseries. That King did give him Liberty of *Access* unto him, whenever he desired it, and with many *Good Words* promised him to relieve the Oppressed People in many *Instances* that were proposed: But when the *Revolution* had brought the Prince and Princess of *Orange* to the Throne, Mr. *Mather* having the Honour divers times to wait upon the King, he still prayed for no less a Favour to *New-England*, than the full Restoration of their *Charter-Priviledges:* And Sir *William Phips* happening to be then in *England*, very generously joined with Mr. *Mather* in some of those Addresses: Whereto His Majesty's Answers were always very expressive of his Gracious Inclinations. Mr. *Mather*, herein assisted also by the Right Worshipful Sir *Henry Ashurst*, a most Hearty Friend of all such good Men as those that once filled *New-England*, solicited the Leading Men of both Houses in the Convention-Parliament, until a Bill for the Restoring of the Charters belonging to *New-England*, was fully passed by the Commons of

England; but that Parliament being Prorogu'd, and
then Dissolved, all that *Sisyphæan* Labour came to
nothing. The Disappointments which afterwards
most wonderfully blasted all the hopes of the Petitioned
Restoration, obliged Mr. *Mather*, not without the
Concurrence of other Agents, now also come from
New-England, unto that Method of Petitioning the
King for a *New* Charter, that should contain more
than all the Priviledges of the *Old;* and Sir *William
Phips*, now being again returned into *England*, lent his
utmost assistance hereunto.

The King taking a Voyage for *Holland* before this
Petition was answered; Mr. *Mather*, in the mean while,
not only waited upon the greatest part of the Lords of
His Majesties most Honourable Privy Council, offering
them a Paper of *Reasons for the Confirmation of the*
Charter-Priviledges *granted unto the* Massachuset-
Colony; but also having the Honour to be introduc'd
unto the Queen, he assured Her Majesty, That there
were none in the World better affected unto their
Majesties Government than the People of *New-England*,
who had indeed been exposed unto great Hardships
for their being so; and entreated, that since the King
had referred the *New-English* Affair unto the Two Lord
Chief Justices, with the Attorney and Solicitor General,
there might be granted unto us what they thought was
reasonable. Whereto the Queen replied, That the
Request was reasonable; and that she had spoken
divers times to the King on the behalf of *New-England;*
and that for her own part, she desired that the People
there might not meerly have Justice, but *Favour* done
to them. When the King was returned, Mr. *Mather*,
being by the Duke of *Devonshire* brought into the
King's Presence on *April* 28. 1691. humbly pray'd

His Majesties Favour to *New-England;* urging, That
if their Old Charter-Priviledges might be restored
unto them, his *Name* would be great in those Parts
of the World as long as the World should stand;
adding,

Sir,

YOUR *Subjects there have been willing to venture
their Lives, that they may enlarge your Dominions; the* Expedition *to* Canada *was a Great and
Noble Undertaking.*

*May it please your Majesty, in your great Wisdom
also to consider the Circumstances of that People, as in
your Wisdom you have considered the Circumstances of*
England, *and of* Scotland. *In* New-England *they differ
from other Plantations; they are called* Congregational
and Presbyterian. *So that such a Governour will not
suit with the People of* New-England, *as may be very
proper for other* English *Plantations.*

Two Days after this, the King, upon what was
proposed by certain Lords, was very inquisitive,
whether he might, without breach of Law, set a Governour over *New-England;* whereto the Lord Chief
Justice, and some others of the Council, answered,
That whatever might be the Merit of the Cause,
inasmuch as the *Charter* of *New-England* stood vacated
by a Judgment against them, it was in the King's
Power to put them under what *Form of Government*
he should think best for them.

The King then said, 'That he believed it would be
'for the Advantage of the People in that Colony, to
'be under a Governour appointed by himself: Never-
'theless (because of what Mr. *Mather* had spoken to

him) 'He would have the Agents of *New-England*
'nominate a Person that should be agreeable unto the
'Inclinations of the People there; and notwithstanding
'this, he would have Charter-Priviledges restored and
'confirmed unto them.

The Day following the King began another Voyage
to *Holland;* and when the Attorney General's Draught
of a Charter, according to what he took to be His
Majesties Mind, as expressed in Council, was presented
at the *Council-Board,* on the Eighth of *June,* some
Objections then made, procured an Order to prepare
Minutes for another Draught, which deprived the
New-Englanders of several *Essential Priviledges* in
their other Charter. Mr. *Mather* put in his Objections,
and vehemently protested, That he would sooner part
with his *Life,* than consent unto those *Minutes,* or any
thing else that should infringe any Liberty or Priviledge of Right belonging unto his Country; but he
was answered, That the Agents of *New-England* were
not *Plenipotentiaries* from another Soveraign State;
and that if they would not submit unto the King's
Pleasure in the Settlement of the Country, they must
take what would follow.

The dissatisfactory *Minutes* were, by Mr. *Mather's*
Industry, sent over unto the King in *Flanders;* and
the Ministers of State then with the King were earnestly
applied unto, that every mistake about the good Settlement of *New-England* might be prevented; and the
Queen her self, with her own Royal Hand, wrote unto
the King, that the Charter of *New-England* might
either pass as it was drawn by the Attorney General,
or be deferred until his own Return.

But after all, His Majesties Principal Secretary of
State received a Signification of the King's Pleasure,

that the Charter of *New-England* should run in the Main Points of it as it was now granted: Only there were several Important Articles which Mr. *Mather* by his unwearied Solicitations obtained afterwards to be inserted.

There were some now of the Opinion, that instead of submitting to this New Settlement, they should, in hopes of getting a Reversion of the Judgment against the Old Charter, declare to the Ministers of State, That they had rather have no Charter at all, than such an one as was now proposed unto Acceptance. But Mr. *Mather* advising with many unprejudiced Persons, and Men of the greatest Abilities in the Kingdom, *Noblemen*, *Gentlemen*, *Divines* and *Lawyers*, they all agreed, that it was not only a lawful, but all Circumstances then considered, a Needful thing, and a part of Duty and Wisdom to accept what was now offered, and that a peremptory refusal would not only bring an Inconveniency, but a Fatal, and perhaps, a Final Ruin upon the Country; whereof Mankind would lay the blame upon the Agents.

It was argued, That such a Submission was no Surrender of any thing; that the Judgment, not in the Court of King's *Bench*, but in *Chancery* against the Old Charter, standing on Record, the Pattern[1] was thereby Annihilated; that all attempts to have the Judgment against the Old Charter taken off, would be altogether in vain, as Men and Things were then disposed.

It was further argued, That the Ancient Charter of *New-England* was in the Opinion of the Lawyers very Defective, as to several *Powers*, which yet were abso-

[1] Patent, charter.

lutely necessary to the subsistence of the Plantation:
It gave the Government there no more Power than the
Corporations have in *England*; Power in Capital Cases
was not therein particularly expressed.

It mentioned not an *House of Deputies*, or an *Assembly of Representatives;* the Governour and Company
had thereby (they said) no Power to impose Taxes
on the Inhabitants that were not Freemen, or to erect
Courts of Admiralty. Without such Powers the Colony
could not subsist; and yet the best Friends that *New-England* had of Persons most Learned in the Law,
professed, that suppose the judgment against the
Massachuset-Charter might be Reversed, yet, if they
should again Exert such Powers as they did before
the *Quo Warranto* against their Charter, a new Writ
of *Scire Facias* would undoubtedly be issued out against
them.

It was yet further argued, That if an Act of Parliament should have Reversed the Judgment against the
Massachuset-Charter, without a Grant of some other
Advantages, the whole Territory had been, on many
Accounts, very miserably Incommoded: The Province
of *Main*, with *Hampshire*, would have been taken from
them; and *Plymouth* would have been annexed unto
New-York; so that this Colony would have been
squeezed into an *Atom*, and not only have been render'd
Insignificant in its Trade, but by having its Militia
also, which was vested in the King, taken away, its
Insignificancies would have become out of measure
humbling; whereas now, instead of seeing any Relief
by Act of Parliament, they would have been put under
a Governour, with a Commission, whereby ill Men,
and the King's and Country's Enemies might probably
have crept into Opportunities to have done Ten Thou-

sand ill things, and have treated the best Men in the Land after a very uncomfortable manner.

It was lastly argued, That by the New Charter very great Priviledges were granted unto *New-England;* and in some respects greater than what they formerly enjoyed. The *Colony* is now made a *Province,* and their General Court, has, with the King's Approbation, as much Power in *New-England,* as the King and Parliament have in *England.* They have all *English* Liberties, and can be touched by no Law, by no Tax, but of their own making. All the Liberties of their Holy Religion are for ever se ured,[1] and their Titles to their Lands, once for want of some Forms of Legal Conveyance, contested, are now confirmed unto them If an ill Governour should happen to be imposed on them, what hurt could he do to them? None, except they themselves pleased; for he cannot make one Counsellor, or one Judge, or one Justice, or one Sheriff to serve his Turn: Disadvantages enough, one would think, to Discourage any ill Governour from desiring to be Stationed in those uneasie Regions. The People have a Negative upon all the Executive Part of the Civil Government, as well as the Legislative, which is a vast Priviledge, enjoyed by no other Plantation in *America,* nor by *Ireland,* no, nor hitherto by *England* it self. Why should all of this good be refused or despised, because of somewhat not so good attending it? The Despisers of so much good, will certainly deserve a Censure, not unlike that of *Causabon,*[2] upon some who did not value what that Learned Man counted highly valuable, *Vix illis optari quidquam peius potest, quam*

[1] Secured.
[2] Causabon is either Isaac Casaubon (1559–1614) or Meric Casaubon (1599–1671). Both were Swiss scholars and critics.

ut fatuitate sua fruantur:[1] Much good may do them with their Madness! All of this being well considered, Sir *William Phips*, who had made so many Addresses for the Restoration of the Old Charter, under which he had seen his Country many Years flourishing, will be excused by all the World from any thing of a Fault, in a most unexpected passage of his Life, which is now to be related.

Sir *Henry Ashurst*, and Mr. *Mather*, well knowing the agreeable Disposition to do Good, and the King and his Country Service, which was in Sir *William Phips*, whom they now had with them, all this while Prosecuting his Design for *Canada*, they did unto the Council-Board nominate *him* for the GOVERNOUR of *New-England*. And Mr. *Mather* being by the Earl of *Nottingham* introduced unto His Majesty, said,

Sir,

I Do, *in the behalf of* New-England, *most humbly thank your Majesty, in that you have been pleased, by a* Charter, *to restore* English *Liberties unto them, to confirm them in their Properties, and to grant them some peculiar Priviledges. I doubt not, but that your Subjects there will demean themselves with that dutiful Affection and Loyalty to your Majesty, as that you will see cause to enlarge your Royal Favours towards them. And I do most humbly thank your Majesty, in that you have been pleased to give leave unto those that are concerned for* New-England *to nominate their* Governour.

Sir William Phips *has been accordingly nominated*

---

[1] "Hardly anything worse can be hoped for them, than that they may have the fruit of their folly."

by us at the Council-Board. He hath done a good Service for the Crown, by enlarging your Dominions, and reducing of Nova Scotia *to your Obedience. I know that he will faithfully serve your Majesty to the utmost of his Capacity; and if your Majesty shall think fit to confirm him in that place, it will be a further Obligation on your Subjects there.*

The Effects of all this was, that Sir *William Phips* was now invested with a Commission under the King's Broad-Seal to be *Captain General,* and *Governour in Chief* over the Province of the *Massachuset-Bay* in *New-England:* Nor do I know a Person in the World that could have been proposed more acceptable to the Body of the People throughout *New-England,* and on that score more likely and able to serve the King's Interests among the People there, under the Changes in some things unacceptable, now brought upon them. He had been a *Gideon,* who had more than once ventured his Life to save his Country from their Enemies; and they now, with universal Satisfaction said, *Thou shalt rule over us.* Accordingly, having with Mr. *Mather* kissed the King's Hand on *January* 3d, 1691. he hastned away to his Government; and arriving at *New-England* the Fourteenth of *May* following, attended with the *Non-such-Frigat,* both of them were welcomed with the loud Acclamations of the long *shaken* and *shatter'd* Country, whereto they were now returned with a Settlement so full of happy Priviledges.

§ 15. When *Titus Flaminius* had freed the poor *Grecians* from the Bondage which had long oppressed them, and the Herald Proclaimed among them the Articles of their Freedom, they cried out, *A Saviour!*

A Saviour! with such loud Acclamations, that the very *Birds* fell down from Heaven astonish'd at the Cry. Truly, when Mr. *Mather* brought with him unto the poor *New-Englanders*, not only a *Charter*, which though in divers Points wanting what both *he* and *they* had wished for, yet for ever delivers them from Oppressions on their *Christian* and *English* Liberties, or on their Ancient Possessions, wherein ruining *Writs of Intrusion* had begun to Invade them all, but also a *GOVERNOUR* who might call *New-England* his own *Country*, and who was above most Men in it, full of Affection to the Interests of *his Country;* the sensible part of the People then caused the Sence of the *Salvations* thus brought them to reach as far as *Heaven* it self. The various little Humours then working among the People, did not hinder the *Great and General Court* of the Province to appoint a Day of Solemn *THANKSGIVING* to Almighty God, for *Granting* (as the Printed Order expressed it) *a safe Arrival to his Excellency our Governour, and the Reverend Mr.* Increase Mather, *who have industriously endeavoured the Service of this People, and have brought over with them a Settlement of Government, in which their Majesties have graciously given us distinguishing Marks of their Royal Favour and Goodness.*

And as the obliged People thus gave *Thanks* unto the God of Heaven, so they sent an Address of *Thanks* unto Their Majesties, with other Letters of *Thanks* unto some Chief Ministers of State, for the *Favourable Aspect* herein cast upon the Province.

Nor were the People mistaken, when they promised themselves all the kindness imaginable from this *Governour,* and expected, *Under his shadow we shall live easie among the Heathen:* Why might they not look for *Halcyon*-days, when they had such a *King's-Fisher*, for their Governour?

Governour *Phips* had, as every raised and useful Person must have, his *Envious Enemies;* but the palest Envy of them, who turned their worst Enmity upon him, could not hinder them from confessing, *That according to the best of his Apprehension, he ever sought the good of his Country:* His Country quickly felt this on innumerable Occasions; and they had it eminently demonstrated, as well in his promoting and approving the Council's choice of good *Judges, Justices* and *Sheriffs,* which being once established, no *Successor* could remove them, as in his urging the *General Assembly* to make themselves happy by preparing a Body of good Laws as fast as they could, which being passed by him in his time, could not be nulled by any other after him.

He would often speak to the Members of the general Assembly in such Terms as these, *Gentlemen, You may make your selves as easie as you will for ever; consider what may have any tendency to your welfare; and you may be sure, that whatever Bills you offer to me, consistent with the Honour and Interest of the Crown, I'll pass them readily; I do but seek Opportunities to serve you; had it not been for the sake of this thing, I had never accepted the Government of this Province; and whenever you have settled such a Body of good Laws, that no Person coming after me may make you uneasie, I shall desire not one Day longer to continue in the Government.* Accordingly he ever passed every Act for the welfare of the Province proposed unto him; and instead of ever putting them upon Buying his Assent unto any good Act, he was much forwarder to give it, than they were to ask it:

Nor indeed, had the *Hunger of a Salary* any such
Impression upon him, as to make him decline doing
all possible Service for the Publick, while he was not
sure of having any Proportionable or Honourable
Acknowledgments.

But yet he minded the Preservation of the King's
Rights with as careful and faithful a Zeal as became a
good Steward for the Crown: And, indeed, he studied
nothing more than to observe such a Temper in all
things, as to extinguish what others have gone to
distinguish; even the Pernicious Notion of a separate
Interest. There was a time when the *Roman* Empire
was infested with a vast number of Governours, who
were Infamous for Infinite Avarice and Villany; and
referring to this time, the Apostle *John* had a Vision
of *People killed with the Beasts of the Earth.*

But Sir *William Phips* was none of those Governours;
wonderfully contrary to this wretchedness was the
Happiness of *New-England*, when they had Governour
Phips, using the tenderness of a Father towards the
People; and being of the Opinion, *Ditare magis esse
Regium quam Ditescere*,[1] that it was a braver thing to
enrich the People, than to grow rich himself. A *Father*,
I said; and what if I had said an *Angel* too? If I should
from *Clemens Alexandrinus*, from *Theodoret*, and from
Jerom, and and [sic] others among the Ancients, as well
as from *Calvin*, and *Bucan*, and *Peter Martyr*, and *Chem-
nitius*, and *Bullinger*, and a Thousand more among the
Moderns, bring Authorities for the Assertion, *That each
Country and Province is under the special Care of some
Angel, by a singular Deputation of Heaven assigned
thereunto*, I could back them with a far greater Authority than any of them all. The Scripture it self does

---

[1] "It is more king-like to enrich than to be enriched."

plainly assert it: And hence the most Learned *Grotius*, writing of *Commonwealths*, has a Passage to this purpose, *His singulis, suos Attributos, esse Angelos, ex Daniele, magno consensu, & Judæi & Christiani veteres colligebant.*[1]

But *New-England* had now, besides the *Guardian-Angel*, who more invisibly intended its welfare, a *Governour* that became wonderfully agreeable thereunto, by his whole Imitation of such a Guardian-Angel. He employed his whole Strength to guard his People from all Disasters, which threatned them either by Sea or Land; and it was remark'd, that nothing remarkably Disastrous did befal that People from the time of his Arrival to the Government, until there arrived an Order for his leaving it: (Except one thing which was begun before he entred upon the Government:) But instead thereof, the *Indians* were notably defeated in the Assaults which they now made upon the *English*, and several *French* Ships did also very advantageously fall into his Hands; yea, there was by his means a Peace restored unto the Province, that had been divers Years languishing under the Hectic Feaver of a lingring War.

And there was this one thing more that rendred his Government the more desirable; that whereas 'tis impossible for a meer Man to govern without some *Error;* whenever this Governour was advised of any Error in any of his Administrations, he would immediately retract it, and revoke it with all possible Ingenuity; so that if any occasion of just Complaint arose, it was usually his endeavour that it should not long be complain'd of.

[1] "Old writers, both Jewish and Christian, agree, on the evidence of Daniel that individuals have angels assigned to them."

———*O, Fœlices nimium, sua si Bona, norant, Nov-
Angli* ———¹

But having in a *Parenthesis* newly intimated, that
his Excellency, when he entred on his Government,
found one thing that was *remarkably Disastrous* begun
upon it: Of that one thing we will now give some account.

Reader, prepare to be entertained with as prodigious
Matters as can be put into any History! And let him,
that writes the next *Thaumatographia Pneumatica*,²
allow to these Prodigies the chief place among the Wonders.

§ 16. About the time of our Blessed Lord's coming
to reside on Earth, we read of so many *possessed with
Devils*, that it is commonly thought the *Number* of
such miserable *Energumens*³ was then encreased above
what has been usual in other Ages; and the *Reason* of
that Increase has been made a Matter of some Enquiry.
Now though the *Devils* might herein design by *Preternatural Operations* to blast the *Miracles* of our Lord
Jesus Christ, which point they gained among the
Blasphemous *Pharisees;* and the *Devils* might herein
also design a Villanous *Imitation* of what was coming
to pass in the *Incarnation* of our Lord Jesus Christ,
wherein *God* came to *dwell in Flesh;* yet I am not with-

¹ "O most happy New Englanders, if they recognize their blessings." *Norant* is probably for *noscant*.
² "Wonders of the world of spirits." Cotton Mather's own *Wonders
of the Invisible World* is well described by "Thaumatographia Pneumatica," and he applies this title to Chapter VII of the Sixth Book
of the *Magnalia*.
³ Persons possessed by devils.

out suspicion, that there may be something further in the Conjecture of the Learned *Bartholinus* hereupon, who says, It was *Quod judæi præter modum, Artibus Magicis dediti Dæmonem Advocaverint*, the *Jews*, by the frequent use of *Magical Tricks*, called in the *Devils* among them.

It is very certain, there were hardly any People in the World grown more fond of *Sorceries*, than that unhappy People: The *Talmuds* tell us of the little *Parchments* with Words upon them, which were their common *Amulets*, and of the *Charms* which they mutter'd over *Wounds*, and of the various *Enchantments* which they used against all sorts of Disasters whatsoever. It is affirmed in the *Talmuds*, that no less than Twenty-four Scholars in one School were killed by *Witchcraft;* and that no less than *Fourscore* Persons were Hanged for *Witchcraft* by one Judge in one Day. The *Gloss* adds upon it, *That the Women of* Israel *had generally fallen to the Practice of Witchcrafts;* and therefore it was required, that there should be still chosen into the Council one skilful in the *Arts of Sorcerers*, and able thereby to discover who might be guilty of those *Black Arts* among such as were accused before them.

Now the Arrival of Sir *William Phips* to the Government of *New-England*, was at a time when a Governour would have had Occasion for all the Skill in *Sorcery*, that was ever necessary to a *Jewish Councellor;* a time when Scores of poor People had newly fallen under a prodigious *Possession of Devils*, which it was then generally thought had been by *Witchcrafts* introduced. It is to be confessed and bewailed, that many Inhabitants of *New-England*, and Young People especially, had been led away with little *Sorceries*, wherein they *did secretly those things that were not right against the Lord their God;* they would often cure Hurts with *Spells,* and practise detestable Conjurations with *Sieves,* and *Keys,* and *Pease,* and *Nails,* and *Horse-shoes,* and other Implements, to learn the things for which they had a forbidden and impious Curiosity. Wretched Books had stoln into the Land, wherein Fools were instructed how to become able Fortune-Tellers: Among which, I wonder that a blacker Brand is not set upon that Fortune-Telling Wheel, which that Sham-Scribler, that goes under the Letters of *R. B.* has promised in his *Delights for the Ingenious,* as an *honest and pleasant Recreation:*[1] And by these Books, the Minds of many had been so poisoned, that they studied this *Finer Witchcraft,* until, 'tis well, if some of them were not betray'd into what is Grosser, and more Sensible and Capital. Although these *Diabolical Divinations* are more ordinarily committed perhaps all over the *whole World,* than they are in the Country of *New-England,* yet, that being a Country Devoted unto the Worship and Service of the Lord *JESUS CHRIST* above the *rest of the World,* He signalized his Vengeance against these Wickednesses, with such extraordinary Dispensations as have not been often seen in other places.

The *Devils* which had been so play'd withal, and, it may be, by some few Criminals more Explicitely engaged and imployed, now broke in upon the Country, after as astonishing a manner as was ever heard of. Some Scores of People, first about *Salem,* the Centre and First-Born of all the Towns in the Colony, and afterwards in several other places, were Arrested with many *Preternatural Vexations* upon their Bodies, and

[1] Nathaniel Crouch, using the initials R. B. published his *Delights for the Ingenious* in London in 1684.

a variety of cruel Torments, which were evidently inflicted from the *Dæmons*, of the *Invisible World*. The People that were *Infected* and *Infested* with such *Dæmons*, in a few Days time arrived unto such a *Refining Alteration* upon their Eyes, that they could see their Tormentors; they saw a *Devil* of a Little *Stature*, and of a Tawny *Colour*, attended still with *Spectres* that appeared in more Humane Circumstances.

These *Tormentors* tendred unto the afflicted a *Book*, requiring them to *Sign* it, or to *Touch* it at least, in token of their consenting to be Lifted in the Service of the *Devil*; which they refusing to do, the *Spectres* under the Command of that *Blackman*, as they called him, would apply themselves to Torture them with prodigious Molestations.

The afflicted Wretches were horribly *Distorted* and *Convulsed;* they were *Pinched* Black and Blue: *Pins* would be run every where in their Flesh; they would be *Scalded* until they had *Blisters* raised on them; and a Thousand other things before Hundreds of Witnesses were done unto them, evidently *Preternatural:* For if it were *Preternatural* to keep a rigid *Fast* for *Nine*, yea, for *Fifteen* Days together; or if it were *Preternatural* to have one's Hands *ty'd* close together with a *Rope* to be plainly seen, and then by *unseen Hands* presently pull'd up a great way from the Earth before a Croud of People; such *Preternatural* things were endured by them.

But of all the *Preternatural* things which befel these People, there were none more *unaccountable* than those, wherein the prestigious *Dæmons* would ever now and then cover the most *Corporeal* things in the World with a *Fascinating Mist* of *Invisibility*. As now; a Person was cruelly assaulted by a *Spectre*, that, she said, run at her with a *Spindle*, though no Body else in the room could see either the *Spectre* or the *Spindle:* At last, in her Agonies, giving a snatch at the *Spectre*, she pulled the *Spindle* away; and it was no sooner got into her Hand, but the other Folks then present beheld that it was indeed a Real, Proper, Iron *Spindle;* which when they locked up very safe, it was nevertheless by the *Dæmons* taken away to do farther Mischief.

Again, a Person was haunted by a most abusive *Spectre*, which came to her, she said, with a *Sheet* about her, though seen to none but her self. After she had undergone a deal of Teaze from the Annoyance of the *Spectre*, she gave a violent *Snatch* at the *Sheet* that was upon it; where-from she tore a Corner, which in her Hand immediately was beheld by all that were present, a palpable Corner of a *Sheet:* And her Father, which was now holding of her, *catch'd*, that he might *keep* what his Daughter had so strangely seized; but the *Spectre* had like to have wrung his Hand off, by endeavouring to wrest it from him: However he still held it; and several times this odd Accident was re-newed in the Family. There wanted not the *Oaths* of good credible People to these particulars.

Also, it is well known, that these wicked *Spectres* did proceed so far as to steal several Quantities of Money from divers People, part of which Individual Money was dropt sometimes out of the Air, before sufficient *Spectators*, into the Hands of the Afflicted, while the *Spectres* were urging them to subscribe their *Covenant with Death.* Moreover, *Poisons* to the Standers-by, wholly *Invisible*, were sometimes forced upon the Af-flicted; which when they have with much Reluctancy swallowed, they have *swoln* presently, so that the com-mon Medicines for *Poisons* have been found necessary to relieve them: Yea, sometimes the *Spectres* in the *struggles* have so dropt the *Poisons*, that the Standers-by have smelt them, and view'd them, and beheld the *Pillows* of the miserable stained with them.

Yet more, the miserable have complained bitterly of *burning Rags* run into their forceably distended *Mouths;* and though no Body could see any such *Clothes*, or indeed *any Fires* in the Chambers, yet presently the *scalds* were seen plainly by every Body on the Mouths of the Complainers. and not only the *Smell*, but the *Smoke* of the Burning sensibly fill'd the Chambers.

Once more, the miserable exclaimed extreamly of *Branding Irons* heating at the Fire on the Hearth to mark them; now though the Sanders-by[1] could see no *Irons*, yet they could see distinctly the *Print* of them in the Ashes, and *smell* them too as they were carried by the *not-seen Furies*, unto the Poor Creatures for whom they were intended; and those Poor Creatures were thereupon so *Stigmatized* with them, that they will bear the *Marks* of them to their Dying Day. Nor are these the *Tenth Part* of the *Prodigies* that fell out among the Inhabitants of *New-England*.

Flashy People may *Burlesque* these Things, but when Hundreds of the most sober People in a Country, where they have as much *Mother-Wit* certainly as the rest of Mankind, know them to be *True*, nothing but the absurd and froward Spirit of *Sadducism*[2] can Question them. I have not yet mentioned so much as one Thing that will not be justified, if it be required by the *Oaths* of more considerate Persons than any that can ridicule these odd *Phænomena*.

But the worst part of this astonishing *Tragedy* is

---

[1] Standers-by.

[2] The spirit of the Sadducees, who denied the existence of angels and spirits.

yet behind; wherein Sir *William Phips*, at last being dropt, as it were from the *Machin of Heaven*,[1] was an Instrument of easing the Distresses of the Land, now *so darkned by the Wrath of the Lord of Hosts*. There were very worthy Men upon the Spot where the *assault from Hell* was first made, who apprehended themselves call'd from the *God of Heaven*, to sift the business unto the bottom of it; and indeed, the continual *Impressions*, which the outcries and the havocks of the *afflicted People* that lived nigh unto them caused on their Minds, gave no little Edge to this Apprehension.

The Persons were Men eminent for *Wisdom* and *Virtue*, and they went about their enquiry into the matter, as *driven* unto it by a *Conscience* of Duty to God and the World. They did in the first Place take it for granted, that there are *Witches*, or wicked Children of Men, who upon *Covenanting* with, and *Commissioning* of *Evil Spirits*, are attended by their Ministry to accomplish the things desired of them: To satisfie them in which Perswasion, they had not only the *Assertions* of the *Holy Scripture*; Assertions, which the *Witch-Advocates* cannot evade without Shifts, too foolish for any *Prudent*, or too profane for any *Honest* Man to use; and they had not only the well-attested *Relations* of the gravest Authors from *Bodin* to *Bovet*, and from *Binsfeld* to *Bromhal* and *Baxter*;[2] to deny all which, would be as reasonable as to turn the Chronicles of all Nations into Romances of *Don Quixot* and the *Seven Champions*;[3] but they had also an *Ocular Demon-*

[1] *Cf.* "deus ex machina."

[2] Mather might easily have extended indefinitely his list of learned writers who had upheld the reality of witchcraft.

[3] *The Famous History of the Seven Champions of Christendom*, by Richard Johnston, a romance first printed in 1596.

stration in one, who a little before had been executed for *Witchcraft*, when *Joseph Dudley*, Esq; was the Chief Judge. There was one whose *Magical Images* were found, and who *confessing her Deeds*, (when a Jury of Doctors returned her *Compos Mentis*) actually shewed the whole Court, by what *Ceremonies* used unto them, she directed her *Familiar Spirits* how and where to Cruciate [1] the Objects of her Malice; and the Experiments being made over and over again before the whole Court, the *Effect* followed exactly in the Hurts done to People at a distance from her. The Existence of such *Witches* was now taken for granted by those good Men, wherein so far the generality of reasonable Men have thought *they ran well;*[2] and they soon received the *Confessions* of some *accused* Persons to confirm them in it; but then they took one thing more for granted, wherein 'tis now as generally thought they *went out of the Way.* The Afflicted People vehemently accused several Persons in several Places, that the *Spectres* which afflicted them, did exactly resemble *them;* until the Importunity of the Accusations did provoke the Magistrates to examine them. When many of the *accused* came upon their Examination, it was found, that the *Dæmons* then a thousand ways abusing of the poor *afflicted* People, had with a marvellous exactness *represented* them; yea, it was found, that many of the *accused*, but casting their Eye on the *afflicted*, the *afflicted*, though their Faces were never so much another way, would fall down and lye in a sort of a Swoon, wherein they would continue, whatever Hands were laid upon them, until the Hands of the *accused* came to touch them, and *then* they would revive immediately:

[1] Torment.
[2] *I. e.*, they were right.

And it was found, that various kinds of *natural Actions*, done by many of the *accused* in or to their own Bodies, as *Leaning*, *Bending*, *Turning* Awry, or *Squeezing* their Hands, or the like, were presently attended with the like things *preternaturally* done upon the Bodies of the *afflicted*, though they were so far asunder, that the *afflicted* could not at all observe the *accused*.

It was also found, that the Flesh of the Afflicted was often *Bitten* at such a rate, that not only the *Print of Teeth* would be left on their *Flesh*, but the very *Slaver* of Spittle too: And there would appear just such a *set of Teeth* as was in the *accused*, even such as might be clearly distinguished from other Peoples. And usually the *afflicted* went through a terrible deal of seeming Difficulties from the tormenting *Spectres*, and must be long waited on, before they could get a Breathing Space from their *Torments* to give in their Testimonies.

Now many good Men took up an Opinion, That the *Providence* of God would not permit an *Innocent Person* to come under such a *Spectral Representation;* and that a concurrence of so many Circumstances would prove an *accused* Person to be in a *Confederacy* with the *Dæmons* thus afflicting of the Neighbours; they judged, that except these things might amount unto a *Conviction*, it would scarce be possible ever to *Convict* a *Witch;* and they had some *Philosophical Schemes* of *Witchcraft*, and of the Method and Manner wherein *Magical Poisons* operate, which further supported them in their Opinion.

Sundry of the *accused* Persons were brought unto their *Trial*, while this Opinion was yet prevailing in the Minds of the *Judges* and the *Juries*, and perhaps the most of the People in the Country, then mostly

Suffering; and though against some of them that were Tried there came in so much *other Evidence* of their Diabolical Compacts that some of the most *Judicious*, and yet *Vehement* Opposers of the Notions then in Vogue, publickly declared, *Had they themselves been on the Bench, they could not have Acquitted them;* nevertheless, divers were Condemned, against whom the *chief Evidence* was founded in the *Spectral Exhibitions*.

And it happening, that some of the *Accused* coming to confess themselves *Guilty*, their *Shapes* were no more seen by any of the *afflicted*, though the Confession had been kept never so Secret, but instead thereof the *Accused* themselves became in all Vexations just like the *Afflicted;* this yet more confirmed many in the Opinion that had been taken up.

And another thing that quickned them yet more to Act upon it, was, that the Afflicted were frequently entertained with *Apparitions* of *Ghosts* at the same time that the *Spectres* of the supposed *Witches* troubled them: Which *Ghosts* always cast the Beholders into far more Consternation than any of the *Spectres;* and when they exhibited themselves, they cried out of being *Murdered* by the *Witchcrafts*, or other Violences of the Persons represented in the *Spectres*. Once or Twice these Apparitions were seen by others at the very same time that they shew'd themselves to the *afflicted;* and seldom were they seen at all, but when something unusual and suspicious had attended the Death of the Party thus appearing.

The *afflicted* People many times had never heard any thing before of the Persons appearing in *Ghost*, or of the Persons *accused* by the *Apparitions;* and yet the accused upon Examination have confessed the Murders of those very Persons, though these *accused* also knew nothing of the *Apparitions* that had come in against them; and the *afflicted* Persons likewise, without any private Agreement or Collusion, when successively brought into a Room, have all asserted the same *Apparitions* to be there before them: These *Murders* did seem to call for an Enquiry.

On the other Part, there were many Persons of great Judgment, Piety and Experience, who from the beginning were very much dissatisfied at these Proceedings; they feared lest the *Devil* would get so far into the *Faith* of the People, that for the sake of many *Truths*, which they might find him telling of them, they would come at length to believe all his *Lies*, whereupon what a Desolation of *Names*, yea, and of *Lives* also, would ensue, a Man might without much *Witchcraft* be able to Prognosticate; and they feared, lest in such an extraordinary Descent of *Wicked Spirits* from their *High Places* upon us, there might such *Principles* be taken up, as, when put into *Practice*, would unavoidably cause the *Righteous to perish with the Wicked*, and procure the Blood-shed of Persons like the *Gibeonites*, whom some learned Men suppose to be under a false Pretence of *Witchcraft*, by *Saul* exterminated.

However uncommon it might be for *guiltless Persons* to come under such unaccountable Circumstances, as were on so many of the Accused, they held *some things there are, which if suffered to be Common, would subvert Government, and Disband and Ruin Humane Society, yet God sometimes may suffer such Things to evene, that we may know thereby how much we are beholden to him for that restraint which he lays upon the Infernal Spirits, who would else reduce a World into a* Chaos. They had already known of one at the Town of *Groton* hideously agitated by *Devils*, who in her Fits cried out

much against a very Godly Woman in the Town, and
when that Woman approached unto her, though the
Eyes of the Creature were never so shut, she yet manifested a violent Sense of her approach: But when
the Gracious Woman thus Impeached, had prayed
earnestly with and for this Creature, then instead of
crying out against her any more, she owned, that she
had in all been deluded by the *Devil*. They now saw,
that the more the *Afflicted* were Hearkned unto, the
more the number of the *Accused* encreased; until at
last many scores were *cried out* upon, and among them,
some, who by the *Unblameableness*, yea, and *Serviceableness* of their whole Conversation, had obtained the
Just Reputation of *Good People* among all that were
acquainted with them. The Character of the *Afflicted*
likewise added unto the common Distaste; for though
some of *them* too were *Good People*, yet others of them,
and such of them as were most Flippent at *Accusing*,
had a far other Character.

In fine, the Country was in a dreadful *Ferment*, and
wise Men foresaw a long Train of Dismal and Bloody
Conequences. Hereupon they first advised, that the
afflicted might be kept asunder in the closest Privacy;
and one particular Person (whom I have cause to know)
in pursuance of this Advice, offered himself singly to
provide Accommodations for any *six* of them, that so
the Success of more than ordinary *Prayer* with *Fasting*,
might, with *Patience*, be *experienced*, before any other
Courses were taken.[1]

And Sir *William Phips* arriving to his Government,
after this *ensnaring horrible Storm* was begun, did
consult the neighbouring Ministers of the Province,
who made unto his Excellency and the Council a return,

---

[1] Mather here refers to himself.

(drawn up at their desire by Mr. *Mather* the Younger,[1] as I have been inform'd) wherein they declared.

We judge, that in the Prosecution of these and all such Witchcrafts, *there is need of a very Critical and Exquisite Caution: Lest by too much Credulity for things received only upon the* Devil's Authority, *there be a Door opened for a long Train of miserable Consequences, and Satan get an Advantage over us; for* we should not be Ignorant of his Devices.

As in complaints upon Witchcrafts, *there may be Matters of* Enquiry, *which do not amount unto Matters of* Presumption; *and there may be Matters of* Presumption, *which yet may not be reckoned Matters of* Conviction; *so 'tis necessary that all Proceedings thereabout be managed with an* exceeding Tenderness *towards those that may be complained of; especially if they have been Persons formerly of an* unblemished Reputation.

When the first Enquiry *is made into the Circumstances of such as may lye under any just Suspicion of* Witchcrafts, *we could wish that there may be admitted as little as is possible of such* Noise, Company, *and* Openness, *as may too hastily expose them that are Examined; and that there may nothing be used as a* Test *for the Trial of the Suspected, the lawfulness whereof may be doubted among the People of God: But that the Directions given by such judicious Writers as* Perkins *and* Bernard, *be consulted in such a Case.*

Presumptions, *whereupon Persons may be committed,*

[1] Cotton Mather. The "as I have been inform'd" is part of his attempt to retain his anonymity, since the life of Phips was first published with no author's name. When it appeared in the *Magnalia*, Mather was known as its author, but he did not alter the phrasing of the original edition.

and much more Convictions, *whereupon Persons may be condemned as guilty of* Witchcrafts, *ought certainly to be more considerable, than barely the* accused *Persons being* represented *by a* Spectre *to the afflicted: Inasmuch as it is an undoubted and a notorious Thing, that a* Dæmon *may, by God's Permission, appear even to ill Purposes in the shape of an* Innocent, *yea, and a* Virtuous *Man: Nor can we esteem* Alterations *made in the* Sufferers, *by a* look *or* touch *of the* accused, *to be an infallible Evidence of Guilt; but frequently liable to be abused by the Devil's* Legerdemains.

We know not whether some remarkable Affronts *given to the* Devils, *by our dis-believing of those Testimonies whose whole Force and Strength is from* them *alone, may not put a Period unto the Progress of a direful Calamity begun upon us, in the* accusation *of so many Persons, whereof, we hope, some are yet* clear *from the* great Transgression *laid unto their Charge.*

The Ministers of the Province also being Jealous lest this *Counsel* should not be duly followed, requested the President of *Harvard*-Colledge to Compose and Publish (which he did) some *Cases of Conscience* referring to these Difficulties: In which Treatise he did, with Demonstrations of incomparable *Reason* and *Reading*, evince it, that *Satan* may appear in the Shape of an *Innocent* and a *Virtuous* Person, to afflict those that suffer by the *Diabolical Molestations:* And that the *Ordeal* of the *Sight*, and the *Touch*, is not a Conviction of a *Covenant* with the Devil, but liable to great Exceptions against the *Lawfulness*, as well as the *Evidence* of it: And that either a Free and Fair *Confession* of the Criminals, or the Oath of two Credible Persons proving such Things against the Person accused, as none but such as have a Familiarity with the Devil can know, or do, is necessary to the Proof of the Crime.[1] Thus,

Cum misit Natura Feras, & Monstra per Orbem,
Misit & Alciden qui Fera Monstra domet.[2]

The *Dutch* and *French* Ministers in the Province of *New York*, having likewise about the same time their Judgment asked by the *Chief Judge* of that Province, who was then a Gentleman of *New-England*, they gave it in under their Hands, that if we believe no *Venefick Witchcraft*, we must Renounce the *Scripture* of God, and the *Consent* of almost all the World; but that yet the *Apparition* of a Person afflicting another, is a very Insufficient Proof of a *Witch;* nor is it Inconsistent with the Holy and Righteous Government of God over Men, to permit the Affliction of the Neighbours, by Devils in the *Shape* of *Good Men;* and that a *Good Name*, obtained by a *Good Life*, should not be Lost by Meer *Spectral Accusations*.

Now upon a Deliberate Review of these things, his Excellency first *Reprieved*, and then *Pardoned* many of them that had been Condemned; and there fell out several strange things that caused the Spirit of the Country to run as vehemently upon the *Acquitting* of all the *accused*, as it by mistake ran at first upon the *Condemning* of them. Some that had been zealously of the Mind, that the *Devils* could not in the *Shapes*

[1] Increase Mather's *Cases of Conscience*, here referred to, was a perfectly explicit statement of certain rules for trying witches, and if its counsels had been followed, many lives would have been saved. As it was, after it appeared, people quickly saw the errors of the court and reformed them.

[2] "When Nature sent animals and monsters throughout the world, she sent also Hercules to subjugate them."

of good Men afflict other Men, were terribly Confuted, by having their own *Shapes*, and the *Shapes* of their most intimate and valued Friends, thus abused. And though more than twice Twenty had made such voluntary, and harmonious, and uncontroulable Confessions, that if they were all *Sham*, there was therein the greatest Violation made by the Efficacy of the *Invisible World*, upon the *Rules of Understanding Humane Affairs*, that was ever seen since *God made Man upon the Earth*, yet they did so recede from their *Confessions*, that it was very clear, some of them had been hitherto, in a sort of a *Præternatural Dream*, wherein they had said *of themselves*, they *knew not what themselves*.

In fine, The last Courts that sate upon this *Thorny Business*, finding that it was impossible to Penetrate into the whole Meaning of the things that had happened, and that so many *unsearchable Cheats* were interwoven into the *Conclusion* of a Mysterious Business, which perhaps had not crept thereinto at the *Beginning* of it, they *cleared* the *accused* as fast as they *Tried* them; and within a little while the *afflicted* were most of them delivered out of their *Troubles* also: And the Land had Peace restored unto it, by the *God of Peace, treading Satan under Foot*. *Erasmus*, among other Historians, does tell us, that at a Town in *Germany*, a *Dæmon* appearing on the Top of a Chimney, threatned that he would set the Town on *Fire*, and at length scattering some Ashes abroad, the whole Town was presently and horribly Burnt unto the Ground.

Sir *William Phips* now beheld such *Dæmons* hideously scattering *Fire* about the Country, in the Exasperations which the Minds of Men were on these things rising unto; and therefore when he had well Canvased a *Cause*, which perhaps might have puzzled the Wisdom of the wisest Men on Earth to have managed, without any *Error* in their Administrations, he thought, if it would be any *Error* at all, it would certainly be the *safest* for him to put a stop unto all future Prosecutions, as far as it lay in him to do it.

He did so, and for it he had not only the Printed Acknowledgments of the *New-Englanders,* who publickly thanked him, *As one of the Tribe of* Zebulun, *raised up from among themselves, and* Spirited *as well as* Commissioned *to be the* Steers-man *of a Vessel befogg'd in the* Mare Mortuum[1] *of* Witchcraft, *who now so happily* steered *her Course, that she escaped Shipwrack, and was safely again Moored under the Cape of* Good Hope; *and cut asunder the* Circæan *Knot of Enchantment, more difficult to be Dissolved than the famous* Gordian *one of Old.*

But the *QUEEN* also did him the Honour to write unto him those Gracious Letters, wherein her Majesty commended his Conduct in these *Inexplicable* Matters. And I did right in calling these Matters *Inexplicable.* For if, after the Kingdom of *Sweden* (in the Year 1669, and 1670.) had some Hundreds of their Children by Night often carried away by *Spectres* to an *Hellish Rendezvous*, where the Monsters that so *Spirited* them, did every way *Tempt* them to Associate with them; and the Judges of the Kingdom, after *extraordinary Supplications* to Heaven, upon a strict Enquiry, were so satisfied with the *Confessions* of more than Twenty of the *accused*, agreeing exactly unto the *Depositions* of the *afflicted*, that they put several Scores of *Witches* to Death, whereupon the Confusions came unto a Period; yet after all, the chiefest Persons in the Kingdom would Question whether there were any *Witch-*

[1] "Dead Sea."

crafts at all in the whole Affair; it must not be wondred at, if the People of *New-England* are to this Hour full of *Doubts*, about the *Steps* which were taken, while a *War* from the *Invisible World* was Terrifying of them; and whether they did not kill some of their *own side* in the *Smoke* and *Noise* of this Dreadful *War*. And it will be yet less wondred at, if we consider, that we have seen the whole *English Nation* alarumed with a *Plot*, and both *Houses of Parliament*, upon good Grounds, Voting their Sense of it, and many Persons most justly *Hang'd, Drawn and Quarter'd,* for their share in it: When yet there are enough, who to this Day will pretend, that they cannot comprehend how much of it is to be accounted *Credible*. However, having related these wonderful Passages, whereof, if the *Veracity* of the Relator in any one Point be contested, there are whole *Clouds of Witnesses* to vindicate it, I will take my leave of the Matter with an wholesome Caution of *Lactantius*, which, it may be, some other Parts of the World besides *New-England* may have occasion to think upon; *Efficiunt Dæmones, ut quæ non sint, sic tamen, quasi sint, conspicienda Hominibus exhibeant.*[1]

But the *Devils* being thus vanquished, we shall *next* hear, that some of his most devoted and resembling *Children* are so too.

§ 17. As one of the first Actions *done* by Sir *William*, after he came to the Age of *Doing*, was to save the Lives of many poor People from the Rage of the *Diabolical Indians* in the *Eastern* Parts of the Country, so now he was come to the Government, his Mind was very vehemently set úpon recovering of those Parts from

[1] "Devils so work that things which are not appear to men as if they were real."

the Miseries, which a New and a Long War of the *Indians* had brought upon them   His *Birth* and *Youth* in the *East*, had rendred him well known unto the *Indians* there; he had Hunted and Fished many a weary Day in his Childhood with them; and when those rude Savages had got the Story by the End, that *he had found a Ship full of Money, and was now become all one-a-King!* [1] They were mightily astonished at it: But when they farther understood that he was become the Governour of *New-England*, it added a further Degree of Consternation to their Astonishment.   He likewise was better acquainted with the Scituation of those Regions than most other Men; and he consider'd what vast Advantages might arise to no less than the whole *English* Nation, from the *Lumber*, and *Fishery*, and *Naval-stores*, which those Regions might soon supply the whole Nation withal, if once they were well settled with good Inhabitants.

Wherefore Governour *Phips* took the first Opportunity to raise an Army, with which he Travelled in Person, unto the *East Country*, to find out and cut off the Barbarous Enemy, which had continued for near four Years together, making horrible Havock on the Plantations that lay all along the Northern *Frontiers* of *New-England:* And having pursued those worse than *Scythian Wolves*, till they could be no longer followed, he did with a very laudable *Skill*, and unusual *Speed*, and with less *Cost* unto the Crown, than perhaps ever such a thing was done in the World, erect a strong *Fort* at *Pemmaquid.*

This *Fort* he contrived so much in the very Heart of the Country now possessed by the Enemy, as very

[1] Presumably Mather here quotes directly what the Indians said. "All one-a-King" seems to mean, " just like a king."

much to hinder the several Nations of the Tawnies from *Clanning* together for the Common Disturbance; and his Design was, that a sufficient Garrison being here posted, they might from thence, upon Advice, issue forth to surprise that Ferocient[1] Enemy. At the same time he would fain have gone in Person up the Bay of *Funda*,[2] with a convenient *Force*, to have spoiled the Nest of Rebellious *Frenchmen*, who being Rendezvouzed at St. *John*'s had a yearly Supply of Ammunition from *France*, with which they still supplied the *Indians*, unto the extream Detriment of the *English;* but his Friends for a long time would not permit him to expose himself unto the Inconveniencies of that Expedition.

However, he took such Methods, that the *Indian Kings of the* East, within a little while had their Stomachs brought down, to sue and beg for a *Peace:* And making their appearance at the New-Fort in *Pemmaquid*, *Aug.* 11. 1693. they did there Sign an Instrument, wherein, lamenting the Miseries which their Adherence to the *French Counsels* had brought them into, they did for themselves, and with the Consent of all the *Indians* from the River of *Merrimack*, to the most Easterly Bounds of all the Province, acknowledge their Hearty Subjection and Obedience unto the Crown of *England*, and Solemnly Covenant, Promise and Agree, to and with Sir *William Phips*, Captain General and Governour in Chief over the Province, and his Successors in that place, *That* they would for ever cease all Acts of Hostility towards the Subjects of the Crown of *England*, and hold a constant Friendship with all the *English*. *That* they would utterly abandon

[1] Ferocious.
[2] Bay of Fundy,

the *French* Interests, and not Succour or Conceal any Enemy *Indians*, from *Canada* or elsewhere, that should come to any of their Plantations within the *English* Territories: *That* all *English* Captives, which they had among them, should be returned with all possible speed, and no Ransom or Payment be given for any of them: *That* Their Majesties Subjects the *English*, now should quietly enter upon, and for ever improve and enjoy all and singular their Rights of Lands, and former Possessions, within the Eastern Parts of the Province, without any Claims from any *Indians* or being ever disturbed therein: *That* all Trade and Commerce, which hereafter might be allowed between the *English* and the *Indians*, should be under a Regulation stated by an Act of the *General Assembly*, or as limited by the Governour of the Province, with the Consent and Advice of his Council. And *that* if any Controversie hereafter happen between any of the *English* and the *Indians*, no private Revenge was to be taken by the *Indians*, but proper Applications to be made unto His Majesties Government, for the due remedy thereof: *Submitting themselves herewithal to be Governed by His Majesties Laws.*

And for the Manifestation of their *Sincerity* in the *Submission* thus made, the *Hypocritical Wretches* delivered *Hostages* for their Fidelity; and then set their *Marks* and *Seals*, no less than Thirteen *Sagamores* of them, (with *Names* of more than a *Persian* length) unto this Instrument.

The first Rise of this *Indian War* had hitherto been almost as dark as that of the River *Nilus*:[1] 'Tis true, if any *Wild English* did rashly begin to provoke and affront the *Indians*, yet the *Indians* had a fairer way

[1] The course of the upper Nile was long unknown.

to obtain Justice than by Bloodshed: However, upon the *New-English Revolution*, the State of the *War* became wholly *New:*   The Government then employed all possible ways to procure a good Understanding with the *Indians;* but all the *English* Offers, Kindnesses, Courtesies were barbarously requited by them, with New Acts of the most perfidious Hostility.   Notwithstanding all this, there were still some *Nice People* that had their Scruples about the *Justice of the War;* but upon this New Submission of the *Indians*, if ever those *Rattle-snakes* (the only *Rattle-snakes*, which, they say, were ever seen to the Northward of *Merimack-River*) should stir again, the most scrupulous Persons in the World must own, *That it must be the most unexceptionable piece of Justice in the World for to extinguish them.*

Thus did the God of Heaven bless the unwearied Applications of Sir *William Phips*, for the restoring of *Peace* unto *New-England*, when the Country was quite *out of Breath*, in its Endeavours for its own Preservation from the continual Outrages of an inaccessible Enemy, and by the *Poverty coming in so like an armed Man*, from the unsuccessfulness of their former *Armies*, that it could not imagine how to take one step further in its Wars.   The most happy Respite of *Peace* beyond *Merimack-River* being thus procured, the Governour immediately set himself to use all possible Methods, that it might be *Peace, like a River*, nothing short of *Everlasting*.

He therefore prevailed with Two or Three Gentlemen to join with him, in sending a Supply of *Necessaries for Life* unto the *Indians*, until the General Assembly could come together to settle the *Indian-Trade* for the Advantage of the Publick, that the *Indians* might not by

Necessity be driven again to become a *French* Propriety; altho' by this Action, as the Gentlemen themselves were great *Losers* in their Estates, thus *he* himself declared unto the Members of the General Assembly, that he would upon Oath give an Account unto them of all his own Gains, and count himself a Gainer, if in lieu of all they would give him *one Beaver-Hat*. The same Generosity also caused him to take many a tedious Voyage, accompanied sometimes with his *Fidus Achates*, and very dear Friend, Kinsman and Neighbour, Colonel *John Philips*, between *Boston* and *Pemmaquid;* and this in the bitter Weeks of the *New-English*, which is almost a *Russian* Winter.

He was a sort of *Confessor* under such Torments of *Cold*, as once made the *Martyrdom* of *Muria*, and others, Commemorated in Orations of the Ancients; and the *Snow* and *Ice* which *Pliny* calls, *The Punishment of Mountains*, he chearfully endured, without any other *Profit* unto himself, but only the *Pleasure* of thereby establishing and continuing unto the People the Liberty to *Sleep* quietly in their *warm Nests* at home, while he was thus concerned for them abroad. *Non mihi sed Populo*, the Motto of the Emperor *Hadrian*, was Engraved on the Heart of Sir *William:* NOT FOR MY SELF, BUT FOR MY PEOPLE: Or that of *Maximin*, *Quo major, hoc Laboriosior*, the more Honourable, the more Laborious.

Indeed the *Restlesness* of his Travels to the *Southern* as well as the *Eastern* Parts of the Country, when the Publick Safety call'd for his Presence, would have made one to think on the Translation which the King of *Portugal*, on a very Extraordinary Occasion, gave the Fourth Verse in the Hundred and Twenty-first *Psalm*. *He will not Slumber, nor will he suffer to Sleep the Keeper of* Israel. Nor did he only try to *Cicurate* [1] the *Indians* of the *East*, by other Prudent and Proper Treatments; but he also furnished himself with an *Indian* Preacher of the Gospel, whom he carried unto the *Eastward*, with an Intention to Teach them the Principles of the *Protestant Religion*, and Unteach them the mixt *Paganry* and *Popery* which hitherto *Diaboliz'd* them. To *Unteach* them, I say; for they had been *Taught*, by the *French* Priests *this* among other things, that the Mother of our Blessed Saviour was a *French Lady*, and that they were *Englishmen* by whom our Saviour was Murdered; and that it was therefore a *Meritorious* thing to destroy the *English* Nation. The Name of the Preacher whom the Governour carried with him, was *Nahauton*, one of the Natives; and because the passing of such Expressions from the Mouth of a poor *Indian*, may upon some Accounts be worthy of *Remembrance*; let it be *Remembred*, that when the Governour propounded unto him such a *Mission* to the *Eastern Indians*, he replied, *I know that I shall probably Endanger my Life, by going to Preach the Gospel among the Frenchified* Indians; *but I know that it will be a Service unto the Lord Jesus Christ, and therefore I will venture to go.*

God grant that his *Behaviour* may be in all things, at all times, according to these his *Expressions!* While these things were doing, having Intelligence of a *French* Man of War expected at St. *John's*, he dispatched away the *Non-such-Frigat* thither to intercept him; nevertheless by the gross *Negligence*, and perhaps *Cowardice* of the Captain, who had lately come from *England* with Orders to take the Command of her, instead of one who had been by Sir *William* a while before put in, and one who had signalized himself by doing of notable

[1] Tame.

Service for the King and Country in it, the *Frenchman* arrived unladed, and went away untouch'd. The Governour was extreamly offended at this notorious *Deficiency;* it cast him into a great Impatience to see the *Nation* so wretchedly served; and he would himself have gone to Saint *John's* with a Resolution to *Spoil* that Harbour of *Spoilers*, if he had not been taken off, by being sent for home to *Whitehall*, in the very midst of his Undertakings.

But the Treacherous *Indians* being *poisoned* with the *French Enchantments*, and furnished with brave *New Coats*, and *New Arms*, and all new Incentives to *War*, by the *Man of War* newly come in; they presently and perfidiously fell upon two *English* Towns, and Butchered and Captived many of the Inhabitants, and made a *New War*, which the *New-Englanders* know not whether it will end until either *Canada* become an *English Province*, or that State arrive, wherein they *shall beat Swords into Plough-shares, and Spears into Purning-hooks.* And no doubt, the taking off Sir *William Phips* was no small Encouragement unto the *Indians* in this Relapse, into the Villanies and Massacres of a *New Invasion* upon the Country.

§ 18. Reader, 'tis time for us to view a little more to the *Life*, the *Picture* of the Person, the *Actions* of whose *Life* we have hitherto been looking upon. Know then, that for his *Exterior*, he was one *Tall*, beyond the common Set of Men, and *Thick* as well as *Tall*, and *Strong* as well as *Thick:* He was, in all respects, exceedingly *Robust*, and able to Conquer such Difficulties of *Diet* and of *Travel*, as would have kill'd most Men alive: Nor did the *Fat*, whereinto he grew very much in his later Years, take away the Vigour of his Motions.

He was Well-set, and he was therewithal of a very *Comely*, though a very *Manly* Countenance: A Countenance where any true skill in *Physiognomy* would have read the Characters of a *Generous Mind*. Wherefore passing to his *Interior*, the very first thing which there offered it self unto Observation, was a most Incomparable *Generosity*.

And of this, besides the innumerable Instances which he gave in his usual Hatred of *Dirty* or *Little* Tricks, there was one Instance for which I must freely say, *I never saw Three Men in this World that Equall'd him*; this was his wonderfully *Forgiving Spirit*. In the vast Variety of *Business*, through which he *Raced* in his time, he met with many and mighty *Injuries;* but although I have heard all that the most venemous *Malice* could ever *Hiss* at his Memory, I never did hear unto this Hour, that he did ever once deliberately *Revenge an Injury*.

Upon certain *Affronts* he has made sudden *Returns* that have shewed *Choler* enough, and he has by *Blow*, as well as by *Word*, chastised *Incivilities*: He was, indeed, sufficiently impatient of being *put upon*; and when *Base Men*, surprizing him at some *Disadvantages* (for else few Men durst have done it) have sometimes drawn upon him, he has, without the *Wicked Madness* of a *Formal Duel*, made them feel that he knew how to *Correct Fools*. Nevertheless, he ever declined a *Deliberate Revenge* of a *Wrong* done unto him; though few Men upon *Earth* have, in their *Vicissitudes*, been furnished with such frequent *Opportunities* of *Revenge*, as *Heaven* brought into the Hands of this *Gentleman*.

Under great Provocations, he would commonly say, *'Tis no Matter, let them alone; some time or other they'll see their Weakness and Rashness, and have occasion for*

*me to do them a Kindness: And they shall then see I
have quite forgotten all their Baseness.* Accordingly
'twas remarkable to see it, that few Men ever did *him*
a Mischief, but those Men afterwards had occasion for
him to do *them* a *Kindness;* and he did the *Kindness*
with as forgetful a *Bravery,* as if the *Mischief* had never
been done at all. The Emperor *Theodosius* himself
could not be readier to *Forgive*,[1] so worthily did he
verifie that Observation.

*Quo quisque est Major, magis est Placabilis Ira,
Et Faciles Motus, Mens Generosa capit.*[2]

In those Places of *Power* whereto the Providence of
God by several *Degrees* raised him, it still fell out so, that
before his *Rise* thereunto he underwent such things as
he counted very hard *Abuses,* from those very Persons
over whom the Divine Providence afterwards gave him
the *Ascendant.*

By such *Trials,* the Wisdom of Heaven still prepared
him, as *David* before him, for *successive Advancements;*
and as he behaved himself with a marvellous *Long-
suffering,* when he was *Tried,* by such Mortifications,
thus when he came to be *advanced,* he convinced all
Mankind, that he had perfectly Buried all the old
Offences in an Eternal *Amnesty.* I was my Self an
Ear-witness, that one, who was an *Eye-witness* of his
Behaviour under such *Probations* of his Patience, did,
long before his Arrival to that Honour, say unto him,
Sir, Forgive those that give you these Vexations, and

[1] An allusion to Theodosius I, who won over the Goths, by honors
paid to their fallen leader, Athanaric.
[2] "The greater one is, the more one is placable in wrath, and a
generous mind is easily moved."

know that the God of Heaven intends, before he has done with you, to make you the Governour of New-England! And when he did indeed become the *Governour of* New-England, he shew'd that he still continued a *Governour of himself,* in his Treating all that had formerly been in ill Terms with him, with as much *Favour* and *Freedom,* as if there had never happened the least Exasperations: Though any Governour that Kens *Hobbianism,*[1] can easily contrive Ways enough to wreak a *Spite,* where he owes it.

It was with some *Christian Remark,* that he read the *Pagan-story* of the Renowned *Fabius Maximus,* who being preferred unto the highest Office in the Commonwealth, did, through a Zeal for his Country, overcome the greatest Contempts that any Person of Quality could have received. *Minutius* the Master of the Horse, and the next Person in Dignity to himself, did first privately Traduce him, as one that was *no Soldier,* and less Politician; and he afterwards did both by Speeches and Letters prejudice not only the *Army,* but also the *Senate* against him, so that *Minutius* was now by an unpresidented[2] Commission brought into an *Equality* with *Fabius.*

All this while the great *Fabius* did not throw up his Cares for the Commonwealth, but with a wondrous *Equality of Mind* endured equally the Malice of the *Judges,* and the Fury of the *Commons;* and when *Minutius* a while after was with all his Forces upon the Point of perishing by the victorious Arms of *Hannibal,* this very *Fabius,* not listening to the Dictates of *Revenge,* came in and helped him, and saved him;

---

[1] *I. e.,* any governor that knows the doctrines of Hobbes, who advocated arbitrary government.

[2] Unprecedented.

and so by a rare Virtue, he made his worst *Adversaries* the Captives of his *Generosity.*

One of the Antients upon such an History, cried out, *If Heathens can do thus much for the Glory of their Name, what shall not Christians do for the Glory of Heaven!* And Sir *William Phips* did so *much more* than *thus much,* that besides his meriting the *Glory* of such a *Name,* as *PHIPPIUS MAXIMUS,*[1] he therein had upon him the Symptoms of a Title to the *Glory of Heaven,* in the *Seal* of his own *Pardon* from God. Nor was this *Generosity* in His EXCELLENCY the Governour of *New-England,* unaccompanied with many other *Excellencies;* whereof the *Piety* of his Carriage towards *God* is worthy to be first Mentioned.

It is true, He was very Zealous for all Men to enjoy such a *Liberty of Conscience,* as he judged a *Native Right of Mankind:* And he was extreamly Troubled at the *over-boiling Zeal* of some good Men, who formerly took that wrong Way of reclaiming *Hereticks* by *Persecution.* For this *Generosity,* it may be, some would have compared him unto *Gallio,* the Governour of *Achaia,* whom our Preachers, perhaps with Mistake enough, think to be condemned in the Scripture, for his not appearing to be a *Judge,* in Matters which indeed fell not under his Cognizance.

And I shall be content that he be compared unto that Gentleman; for that *Gallio* was the Brother of *Seneca,* who gives this Character of him, *That there was no Man who did not love him too little, if he could Love him any more*; and, *That there was no Mortal so Dear to any, as he was to all;* and, *That he hated all Vices, but none more than Flattery.*

But while the *Generosity* of Sir *William* caused

[1] "The very great Phips."

him to desire a *Liberty of Conscience*, his *Piety* would not allow a *Liberty of Prophaneness*, either to himself or others. He did not affect any mighty *show* of Devotion; and when he saw any that were *evidently careful* to make a *show*, and especially, if at the same Time they were notoriously Defective in the Duties of *Common Justice* or *Goodness*, or the Duties of the *Relations* wherein God had *stationed* them, he had an extream Aversion for them.

Nevertheless he did show a Consciencious Desire to observe the Laws of the Lord Jesus Christ in his *Conversation;* and he Conscienciously attended upon the Exercises of *Devotion* in the Seasons thereof, on *Lectures*, as well as on *Lord's Days*, and in the *Daily Sacrifice*, the Morning and Evening Service of his own Family; yea, and at the *Private Meetings* of the Devout People kept every *Fortnight* in the Neighbourhood.

Besides all this, when he had *great Works* before him, he would invite good Men to come and *Fast* and *Pray* with him at his House for the Success thereof; and when he had succeeded in what he had undertaken, he would prevail with them to come and keep a Day of Solemn *Thansgiving* [*sic*] with him.   His *Love* to Almighty *God*, was indeed manifested by nothing more than his *Love* to those that had the *Image* of God upon them; he heartily, and with real *Honour* for them, *Loved all Godly Men;* and in so doing, he did not confine *Godliness* to this or that Party, but where-ever he saw the *Fear of God*, in one of a *Congregational*, or *Presbyterian*, or *Antipædobaptist*,[1] or *Episcopalian* Perswasion, he did, without any Difference, express towards them a Reverent Affection.

But he made no Men more welcome than those

---

[1] One opposed to infant baptism; a Baptist.

good *Men*, whose *Office* 'tis to promote and preserve *Goodness* in all other Men; even the *Ministers* of the Gospel: Especially when they were such as faithfully discharged their Office: And from these at any time, the least Admonition or Intimation of any good thing to be done by him, he entertained with a most obliging Alacrity. His *Religion* in truth, was one Principle that added *Virtue* unto that vast *Courage*, which was always in him to a Degree *Heroical*. Those terrible Nations which made their Descents from the *Northern* on the *Southern* Parts of *Europe*, in those Elder Ages, when so to *swarm out* was more frequent with them, were inspired with a *Valiant Contempt of Life*, by the Opinion wherein their Famous *Odin* instructed them. *That their Death was but an Entrance into another Life, wherein they who died in Warlike Actions, were bravely Feasted with the God of War for ever:* 'Tis inexpressible how much the *Courage* of those fierce Mortals was fortified by that Opinion.

But when Sir *William Phips* was asked by some that observed his *Valiant Contempt of Death*, what it was that made him so little afraid of *Dying*, he gave a better grounded Account of it than those *Pagans* could; his Answer was, *I do humbly believe, that the Lord Jesus Christ shed his Precious Blood for me, by his Death procuring my Peace with God: And what should I now be afraid of dying for?*

But this leads me to mention the *Humble* and *Modest* Carriage in him towards other *Men*, which accompanied this his *Piety*. There were certain *Pomps* belonging unto the several *Places of Honour*, through which he passed; *Pomps* that are very taking to Men of *little Souls:* But although he rose from so *little*, yet he discovered a Marvellous *Contempt* of those Airy things,

and as far as he handsomely could, he declined, being
Ceremoniously, or any otherwise than with a *Dutch
Modesty* waited upon.   And it might more truly be
said of him, than it was of *Aristides, He was never seen
the Prouder for any Honour that was done him from his
Countrymen.*

Hence, albeit I have read that Complaint, made by a
Worthy Man, *I have often observed, and this not without
some blushing, that even good People have had a kind of
Shame upon them, to acknowledge their low beginning, and
used all Arts to hide it.*   I could never *observe* the least of
that Fault in this Worthy Man; but he would speak
of his own *low beginning* with as much Freedom and
Frequency, as if he had been afraid of having it forgotten.

It was counted an Humility in King *Agathocles*, the
Son of a *Potter*, to be served therefore in *Earthen Vessels*,
as *Plutarch* hath informed us: It was counted an
Humility in Archbishop *Willigis*,[1] the Son of a *Wheel-
wright*, therefore to have *Wheels* hung about his Bed-
Chamber, with this Inscription, *Recole unde Veneris*,
i. e. *Remember thy Original.*   But such was the *Humility* and *Lowliness* of this *Rising Man!*   Not only
did he after his return to his Country in his Greatness,
one Day, make a splendid Feast for the *Ship-Carpenters*
of *Boston*, among whom he was willing at his Table to
Commemorate the Mercy of God unto him, who had
once been a *Ship-Carpenter* himself, but he would on
all Occasions *Permit*, yea, *Study* to have his *Meannesses* [2]
remembered.

Hence upon frequent Occasions of Uneasiness in
his Government, he would chuse thus to express

[1] Archbishop of Mainz, 975–1011.
[2] That is, his past low rank in the world.

himself, *Gentlemen, were it not that I am to do Service for the Publick, I should be much easier in returning unto my broad Ax again!* And hence, according to the *Affable* Courtesie which he ordinarily used unto all sorts of Persons, (quite contrary to the *Asperity* which the old Proverb expects in the *Raised*) he would particularly, when Sailing in sight of *Kennebeck*, with Armies under his Command, call the Young *Soldiers* and *Sailors* upon Deck, and speak to them after this Fashion; *Young Men, It was upon that Hill that I kept Sheep a few Years ago; and since you see that Almighty God has brought me to something, do you learn to Fear God, and be Honest, and mind your Business, and follow no bad Courses, and you don't know what you may come to!* A Temper not altogether unlike what the advanced *Shepherd* had, when he wrote the *Twenty-third* Psalm; or when he Imprinted on the *Coin* of his Kingdom the Remembrance of his Old Condition: For *Christianus Gerson*, a Christianized *Jew*, has informed us, That on the one side of *David*'s Coin were to be seen his old *Pouch* and *Crook*, the Instruments of *Shepherdy;* on the other side were enstamped the Towers of *Zion*.

In fine, our Sir *William* was a Person of so sweet a Temper, that they who were most intimately acquainted with him, would commonly pronounce him, *The best Conditioned Gentleman in the World!* And by the continual Discoveries and Expressions of such a *Temper*, he so gained the Hearts of them who waited upon him in any of his Expeditions, that they would commonly profess themselves willing still, *to have gone with him to the end of the World*.

But if all other People found him so kind a *Neighbour*, we may easily infer what an Husband he was unto his *Lady*. Leaving unmentioned that *Virtue* of his *Chastity*, which the Prodigious Depravation brought by the Late Reigns upon the Manners of the Nation, has made worthy to be mentioned as a *Virtue* somewhat *Extraordinary;*[1] I shall rather pass on to say, That the *Love*, even to *Fondness*, with which he always treated her, was a Matter not only of *Observation*, but even of such *Admiration*, that every one said, *The Age afforded not a kinder Husband!*

But we must now return to our Story.

§ 19. When Persons do by Studies full of *Curiosity*, seek to inform themselves of things about which the God of Heaven hath forbidden our *Curious Enquiries*, there is a marvellous *Impression*, which the *Dæmons* do often make on the Minds of those their Votaries, about the *Future* or *Secret* Matters unlawfully enquired after, and at last there is also an horrible *Possession*, which those *Fatidic*[2] *Dæmons* do take of them. The *Snares* of Hell, hereby laid for miserable Mortals, have been such, that when I read the Laws, which *Agellius* affirms to have been made, even in *Pagan Rome*, against the *Vaticinatores;*[3] I wonder that no *English* Nobleman or Gentleman signalizes his regard unto *Christianity*, by doing what even a *Roman Tully* would have done, in promoting *An Act of Parliament* against that *Paganish* Practice of *Judicial Astrology*,[4] whereof, if such Men as *Austin* were now living, they would assert, *The Devil first found it, and they that profess it are Enemies of Truth and of God.*

---

[1] An allusion to the moral decline in England during the Restoration period.

[2] Prophetic.

[3] "Soothsayers."

[4] The supposed act of determining occult influences of the stars and planets on human lives and affairs.

In the mean time, I cannot but relate a wonderful Experience of Sir *William Phips,* by the Relation whereof something of an *Antidote* may be given against a *Poison,* which the Diabolical *Figure-Flingers* and *Fortune-Tellers* that swarm all the World over may insinuate into the Minds of Men. Long before Mr. *Phips* came to be Sir *William,* while he sojourned in in [*sic*] *London,* there came into his Lodging an Old *Astrologer,* living in the Neighbourhood, who making some *Observation* of him, though he had small or no *Conversation* with him, did (howbeit by him wholly undesired) one Day send him a Paper, wherein he had, with Pretences of a Rule in *Astrology* for each Article, distinctly noted the most material Passages that were to befal this our *Phips* in the remaining part of his Life; it was particularly Asserted and Inserted, That he should be engaged in a Design, wherein by Reason of Enemies at *Court,* he should meet with much delay; that nevertheless in the *Thirty-Seventh* Year of his Life, he should find a *mighty Treasure;* that in the *Forty-First* Year of his Life, his *King* should employ him in as great a *Trust beyond Sea,* as a Subject could easily have: That soon after this he should undergo an hard *Storm* from the Endeavours of his Adversaries to *reproach* him and *ruin* him; that his Adversaries, though they should go very *near* gaining the Point, should yet *miss* of doing so; that he should hit upon a vastly *Richer Matter* than any that he had hitherto met withal; that he should continue *Thirteen Years* in his *Publick Station,* full of Action, and full of Hurry; and the rest of his Days he should spend in the Satisfaction of a *Peaceable Retirement.*

Mr. *Phips* received this undesired Paper with Trouble and with Contempt, and threw it by among certain

loose Papers in the bottom of a Trunk, where his Lady
some Years after accidentally lit upon it. His Lady
with Admiration saw, step after step, very much of it
accomplished; but when she heard from *England*,
that Sir *William* was coming over with a Commission
to be Governour of *New-England*, in that very Year of
his Life, which the Paper specified; she was afraid of
letting it lye any longer in the House, but cast it into
the *Fire*.

Now the thing which I must invite my Reader to
remark, is this, That albeit Almighty God may permit
the *Devils* to *Predict*, and perhaps to *Perform* very many
particular things to Men, that shall by such a *Presump-
tuous and Unwarrantable Juggle* as *Astrology* (so Dr.
Hall well calls it!) or any other *Divination*, consult
them, yet the *Devil* [1] which *foretel* many *True* things,
do commonly *foretel* some that are *False*, and it may be,
propose by the things that are *True* to betray Men into
some fatal Misbelief and Miscarriage about those
that are *False*.

Very singular therefore was the Wisdom of Sir
William Phips, that as he ever Treated these *Prophesies*
about him with a most *Pious Neglect*, so when he had
seen all but the *Two last* of them very punctually
fulfilled, yea, and seen the beginning of a Fulfilment
unto the *last but one* also, yet when I pleasantly mentioned them unto him, on purpose to *Try* whether there
were any occasion for me humbly to give him the
serious *Advice*, necessary in such a Case to Anticipate
the *Devices of Satan*, he prevented my Advice, by saying
to me, Sir, *I do believe there might be a cursed Snare
of Satan in those Prophesies: I believe Satan might have
leave to foretel many things, all of which might come to*

[1] Devils.

*pass in the beginning, to lay me asleep about such things
as are to follow, especially about the main Chance of all;
I do not know but I am to die this Year: For my part,
by the help of the Grace of God, I shall endeavour to live
as if I were this Year to die.* And let the Reader now
attend the Event!

§ 20. 'Tis a Similitude which I have Learned from
no less a Person than the great *Basil:* That *as* the
Eye sees not those Objects which are applied close
unto it, and even lye upon it; but when the Objects
are to some distance removed, it clearly discerns them:
So, we have little sense of the Good which we have in
our Enjoyments, until God, by the removal thereof,
teach us better to prize what we once enjoyed. It is
true, the Generality of sober and thinking People
among the *New-Englanders,* did as highly value the
Government of Sir *William Phips,* whilst he lived, as
they do his *Memory,* since his Death; nevertheless it
must be confessed, that the Blessing which the Country
had in his indefatigable Zeal, to serve the Publick in
all it's Interests, was not so valued as it should have
been.

It was mention'd long since as a notorious Fault in
Old Egypt, that it was *Loquax & Ingeniosa in Contumeliam Præfectorum Provincia; si quis forte vitaverit Culpam,
Contumeliam non effugit:*[1] And *New-England* has been
at the best always too faulty, in that very Character,
*A Province very Talkative, and Ingenious for the vilifying
of its Publick Servants.*

But Sir *William Phips,* who might in a *Calm* of the
Commonwealth have administred all things with as
General an Acceptance as any that have gone before

---

[1] "Free-spoken and ingenious in slandering the rulers in the province; if by chance anyone avoided guilt, he did not escape slander."

him, had the Disadvantage of being set at *Helm* in a time as full of *Storm* as ever that *Province* had seen; and the People having their Spirits put into a *Tumult* by the discomposing and distempering Variety of Disasters, which had long been rendring the time Calamitous, it was natural for them, as 'tis for all Men *then*, to be *complaining;* and you may be sure, the *Rulers* must in such Cases be always *complained* of, and the chief Complaints must be heaped upon those that are *Commanders in Chief.* Nor has a certain Proverb in *Asia* been improper in *America, He deserves no Man's good Word, of whom every Man shall speak well.*

Sir *William* was very hardly *Handled* (or *Tongued* at least) in the Liberty which People took to make most unbecoming and injurious Reflections upon his Conduct, and Clamour against him, even for those very Actions which were not only *Necessary* to be done, but highly *Beneficial* unto themselves; and though he would ordinarily smile at their *Frowardness,* calling it *his Country Pay,* yet he sometimes resented it with some uneasiness; he seem'd unto himself sometimes almost as bad as Rolled about in *Regulus's* Barrel; [1] and had occasion to think on the *Italian* Proverb, *To wait for one who does not come; to lye a Bed not able to sleep; and to find it impossible to please those whom we serve; are three Griefs enough to kill a Man.*

But as *Froward* as the People were, under the *Epedemical Vexations* of the Age, yet there were very few but would acknowledge unto the very Last, *It will be hardly possible for us to see another Governour that shall more intirely Love and Serve the Country:* Yea, had the Country had the Choice of their own *Governour,* 'tis

---

[1] Regulus was tortured by being placed in a barrel or chest which was studded with nails pointing inward.

judged their *Votes*, more than Forty to One, would have still fallen upon him to have been the Man: And the *General Assembly* therefore on all occasions renewed their Petitions unto the King for his Continuance.

Nevertheless, there was a little Party of Men, who thought they must not *sleep till they had caused him to fall:* And they so vigorously prosecuted certain Articles before the Council-board at *Whitehall* against him, that they imagined they had gained an *Order* of His Majesty in Council, to suspend him immediately from his Government, and appoint a *Committee* of Persons nominated by his Enemies, to hear all *Depositions* against him; and so a Report of the whole to be made unto the King and Council.

But His Majesty was too well informed of Sir *William*'s Integrity to permit such a sort of Procedure; and therefore he signified unto His most Honourable Council, that nothing should be done against Sir *William*, until he had Opportunity to clear himself; and thereupon he sent His Royal Commands unto Sir *William* to come over. To give any retorting Accounts of the Principal Persons who thus adversaried him, would be a Thing so contrary to the Spirit of Sir *William Phips* himself, who at his leaving of *New-England* bravely declared that he *freely forgave them all;* and if he had returned thither again, would never have taken the least revenge upon them, that *This* alone would oblige me, if I had no other Obligations of Christianity upon me, to forbear it; and it may be, for some of them, it would be *to throw Water upon a drowned Mouse.*

Nor need I to produce any more about the *Articles* which these Men exhibited against him, than *This;* that it was by most Men believed, that if he would have connived at some *Arbitrary Oppressions* too much used by some kind of Officers on the King's Subjects, *Few* perhaps, or *None* of those Articles had ever been formed; and that he apprehended himself to be provided with a full *Defence* against them all.

Nor did His Excellency seem loth to have had his Case Tried under the Brazen Tree of *Gariac*, if there had been such an one, as that mentioned by the Fabulous *Murtadi*, in his Prodigies of *Egypt*, a Tree which had Iron Branches with sharp *Hooks* at the end of them, that when any false Accuser approached, as the Fabel says, immediately flew at him, and stuck in him, until he had ceased Injuring his Adversary.

Wherefore in Obedience unto the King's Commands, he took his leave of *Boston* on the seventeenth of *November*, 1694. attended with all proper Testimonies of Respect and Honour from the *Body* of the People, which he had been the *Head* unto; and with *Addresses* unto their Majesties, and the Chief Ministers of State from the General Assembly, humbly imploring, that they might not be deprived of the Happiness which they had in such an *Head*.

Arriving at *Whitehall*, he found in a few Days, that notwithstanding all the Impotent Rage of his Adversaries particularly vented and printed in a *Villanous Libel*, as well as almost in as many other ways as there are Mouths, at which Fyal[1] sometimes has vomited out its Infernal Fires, he had all *Humane Assurance* of his returning in a very few Weeks again the Governour of *New-England*.

Wherefore there were especially *two Designs*, full of Service to the whole *English* Nation, as well as his own particular Country of *New-England*, which he applied his *Thoughts* unto. *First*, He had a new *Scene*

[1] Fayal, a volcánic island in the Azores.

of Action opened unto him, in an opportunity to supply the Crown with all *Naval Stores* at most *easie Rates*, from those *Eastern* Parts of the *Massachuset* Province, which through the Conquest that *he* had made thereof, came to be Inserted in the *Massachuset*-Charter. As no Man was more *capable* than *he* to improve this Opportunity unto a vast Advantage, so his *Inclination* to it was according to his *Capacity*.

And he longed with some Impatience to see the King furnished from his *own Dominions*, with such floating and stately Castles, those *Wooden-Walls* of Great *Britain*, for much of which he has hitherto Traded with *Foreign Kingdoms*. *Next*, if I may say *next* unto this, he had an Eye upon *Canada*; all attempts for the reducing whereof had hitherto proved Abortive.

It was but a few Months ago that a considerable Fleet, under Sir *Francis Wheeler*, which had been sent into the *West-Indies* to subdue *Martenico*,[1] was ordered then to call at *New-England*, that being recruited there, they might make a further Descent upon *Canada*; but Heaven frowned upon that Expedition, especially by a terrible Sickness, the most like the *Plague* of any thing that has been ever seen in *America*, whereof there Died, e'er they could reach to *Boston*, as I was told by Sir *Francis* himself, no less than *Thirteen* Hundred Sailers out of *Twenty One*, and no less than *Eighteen* Hundred Soldiers out of *Twenty-four*.

It was now therefore his desire to have satisfied the King, that his whole Interest in *America* lay at Stake, while *Canada* was in *French* Hands: And therewithal to have laid before several Noblemen and Gentlemen, how beneficial an Undertaking it would have been for them to have pursued the *Canadian*-Business, for

---

[1] Martinique.

which the *New-Englanders* were now grown too Feeble; their Country being too far now, as *Bede* says *England* once was, *Omni Milite & floridæ Juventutis Alacritate spoliata.*[1]

Besides these *two* Designs in the *Thoughts* of Sir *William*, there was a *Third*, which he had Hopes that the King would have given him leave to have pursued, after he had continued so long in his Government, as to have obtained the more *General Welfare* which he designed in the former Instances. I do not mean the making of *New-England* the Seat of a *Spanish Trade*, though so vastly profitable a thing was likely to have been brought about, by his being one of an Honourable Company engaged in such a Project.

But the *Spanish Wreck*, where Sir *William* had made his first *good Voyage*, was not the *Only*, nor the *Richest* Wreck, that he knew to be lying under the Water. He knew particularly, that when the Ship which had Governour *Boadilla* Aboard, was cast away, there was, as *Peter Martyr* says, an entire Table of *Gold* of *Three Thousand Three Hundred and Ten Pound Weight.*

The Duke of *Albemarle*'s Patent for all such *Wrecks* now expiring, Sir *William* thought on the *Motto* which is upon the Gold *Medal*, bestowed by the late King, with his *Knighthood* upon him, *Semper Tibi pendeat Hamus:*[2] And supposing himself to have gained sufficient Information of the right Way to such a *Wreck*, it was his purpose upon his Dismission from his Government, once more to have gone unto his old *Fishing-Trade*, upon a mighty Shelf of Rocks and Bank of Sands that lye where he had informed himself.

[1] " Despoiled of young and active soldiery."
[2] "May your fish-hook always hang out."

But as the Prophet *Haggai* and *Zechariah*, in their *Psalm* upon the Grants made unto their People by the Emperors of *Persia* have that Reflection, *Man's Breath goeth forth, he returns to his Earth; in that very Day his thoughts perish.* My Reader must now see what came of all these considerable *Thoughts.* About the middle of *February*, 1694. Sir *William* found himself indisposed with a Cold, which obliged him to keep his Chamber; but under this Indisposition he received the Honour of a Visit from a very Eminent Person at *Whitehall*, who upon sufficient Assurance, bad him *Get well as fast as he could, for in one Months time he should be again dispatched away to his Government of* New-England.

Nevertheless his Distemper proved a sort of *Malignant Feaver*, whereof many about this time died in the City; and it suddenly put an End at once unto his *Days* and *Thoughts*, on the Eighteenth of *February;* to the extream surprize of his Friends, who Honourably Interr'd him in the Church of St. *Mary Woolnoth*, and with him, how much of *New-England's* Happiness!

§ 21. Although he has now *no more a Portion for ever in any Thing that is done under the Sun*, yet Justice requires that *his Memory be not forgotten.* I have not all this while said *He was Faultless*, nor am I unwilling to use for him the Words which Mr. *Calamy* had in his Funeral Sermon for the Excellent Earl of *Warwick, It must be confessed, lest I should prove a Flatterer, he had his Infirmities, which I trust Jesus Christ hath covered with the Robe of his Righteousness: My Prayer to God is, that all his Infirmities may be Buried in the Grave of Oblivion, and that all his Virtues and Graces may Supervive;* although perhaps they were no *Infirmities* in that Noble Person, which Mr. *Calamy* counted so.

Nevertheless I must also say, That if the Anguish

of his Publick Fatigues threw Sir *William* into any *Faults* of *Passion;* they were but *Faults* of *Passion* soon Recall'd: And *Spots* being soonest seen in *Ermin,* there was usually the *most* made of them that could be, by those that were least *Free* themselves.

After all, I do not know that I have been, by any personal Obligations or Circumstances, charmed into any *Partiality* for the *Memory* of this Worthy Man; but I do here, from a real Satisfaction of Conscience concerning him, declare to all the World, that I reckon him to have been really a very *Worthy Man;* that few Men in the World rising from so mean an *Original* as he, would have acquitted themselves with a Thousand Part of his *Capacity* or *Integrity;* that he left unto the World a notable Example of a Disposition to *do Good,* and encountred and overcame almost invincible *Temptations* in doing it.

And I do most solemnly Profess, that I have most conscienciously endeavoured the utmost Sincerity and Veracity of a *Christian,* as well as an *Historian,* in the *History* which I have now given of him. I have not written of Sir *William Phips,* as they say *Xenophon* did of *Cyrus, Non ad Historiæ Fidem, sed ad Effigiem veri imperii;*[1] what *should* have been, rather than what really *was.* If the *Envy* of his *few Enemies* be not now *Quiet,* I must freely say it, That for many Weeks before he died, there was not one Man among his *personal Enemies* whom *he* would not readily and chearfully have done all the kind Offices of a *Friend* unto: Wherefore though the Gentleman in *England* that once published a Vindication of Sir *William Phips* against some of his Enemies, chose to put the Name of *Publicans* upon them, they must in *this* be counted

[1] "Aiming not at truth of history, but at a picture of true empire."

worse than the *Publicans* of whom our Saviour says, *They Love those that Love them.*

And I will say this further, That when certain Persons had found the *Skull* of a *Dead Man*, as a *Greek* Writer of Epigrams has told us, they all fell a Weeping, but only one of the Company, who Laughed and Flouted, and through an unheard-of Cruelty, threw *Stones* at it, which *Stones* wonderfully rebounded back upon the Face of him that threw them, and miserably wounded him: Thus if any shall be so *Unchristian*, yea, so *Inhumane*, as libellously to throw Stones at so deserved a Reputation as this Gentleman has died withal, they shall see a *Just Rebound* of all their Calumnies.

But the Name of Sir *WILLIAM PHIPS* will be heard Honourably mentioned in the *Trumpets* of *Immortal Fame*, when the Names of many that *Antipathied* him will either be Buried in Eternal Oblivion, without any *Sacer Vates* [1] to preserve them; or be remembred, but like that of *Judas* in the Gospel, or *Pilate* in the Creed, with Eternal Infamy.

The old *Persians* indeed, according to the Report of *Agathias*, exposed their *Dead* Friends to be Torn in Pieces by *Wild Beasts*, believing that if they lay long *unworried*, they had been *unworthy* Persons; but all attempts of surviving Malice to demonstrate in that way the *worth* of this *Dead* Gentleman, give me leave to *Rate off* with Indignation.

And I must with a like Freedom say, That great was the Fault of *New-England* no more to value a Person, whose *Opportunities* to serve all their Interests, though very Eminent, yet were not so Eminent as his *Inclinations.* If this whole Continent carry in its very Name of

[1] "Sacred poet."

AMERICA, an unaccountable *Ingratitude* unto that Brave Man who first led any numbers of *Europeans* thither, it must not be wondred at, if now and then a particular Country in that Continent afford some Instances of *Ingratitude:* But I must believe, that the Ingratitude of many, both to God and Man, for such *Benefits* as that Country of *New-England* enjoy'd from a Governour of their own, by whom they enjoyed *great quietness, with very worthy Deeds done unto that Nation by his Providence,* was that which hastned the Removal of such a *Benefactor* from them.

However, as the *Cyprians* buried their Friends in *Honey,* to whom they gave *Gall* when they were Born; thus whatever *Gall* might be given to this Gentleman while he lived, I hope none will be so base, as to put any thing but *Honey* into their Language of him now after his Decease. And indeed, since 'tis a frequent thing among Men to wish for the Presence of our *Friends,* when they are *dead* and *gone,* whom, while they were present with us, we undervalued; there is no way for us to fetch back our Sir *William Phips,* and make him yet Living with us, but by setting up a *Statue* for him, as 'tis done in these Pages, that may out-last an ordinary *Monument.*

Such was the Original Design of erecting *Statues,* and if in *Venice* there were at once no less than an Hundred and Sixty-two Marble, and Twenty-three Brazen *Statues,* erected by the Order, and at the Expence of the Publick, in Honour of so many Valiant Soldiers, who had merited well of that Commonwealth, I am sure *New-England* has had those, whose Merits call for as good an acknowledgment; and, whatever they did *before,* it will be well, if *after* Sir *William Phips,* they find many as meritorious as he to be so acknowledged.

Now I cannot my self provide a better *Statue* for this Memorable Person, than the *Words* uttered on the occasion of his Death in a very great Assembly, by a Person of so Diffus'd and Embalm'd a Reputation in the Church of God, that such a Character from *him* were enough to Immortalize the Reputation of the Person upon whom he should bestow it.

The *Grecians* employ'd still the most Honourable and Considerable Persons they had among them, to make a *Funeral Oration* in Com•nendation of Soldiers that had lost their Lives in the Service of the Publick: And when Sir *William Phips*, the Captain General of *New-England*, who had often ventured his Life to serve the Publick, did expire, that Reverend Person, who was the President of the only University then in the *English America*,[1] Preached a Sermon on that Passage of the Sacred Writ, Isa. 57. 1. *Merciful Men are taken away, none considering that the Righteous are taken away from the Evil to come;* and in it gave Sir *William Phips* the following Testimony.

'This *Province* is Beheaded, and lyes a Bleeding.
'A GOVERNOUR is *taken away*, who was a *Merciful* 'Man;* some think *too Merciful:* And if so, 'tis best 'Erring on *that* Hand; and a *Righteous Man;* who, 'when he had great Opportunities of gaining by *In-* 'justice,* did refuse to do so.

'He was a known Friend unto the best Interests, 'and unto the *Churches* of God: Not *ashamed* of owning 'them: No, how often have I heard him expressing 'his Desires to be an Instrument of *Good* unto them! 'He was a Zealous *Lover* of his *Country*, if any Man in 'the World were so: He exposed *himself* to serve it; 'he ventured his *Life* to save it: In *that*, a true *Nehe-*

[1] Increase Mather.

'*miah*, a Governour that *sought the welfare of his* '*People*.

'He was one who did not *seek* to have the Govern-'ment cast upon him: No, but instead thereof to my 'Knowledge he did several times Petition the King, 'that this People might always enjoy the *great Privi-* '*ledge of chusing their own Governour;* and I have heard 'him express his Desires, that it might be so, to several 'of the Chief Ministers of State in the Court of *England*.

'He is now Dead, and not capable of being *Flattered:* 'But this I must testifie concerning him, That though 'by the Providence of God I have been with him at 'Home and Abroad, near at Home, and afar off, by 'Land and by Sea, *I never saw him do any evil Action,* '*or heard him speak any thing unbecoming a Christian*.

'The Circumstances of his Death seem to intimate 'the *Anger* of God, in that he was *in the Midst of his* '*Days* removed; and I know (though *Few* did) that he 'had *great Purposes* in his Heart, which probably would 'have taken Effect, if he had lived a few Months longer, 'to the great Advantage of this Province; but now he 'is gone, there is not a Man Living in the World 'capacitated for those Undertakings; *New-England* 'knows not yet what they have lost!

The Recitation of a Testimony so *great*, whether for the *Author*, or the *Matter* of it, has now made a *Statue* for the Governour of *New-England*, which

Nec poterit Ferrum, nec edax abolere vetustas.[1]

And there now remains nothing more for *me* to do about it, but only to recite herewithal a well-known Story related by *Suidas*, That an *Envious* Man, once going to pull down a *Statue* which had been raised unto

[1] "No sword nor greedy time can destroy."

the Memory of one whom he maligned, he only got this by it, that the *Statue* falling down, knock'd out his Brains.

But *Poetry* as well as *History* must pay it's Dues unto him. If *Cicero*'s Poem intituled, *Quadrigæ*, wherein he did with a *Poetical Chariot* extol the Exploits of *Cæsar* in *Britain* to the very Skies, were now Extant in the World, I would have Borrowed some *Flights* of *That* at least, for the Subject now to be Adorned.

But instead thereof, let the Reader accept the ensuing *Elegy*.

UPON THE

DEATH

OF

Sir 𝖂𝖎𝖑𝖑𝖎𝖆𝖒 𝕻𝖍𝖎𝖕𝖘, Knt.

Late Captain General and Governour in Chief of the
Province of the *Massachuset-Bay* in *New-England*,
Who Expired in *London, Feb.* 18. 169$\frac{4}{5}$.

> *And to* Mortality *a Sacrifice*
> *Falls He, whose Deeds must Him* Immortalize!

R*Ejoice* Messieurs; Netops [1] *rejoice; 'tis true,*
    Ye Philistines, *none will rejoice but* You:
    Loving of All *He Dy'd; who Love* him *not*
Now, have the Grace of Publicans *forgot.*
Our Almanacks *foretold a great* Eclipse,
This they foresaw~not, of our greater PHIPS.
PHIPS *our great* Friend, *our Wonder, and our Glory,*
The Terror of our Foes, *the World's rare Story.*
England *will Boast him too, whose Noble Mind*
Impell'd by Angels, *did those* Treasures *find,*
Long in the Bottom of the Ocean *laid,*
Which her Three Hundred Thousand *Richer made,*
By Silver *yet ne'er Canker'd, nor defil'd*
By Honour, *nor Betray'd when* Fortune *smil'd.*
Since this bright Phœbus *visited our Shoar,*

---

[1] "Messieurs"—the French, Phips' enemies.   Netop is an Indian
word, used by Indians in greeting one another.

We saw no Fogs *but what were rais'd before:*
Those vanish'd too; harrass'd by Bloody Wars
Our Land saw Peace, *by his most generous Cares.*
The Wolvish Pagans *at his dreaded Name,*
Tam'd, shrunk before him and his Dogs became!
Fell Moxus *and fierce* Dockawando *fall,*[1]
Charm'd at the Feet of our Brave General.

Fly-blow the Dead, *Pale* Envy, *let him not*
(*What* Hero *ever did?*) *escape a Blot.*
All is Distort[2] *with an* Inchanted Eye,
And Heighth *will make what's* Right *still stand awry.*
He was, Oh that He was! His Faults *we'll tell,*
Such Faults *as these we* knew, *and lik'd them well.*

Just *to an Injury; denying none*
Their Dues; but Self-denying *oft his own.*

Good *to a Miracle; resolv'd to do*
Good *unto All, whether they would or no.*
To make Us Good, Great, Wise, *and all Things else,*
He wanted but the Gift *of Miracles.*
On him, vain Mob, *thy Mischiefs cease to throw;*
Bad, *but alone in This, the Times were so.*

Stout *to a Prodigy; living in Pain*
To send back Quebeck-Bullets *once again.*
Thunder, his Musick, sweeter than the Spheres,
Chim'd Roaring Canons *in his Martial Ears.*
Frigats *of armed Men could not withstand,*
'Twas try'd, the Force of his one Swordless Hand:
Hand, *which in one, all of* Briareus *had,*
And Hercules's *twelve* Toils *but Pleasures made.*

[1] Moxus and Dockawando, (or Madockawando) were Indian chiefs.
[2] Distorted.

Too Humble; *in brave* Stature *not so Tall,*
As low in Carriage, *stooping unto all.*
Rais'd in Estate, in Figure and Renown,
Not Pride; Higher, *and yet not* Prouder *grown.*
Of Pardons *full; ne'er to* Revenge *at all,*
W as that which He would Satisfaction *call.*

True *to his Mate; from whom though often flown.*
A Stranger yet to every Love but one.
Write Him not Childness,[1] *whose whole People were*
Sons, Orphans *now, of His Paternal Care.*

Now lest ungrateful Brands *we should incur,*
Your Salary we'll pay in Tears, *GREAT SIR!*

To England *often blown, and by his Prince*
Often sent laden with Preferments *thence.*
Preferr'd each Time He went, when all was done
That Earth *could do, Heaven fetch'd Him to a Crown.*

'Tis He: With Him *Interr'd how great designs!*
Stand Fearless now, ye Eastern Firrs *and* Pines.
With Naval Stores *not to enrich the Nation,*
Stand, for the Universal Conflagration.
Mines, *opening unto none but Him, now stay*
Close under Lock and Key, till the Last Day:
In this, like to the Grand Aurifick Stone,
By any but Great Souls *not to be known.*
And Thou Rich Table, with Bodilla *lost,*
In the Fair Galeon, *on our Spanish Coast.*
In weight Three Thousand and Three Hundred Pound,
But of pure Massy Gold, lye Thou, *not found,*
Safe, since He's *laid under the* Earth *asleep,*
Who learnt where Thou dost under Water *keep.*

[1] Childless.

But Thou Chief Loser, Poor NEW-ENGLAND,
 speak
Thy Dues to such as did thy Welfare seek,
The Governour that vow'd to Rise and Fall
With Thee, Thy *Fate shows in* His *Funeral.*
Write now His *Epitaph,* '*twill be* Thine own,
Let it be this, A PUBLICK SPIRIT 's GONE.
Or, but Name PHIPS; *more needs not be exprest;*
Both Englands, *and next* Ages, *tell the Rest.*

The End of the Second B O O K.

SELECTIONS FROM "THE CHRISTIAN PHILOSOPHER"

THE PREFACE

R ELIGIO P HILOSOPHICA; [1]

OR, THE

Christian Philosopher:

BEING

A Commentary, of the more Modern and Certain P HILOSOPHY,[2] upon that Instruction,

J OB xxxvi. 24.

Remember that thou magnify His Work which Men behold.

T HE Works of the Glorious GOD in the *Creation* of the World, are what I now propose to exhibit; in brief *Essays* to enumerate *some of them,* that He may be glorified in them: And indeed my *Essays* may pretend unto no more than *some of them;* for, *Theophilus* [3] writing, *of the Creation,* to his Friend *Antolycus,* might very justly say, That if he should have a *Thousand Tongues,* and live a *Thousand Years,* yet he were not able to describe the admirable Order of the Creation, διὰ τὸ ὑπερβᾶλλον μεγεθὸς καὶ τὸν πλοῦτον σοφίας τοῦ Θεοῦ. *Such a Tran-*

---

[1] "Philosophic (or Scientific) Religion."
[2] Philosophy in the sense of science in general.
[3] Theophilus of Antioch, died 190 A. D.

scendent Greatness of God, and the Riches of his Wisdom appearing in it!

Chrysostom, I remember, mentions a *Twofold Book* of GOD; the Book of the *Creatures*, and the Book of the *Scriptures:* GOD having taught first of all us διὰ πραγμάτων, by his *Works*, did it afterwards διὰ γραμμάτων, by his *Words*. We will now for a while read the *Former* of these *Books*, 'twill help us in reading the *Latter:* They will admirably assist one another. The Philosopher being asked, What his *Books* were; answered, *Totius Entis Naturalis Universitas*.[1] All Men are accommodated with that *Publick Library*. *Reader*, walk with me into it, and see what we shall find so legible there, *that he that runs may read it*. Behold, a Book, whereof we may agreeably enough use the words of honest *Ægardus; · Lectu hic omnibus facilis, etsi nunquam legere didicerint, & communis est omnibus, omniumque oculis expositus*.[2]

THE

INTRODUCTION

THE Essays now before us will demonstrate, that *Philosophy* is no *Enemy*, but a mighty and wondrous *Incentive* to *Religion;* and they will exhibit that PHILOSOPHICAL RELIGION, which will carry with it a most sensible *Character*, and victorious *Evidence* of a *reasonable Service*. GLORY

[1] "The natural university of all the existing universe."

[2] "Here is reading easy for everyone even though they have not learned to read, and it is open to all, and set out before everyone's eyes."

TO GOD IN THE HIGHEST, and *GOOD-WILL TOWARDS MEN*, animated and exercised; and a Spirit of *Devotion* and of *Charity* inflamed, in such Methods as are offered in these *Essays*, cannot but be attended with more Benefits, than any *Pen* of ours can declare, or any *Mind* conceive.

In the *Dispositions* and *Resolutions* of PIETY thus enkindled, a *Man* most effectually *shews himself a* MAN, and with unutterable Satisfaction answers the grand END of his Being, which is, *To glorify GOD*. He discharges also the Office of a *Priest* for the *Creation*, under the Influences of an admirable Saviour, and therein asserts and assures his Title unto that *Priesthood*, which the Blessedness of the *future State* will very much consist in being advanced to. The whole *World* is indeed a *Temple* of GOD, *built* and *filled* by that Almighty *Architect;* and in this *Temple*, every such one, affecting himself with the Occasions for it, will *speak of His Glory*. He will also rise into that *Superior Way* of *Thinking* and of *Living*, which the *Wisest* of Men will chuse to take; which the more *Polite Part* of Mankind, and the *Honourable of the Earth*, will esteem it no Dishonour for them to be acquainted with. Upon that Passage occurring in the best of Books, *Ye Sons of the Mighty, ascribe unto the Lord Glory and Strength;* it is a Gloss and an Hint of *Munster*, which carries with it a Cogency: *Nihil est tam sublime, tamque magnificum, quod non teneatur laudare & magnificare Deum Creatorem suum.*[1] Behold, a *Religion*, which will be found *without Controversy;* a *Religion*, which will challenge all possible Regards from the *High*, as well as the *Low*, among the People; I will

[1] "Nothing is so sublime or magnificent as not to be bound to magnify and praise the Lord, its creator."

resume the Term, a PHILOSOPHICAL RELIGION: And yet how *Evangelical!*

In prosecuting this *Intention*, and in introducing almost every *Article* of it, the Reader will continually find some *Author* or other *quoted*. This constant Method of *Quoting*, 'tis to be hoped, will not be censured, as proceeding from an *Ambition to intimate and boast a Learning*, which the *Messieurs du Port-Royal*[1] have rebuked; and that the Humour for which *Austin* reproached *Julian*, will not be found in it: *Quis hæc audiat, & non ipso nominum strepitu terreatur, si est ineruditus, qualis est hominum multitudo, & existimet te aliquem magnum qui hæc scire potueris?*[2]   Nor will there be discernible any Spice of the impertinent Vanity, which *La Bruyere* hath so well satirized: '*Herillus* 'will always *cite*, whether he speaks or writes.   He makes 'the *Prince of Philosophers* to say, *That Wine inebriates;* 'and the *Roman Orator, That Water temperates it*.   If he 'talks of *Morality*, it is not he, but the Divine *Plato*, 'who affirms, *That Virtue is amiable, and Vice odious*. 'The most common and trivial things, which he himself 'is able to think of, are ascribed by him to *Latin* and 'Greek Authors.'   But in these *Quotations*, there has been proposed, first, a due *Gratitude* unto those, who have been my *Instructors;* and indeed, *something within me* would have led me to it, if *Pliny*, who is one of them, had not given me a Rule; *Ingenuum est profiteri per quos profeceris*.[3]   It appears also but a piece

[1] Port-Royal, a famous community in France, including among its members some of the most learned men of the 17th century.

[2] "Who can hear this and not be frightened by the very sound of the names—provided he is not learned, as most men are not—and who but will consider you great because you know so much?"

[3] "It is noble to acknowledge by whom you have profited."

of *Justice*, that the *Names* of those whom the Great GOD has distinguished, by employing them to make those *Discoveries*, which are here collected, should live and shine in every such Collection. Among these, let it be known, that there are especially Two, unto whom I have been more indebted, than unto many others; the Industrious Mr. RAY, and the Inquisitive Mr. DERHAM; *Fratrum dulce par:*[1] upon whom, in divers Paragraphs of this *Rhapsody*,[2] I have had very much of my Subsistence; (I hope without doing the part of a *Fidentinus* upon them) and I give thanks to Heaven for them.

'Tis true, some Scores of other *Philosophers* have been consulted on this Occasion; but an *Industry* so applied, has in it very little to bespeak any *Praises* for him that has used it: He earnestly renounces them, and sollicits, that not only *he*, but the *Greater Men*, who have been his *Teachers*, may disappear before the Glorious GOD, whom these *Essays* are all written to represent as *worthy to be praised*, and by whose *Grace we are what we are;* nor have we *any thing but what we have received* from Him.

A considerable Body of Men (if the *Jansenists*[3] may now be thought so) in *France*, have learnt of Monsieur *Pascal*, to denote themselves by the *French* Impersonal Particle *On;* and it was his opinion, that an honest Man should not be fond of *naming himself*, or using the word I, and ME; that *Christian Piety* will annihilate our I, and ME, and *Human Civility* will suppress it, and conceal it.

---

[1] "A sweet pair of brothers." See Introduction, pages xlix–l.
[2] A collection, a literary work without definite form.
[3] A school of Roman Catholic theologians, whose views dominated Port-Royal.

Most certainly there can be very little Pretence to
an I, or ME, for what is done in these *Essays*. *'Tis
done*, and entirely, *by the Help of God:* This is all that
can be pretended to.

There is very little, that may be said, really to be
performed by the Hand that is now writing; but only
the *Devotionary Part* of these *Essays*, tho they are
not altogether destitute of *American* Communications:
And if the *Virtuoso's*, and all the *Genuine Philosophers*
of our Age, have approved the Design of the devout
RAY and DERHAM, and others, in their Treatises; it
cannot be distasteful unto them, to see what was more
generally hinted at by those Excellent Persons, here more
particularly carried on, and the more *special Flights* of
the true PHILOSOPHICAL RELIGION exemplified.   Nor
will they that value the Essays of the memorable
Antients, *Theodoret*, and *Nazianzen*, and *Ambrose*,
upon *the Works of the six Days*, count it a Fault, if among
lesser Men in our Days, there be found those who say,
Let me run after them.   I remember, when we read,
Praise is comely for the Upright, it is urged by *Kimchi*,
that the Word which we render *comely*, signifies *desirable*,
and *acceptable;* and the Sense of that Sentence is,
that *Qui recti sunt, aliud nihil desiderant quam Laudem &
Gloriam Dei.*[1]   Sure I am, such *Essays* as these, to observe, and proclaim, and publish the *Praises* of the
Glorious GOD, will be *desirable* and *acceptable* to all
that have a *right Spirit* in them; *the rest*, who are *blinded*,
are Fools, and unregardable: As little to be regarded
as a *Monster* flourishing a *Broomstick! Vix illis optari
quidquam pejus potest, quam ut fatuitate sua fruantur.*[2]

[1] "The righteous desire nothing but the praise and glory of God."
[2] "Hardly anything worse can be hoped for them, than that they
may have the fruit of their folly."

For such *Centaurs* to be found in the Tents of professed *Christianity!*—*Good God, unto what Times hast thou reserved us!* If the *self-taught Philosopher* will not, yet *Abubeker*, a *Mahometan* Writer, by whom such an one was exhibited more than five hundred Years ago, will *rise up in the Judgment with this Generation, and condemn it.* Reader, even a *Mahometan* will shew thee one, without any *Teacher*, but *Reason* in a serious View of *Nature*, led on to the Acknowledgment of a Glorious GOD. Of a Man, supposed as but using his *Rational Faculties* in viewing the Works of GOD, even the *Mahometan* will tell thee; 'There appeared unto him 'those Fooststeps of Wisdom and Wonders in the '*Works of Creation*, which affected his Mind with an 'excessive Admiration; and he became hereby assured, 'that all these things must proceed from such a *Volun-* '*tary Agent* as was *infinitely perfect*, yea, above all 'Perfection: such an one to whom the Weight of the 'least Atom was not unknown, whether in Heaven or 'Earth. Upon his viewing of the *Creatures*, whatever '*Excellency* he found of any kind, he concluded, it must 'needs proceed from the Influence of that *Voluntary* '*Agent*, so illustriously glorious, the *Fountain of Being*, 'and of *Working*. He knew therefore, that whatsoever 'Excellencies were by Nature in *Him*, were by so 'much the greater, the more perfect, and the more 'lasting; and that there was no proportion between 'those Excellencies which were in *Him*, and those 'which were found in the *Creatures*. He discerned 'also, by the virtue of that more Noble Part of his, 'whereby he knew the *necessarily existent Being*, that 'there was in him a certain Resemblance thereof: And 'he saw, that it was his Duty to labour by all manner 'of Means, how he might obtain the Properties of

'that *Being*, put on *His Qualities*, and imitate *His*
'*Actions;* to be diligent and careful also in promoting
'*His Will;* to commit all his Affairs unto *Him*, and
'heartily to acquiesce in all those *Decrees* of *His* which
'concerned him, either from within, or from without:
'so that he pleased himself in *Him*, tho he should
'*afflict* him, and even *destroy* him.'   I was going to say,
O Mentis aureæ Verba bracteata! [1]   But the Great
Alsted instructs me, that we *Christians*, in our valuable
Citations from them that are Strangers to *Christianity*,
should seize upon the Sentences as containing *our*
Truths, detained in the hands of *Unjust Possessors*;
and he allows me to say, *Audite Ciceronem, quem Natura*
docuit. [2]   However, this I may say, *God has thus far*
taught a Mahometan!   And this I will say, *Christian*,
beware lest a *Mahometan* be called in for thy *Condem-*
nation!

Let us conclude with a Remark of *Minutius Fœlix:* [3]
'If so much Wisdom and Penetration be requisite to
'*observe* the wonderful Order and Design in the Struc-
'ture of the World, how much more were necessary
'to *form* it!'   If Men so much admire Philosophers,
because they *discover* a small Part of the *Wisdom* that
made all things; they must be stark blind, who do not
admire that *Wisdom* itself!

[1] "O golden words of a golden mind."
[2] "Hear Cicero, whom Nature taught."
[3] Marcus Minucius Felix, Latin apologist for Christanity, in the
third century.

ESSAY XXIII. *Of the* EARTH.

THE *Lord by Wisdom has founded the Earth.* A poor Sojourner on the *Earth* now thinks it his Duty to behold and admire the *Wisdom* of his glorious Maker there.

The *Earth,* which is the Basis and Support of so many Vegetables and Animals, and yields the alimentary Particles, whereof *Water* is the Vehicle, for their Nourishment: *Quorum omnium* (as *Tully* saith well) *incredibilis Multitudo, insatiabili Varietate distinguitur.*[1]

The various Moulds and Soils of the Earth declare the admirable Wisdom of the Creator, in making such a provision for a vast variety of Intentions. *God said, Let the Earth bring forth!*

And yet,

Nec vero Terræ ferre omnes omnia possunt.[2]

It is pretty odd; they who have written *de Arte Combinatoria,* reckon of no fewer than one hundred and seventy-nine Millions, one thousand and sixty different sorts of Earth: But we may content ourselves with Sir *John Evelyn*'s Enumeration, which is very short of *that.*[3]

However, the *Vegetables* owe not so much of their Life and Growth to the *Earth* itself, as to some agreeable Juices or Salts lodg'd in it. Both Mr. *Boyle* and *Van Helmont,* by Experiments, found the Earth scarce

[1] "Of all these an incredible number, divided with inexhaustible variety."

[2] "Not all lands can bear all things."

[3] Mather here draws on Evelyn's *Terra,* whence he takes his reference to the *De Arte Combinatoria.*

at all diminished when *Plants*, even *Trees*, had been for divers Years growing in it.

The *Strata* of the Earth, its *Lays* and *Beds*, afford surprizing Matters of Observation: the *Objects* lodged in them; the *Uses* made of them; and particularly the *Passage* they give to *sweet Waters*, as being the *Calanders*[1] wherein they are sweetned. It is asserted that these are found all to lie very much according to the Laws of *Gravity*. Mr. *Derham* went far to demonstrate this Assertion.

The *vain Colts of Asses*, that *fain would be wise*, have cavill'd at the *unequal Surface of the Earth*, have open'd against the *Mountains*, as if they were *superfluous Excrescences;* but *Warts* deforming the Face of the Earth, and Proofs the *Earth* is but an Heap of Rubbish and Ruins. *Pliny* had more of Religion in him.

The sagacious Dr. *Halley* has observed, That the Ridges of *Mountains* being placed thro the midst of their Continents, do serve as *Alembicks*, to distil fresh Waters in vast Quantities for the Use of the World: And their *Heights* give a Descent unto the *Streams*, to run gently, like so many Veins of the *Macrocosm*, to be the more beneficial to the Creation. The generation of *Clouds*, and the distribution of *Rains*, accommodated and accomplished by the *Mountains*, is indeed so observable, that the learned *Scheuchzer* and *Creitlovius* can't forbear breaking out upon it with a *Mirati summam Creatoris Sapientiam!* [2]

What *Rivers* could there be without those admirable *Tools of Nature!*

Vapours being raised by the *Sun*, acting on the Sur-

[1] *I. e.*, colanders, strainers.

[2] "Wonderful is the lofty wisdom of the Creator." The quotation and the names of the two authorities, are taken direct from Derham.

face of the *Sea*, as a *Fire* under an Alembick, by rarefy-
ing of it, makes the lightest and freshest Portions
thereof to rise first; which *Rarefaction* is made (as Dr.
Cheyne observes)[1] by the insinuation of its active Particles among the porous Parts thereof, whereby they are
put into a violent Motion many different ways, and
so are expanded into little Bubbles of larger Dimensions
than formerly they had; and so they become specifically
lighter, and the weightier *Atmosphere* buoys them up.
The Streams of these *Vapours* rest in places where the
Air is of equal *Gravity* with them, and are carried up
and down the *Atmosphere* by the course of that Air,
till they hit at last against the sides of the *Mountains*,
and by this Concussion are condensed, and thus become
heavier than the Air they swum in, and so gleet down
the rocky Caverns of these *Mountains*, the inner parts
whereof being hollow and stony, afford them a *Bason*,
until they are accumulated in sufficient Quantities, to
break out at the first *Crany:* whence they descend
into Plains, and several of them uniting, form Rivulets;
and many of those uniting, do grow into *Rivers*. This
is the Story of them; this their *Pedigree!*

Minerals are dug out of *Mountains;* which, if they
were sought only in level Countries, the Delfs would
be so flown with Waters, that it would be impossible
to make *Addits* or *Soughs* to drein them.[2] Here is, as
Olaus Magnus expresses it, *Inexhausta pretiosorum
Metallorum ubertas.*[3]

A *German* Writer, got upon the *Mountains*, gives this
Account of them: *Sunt ceu tot naturales Fornaces Chymi-*

---

[1] Mather refers to Dr. George Cheyne's *Philosophical Principles
of Religion, Natural and Revealed.*

[2] Delf = a ditch; addits and soughs = drains, gutters.

[3] "Inexhaustible plenty of precious minerals."

cæ, in quibus Deus varia Metalla & Mineralia excoquit & maturat.[1]

The *Habitations* and *Situations* of Mankind are made vastly the more comfortable for the *Mountains*. There is a vast Variety of *Plants* proper to the *Mountains:* and many Animals find the *Mountains* their most proper places to breed and feed in. *The highest Hills a Refuge to the wild Goats!* A Point Mr. *Ray* has well spoken to.

They report that *Hippocrates* did usually repair to the *Mountains* for the *Plants,* by which he wrought the chief of his Cures.

Mountains also are the most convenient Boundaries to Territories, and afford a Defence unto them. One calls them *the Bulwarks of Nature, cast up at the Charges of the Almighty; the Scorns and Curbs of the most victorious Armies.* The *Barbarians* in *Curtius* [2] were confidently sensible of this!

Yea, we may appeal to the Senses of all Men, whether the grateful Variety of *Hills* and *Dales* be not more pleasing than the largest continued *Plains.*

'Tis also a *salutary Conformation* of the Earth; some Constitutions are best suited *above,* and others *below.*

Truly these massy and lofty Piles can by no means be spared.

Galen, thou shalt chastize the *Pseudo-Christians,* who reproach the Works of God. Say!——*Accusandi sanè meâ Sententiâ hic sunt Sophistæ, qui cùm nondum invenire neque exponere Opera Naturæ queant, eam tamen inertia atque inscitia condemnant.*[3]

[1] "They are like so many natural chemical furnaces in which God tempers and ripens various metals and minerals."

[2] Quintus Curtius, historian.

[3] "Those sophists are blameable, who, since they cannot discover or make clear the works of nature, condemn it from laziness and ignorance."

Say now, *O Man*, say, under the sweet Constraints of Demonstration, *Great GOD, the Earth is full of thy Goodness!*

And Dr. *Grew* shall carry on the more general Observation for us. 'How little is the Mischief which the '*Air, Fire*, or *Water* sometimes doth, compared with 'the innumerable *Uses* to which they daily serve? Be-'sides the *Seas* and *Rivers*, how many *wholesome Springs* 'are there for one that is *poisonous?* Are the Northern 'Countries subject to *Cold?* They have a greater 'plenty of *Furs* to keep the People warm. Would those 'under or near the Line be subject to *Heat?* They have 'a constant *Easterly Breeze*, which blows strongest in 'the Heat of the Day, to refresh them: And with this 'Refreshment *without*, they have a variety of excellent '*Fruits* to comfort and cool them *within*. How admir-'ably are the *Clouds* fed with Vapours, and carried 'about with the *Winds*, for the gradual, equal, and 'seasonable watering of most Countries? And in 'those which have less *Rain*, how abundantly is the 'want of that supplied with noble *Rivers?*'

Even the subterraneous *Caverns* have their Uses. And so have the *Ignivomous Mountains:* Those terrible things are *Spiracles*, to vent the *Vapours*, which else might make a dismal Havock. Dr. *Woodward* observes, That tho Places which are very subject unto *Earthquakes* usually have these *Volcano's*, yet without these *fiery Vents* their *Earthquakes* would bring more tremendous Desolations upon them.

Those two flammivomous Mountains, *Vesuvius* and *Ætna*, have sometimes terrified the whole World with their tremendous Eruptions. *Vesuvius* transmitted its frightful Cinders as far as *Constantinople*, which obliged the Emperor to leave the City; and Historians tell us there was kept an Anniversary Commemoration of it. *Kircher* has given us a Chronicle of what furious things have been done by *Ætna;* the melted Matter which one time it poured forth, spreading in breadth six Miles, ran down as far as *Catanea*,[1] and forced a Passage into the Sea.

Asia abounds in these *Volcano's*. *Africa* is known to have eight at least. In *America* 'tis affirmed that there are not less than fifteen, among that vast Chain of Mountains called the *Andes*. One says, 'Nature 'seems here to keep house under ground, and the 'Hollows of the *Mountains* to be the *Funnels* or *Chim-* 'neys, by which the fuliginous Matter of those ever- lasting Fires ascends.'

The *North* too, that seems doom'd unto *eternal Cold*, has its famous *Hecla*. And *Bartholomew Zenet*[2] found one in *Greenland*, yet nearer to the Pole; the Effects whereof are very surprizing.

A reasonable and religious Mind cannot behold these formidable *Mountains*, without some Reflections of this importance: *Great GOD, who knows the Power of thine Anger? Or what can stand before the powerful Indignation of that God, who can kindle a Fire in his .Anger that shall burn to the lowest Hell, and set on fire the Foundations of the Mountains!*

The *Volcano's* would lead us to consider the *Earth- quakes*, wherein the *Earth* often suffers violent, and sometimes very destructive Concussions.

The History of Earthquakes would be a large, as well as a sad Volume. Whether a *Colluctation*[3] of *Minerals*

---

[1] Catania.

[2] Possibly a reference to Nicolo Zeno, who, in the 14th century is said to have gone to Greenland, and to have discovered a volcano there.   [3] Conflict.

in the Bowels of the Earth is the cause of those direful Convulsions, may be considered: As we know a Composition of Gold which *Aqua Regia* has dissolved; *Sal Armoniack*, and *Salt of Tartar*, set on fire, will with an horrible crack break thro all that is in the way. But Mankind ought herein to tremble before the Justice of God. Particular *Cities* and *Countries*, what fearful Desolations have been by Earthquakes brought upon them!

The old sinking of *Helice* and *Buris*, absorbed by *Earthquakes* into the Sea, mention'd by *Ovid*, or the twelve Cities that were so swallow'd up in the Days of *Tiberius*, are small things to what *Earthquakes* are to do on our Globe; yea, have already done. I know not what we shall think of the huge *Atlantis*, mentioned by *Plato*, now at the bottom of the *Atlantick* Ocean: But I know *Varenius* thinks it probable, that the Northern Part of *America* was joined unto *Ireland*, till Earthquakes made the vast and amazing Separation. Others have thought so of *England* and *France;* of *Spain* and *Africa;* of *Italy* and *Sicily*.

Ah, *Sicily!* Art thou come to be spoken of? No longer ago than t'other day what a rueful Spectacle was there exhibited in the Island of *Sicily* by an *Earthquake*,[1] in which there perished the best part of two hundred thousand Souls!

Yea, *Ammianus Marcellinus* tells us, in the Year 365, *Horrendi Tremores per omnem Orbis Ambitum grassati sunt*.[2]

O Inhabitants of the Earth, how much ought you to fear the things that will bring you into ill Terms with the Glorious GOD! *Fear*, lest the *Pit* and the *Snare*

[1] Probably the earthquakes in January, 1693.
[2] "Fearful shakings went through all the surface of the earth."

be upon you! Against all other Strokes there may some
Defence or other be thought on: There is none against
an *Earthquake!* It says, *Tho they hide in the top of*
Carmel, *I will find them there!*

But surely the *Earthquakes* I have met with will
effectually instruct me to avoid the Folly of setting my
Heart inordinately on any *Earthly* Possessions or Enjoyments. Methinks I hear Heaven saying *Surely he*
will receive this Instruction!

A modern Philosopher speaks at this rate, 'We do
'not know when and where we stand upon *good Ground:*
'It would amaze the stoutest Heart, and make him
'ready to die with Fear, if he could see into the *sub-*
'*terraneous World*, and view the dark Recesses of Nature
'under ground; and behold, that even the strongest
'of our Piles of Building, whose Foundation we think
'is laid firm and fast, yet are set upon an Arch or
'Bridge, made by the bending Parts of the Earth one
'upon another, over a prodigious Vault, at the bottom
'of which there lies an unfathomable Sea, but its upper
'Hollows are filled with stagnating Air, and with Ex-
'pirations of sulphureous and bituminous Matter.
'Upon such a *dreadful Abyss* we walk, and ride, and
'sleep; and are sustained only by an *arched Roof*, which
'also is not in all places of an equal Thickness.'

Give me leave to say, I take *Earthquakes* to be very
moving Preachers unto *worldly-minded Men:* Their
Address may be very agreeably put into the Terms of
the Prophet; *O Earth, Earth, Earth, hear the Word of*
the Lord!

'*Chrysostom* did well, among his other Epithets, to
'call the Earth *our Table;* but it shall *teach* me as
'well as *feed* me: May I be a *Deipnosophist* [1] upon it.

[1] "A master of the art of dining."

'Indeed, what is the Earth but a *Theatre*, as has
'been long since observed? *In quo Infinita & Illustria,*
'*Providentiæ, Bonitatis, Potentiæ ac Sapientiæ Divinæ*
Spectacula contemplanda! [1] But I must not forget that
'this *Earth* is very shortly to be my *sleeping-place;* it
has a *Grave* waiting for me: *I will not fear to go down,*
'*for thou hast promised, O my Saviour, to bring me up*
'*again.*'

APPENDIX.

§.   Having arrived thus far, I will here make
a Pause, and acknowledge the Shine of
Heaven on *our Parts of the Earth*, in the
Improvements of our *modern Philosophy*.

To render us the more sensible hereof, we will propose
a few Points of the *Mahometan Philosophy*, or Secrets
reveal'd unto *Mahomet*, which none of his Followers,
who cover so much of the Earth at this Day, may dare
to question.

The *Winds;* 'tis an *Angel* moving his *Wings* that
raises them.

The *Flux* and *Reflux* of the *Sea*, is caused by an
Angel's putting his Foot on the middle of the *Ocean*,
which compressing the Waves, the Waters run to the
Shores; but being removed, they retire into their
proper Station.

Falling Stars are the *Firebrands* with which the *good
Angels* drive away the *bad*, when they are too saucily
inquisitive, and approach too near the Verge of the
Heavens, to eves-drop the Secrets there.

Thunder is nothing else but the cracking of an *Angel's*

[1] "In which are to be contemplated infinite and glorious spectacles
of the Divine providence, goodness, power, and wisdom."

Whip, while he slashes the dull Clouds into such and such places, when they want *Rains* to fertilize the Earth.

Eclipses are made thus: The *Sun* and *Moon* are shut in a *Pipe*, which is turned up and down; from each Pipe is a Window, by which they enlighten the World; but when God is angry at the Inhabitants of it for their Transgressions, He bids an *Angel* clap to the Window, and so turn the Light towards Heaven from the Earth: for this Occasion *Forms of Prayer* are left, that the Almighty would avert his Judgments, and restore Light unto the World.

The thick-skull'd Prophet sets another *Angel* at work for *Earthquakes;* he is to hold so many *Ropes* tied unto every Quarter of the Globe, and when he is commanded, he is to pull; so he shakes that part of the Globe: and if a City, or Mountain, or Tower, is to be overturned, then he tugs harder at the Pulley, till the Rivers dance, and the Valleys are filled with Rubbish, and the Waters are swallowed up in the Precipices.

May our Devotion exceed the Mahometan *as much as our Philosophy!*

ESSAY XXIV. *Of* MAGNETISM.

SUCH an unaccountable thing there is as *the* MAGNETISM *of the Earth*. A Principle very different from that of *Gravity*.

The Operations of this amazing Principle, are principally discovered in the communion that *Iron* has with the *Loadstone;* a rough, coarse, unsightly Stone, but of more Value than all the *Diamonds* and *Jewels* in the Universe.

It is observed by *Sturmius,* That the *attractive Quality* of the *Magnet* was known to the Antients, even beyond all History. Indeed, besides what *Pliny* says of it, *Aristotle* speaks of *Thales,* as having said, the *Stone* has a *Soul,* ὅτι τὸν σιδηρὸν κινεῖ· be*cause it moves Iron.*

It was *Roger Bacon* who first of all discovered the *Verticity* of the *Magnet,* or its Property of pointing towards the *Pole,* about four hundred Years ago.

The Communication of its Vertue to *Iron* was first of all discovered by the *Italians.* One *Goia* first lit upon the Use of the *Mariner's Compass,* about *A. C.* 1300. After this, the various *Declination* of the *Needle* under different Meridians, was discovered by *Cabot* and *Norman.* And then the Variation of the Declination, so as to be not always the same in one and the same place, by *Hevelius, Auzot, Volckamer,* and others.[1]

The inquisitive Mr. *Derham* says, The *Variation of the Variation* was first found out by our *Gellibrand, A. C.* 1634.

And he himself has added a further Discovery; That as the *Common Needle* is continually varying towards the *East* and *West,* so the *Dipping Needle* varies up and down, towards the *Zenith,* or fromwards, with a *magnetick* Tendency, describing a Circle round the Pole of the World, or some other Point; a Circle, whereof the *Radius* is about 13 Degrees.

In every *Magnet* there are *two Poles,* the one pointing to the *North,* and the other to the *South.*

The *Poles,* in divers Parts of the Globe, are diversly inclined towards the *Center* of the Earth.

[1] All three of these scientists had communicated papers to the *Philosophical Transactions* of the Royal Society, whence Mather draws much of his material about magnets.

These *Poles*, tho contrary to one another, do mutually help towards the *Magnet's* Attraction, and suspension of *Iron*.

If a *Stone* be cut or broke into ever so many pieces, there are these *two Poles* in each of the *pieces*.

If two *Magnets* are spherical, one will conform itself to the other, so as either of them would do to the *Earth;* and after they have so turned themselves, they will endeavour to approach each other: but placed in a contrary Position, they avoid each other.

If a *Magnet* be cut thro the *Axis*, the Segments of the Stone, which before were joined, will now avoid and fly each other.

If the *Magnet* be cut by a Section perpendicular to its *Axis*, the two Points, which before were conjoined, will become contrary Poles; one in one, t'other in t'other Segment.

Iron receives Vertue from the *Magnet*, by application to it, or barely from an approach near it, tho it do not touch it; and the *Iron* receives this Vertue variously, according to the Parts of the Stone it is made to approach to.

The *Magnet* loses none of its own Vertue by communicating any to the *Iron*. This Vertue it also communicates very speedily; tho the longer the *Iron* joins the Stone, the longer its communicated Vertue will hold. And the better the *Magnet*, the sooner and stronger the communicated Vertue.

Steel receives Vertue from the *Magnet* better than *Iron*.

A *Needle* touch'd by a *Magnet*, will turn its Ends the same way towards the Poles of the World as the *Magnet* will do it. But neither of them conform their Poles exactly to those of the World; they have usually some *Variation*, and this *Variation* too in the same place is not always the same.

A *Magnet* will take up much more *Iron* when *arm'd* or *cap'd* than it can alone. And if the *Iron Ring* be suspended by the *Stone*, yet the magnetical Particles do not hinder the Ring from turning round any way, to the Right or Left.

The best *Magnet*, at the least distance from a lesser or a weaker, cannot draw to it a piece of Iron adhering actually to a much weaker or lesser Stone; but if it come to touch it, it can draw it from the other. But a weaker *Magnet*, or even a little piece of *Iron*, can draw away or separate a piece of *Iron* contiguous to a better and greater *Magnet*.

In our Northern Parts of the World, the *South Pole* of a *Loadstone* will raise more *Iron* than the *North Pole*.

A Plate of *Iron* only, but no other Body interposed, can impede the Operation of the *Loadstone*, either as to its attractive or directive Quality.

The Power and Vertue of the *Loadstone* may be impair'd by lying long in a wrong posture, as also by Rust, and Wet, and the like.

A *Magnet* heated *red-hot*, will be speedily deprived of its *attractive* Quality; then cooled, either with the *South Pole* to the *North*, in an horizontal position, or with the *South Pole* to the *Earth* in a perpendicular, it will change its *Polarity;* the *Southern* Pole becoming the *Northern*, and *vice versâ*.

By applying the Poles of a very *small Fragment* of a *Magnet* to the opposite vigorous ones of a larger, the Poles of the Fragment have been speedily changed.

Well temper'd and harden'd *Iron* Tools, *heated* by Attrition, will attract Filings of *Iron* and *Steel*.

The *Iron Bars* of *Windows*, which have stood long

in an erect position, do grow permanently *magnetical;* the lower ends of such Bars being the *Northern Poles,* and the upper the *Southern.*

Mr. *Boyle* found *English Oker,* heated red-hot, and cooled in a proper posture, plainly to gain a *magnetick* Power.

The illustrious Mr. *Boyle,* and the inquisitive Mr. *Derham,* have carried on their Experiments, till we are overwhelmed with the *Wonders,* as well as with the *Numbers* of them.

That of Mr. *Derham,* and *Grimaldi,* That a piece of well-touch [1] *Iron Wire,* upon being bent round in a Ring, or coiled round upon a Stick, loses its Verticity; is very admirable.

The Strength of some *Loadstones* is very surprizing.

Dr. *Lister* [2] saw a Collection of *Loadstones,* one of them weighed naked not above a *Dram,* yet it would raise a *Dram and half* of *Iron;* but being shod, it would raise *one hundred and forty and four Drams.* A smooth *Loadstone,* weighing 65 Grains, drew up 14 Ounces; that is, 144 times its own weight. A *Loadstone* that was no bigger than an Hazel-nut, fetch'd up an huge bunch of Keys.

The *Effluvia* of a *Loadstone* seem to work in a *Circle.* What flows from the *North Pole,* comes round, and enters the *South Pole;* and what flows from the *South Pole,* enters the *North Pole.*

Tho a minute *Loadstone* may have a prodigious force, yet it is very strange to see what a *short Sphere of Activity* it has; it affects not the *Iron* sensibly above an Inch or two, and the biggest little more than a

---

[1] Probably a misprint for " well-touched," *i. e.,* well magnetized.

[2] Dr. Martin Lister, 1638?–1712, published in 1698 an account of his travels.

Foot or two. The *magnetick Effluvia* make haste to return to the Stone that emitted them, and seem afraid of leaving it, as a Child the Mother before it can go alone.

On that astonishing Subject, *The Variation of the Compass*, what if we should hear the acute Mr. *Halley*'s [1] Proposals?

He proposes, That our whole Globe should be looked upon as a *great Magnet*, having four *magnetical Poles*, or Points of Attraction, two near each Pole of the Equator. In those Parts of the World which lie near adjacent unto any one of these *magnetical Poles*, the Needle is governed by it; the nearer Pole being always predominant over the remoter. The *Pole* which at present is nearest unto *Britain*, lies in or near the Meridian of the Lands-end of *England*, and not above seven Degrees from the *Artick Pole*. By this *Pole* the Variations in all *Europe*, and in *Tartary*, and in the *North Sea*, are principally governed, tho' with some regard to the other *Northern Pole*, which is in a Meridian passing about the middle of *Calefornia*,[2] and about fifteen Degrees from the *North Pole* of the World. To this the Needle pays its chief respect in all the North *America*, and in the two Oceans on either side, even from the *Azores* Westward, unto *Japan*, and further. The two *Southern Poles* are distant rather further from the *South* Pole of the World; the one is about sixteen Degrees therefrom, and is under a *Meridian* about twenty Degrees to the Westward of the *Magellanick*

---

[1] Edmund Halley, the astronomer, 1656–1742, communicated to the Royal Society an article on "a theory of the variation of the magnetical compass," printed in the Society's *Philosophical Transactions*, vol. xiii.

[2] *I. e.*, the old Mexican province of California.

Streights; this commands the Needle in all the South *America*, in the *Pacifick Sea*, and in the greatest part of the *Ethiopick Ocean*. The fourth and last Pole seems to have the greatest Power and the largest Dominions of all, as it is the most remote from the Pole of the World; for 'tis near twenty Degrees from it, in the Meridian which passes thro *Hollandia Nova*, and the Island *Celebes*. This Pole has the mastery in the South part of *Africa*, in *Arabia*, and the *Red Sea*, in *Persia*, in *India*, and its Islands, and all over the *Indian Sea*, from the *Cape of Good Hope* Eastwards, to the middle of the great *South Sea*, which d vides *Asia* from *America*.

Behold, the Disposition of the *magnetical Vertue*, as it is throughout the whole Globe of the *Earth* at this day!

But now to solve the *Phœnomena!*

We may reckon the external Parts of our Globe as a *Shell*, the internal as a *Nucleus*, or an *inner Globe* included within ours; and between these a *fluid Medium*, which having the same common Center and Axis of diurnal Rotation, may turn about with our Earth every four and twenty Hours: only this outer Sphere having its turbinating Motion some small matter either swifter or slower than the internal Ball, and a very small difference becoming in length of Time sensible by many Repetitions; the internal Parts will by degrees recede from the external, and not keeping pace with one another, will appear gradually to move, either East-wards or Westwards, by the difference of their Motions. Now if the exterior Shell of our Globe should be a *Magnet*, having its Poles at a distance from the Poles of diurnal Rotation; and if the internal *Nucleus* be likewise a *Magnet*, having its Poles in two other places, distant also from the Axis, and these latter, by a slow

and gradual Motion, change their place in respect of
the external, we may then give a reasonable account
of the *four magnetical Poles*, and of the *Changes of the
Needle's Variations*. Who can tell but the *final Cause*
of the Admixture of the *magnetical Matter* in the Mass
of the terrestrial Parts of our Globe, should be to maintain the concave Arch of this our Shell? Yea, we may
suppose the Arch lined with a *magnetical Matter*, or to
be rather one great *concave Magnet*, whose *two Poles*
are fixed in the Surface of our Globe? Sir *Isaac Newton*
has demonstrated the *Moon* to be more solid than our
Earth, as nine to five; why may we not then suppose
four Ninths of our Globe to be Cavity? Mr. *Halley*
allows there may be Inhabitants of the lower Story,
and many ways of producing *Light* for them. The
Medium itself may be always luminous; or the concave
Arch may shine with such a Substance as does invest
the Surface of the *Sun;* or they may have peculiar
Luminaries, whereof we can have no Idea: As *Virgil*
and *Claudian* enlighten their *Elysian* Fields; the latter,

> *Amissum ne crede Diem; sunt altera nobis*
> *Sydera; sunt Orbes alii; Lumenque videbis*
> *Purius, Elysiumque magis mirabere Solem.*[1]

The Diameter of the Earth being about eight thou-
sand *English* Miles, how easy 'tis to allow five hundred
Miles for the Thickness of the Shell! And another
five hundred Miles for a Medium capable of a vast
Atmosphere, for the Globe contained within it! ——
But it's time to stop, we are got beyond *Human Pene-*

[1] "Do not suppose that light is lost; there are other stars for us,
and other courses, and you shall see a clearer light and wonder at
the sun of Elysium."

tration; we have *dug* as far as 'tis fit any *Conjecture* should carry us!

It is a little surprizing that the Orb of the Activity of *Magnets*, as Mr. *Derham* observes, is larger or lesser at different times. There is a noble and a mighty *Loadstone* reserved in the Repository at *Gresham*-College, which will keep a Key, or other piece of *Iron*, suspended unto another, sometimes at the distance of eight or ten Foot from it, but at other times not above four.

[A *Digression*, if worthy to be called so!]

§. But is it possible for me to go any further without making an *Observation*, which indeed would ever now and then break in upon us as we go along?

Once for all; *Gentlemen Philosophers*, The MAGNET has quite *puzzled* you. It shall then be no indecent *Anticipation* of what should have been observed at the Conclusion of this Collection, here to demand it of you, that you glorify the infinite Creator of this, and of all things, as *incomprehensible.* You must acknowledge that *Human Reason* is too feeble, too narrow a thing to comprehend the *infinite* God. The Words of our excellent *Boyle* deserve to be recited on this Occasion: 'Such is the *natural Imbecillity* of the *Human* 'Intellect*, that the most piercing Wits and excellent 'Mathematicians are forced to confess, that not only 'their own *Reason*, but that of Mankind, may be 'puzzled and nonplus'd about QUANTITY, which 'is an Object of Contemplation natural, nay, mathe-'matical. Wherefore why should we think it unfit 'to be believed, and to be acknowledged, that in the 'Attributes* of God [it may be added, *and in His Dis-'pensations towards the Children of Men*] there should be 'some things which our finite Understandings cannot

'clearly *comprehend?* And we who cannot clearly
'comprehend how in ourselves two such distant Na-
'tures, as that of a *gross Body* and an *immaterial Spirit*
'should be so united as to make up *one Man*, why
'should we grudge to have our REASON Pupil to an
'*omniscient Instructor*, who can teach us such things,
'as neither our own mere Reason, nor any others,
'could ever have discovered to us?'

I will now single out a few plain *Mathematical Instances* wherein, Sirs, you will find your finest *Reason* so
transcended, and so confounded, that it is to be hoped
a *profound Humility* in the grand Affairs of our *holy
Religion* will from this time for ever *adorn* you.

Mr. *Robert Jenkin*[1] discoursing on *the Reasonableness
of the Christian Religion*, gives two Instances *how much
we may lose ourselves in the Speculation of material
things*.

First, Nothing seems more evident, than that *all
Matter is divisible;* yea, the *least Particle* of *Matter*
must be so, because it has the Nature and Essence of
Matter: it can never be so *divided* that it shall cease to
be *Matter*. But then, on the other side, it is plain,
Matter cannot be *infinitely divisible;* because whatever
is *divisible*, is *divisible* into *Parts;* and no *Parts* can be
infinite, because no *Number* can be so. A *numberless
Number* is a Contradiction; all Parts are capable of
being *numbred;* they are *more* or *fewer*, *odd* or *even*. It
is not enough to say, that *Matter* is only capable of
such a *Division*, but never can be *actually divided into
infinite Parts;* for the Parts into which it is *divisible*
must be *actually existent*, tho they be not *actually divided*.
And last of all to say, these Parts of Matter are *indef-*

---

[1] Robert Jenkin, 1656–1727, master of St. John's College, Cambridge.

inite, but not *infinite*, is only to confess *we know not
what to say*.

Secondly, We all agree that all the *Parts* into which
the *Whole* is divided, being taken together are *equal to
the Whole*. But it seems any *single Part* is *equal to the
Whole*. It is granted, that in any *Circle* a *Line* may be
drawn from *every Point* of the Circumference to the
Center. Suppose the Circle to be the *Equator*, and a
million lesser Circles are drawn within the *Equator*,
about the same *Center*, and then a *right Line* drawn
from *every Point* of the *Equator* to the Center of the
Globe; every such *right Line* drawn from the *Equator*
to the *Center*, must of necessity cut thro the million
lesser Circles, about the same *Center:* consequently there
must be the same number of Points in a Circle a million
of times less than the *Equator*, as there is in the *Equator*
itself. The *lesser Circles* may be multiplied into as
many as there are *Points* in the *Diameters;* and
so the *least Circle* imaginable may have *as many Points*
as the greatest; that is, be as big as the greatest, as
big as one that is millions of times as big as itself.

Yet more; What will you say to this? Let a *Radius*
be moved as a *Radius* upon a *Circle;* 'tis a Case of
Dr. *Grew*'s proposing: whether we suppose it *wholly*
moved, or but *in part*, the Supposition will bring us
to an *Absurdity;* if it be in a part *movent*,[1] and in a
part *quiescent*, it will be a *curve Line*, and no *Radius;*
if it be wholly *movent*, then it moves either *about* or
upon the Center; if it moves *about* it, it then comes
short of it, and so again is no *Radius:* it cannot move
upon it, because all motion having parts, there can be
no motion upon a *Point*.

More yet; We cannot conceive how the *Perimeter*

[1] Moving.

of a Circle, or other *curve Figure*, can consist without
being infinitely *angular;* for the *parts* of a *Line* are
Lines: But we cannot conceive how those Lines can
have, as here they have, a different direction, and therefore an inclination, without making an *Angle.* And yet if
you suppose a *Circle* to be *angular*, you destroy the
Definition of a *Circle*, and the Theorems depending on it.

Once more; I will offer a Case of my own. The
Line on which I am now writing is a *Space* between
two Points; it will be doubtless allowed me, that my
Pen in passing over this Line, from the one point unto
the other, must *pass over the half of the Line before it
passes over the whole;* and so the *half* of the remaining
half, and so the half of the quarter that remains: so
still the half of the remaining space, the *half before the
whole;* and yet when it comes to execution, you find
it is not so. If the Position you allowed me had been
true, my Pen would not have reach'd unto the *end* of
the *Line* before the *End* of my *Life;* or in a Term
wherein it might have written ten Books as big as old
Zoroaster's, or more Manuscripts than ever were in
the *Alexandrian* Library.

It is then evident, that all Mankind is to this day
in the dark as to the *ultimate Parts* of *Quantity*, and of
Motion.

Go on my learned *Grew*, and maintain [who more
fit than one of thy *recondite Learning?*] *that there is
hardly any one thing in the World, the Essence whereof
we can perfectly comprehend.* But then to the *natural
Imbecillity* of REASON, add the *moral Depravations* of
it, by our Fall from God, and the Ascendant which a
corrupt and vicious *Will* has obtain'd over it, how much
ought this Consideration to warn us against the Conduct
of an *unhumbled Understanding* in things relating to the

Kingdom of God? I am not out of my way, I have had a *Magnet* all this while *steering* of this Digression: I am now returning to *that*.

¶. God forbid I should be, *Tam Lapis ut Lapidi Numen inesse putem.*[1] To fall down before a *Stone*, and say, *Thou art a God*, would be an *Idolatry*, that none but a Soul more senseless than a *Stone* could be guilty of. But then it would be a very agreeable and acceptable *Homage* unto the Glorious GOD, for me to see much of Him in such a wonderful *Stone* as the MAGNET. They have done well to call it the *Loadstone*, that is to say, the *Lead-stone: May it lead me unto Thee, O my God and my Saviour! Magnetism* is in this like to *Gravity*, that it leads us to GOD, and brings us very near to Him. When we see *Magnetism* in its Operation, we must say, *This is the Work of God!* And of the *Stone*, which has proved of such vast use in the Affairs of the *Waters that cover the Sea*, and will e'er long do its part in bringing it about that the *Glory of the Lord shall cover the Earth*, we must say, *Great God, this is a wonderful Gift of Thine unto the World!*

I do not propose to exemplify the *occasional Reflections* which a devout Mind may make upon all the *Creatures* of God, their *Properties*, and *Actions*, and *Relations;* the *Libri Elephantini*[2] would not be big enough to contain the thousandth part of them. If it were lawful for me here to pause with a particular *Exercise upon the Loadstone*, my first Thoughts would be those of the

---

[1] "Such a stone as to think that there is in a stone any divine authority."

[2] The elephantine books were made up of ivory tablets on which were kept certain governmental records of the ancient Romans. "Elephantine" means "made of ivory" but Mather takes it here as referring to "elephantine" size.

holy *Scudder*,[1] whose Words have had a great Impression
on me ever since my first reading of them in my Childhood: 'An upright Man is like a *Needle* touch'd with
'the *Loadstone;* tho he may thro boisterous *Temptations*
'and strong *Allurements* oftentimes look towards the
'Pleasure, Gain and Glory of this *present World*, yet
'because he is truly touch'd with the sanctifying Spirit
'of God, he still inclineth *God-ward*, and hath no Quiet
'till he stand *steady towards Heaven.*'——However, to
animate the Devotion of my *Christian* Philosopher, I
will here make a Report to him. The ingenious *Ward*
wrote a pious Book, as long ago as the Year 1639,
entitled, *Magnetis Reductorium Theologicum.*[2] The
Design of his Essay, is, to *lead* us from the Consideration of the *Loadstone*, to the Consideration of our
Saviour, and of his incomparable *Glories;* whereof
the *Magnet* has in it a notable Adumbration. In his
Introduction he has a Note, worthy to be transcribed
here, as religiously asserting the Design, of which our
whole Essay is a Prosecution. *Hic præcipuus & poten-
tissimus Creaturarum omnium Finis est, cum Scalæ nobis
& Alæ fiunt, quibus Animæ nostraæ suprà Dumeta &
Sterquilinia Mundi hujus volitantes, faciliùs ad Cælum
ascendunt, & ad Deum Creatorem aspirant.*[3] For what is
now before us, if our *Ward* may be our Adviser; *Christian*, in the *Loadstone* drawing and lifting up the *Iron*,
behold thy *Saviour* drawing us to himself, and raising

[1] Henry Scudder, divine and writer, who died about 1659.

[2] Samuel Ward, who died in 1643, was the brother of Nathaniel
Ward, who wrote in New England the famous *Simple Cobler of
Aggawamm.*

[3] "This is the special and most important end of all creatures,
since stairs and wings are made for us, by which our souls, flying
above the thorn-bushes and dunghills of this world, may ascend
to Heaven and aspire toward God the Creator."

us above the secular Cares and Snares that ruin us. In its ready *communication* of its Vertues, behold a shadow of thy *Saviour* communicating his holy Spirit to his chosen People; and his *Ministers* more particularly made Partakers of his *attractive Powers*. When *Silver* and *Gold* are neglected by the *Loadstone*, but coarse *Iron* preferred, behold thy *Saviour* passing over the *Angelical World*, and chusing to take *our Nature* upon him. The *Iron* is also undistinguished, whether it be lodged in a fine Covering, or whether it be lying in the most squalid and wretched Circumstances; which invites us to think how little *respect of Persons* there is with our *Saviour*. However, the *Iron* should be *cleansed*, it should not be *rusty;* nor will our *Saviour* embrace those who are not so far *cleansed*, that they are at least *willing to be made clean*, and have his *Files* pass upon them. The *Iron* is at first *merely passive*, then it *moves* more feebly towards the *Stone;* anon upon Contact it will fly to it, and express a marvellous Affection and Adherence. Is not here a Picture of the Dispositions in our Souls towards our Saviour? It is the Pleasure of our Saviour to work by *Instruments*, as the *Loadstone* will do most when the Mediation of a *Steel Cap* is used about it. After all, whatever is done, the whole *Praise* is due to the *Loadstone* alone. But there would be *no end*, and indeed there should be *none*, of these Meditations!——Our *Ward* in his Dedication of his Book to the King, has one very true Compliment. *Hoc ausim Majestati tuæ bonâ fide spondere; si unicus unicum possideres, Mundi totius te facile Monarcham efficeret.*[1]   But what a Great KING

---

[1] "This I might venture to promise in good faith to your Majesty: that if you alone possessed the only magnet, you might easily make yourself ruler of the whole world."

is He, who is the Owner, yea, and the Maker of all the *Magnets* in the World! *I am a Great KING, saith the Lord of Hosts, and my Name is to be feared among the Nations!* May the *Loadstone* help to carry it to them.

ESSAY XXV. *Of* MINERALS.

OPERUM *Dei Cognitionem* (says my dear *Arndt*) *quilibet ex sincero erga Deum amore & gratitudine sibi acquirere studeat, ut sciat, quæ Deus nostri causa creaverit.*[1] He smiles at the trifling *Logicians*, who, *totam ætatem inter inanes Subtilitates transigentes*,[2] wholly taken up with *Trifles*, overlook the glorious Works of God.

Our *Earth* is richly furnished with a Tribe of *Minerals*, called so because dug out of *Mines;* and because *dug*, therefore also called *Fossils*. Many things to be written of these, ought to have a *Nimok* [3] in the Margin!

The *adventitious Fossils*, which are but the *Exuviæ* [4] of *Animals* have been erroneously thought a sort of *peculiar Stones*. These must be excluded.

But then the *Natives of the Earth* are to be found in a vast variety. The inquisitive Dr. *Woodward*[5] has prepared us a noble *Table* of them.

[1] "Let everyone seek to acquire knowledge of the works of God, out of a true love and gratitude toward Him, in order to know what He created on our account."

[2] "Spending all their time in trifling subtleties."

[3] Mather's "Nimok," is probably a misprint for Nichols. To read "ch" as "m" and "ls" as "k" is easy, in his handwriting. Thomas Nichols, who flourished about 1650, wrote three books on gems and precious stones.

[4] "Parts sloughed off."

[5] John Woodward, geologist and physician, published in 1695 his *Essay toward a Natural History of the Earth.*

There are near twenty several sorts of *Earth*. Of these, besides the *Potter's Earth*, and the *Fuller's Earth*, how exceedingly useful is the *Chalk* to us! 'Tis a πολύχρηστον.[1]

There are above a dozen several sorts of *Stones*, that are found in *larger* Masses.

What *Vessels*, what *Buildings*, what *Ornaments*, do these afford us; especially the *Slate*, the *Marble*, the *Free-stone*, and the *Lime-stone?*

How helpful the *Warming-stone?*

How needful the *Grind-stone* and *Mill-stone?*

To the *Service* of our Maker we have so many Calls from the *Stones* themselves, [for if *Men* should be silent at proclaiming the Glory of God, the *very Stones would speak*] that a learned and a pious *German* so addresses us: *Audis tibi loquentes Lapides; tu ne sis Lapis in hac parte, sed ipsorum Vocem audi, & in illis Vocem Dei.*[2]

The *Whetstone* gives me a particular Admonition, which I have somewhere met with: *Multi multa docent alios, quæ ipsi præstare nequeunt.*[3] The worst Motto for a *Divine* that can be! *Lord, save me from it!*

How astonishing the *Figures*, which Dr. *Robinson* and Mr. *Ray* report, as naturally delineated upon several kinds of *Stones;* almost every thing in Nature described in them, so as could not be out-done by any Sculptor or Painter! The *Colaptice*,[4] such as no *Human Skill* could arise to!

---

[1] "Something useful in many ways."

[2] "You hear the stones speaking; be not a stone but hear their voice and in them the voice of God."

[3] "Many teach much to others, which they themselves can not do well."

[4] Carving.

Yea, in *Stones* there has been sometimes found so much of an *Human Shape*, that every thing really in it has been astonished at it. *Zeiler* and *Kircher* mention some famous *Rocks*, which so resemble *Monks*, that all People call them so. *Olaus Wormius* was Possessor of a large *Stone*, which had exactly the Head, Face, Neck and Shoulders of a *Man*. *Monconnys* and others relate the several *Parts* of a Man, which many *Stones* have exactly exhibited.[1] *Oh! how happy we, if Men and Stones had less Resemblance!*

There are many sorts of *Stones* found in *lesser Masses.*

Of these there are many who do *not* exceed the hardness of *Marble.*

Seven or eight of these are of an *indeterminate Figure.*

Twice as many have a *determinate Figure.*

Among these the Wonders of the *Osteo-colla,* to join and heal our *broken Brones* [*sic*].

But then there are others which *do* exceed *Marble* in hardness.

To this Article belong those that are usually called *Gems* or *precious Stones.*

[*Pebbles* and *Flints* are of the *Agate-kind.*]

Some of these are *opake.*

Three of the opake have a Body of *one Colour.*

Here the Wonders of the *Nephritick Stone!*

Three of the *opake* have *different Colours* mixed in the same Body.

Here the Wonders of the *Blood-stone!*

Some are *pellucid.*

---

[1] Olaus Worm (Wormius), 1588–1654, was a Danish physician. Balthasar de Monconys, 1611–1665, was a French traveller to the Orient. Martin Zeiller was a German geographer, and writer of books of travel in the 17th century. Kircher is probably Athanasius Kircher, 1602–1680, German antiquary and writer.

Two with *Colours changeable*, according to their different position in the Light.

Nine or ten with *Colours permanent*.

Some are *diaphanous*.

Two *yellow* (or partaking of it.)

Three *red*.

Three *blue*.

Two *green*.

Four *without any Colours*.

'But an excellent Writer observing, *Deus est Figu-*
'*lus Lapidum*,[1] carries on his Observation, That the
'God who makes *precious* as well as *common Stones*, has
'made *Men* with as much of a *Difference*, and not al-
'together without such a *Proportion*.'

'Good God, *Thy heavenly Graces in the Soul are brighter*
'*Jewels than any that are dug out of the Earth!* A *poor*
'Man may be adorn'd with these; those who are so,
'*they shall be mine, saith the Lord, in the Day when I*
'*make up my Jewels*.'

'How often have I seen a Jewel in the *Snout of a*
'*Swine!*'

'And how many *Counterfeits* in the World!'

There are seven sorts of *Salts* to be met withal.

But the *Salt* of our *Table*, of how much consequence
this to us! The Uses of it are too many to be by any
reckoned: Very many are well known to all. To
which add the Experience which *Bickerus* affirms the
Army of the Emperor *Charles* V. had, that they must
have perish'd on the *African* Shore, if they had not
found a Grain of *Salt* in their Mouths; an Antidote
not only against *Thirst*, but *Hunger* too.

He deserves to be herded with the Creatures, which

[1] "God is the potter who makes the stones."

OF MINERALS

Animam habent pro Sale,[1] who shall be so *insipid* an Animal, as to be insensible that the Benefits of *Salt* call for very great Acknowledgments. *My God, save me from what would render me unsavory Salt!*

There are three liquid *Bitumens,* six or seven solid.

There are about a dozen *metallick Minerals. Mercury* is one of these, but how astonishing an one! The Particles whereof how small, how smooth, how solid! The Corpuscles of it have Diameters much less than those of *Air;* yea, than those of *Water;* and not much greater than those of *Light* itself!

At last we come to *Metals; Iron,* with its Attendants; *Tin, Lead, Copper, Silver* and GOLD.

'I shall not consider the Reasons which moved 'Cardan[2] to assert that *Metals* have a *Soul;* but I am 'sure that I myself have a *Soul,* and am one that is '*reasonable;* if so, what can be more agreeable to me, 'than a Consideration which I find hinted by a curious 'Writer of *natural Theology:* We should admire the '*Munificence* of one who would bestow a considerable 'Quantity of enriching *Metals* upon us. But then 'how much cause have we to adore the *Munificence* 'of our bountiful GOD, who has enrich'd us with '*Metals* in so vast a Quantity, and with so much 'Profusion from His *hidden Treasures! Quotusquisque* '*est qui non videt, quid Ratio officii sui postulat?*'[3]

How amazingly serviceable is our *Iron* to us! In our *mechanical* Arts, in our *Agriculture,* in our *Navigation,* in our *Architecture;* in *all,* I say, *all* our Business! What a *sordid Life* do those *Barbarians* lead, who are kept

[1] "Have a desire for salt."
[2] Girolamo Cardan, Italian philosopher and scientist, 1501–1576.
[3] "How few are the men, who do not see what reason demands."

ignorant of it! Unthankful for this, *O Man*, you deserve *Heaven* should become as *Iron* over you.

It is from GOD that the *Metals* of most necessary Uses are the most plentiful; others that may be better spared, there is a rarity of them.

That one single *Metal*, Iron, as Dr. *Grew* observes, it sets on foot above an hundred sorts of manual Operations.

Tho the *Love of Money* be the *Root of all Evil*, yet the ingenious Dr. *Cockburn* has discoursed very justly on the vast Importance whereof the Use of *Money* is to Mankind. And indeed where the Use of *Money* has not been introduced, Men are brutish and savage, and nothing that is good has been cultivated.

There is a surprizing Providence of GOD in keeping up the Value of *Gold* and *Silver*, notwithstanding the vast Quantities dug out of the Earth in all Ages, ever since the Trade begun of *effodiuntur Opes;*[1] and so continuing them fit Materials to make *Money* of.

Among the marvellous Qualities of *Gold*, its *Ductility* deserves to have a particular Notice taken of it.

The *Wire-drawers*, to every 48 Ounces of *Silver*, allow one of *Gold*. Now *two Yards* of the superfine Wire weigh a *Grain*. In the Length of 98 Yards there are 49 Grains of Weight. A single Grain of *Gold* covers the said 98 Yards. The 10000th part of a *Grain* is above one third of an Inch long, which yet may be actually divided into ten; and so the 100000th part of a *Grain of Gold* may be visible without a *Microscope*.

It is a marvellous thing that *Gold*, after it has been divided by corrosive Liquors into *invisible Parts*, yet may presently be so precipitated, as to appear in its own *golden Form* again.

[1] "Riches are dug," *i. e.*, the trade of mining.

But, as Dr. *Grew* observes, the same *Immutability* which belongs to the Composition of *Gold*, much more belongs to the *Principles* of *Gold*, and of all other Bodies, when their Composition is destroyed. *Dampier*,[1] an ingenious Traveller all round the Globe, has an Observation; *I know no Place where Gold is found, but what is very unhealthy.*

'Possessor of *Gold!* Beware lest the Observation be 'verified in the *unhealthy* Influences of thy *Gold* upon 'thy *Mind;* and lest the *love* of it betray thee into 'many *foolish and hurtful Lusts*, which will drown thee 'in *Destruction and Perdition.*'

'The *Auri sacra Fames* [2] is the worst of all Distempers.'

My God, I bless Thee; I know something that is better than fine Gold, something that cannot be gotten for Gold, neither shall Silver be weighed for the Price thereof.

If *Gold* could speak, it would rebuke the *Idolatry* wherewith Mankind adores it, in much such Terms as I find a devout Writer assigning to it. *Non Deus sum, sed Dei Creatura; Terra mihi Mater. Ego servio tibi, ut tu servias Creatori.*[3]

¶. 'Finally, The antient Pagans not only worshipped 'the *Host of Heaven*, [justly called *Zabians*][4] but what-'soever they found *comfortable* to Nature, they also 'deified, even, *Quodcunque juvaret.*[5] The River *Nilus* 'too must at length become a Deity; yea, *Nascuntur* 'in *hortis Numina.*'[6]

[1] William Dampier, 1652–1715, English voyager.

[2] "Accursed hunger for gold."

[3] "I am not God, but a creature of God; the earth is my mother. I serve thee, that thou mayst serve the Creator."

[4] Zabians, or Sabians, a religious sect. In erroneous use the name was applied to star-worshippers, as it is here.

[5] "Whatever was pleasing."

[6] "Gods are born in gardens."

'And according to *Pliny, a Man that helps a Man
'becomes a God.'*

'God save us from the Crime stigmatiz'd by our
'Apostle, *to adore the Creatures more than the Creator!*
'By no means let us be as *Philo* speaks, Κοσμον μαλλὸν
'ἠ κοσμοπόιον θαυμάσαντες, *more admiring the World,
than the maker of the World.'*

'We will glorify the GOD who has bestowed things
'upon us; *for the Silver is mine, and the Gold is mine,*
'*saith the Lord of Hosts.'*

ESSAY XXVI. *Of the* VEGETABLES.

THE Contrivance of our most Glorious Creator,
in the VEGETABLES growing upon this Globe,
cannot be wisely observed without Admiration and Astonishment.

We will single out some Remarkables, and glorify
our GOD!

First, In *what manner* is *Vegetation* performed? And
how is the Growth of *Plants* and the Increase of their
Parts carried on? The excellent and ingenious Dr.
John Woodward[1] has, in the way of nice Experiment,
brought this thing under a close Examination. It is
evident that *Water* is necessary to *Vegetation;* there is
a *Water* which ascends the Vessels of the *Plants*, much
after the way of a *Filtration;* and the Plants take up a
larger or lesser Quantity of this Fluid, according to
their Dimensions. The much greater part of that
fluid Mass which is conveyed to the Plants, does not
abide there, but exhale thro them up into the *Atmos-*

[1] . *Cf.* John Woodward's "Some Thoughts and Experiments concerning Vegetation," in *Philosophical Transactions*, vol. xxi.

phere. Hence Countries that abound with *bigger Plants* are obnoxious to greater Damps, and Rains, and inconvenient Humidities. But there is also a *terrestrial Matter* which is mixed with this *Water*, and ascends up into the *Plants* with the *Water:* Something of this Matter will attend *Water* in all its motions, and stick by it after all its Percolations. Indeed the Quantity of this *terrestrial Matter*, which the Vapours carry up into the *Atmosphere*, is very *fine*, and not very *much*, but it is the truest and the best prepared *vegetable Matter;* for which cause it is that *Rain-water* is of such a singular Fertility. 'Tis true there is in *Water* a *mineral Matter* also, which is usually too scabrous, and ponderous, and inflexible, to enter the Pores of the *Roots.* Be the *Earth* ever so rich, 'tis observed little good will come of it, unless the Parts of it be loosened a little, and separated. And this probably is all the use of *Nitre* and other *Salts* to Plants, to loosen the Earth, and separate the Parts of it. It is this *terrestrial Matter* which fills the *Plants;* they are more or less nourished and augmented in proportion, as their *Water* conveys a greater or lesser quantity of proper *terrestrial Matter* to them. Nevertheless 'tis also probable that in this there is a variety; and all Plants are not formed and filled from the same sort of *Corpuscles.* Every *Vegetable* seems to require a *peculiar and specifick Matter* for its Formation and Nourishment. If the Soil wherein a Seed is planted, have not all or most of the Ingredients necessary for the *Vegetable* to subsist upon, it will suffer accordingly. Thus *Wheat* sown upon a Tract of Land well furnish'd for the Supply of that *Grain*, will succeed very well, perhaps for divers Years, or, as the Husbandman expresses it, *as long as the Ground is in heart;* but anon it will produce no more of that *Corn;* it will of some other, perhaps of *Barley:* and when it will subsist this no more, still *Oats* will thrive there; and perhaps *Pease* after these. When the Ground has lain fallow some time, the *Rain* will pour down a fresh Stock upon it; and the care of the *Tiller* in manuring of it, lays upon it such things as are most impregnated with a Supply for *Vegetation.* It is observ'd that *Spring-water* and *Rain-water* contain pretty near an equal charge of the *vegetable Matter,* but *River-water* much more than either of them; and hence the Inundations of *Rivers* leave upon their Banks the fairest Crops in the World. It is now plain that *Water* is not the *Matter* that composes *Vegetables,* but the *Agent* that conveys that *Matter* to them, and introduces it into the several parts of them. Wherefore the plentiful provision of this Fluid supplied to all Parts of the Earth, is by our *Woodward* justly celebrated with a pious Acknowledgment of that *natural Providence* that superintends over the Globe which we inhabit. The Parts of *Water* being exactly spherical, and subtile beyond all expression, the Surfaces perfectly polite, and the Intervals being therefore the largest, and so the most fitting to receive a *foreign Matter* into them, it is the most proper Instrument imaginable for the Service now assign'd to it. And yet *Water* would not perform this Office and Service to the *Plants,* if it be not assisted with a due quantity of *Heat; Heat* must concur, or *Vegetation* will not succeed. Hence as the *Heat* of several *Seasons* affords a different face of things, the same does the *Heat* of several *Climates.* The *hotter* Countries usually yield the *larger Trees,* and in a greater variety. And in *warmer* Countries, if there be a remission of the *usual Heat,* the Production will in proportion be diminish'd.

That I may a little contribute my *two Mites* to the illustration of the way wherein *Vegetation* is carried on, I will here communicate a couple of Experiments lately made in my Neighbourhood.

My Neighbour planted a Row of Hills in his Field with our *Indian Corn*, but such a Grain as was colour'd *red* and *blue;* the rest of the Field he planted with Corn of the most usual Colour, which is *yellow*. To the most *Windward-side* this Row infected *four* of the next neighbouring Rows, and part of the fifth, and some of the sixth, to render them colour'd like what grew on itself. But on the *Leeward-side* no less than seven or eight Rows were so colour'd, and some smaller impressions were made on those that were yet further distant.

The same Neighbour having his Garden often robb'd of the *Squashes* growing in it, planted some *Gourds* among them, which are to appearance very like them, and which he distinguish'd by certain adjacent marks, that he might not be himself imposed upon; by this means the Thieves 'tis true found a very *bitter Sauce*, but then all the *Squashes* were so infected and embitter'd, that he was not himself able to eat what the Thieves had left of them.

That most accurate and experienc'd Botanist Mr. *Ray* has given us the *Plants* that are more commonly met withal, with certain characteristick Notes, wherein he establishes *twenty-five Genders* of them. These *Plants* are to be rather stiled *Herbs*.

But then of the *Trees* and *Shrubs*, he distinguishes *five Classes* that have their *Flower* disjoined and remote from the *Fruit*, and as many that have their *Fruit* and *Flower* contiguous.

How unaccountably is the *Figure* of *Plants* preserved? And how unaccountably their *Growth* determined? Our excellent *Ray* flies to an intelligent *plastick Nature*, which must understand and regulate the whole Oeconomy.

Every particular *part* of the *Plant* has its astonishing Uses. The *Roots* give it a Stability, and fetch the Nourishment into it, which lies in the Earth ready for it. The *Fibres* contain and convey the Sap which carries up that Nourishment. The *Plant* has also larger Vessels, which entertain the proper and specifick Juice of it; and others to carry the Air for its necessary respiration. The outer and inner *Bark* defend it from Annoyances, and contribute to its Augmentation. The *Leaves* embrace and preserve the *Flower* and *Fruit* as they come to their explication. But the principal use of them, as *Malpighi*, and *Perault*, and *Mariotte*,[1] have observed, is, to concoct and prepare the *Sap* for the Nourishment of the *Fruit*, and of the whole *Plant;* not only that which ascends from the Root, but also what they take in from without, from the Dew, and from the Rain. For there is a *regress* of the *Sap* in Plants from above downwards; and this descendent Juice is that which principally nourishes both Fruit and Plant, as has been clearly proved by the Experiments of Signior *Malpighi* and Mr. *Brotherton.*

How agreeable the *Shade* of *Plants*, let every Man say that *sits under his own Vine, and under his own Fig-tree!*

How charming the Proportion and Pulchritude of the *Leaves*, the *Flowers*, the *Fruits*, he who confesses not, must be, as Dr. *More* says, *one sunk into a forlorn pitch of Degeneracy, and stupid as a Beast.*

Our Saviour says of the *Lillies* (which some, not

[1] Mather here is drawing from Ray's *Wisdom of God*, Part I, whence he derives these references to other authors.

without reason, suppose to be *Tulips*) *that* Solomon *in all his Glory was not arrayed like one of these*. And it is observed by *Spigelius*, that the Art of the most skilful Painter cannot so mingle and temper his *Colours*, as exactly to imitate or counterfeit the *native* ones of the *Flowers* of *Vegetables*.

Mr. *Ray* thinks it worthy a very particular Observation, that *Wheat*, which is the best sort of Grain, and affords the wholesomest Bread, is in a singular manner patient of both Extremes, both Heat and Cold, and will grow to maturity as well in *Scotland*, and in *Denmark*, as in *Egypt*, and *Guiney*, and *Madagascar*. It scarce refuses any Climate. And the exceeding *Fertility* of it is by a Pagan *Pliny* acknowledged as an Instance of the Divine Bounty to Man, *Quod eo maxime Hominem alat;*[1] one Bushel in a fit Soil, he says, yielding one hundred and fifty. A *German* Divine so far plays the Philosopher on this Occasion, as to propose it for a Singularity in *Bread*, that *totum Corpus sustentat, adeo, ut in unicâ Bucellâ, omnium Membrorum totius externi Corporis, nutrimentum contineatur, illiusque Vis per totum Corpus sese diffundat.*[2] A Friend of mine had *thirty-six Ears* of Rye growing from *one Grain*, and on *one Stalk*.

But of our *Indian Corn*, one Grain of *Corn* will produce above a *thousand*. And of *Guiney*[3] *Corn*, one Grain has been known to produce *ten thousand*.

The *Anatomy of Plants*, as it has been exhibited by

[1] "Because he feeds man chiefly with it." Ray, in whose book Mather found this quotation, has "alit."

[2] "It sustains all the body, to such a degree that in one bushel is contained nutriment for all the members of the whole body, and its strength is spread through all the body." Mather adds this quotation to what he finds in Ray.

[3] Guinea.

the incomparable Curiosity of Dr. *Grew*, what a vast *Field of Wonders* does it lead us into!

The most inimitable *Structure* of the Parts!

The particular *Canals*, and most adapted ones, for the conveyance of the lymphatick and essential Juices!

The *Air-Vessels* in all their curious Coylings!

The Coverings which befriend them, a Work unspeakably more curious in reality than in appearance!

The strange Texture of the *Leaves*, the angular or circular, but always most orderly Position of their *Fibres;* the various *Foldings*, with a *Duplicature*, a *Multiplicature*, the *Fore-rowl*, the *Back-rowl*, the *Tre-rowl;* the noble Guard of the *Films* interposed!

The *Flowers*, their Gaiety and Fragrancy; the *Perianthium* or *Empalement* of them; their curious Foldings in the *Calyx* before their Expansion, with a *close Couch* or a *concave Couch*, a *single Plait* or a *double Plait*, or a *Plait* and *Couch* together, or a *Rowl*, or a *Spire*, or *Plait* and *Spire* together; and their luxuriant Colours after their *Foliation*, and the expanding of their *Petala!*

The *Stamina*, with their *Apices;* and the *Stylus* (called the *Attire* by Dr. *Grew*) which is found a sort of *Male Sperm*, to impregnate and fructify the Seed!

At last the whole Rudiments and Lineaments of the *Parent-Vegetable*, surprizingly lock'd up in the little compass of the *Fruit* or *Seed!* [1]

Gentlemen of Leisure, consult my illustrious Doctor, peruse his *Anatomy of Plants*, ponder his numberless Discoveries; but all the while consider that rare Person as inviting you to join with him in adoring the *God of*

---

[1] The substance of the nine preceding paragraphs comes directly from Derham's *Physico-Theology*, in which Mather found the references to Grew.

his Father, and the God who has *done these excellent things*, which ought to be *known in all the Earth*.

Signior *Malpighi* has maintain'd it with cogent Arguments, that the whole *Plant* is actually in the *Seed;* and he answers the grand Objection against it, which is drawn from a degeneracy of one Plant sometimes into another. One of his Answers is, *Ex morboso & monstroso affectu, non licet inferre permanentem statum à Natura intentum*.[1]

But there is no Objection to be made against *Ocular Observation*. Shew us, *Lewenhoeck*, how it is? He will give us to see, a small Particle no bigger than a Sand, contain the *Plant*, and all belonging to it, all actually in that *little Seed;* yea, in the *Nux vomica* it appears even to the naked Eye, and in an astonishing Elegancy! Dr. *Cheyne* expresses himself with good assurance upon it: '*We are certain* that the *Seeds* of *Plants* are nothing 'but *little Plants* perfectly formed, with Branches and 'Leaves duly folded up, and involved in *Membranes*, 'or surrounded with *Walls* proper to defend them in 'this tender state from external Injuries; and *Vegetation* 'is only the unfolding and extending of these Branches 'and Leaves, by the force of Juices raised by *Heat* in 'the slender Tubes of the Plant.'

Those *capillary Plants*, which all the Antients, and some of the Moderns, have taken to be destitute of *Seeds*, are by *Bauhinus* and others now pronounced *Spermatophorous*. Mr. *Ray* says, *Hanc Sententiam verissimam esse Autopsia convincit*.[2]

[1] "It is not permissible to infer from an abnormal and monstrous condition the permanent state designed by Nature." Here as before, Mather simply takes the quotation from Derham. The same applies to the quotation from Lewenhoeck, which follows.

[2] "Examination proves this opinion to be very true." Quoted from Derham.

Fr. Cæsius claims to be the first who discovered the *Seeds* of these *Plants*, with the help of a *Microscope.* One Mr. *Cole* has prosecuted the Observation, and is astonished at the small Dimensions of the *Seeds.* The *Boxes* or Vessels that hold the *Seeds* are not half, perhaps not a quarter, so big as a Grain of Sand; and yet an *hundred Seeds* are found in one of these. *Tantam Plantam è tantillo Semine produci attentum Observatorem merito in Admirationem rapiat!* [1]

Sir *Thomas Brown* observes, That of the Seeds of *Tobacco* a thousand make not one Grain; (tho *Otto de Gueric*, as I remember, says, fifty-two Cyphers with one Figure will give the Number of those, which would fill the Space between us and the Stars!) A Plant which has extended its Empire over the whole World, and has a larger Dominion than any of all the *Vegetable* Kingdom.[2]

Ten thousand Seeds of *Harts-tongue* hardly make the Bulk of a *Pepper-corn.* But now, as Dr. *Grew* notes, the Body, with the Covers of every Seed, the ligneous and parenchymous Parts of both, the Fibres of those Parts, the Principles of those Fibres, and the homogeneous Particles of those Principles, being but moderately multiplied one by another, afford an hundred thousand millions of Atoms formed in the Space of a *Pepper-corn.* But who can define how many more![3]

The Uses of *Trees* in various Works were elegantly celebrated, as long ago as when *Theophrastus* wrote his fifth Book of the *History of Plants.*

And what *stately Trees* do sometimes by their glorious

[1] "That so great a plant is produced from so small a seed, drives the attentive watcher rightly to wonder." Quoted from Derham.

[2] Otto von Guericke was a German scientist, 1602–1686. The rest of the paragraph seems to be drawn from Sir Thomas Browne's *Garden of Cyrus.*

[3] Mather seems here to be using Grew's *Anatomy of Plants.*

Height and *Breadth* recommend themselves to a more singular Observation with us! The *Cabbage*-tree[1] an hundred and forty or fifty Foot high, as if it were aspiring to afford a Diet to the Regions above us; how noble a Spectacle!

The *Trees* which are found sometimes near twenty Foot, or perhaps more, in circumference, what capacious *Canoes* do they afford, when the Traveller makes them change their Element? Near *Scio* there is an Island called *Long-Island*, and on this Island (as *Jo. Pitts*[2] tells us) there is a Tree of a prodigious bigness; under it are *Coffee-houses*, and many Shops of several Intentions, and several Fountains of Water; and it has near forty Pillars of Marble and of Timber to support the Branches of it. It is a Tree famous to a Proverb all over *Turkey*.

Even the most *noxious* and the most *abject* of the *Vegetables*, how useful are they! As of the *Bramble* Dr. *Grew* notes, *If it chance to prick the Owner, it will also tear the Thief. Olaus Magnus* admires the Benefits which the *rotten Barks* of *Oaks* give to the Northern People, by the *Shine*, with which they do in their long Nights direct the Traveller. And Dr. *Merret* celebrates the *Thistles*, and the *Hop-strings*, for the *Glass* afforded by their Ashes![3]

The *frugal Bit* of the old *Britons*, which in the bigness of a *Bean* satisfied the most hungry and thirsty Appetite, is now thrown into the Catalogue of the *Res deperditæ*.[4]

[1] A name given to various palm-trees.

[2] Joseph Pitts, 1663–1735?, English traveller and writer.

[3] All the references in this paragraph are from Derham.

[4] "Things which are lost." Speed, *History of Great Britaine*, (1611), 167, says that the Britons could live "with a kind of meat no bigger then a beane" after eating which they did not hunger or thirst.

The peculiar Care which the great God of Nature has taken for the Safety of the *Seed* and *Fruit*, and so for the Conservation of the *Plant*, is by my ingenious *Derham* considered as a loud Invitation to His Praises.

They which dare shew their Heads all the Year, how securely is their *Seed* or *Fruit* lock'd up in the Winter in their *Gems*,[1] and well cover'd with neat and close *Tunicks* there!

Such as dare not expose themselves, how are they preserved under the Coverture of the *Earth*, till invited out by the kindly Warmth of the Spring!

When the *Vegetable Race* comes abroad, what strange Methods of Nature are there to *guard* them from Inconveniences, by making some to lie down prostrate, by making others, which were by the Antients called *Æschynomenæ*, to close themselves up at the Touch of Animals, and by making the most of them to shut up under their guard in the cool of the Evening, especially if there be foul Weather approaching; which is by *Gerhard*[2] therefore called, *The Countryman's Weatherwiser!*

What various ways has Nature for the *scattering* and the *sowing* of the *Seed!* Some are for this end winged with a light sort of a *Down*, to be carried about with the *Seed* by the Wind. Some are laid in springy cases, which when they burst and crack, dart their Seed to a distance, performing therein the part of an Husbandman. Others by their good Qualities invite themselves to be swallowed by the Birds, and being fertiliz'd by passing thro their Bodies, they are by them transferred to places where they fructify. *Theophrastus*

---

[1] Buds.

[2] John Gerard, 1545–1612, English herbalist. Quoted from Derham.

affirms this of the *Misletoe;* and *Tavernier* of the *Nutmeg.*
Others not thus taken care for, do, by their Usefulness
to *us*, oblige us to look after them.

It is a little surprizing, that *Seeds* found in the
Gizzards of *Wild-fowl*, have afterwards sprouted in the
Earth; and *Seeds* left in the *Dung* of the *Cattel.* The
Seeds of *Marjoram* and *Strammonium*, carelesly kept,
have grown after seven Years.

How nice the provision of Nature for their Support
in *standing* and *growing*, that they may keep their
Heads above ground, and administer to our Intentions!
There are some who stand by their own Strength;
and the ligneous parts of these, tho' like our Bones,
yet are not, like them, inflexible, but of an elastick
nature, that they may dodge the Violence of the Winds:
and their Branches at the top very commodiously have
a tendency to an hemispherical Dilatation, but within
such an Angle as makes an Æquilibration there.
An ingenious Observer upon this one Circumstance,
cannot forbear this just Reflection: *A visible Argument
that the plastick Capacities of Matter are govern'd by an
all-wise and infinite Agent, the native Strictnesses and
Regularities of them plainly shewing from whose Hand
they come.* And then such as are too weak to stand of
themselves, 'tis wonderful to see how they use the Help
of their *Neighbours*, address them, embrace them, climb
up about them, some twisting themselves with a
strange *convolving* Faculty, some catching hold with
Claspers and *Tendrels*, which are like Hands to them;
some striking in rooty *Feet*, and some emitting a natural
Glue, by which they adhere to their Supporters.

But, Oh! the glorious *Goodness* of our GOD in all
these things! Lend us thy Pen, O industrious *Ray*, to
declare a little of it. *Plantarum usus latissimè patet,*

& in omni Vitæ parte occurrit. Sine illis cautè, sine illis commodè, non vivitur; at nec vivitur omnino: quæcunque ad victum necessaria sunt, quæcunque ad Delicias faciunt, è locupletissimo suo Penu abunde subministrant. Quanto ex iis Mensa innocentior, mundior, salubrior, quam ex Animalium Cæde & Laniena! Homo certè Naturâ Animal carnivorum non est; nullis ad Prædam & Rapinam armis instructum; non Dentibus exertis & serratis, non Unguibus aduncis. Manus ad Fructus colligendos, Dentes ad mandendos comparati. Non legimus ei ante Diluvium Carnes ad esum concessas. At non victum tantum nobis suppeditant, sed & Vestitum, & Medicinam, & Domicilia, aliaque Ædificia, & Navigia, & Supellectilem, & Focum, & Oblectamenta Sensuum Animique. Ex his Naribus Odoramenta & Suffumigia parantur: Horum Flores inenarrabili Colorum & Schematum Varietate & Elegantia Oculos exhilarant, & suavissima Odorum quos expirant Fragantia, Spiritus recreant. Horum Fructus, Gulæ illecebræ Mensas secundas instruunt, & languentem Appetitum excitant. Taceo Virorem Oculis Amicum, quem per Prata, Pascua, Agros, Sylvas spatiantibus objiciunt; & Umbras quas contra Æstum & Solis Ardores præbent.[1]

[1] "The use of plants is most pleasantly displayed, and occurs in every part of life. Without them one could not live prudently or conveniently, or, indeed, at all. They afford from their rich store whatever is necessary for food and whatever ministers to delight. With them how much less offensive and how much cleaner and more healthful is a feast, than one with the slaughtering and butchering of animals. Man certainly is not naturally carniverous, he is not supplied with weapons for plundering and preying, nor with bare, sharp teeth, or hooked nails. His hands are prepared for gathering fruit, and his teeth for chewing it. We do not learn that flesh was lawful food for him before the flood. Plants supply not only food for us but also clothing, medicine, houses and other buildings, ships, furniture, the hearth-fire, and the delights of the senses and the mind.

Indeed *all* the *Plants* in the whole *Vegetable Kingdom* are every one of them so *useful*, as to *rise up* for thy Condemnation, *O Man, who dost little Good in the World.* But sometimes the *Uses* of one *single Plant* are so many, so various, that a wise Man can scarce behold it without some *Emulation* as well as *Admiration*, or without some wishing, that if a *Metamorphosis* were to befal him, it might be into one of these. *Plutarch* reports, that the *Babylonians* out of the *Palm-tree* fetch'd more than three hundred several sorts of Commodities.

The *Coco-tree* supplies the *Indians* with Bread, and Water, and Wine, and Vinegar, and Brandy, and Milk, and Oil, and Honey, and Sugar, and Needles, and Thread, and Linnen, and Clothes, and Cups, and Spoons, and Besoms, and Baskets, and Paper, and Nails; Timber, Coverings for their Houses; Masts, Sails, Cordage, for their Vessels; add, Medicines for their Diseases; and what can be desired more? This is more expressively related in the *Hortus Malabaricus*, published by the illustrious *Van Draakenstein*.[1]

The *Aloe Muricata* yields the *Americans* all that their Necessities can call for. *De la Vega* and *Margrave* will inform us how this alone furnishes them with Houses and Fences, and Weapons of many sorts, and Shoes, and Clothes, and Thread, and Needles, and Wine, and Honey, and Utensils that cannot be numbred.

They prepare odors and scents for the nostrils; their flowers please the eye with endless variety and grace of color and form, and their sweet fragrances refresh the spirits. Their fruits make rich feasts with tempting flavors, and stimulate flagging appetite. I say nothing of the friendly greenness they offer to the eyes of those who walk, by means of their meadows, pastures, fields, woods, and the shade they afford against heat and the brightness of the sun." Mather takes this quotation as it is given by Derham.

[1] The reference is from Ray's *Wisdom of God.*

Hernandes will assure us, *Planta hæc unica, quicquid Vitæ esse potest necessarium facile præstare potest, si esset rebus humanis modus.* [1]

What a surprizing Diversity from the *Cinnamon-tree!*

Some will have the *Plantane* to be the *King of all Fruit,* tho the Tree be little more than ten Foot high, and raised not from *Seed,* but from the *Roots* of the old ones. The *Fruit* a delicate Butter, and often the whole Food that a whole Family will subsist upon.

Among the *Uses* of *Plants,* how surprizing an one is that, wherein we find them used for *Cisterns,* to preserve Water for the needy Children of Men!

The *Dropping-tree* in *Guiney,* and on some Islands, is instead of *Rains* and *Springs* to the Inhabitants.

The *Banduca Cingatensium,* at the end of its Leaves has long Sacks or Bags, containing a fine limpid Water, of great use to the People when they want Rains for eight or ten Months together.

The *wild Pine,* describ'd by Dr. *Sloane,* has the Leaves, which are each of them two Foot and an half long, and three Inches broad, so inclosed one within another, that there is formed a large Bason, fit to contain a considerable quantity of Water (*Dampier* says, the best part of a Quart) which in the rainy Season falling upon the utmost parts of the spreading Leaves, runs down by Channels into the Bottle, where the Leaves bending inwards again, come so close to the Stalk, as to hinder the Evaporations of the Water. In the mountainous, as well as in the dry and low Woods, when there is a scarcity of Water, this *Reservatory* is not only necessary and sufficient for the nourishment

---

[1] "This one plant can furnish easily whatever can be necessary for human life." If the first part of the paragraph is from Ray, the quotation is taken from Derham.

of the Plant itself, but it is likewise of marvellous advantage unto Men and Birds, and all sorts of Insects, who then come hither in Troops, and seldom go away without Refreshment.

What tho there are *venomous Plants?* An excellent *Fellow of the College of Physicians* makes a just Remark: 'Aloes has the Property of promoting *Hæmorrhages;* 'but this Property is good or bad, as it is used; a *Medi-* 'cine or a *Poison:* And it is very probable that the most 'dangerous *Poisons,* skilfully managed, may be made 'not only *innocuous,* but of all other Medicines the most 'effectual.' [1]

What admirable Effects of *Opium* well *smegmatized!*[2] Even *poisonous Plants,* one says of them, It may be reasonably supposed that they draw into their visible Bodies that malignant *Juice,* which, if diffused thro the other *Plants,* would make them less wholesome and fit for Nourishment.

In the *Delights* of the *Garden* 'tis not easy to hold a Mediocrity. They afford a Shadow for our *celestial Paradise.* The King of *Persia* has a *Garden* called *Paradise upon Earth.* The antient *Romans* cultivated them to a degree of *Epicurism.* Some confined their *Delights* to a single *Vegetable,* as *Cato,* doting on his *Cabbage.* The *Tulipists* are so set upon their gaudy Flower, that the hard Name and Crime of a *Tulipomania,* is by their own Professors charged upon them; a little odd the Humour of those Gentlemen, who affected Plantations of none but *venomous Vegetables.*[3]

But finally, the vast Uses of *Plants* in *Medicine,* are those which fallen and feeble Mankind has cause to

---

[1] The quotation is from Grew's *Cosmologia Sacra.*
[2] Cleansed, scoured.
[3] Mather draws here from Sir Thomas Browne's *Garden of Cyrus.*

consider, with singular Praises to the merciful God, who so pities us under the sad Effects of our Offences.

Among the eighteen or twenty thousand *Vegetables*, we have ever now and then a single one, which is a *Polychrest*,[1] and almost a *Panacæa;* or at least such an one as obliges us to say of it, as Dr. *Morton* speaks of the *Cortex Peruvianus*; 'tis *Antidotus in Levamen Ærumnarum Vitæ humanæ plurimarum divinitus concessa.* And, *In Sanitatem Gentium proculdubio a Deo optimo maximo condita.*[2]

Among the Antients there were several Plants that bore the Name of *Hercules*, —— called *Heracleum*, or *Heraclea;* probably, as *Le Clerc* thinks, to denote the *extraordinary Force* of the Plants, which they compared to the Strength of *Hercules*.

Cabbage was to the *Romans* their grand *Physick*, as well as *Food*, for six hundred Years together.

Mallows has been esteemed such an *universal Medicine*, as to be called *Malva Omnimorbia.*[3]

Every body has heard,

> *Cur moriatur homo cui Salvia crescit in hortis?* [4]

The *six favourite Herbs* distinguish'd by Sir *William Temple* [5] for the many Uses of them, namely, *Sage*, and *Rue*, and *Saffron*, and *Alehoof*, and *Garlick*, and *Elder*, if they were more frequently used, would no doubt

[1] Something useful for many purposes.

[2] "An antidote divinely granted for the relief of many distresses of human life," and "established doubtless by the great and good God for the health of nations." "Cortex peruvianus," Peruvian bark, is quinine.   Mather draws here from Derham.

[3] "Mallow of all diseases."

[4] "Why should a man die who has sage in his garden?"   *Cf*. the English proverb, "He that would live for aye must eat sage in May."

[5] In his essay *Of Health and Long Life*.

be found vastly beneficial to such as place upon *Health* the Value due to such a *Jewel*.

The *French* do well to be such great Lovers of *Sorrel*, and plant so many Acres of it; it is good against the *Scurvy*, and all ill Habits of Body.

The Persuasion which Mankind has imbib'd of *Tobacco* being good for us, has in a surprizing manner prevail'd! What incredible Millions have *suck'd in* an Opinion, that it is an *useful* as well as a *pleasant* thing, for them to spend much of their Time in drawing thro a Pipe the *Smoke* of that lighted Weed! It was in the Year 1585, that one Mr. *Lane* carried over from *Virginia* some *Tobacco*, which was the first that had ever been seen in *Europe*; [1] and within an hundred Years the *smoking* of it grew so much into fashion, that the very Customs of it brought *four hundred ihousand Pounds a Year* into the *English* Treasury.

It is doubtless a *Plant* of many Virtues. The *Ointment* made of it is one of the best in the Dispensatory. The Practice of *smoking* it, tho a great part of them that use it might very truly say, *they find neither Good nor Hurt by it*; yet it may be fear'd it rather does more *Hurt* than *Good*.

'May God preserve me from the indecent, ignoble, 'criminal *Slavery*, to the mean Delight of *smoking a* '*Weed*, which I see so many carried away with. And 'if ever I should *smoke* it, let me be so wise as to do it, 'not only with *Moderation*, but also with such Employ-'ments of my Mind, as I may make that Action afford 'me a Leisure for!'

---

[1] Ralph Lane, first governor of Virginia, with Sir Francis Drake brought from Virginia tobacco and pipes, and handed them over to Sir Walter Raleigh. Lane is said to have been the first English smoker.

Methinks *Tobacco* is but a poor *Nepenthe*, tho the Takers thereof take it for such an one. It is to be feared the *caustick Salt* in the *Smoke* of this Plant, convey'd by the *Salival Juice* into the Blood, and also the *Vellication* [1] which the continual use of it in *Snuff* gives to the *Nerves* may lay Foundations for Diseases in Millions of unadvised People, which may be commonly and erroneously ascribed to some other Original.

It is very remarkable, that our compassionate God has furnish'd all Regions with *Plants* peculiarly adapted for the relief of the *Diseases* that are most common in those Regions. 'Tis Mr. *Ray*'s Remark, *Tales Plantarum Species in quacunque Regione a Deo creantur, quales Hominibus & Animalibus ibidem natis maxime conveniunt.* [2]

Yea, *Solenander* affirms, that from the Quantity of the *Plants* most plentifully growing in any place, he could give a probable Guess what were the *Distempers* which the People there were most of all subject to.

Benerovinus has written a Book, on purpose to shew that every Country has every thing serving to its Occasions, and particularly *Remedies* for all the Distempers which it may be afflicted with. [3]

Can we be any other than charmed with the Goodness appearing in it, when we see the *Plants* every where starting out of the *Earth*, and hear their courteous Invitation, *Feeble Man, I am a Remedy, which our*

[1] Irritation.

[2] "Such species of plants are created by God in each district as are most suited to the men and animals native there." Mather takes the quotation from Derham.

[3] The references to Solenander and Benerovinus are taken from Derham.

OF THE VEGETABLES

343

gracious Maker has provided for thy Feebleness; take me, know me, use me, thou art welcome to all the Good that is to be found in me!

Yea, such are the Virtues of the *Vegetable World*, that it is no rare thing to see a whole Book written on the Virtues of one single *Vegetable*.

How long is *Rosenbergius* on the Rose, in his *Rhodologia!* *Whitaker* will have the *Vine* to be the *Tree of Life*, in his Treatise on the Blood of it. *Alsted* has entertained us with a yet greater variety on that *Plant of Renown*.[1]

I was going to mention the *Anatomia Sambuci*, written by a *German* Philosopher.

But I presently call to mind such a vast Number of Treatises published, each of them on one *single Vegetable*, by the *Naturæ Curiosi*[2] of *Germany*, that a *Catalogue* would be truly too tedious to be introduced.

If the *Coral* may pass for a *Vegetable*, *Garencieres*[3] has obliged us with a whole Treatise upon it.

But then we have one *far-fetch'd* and *dear-bought* Plant, on which we have so many Volumes written, that they alone almost threaten to become a *Library*. TEA is that charming Plant. Read *Pecklinus's*[4] Book *de Potu Theæ*, and believe the medicinal and balsamick Virtues of it; it strengthens the *Stomach*, it sweetens the *Blood*, it revives the *Heart*, and it refreshes the *Spirits*, and is a Remedy against a World of Distempers.

[1] Johann Carl Rosenberg, physician, fl. c. 1625. Tobias Whitaker, who died in 1666, was the author of *The Tree of Humane Life, or the Bloud of the Grape*, a defense of wine, published in 1638; Johann Heinrich Alsted, 1588–1638, encyclopedic writer and reformed theologian.
[2] Scientists.
[3] Théophile de Garencieres, 1615–1670, French physician.
[4] Johannes Pechlin, 1646–1706, Dutch physician.

Then go to *Waldschmidt*,[1] and you'll find it also to brighten the *Intellectuals*. When *Prose* has done its part, our *Tate*[2] will bring in *Verse* to celebrate the sovereign Virtues of it.

> *Innocuos Calices, & Amicam Vatibus Herbam*
> *Vimque datam Folio.*[3]

At last it shall be the very Θεὰ [4] of the Poet.

> *Whilst TEA, our Sorrows safely to beguile,*
> *Sobriety and Mirth does reconcile:*
> *For to this Nectar we the Blessing owe,*
> *To grow more wise as we more chearful grow.*

There is a Curiosity observed by Mr. *Robinson* of *Ousby*, that should not be left unmentioned; it is, that *Birds* are the *natural Planters* of all sorts of *Trees;* they disseminate the *Kernels* on the Earth, which brings them forth to perfection. Yea, he affirms, that he hath actually seen a great Number of *Crows* together planting a Grove of *Oaks*; they first made little Holes in the Earth with their Bills, going about and about, till the Hole was deep enough, and then they dropt in the *Acorn*, and cover'd it with Earth and Moss. At the time of his writing, this young Plantation was growing up towards a *Grove of Oaks*, and of an height for the *Crows* to build their Nests in.

[1] Probably Johann Jacob Waldschmidt, 1644–1689, German physician and medical writer.

[2] Nahum Tate, 1652–1715.

[3] "Harmless cups, and the herb friendly to poets, and the power given by the leaf." The lines are from the title-page of Tate's *Panacea*, (London, 1700).

[4] "Goddess." The lines quoted are from Tate's "The Tea-Table," printed at the end of his *Panacea*.

In *Virginia* there is a Plant called *The James-Town-Weed*, whereof some having eaten plentifully, turn'd *Fools* upon it for several Days; one would blow up a Feather in the Air, another dart Straws at it; a third sit stark naked, like a Monkey, grinning at the rest; a fourth fondly kiss and paw his Companions, and snear in their Faces. In this frantick State they were confined, lest they should kill themselves, tho there appear'd nothing but Innocence in all their Actions. After eleven Days they return'd to themselves, not remembring any thing that had pass'd.

My Friend, a *Madness* more sensless than that with which this *Vegetable* envenoms the Eaters of it, holds thee in the stupefying Chains thereof, if thou dost not behold in the whole *Vegetable Kingdom* such Works of the glorious Creator, as call for a continual Admiration.

¶. It is a notable Stroke of Divinity methinks which *Pliny* falls upon, *Flores Odoresque indiem gignit Natura, magna (ut palam est) Admonitione hominum.*[1]

'The Man began to be cured of his *Blindness*, who 'could say, *I see Men, like Trees, walking.* That Man 'is yet perfectly *blind* who does not *see Men, like Trees,* 'first *growing* and *flourishing*, then *withering, decaying,* '*dying.*'

'The *Rapæ Anthropomorphæ*, and some other *Plants,* 'that have grown with much of an *Human Figure*, to 'be fancied on them, have been *odd things.* But there 'are Points wherein all *Plants* will exhibit something 'of the *Human Figure.*'

'The *Parts* of *Plants* analogous to those in an *Human* '*Body*, are notably enumerated by *Alsted* in his *Theologia*

[1] "Nature brought forth flowers and fragrance in a day, as a great example, which is plain, to men."

'*Naturalis.* The Analogy between their States and
'ours would be also as *profitable* as *reasonable* a Subject
'of Contemplation.'

'And I hope the *Revival* of the *Plants* in the *Spring*
'will carry us to the Faith of our own *Resurrection*
'*from the Dead.*'

'And of the *Recovery* which the *Church* will one day
'see from a *Winter* of *Adversity*; the *World* from a
'*Winter* of *Impiety:* The *Earth* shall one day be filled
'with the *Fruits of Righteousness*, however barren and
'horrid may be the present Aspect of it.'

'A Man famous in his day (and in ours too) thought
'himself well accommodated for devotionary Studies,
'tho he says, *Nullos se aliquando Magistros habuisse*
'*nisi Quercus & Fagos.*'[1]

'I will hear these *Field-Preachers*, their loud Voice
'to me from the *Earth*, is the same with what would
'be uttered by *Angels flying thro the midst of Heaven;*
'*Fear God, and glorify him!*'

'One thus articulates the Vegetable Sermons: *Ecce*
'*nos, O increduli filii hominum, nuper mortui eramus, at*
'*nunc reviximus. Vetus nostrum Corpus ac Vestimentum*
'*deposuimus, & novæ Creaturæ factæ sumus. Facite vos*
'*nunc aliquid simile.*[2] And again, *Dum in hac miserrima*
'*Vitâ estis, nolite de Corpore esse solliciti; nostri memores*
'*estote, quas Creator honestissime coloratis Vestibus induit,*
'*quotannis per tot Millenarios, jam inde ab exordio*
'*Mundi.*[3] And once more, *Ecce vires nostræ, non nobis*

---

[1] "He had never any masters except the oaks and beeches."

[2] "Lo, unbelieving sons of men, we were lately dead but now we
live again. We put off our old bodies and garments and are made
new creatures. Do you now the same."

[3] "Do not be concerned for your bodies while you are in this
miserable world. Be mindful of us, whom God has dressed nobly in

'*ipsis, sed vobis deserviunt. Non nostro Bono floremus,*
'*sed vestro. Imo Divina Bonitas vobis floret per nos, ut*
'*dicere possitis, Dei Benignitatem in nobis florere, suoque*
'*Odore suavissimo vos recreare.*'[1]

'A famous *German* Doctor of Philosophy declares,
'that he found it impossible for him to look upon the
'*Vegetable World* without those Acclamations, *Psalm*
'cxxxix. 6. *The Knowledge of these things is too wonder-*
'*ful for me, it is high, I cannot attain to it.*'

'The pious *Arndt* observes, that every Creature is
'enstamp'd with Characters of the Divine Goodness,
'and brings Testimonies of a good Creator. Our *Vine*
'so calls upon us, *Scias, O homo, hanc Liquoris mei Sua-*
'*vitatem, qua Cor tuum recreo, a Creatore meo esse.*[2] Our
'*Bread* so calls upon us, *Vis ista, qua famem sublevo, à*
'*Creatore meo, & vestro mihi obtigit.*[3] It is a Saying of
'*Austin's, Deum Creaturas singulas guttula Divinæ suæ*
'*Bonitatis aspersisse, ut per illas homini bene sit.*'[4]

'A devout Writer treats us with such a Thought
'as this: Our God is like a tender Father, who, when
'the Infant complies not presently with his Calls,
'allures him with the Offer of pleasant *Fruits* to him.
'Not that the Child should stop in the Love of the
colored garments yearly through so many ages since the beginning
of the world."

[1] "Lo, our strength is devoted not to ourselves but to you. We do
not bloom for our own good, but for yours. Yes, the divine goodness
blooms for you through us, in order that you may say that the benev-
olence of God flowers in us and that His sweetness refreshes you."

[2] "Know, O man, that the sweetness of my juice, by which I cheer
your heart, is from my creator."

[3] "That power by which I relieve hunger, falls to my lot from my
creator and yours."

[4] "God has sprinkled individual creatures with a little drop of
his divine goodness, in order that through them men might be well
off."

'*Apple*, the *Plumb*, the *Pear*, but be by the *Fruits* drawn
'to the Love and Obedience of the *Father* that gives
'them.   Our heavenly Father calling on us in his *Word*,
'gives us also *Rain from Heaven, and fruitful Seasons,*
'to engage our Love and Obedience.   *Quæ sanè Beneficia*
'*aliud nihil sunt, quam tot manus & Nuncii Dei, parati*
'*ad ipsum Deum nos deducere, illiusque amorem altius*
'*amimis nostris insinuare, ut ipsum tandem Datorem*
'*in Creaturis & Donis suscipere discamus.*' [1]

'Among other Thoughts of Piety upon the *Vegetable*
'*World*, some have allow'd a room for this; the strong
'Passion in almost all Children for *Fruit*;——by ten-
'dring *Fruits* to them, you may draw them to any thing
'in the World.   May not this be a lasting *Signature*
'of the *first Sin*, left upon the Minds of our Children!
'An Appetite for the *forbidden Fruit*.   When we see
'our Children greedy after *Fruits*, a remembrance
'and repentance of *that* Sin may be excited in us.'

Add this: *Quid prodest ope Creaturarum vivere, si Deo
non vivitur?* [2]

A good Thought of a *German* Writer:

*Sol & Luna, totusque Mundus Sydereus, luce sua Deum
collaudunt.   Terra Deum laudat, dum viret & floret.   Sic
Herbæ & Flosculi Opificis sui Omnipotentiam & Sapientiam commendant Odore, Pulchritudine, & Colorum varia
Pictura: Aves Cantu & Modulatione; Arbores Fructibus;
Mare Piscibus; omnes Creaturæ laudant Deum, dum illius
mandata exequuntur.   Colloquuntur nobiscum per divini-*

[1] "Which benefits are nothing but so many hands and messengers
of God, designed to lead us to God himself, and to instil in our minds
a loftier love of Him, in order that we may learn to recognize Him,
the Giver, in His creatures and gifts."

[2] "What is the use of living with riches of the world, if one does not
live with God?"

*tus ipsis insitas Proprietates, manifestantes opificem suum,
& exhortantes nos ad ipsum laudandum.*[1]

ESSAY XXXII. *Of* MAN

[From page 294 of the original edition, to the end of the book.]

¶. *Hear now the Conclusion of the Matter.* To enkindle the *Dispositions* and the *Resolutions* of PIETY in my Brethren, is the *Intention* of all my ESSAYS, and must be the *Conclusion* of them.

Atheism is now for ever chased and hissed out of the World, every thing in the World concurs to a Sentence of *Banishment* upon it. *Fly, thou Monster, and hide, and let not the darkest Recesses of Africa itself be able to cherish thee; never dare to shew thyself in a World where every thing stands ready to overwhelm thee!* A BEING that must be *superior* to *Matter*, even the *Creator* and *Governor* of all *Matter*, is every where so conspicuous, that there can be nothing more *monstrous* than *to deny the God that is above.* No *System* of *Atheism* has ever yet been offered among the Children of Men, but what may presently be convinced of such *Inconsistences*, that a Man must ridiculously believe *nothing certain* before he can imagine them; it must be a *System of Things*

---

[1] "The sun and moon, and all the universe, praise God by their light. The Earth praises God, when it flowers and is green. So the grass and the little flowers commend their maker's omnipotence and wisdom by their fragrance, beauty, and the varied painting of their colors. The birds praise God with song and melody; the trees, with fruit; the sea, with fish; all creatures praise Him while they carry out His commands. They talk to us by means of the properties divinely given them, displaying His handiwork, and urging us to praise Him."

which cannot stand together! A Bundle of *Contradictions* to themselves, and to all *common Sense.* I doubt it has been an *inconsiderate* thing to pay so much of a Compliment to *Atheism,* as to bestow solemn *Treatises* full of learned *Arguments* for the Refutation of a *delirious Phrenzy,* which ought rather to be put out of countenance with the most *contemptuous Indignation.* And I fear such Writers as have been at the pains to put the *Objections* of *Atheism* into the most plausible Terms, that they may have the honour of *laying a Devil when they have raised him,* have therein done too *unadvisedly.* However, to so much notice of the raving *Atheist* we may condescend while we go along, as to tell him, that for a Man to question the *Being* of a GOD, who requires from us an *Homage* of *Affection,* and *Wonderment,* and Obedience to Himself, and a perpetual Concern for the Welfare of the *Human Society,* for which He has in our *Formation* evidently *suited* us, would be an *exalted Folly,* which undergoes especially two Condemnations; it is first condemned by this, that every Part of the *Universe* is continually *pouring in* something for the *confuting* of it; there is not a Corner of the whole World but what supplies a *Stone* towards the Infliction of such a *Death* upon the *Blasphemy* as justly belongs to it: and it has also this condemning of it, that Men would soon become *Canibals* to one another by embracing it; Men being utterly destitute of any Principle to keep them *honest in the Dark,* there would be no *Integrity* left in the World, but they would be as the *Fishes of the Sea to one another,* and worse than *the creeping Things, that have no Ruler over them.* Indeed from every thing in the World there is this Voice more audible than the loudest Thunder to us; *God hath spoken, and these two things have I heard!* First, *Believe and*

*adore a glorious GOD, who has made all these Things,
and know thou that He will bring thee into Judgment!*
And then *be careful to do nothing but what shall be for
the Good of the Community which the glorious GOD has
made thee a Member of.* Were what God *hath spoken*
duly regarded, and were these *two things* duly complied
with, the World would be soon revived into a desirable
Garden of God, and Mankind would be fetch'd up into
very comfortable Circumstances; till *then* the World
continues in a wretched Condition, *full of doleful Creatures,* with *wild Beasts crying* in its *desolate Houses,
Dragons* in its most *pleasant Palaces.* And now declare,
O every thing that is reasonable, declare and pronounce
upon it whether it be possible that *Maxims* absolutely
necessary to the *Subsistence* and *Happiness* of Mankind,
can be *Falsities?* There is no possibility for this, that
Cheats and *Lyes* must be so *necessary,* that the *Ends*
which alone are worthy of a glorious GOD, cannot be
attain'd without having *them* imposed upon us!

Having dispatch'd the *Atheist,* with bestowing on
him *not many* Thoughts, yet *more* than could be deserved
by such an *Idiot;* I will proceed now to propose two
general Strokes of *Piety,* which will appear to a *Christian
Philosopher* as unexceptionable as any Proposals that
ever were made to him.

First, the Works of the glorious God exhibited to
our View, 'tis most certain they do *bespeak,* and they
should *excite* our *Acknowledgments of His Glories* appearing in them: the Great GOD is infinitely *gratified*
in beholding the Displays of His own infinite *Power,*
and *Wisdom,* and *Goodness,* in the Works which He
has made; but it is also a most acceptable Gratifica-
tion to Him, when such of His Works as are the *rational
Beholders* of themselves, and of the rest, shall with

devout Minds *acknowledge* His Perfections, which they see shining there. Never does one endued with *Reason* do any thing more evidently *reasonable*, than when he makes every thing that occurs to him in the vast Fabrick of the World, an *Incentive* to some agreeable Efforts and Salleys of *Religion*. What can any Man living object against the *Piety* of a Mind awaken'd by the sight of God in His Works, to such Thoughts as these: *Verily, there is a glorious GOD! Verily, the GOD who does these things is worthy to be feared, worthy to be loved, worthy to be relied on! Verily, all possible Obedience is due to such a GOD; and most abominable, most inexcusable is the Wickedness of all Rebellion against Him!* A Mind kept under the Impression of such Thoughts as these, is an *holy* and a *noble* Mind, a *Temple* of God, a *Temple filled with the Glory of God.* There is nothing but what will afford an *Occasion* for the *Thoughts*; the oftner a Man improves the *Occasion*, the more does he *glorify GOD*, and answer the *chief End of Man*; and why should he not *seek occasion* for it, by visiting for this purpose the several *Classes* of the Creatures (for *Discipulus in hâc Scholâ erit Peripateticus*)[1] as he may have opportunity for so generous an Exercise! But since the horrid Evil of all *Sin* is to be inferred from this; *it is a Rebellion against the Laws of the glorious GOD, who is the Maker and the Ruler of all Worlds*; and *it is a disturbance of the good Order wherein the glorious Maker and Ruler of all Things has placed them all*; how much ought a quickned *Horror of Sin* to accompany this Contemplation, and produce this most agreeable Resolution, *My God, I will for ever fear to offend thy glorious Majesty!* Nor is this all the *Improvement* which we are to make of what we see in

---

[1] "A disciple of this school must be a Peripatetic."

the *Works of God*; in our *improving* of them, we are
to accept of the *Rebuke* which they give to our *Presumption*, in pretending to criticize upon the *dark things*
which occur in the Dispensations of His *Providence*;
there is not any one of all the *Creatures* but what has
those *fine things* in the *Texture* of it, which have never
yet been reached by our *Searches*, and we are as much at
a loss about the *Intent* as about the *Texture* of them;
as yet we know not what the glorious God *intends* in
His forming of those *Creatures*, nor what *He has to do*
in them, and with them; He therein proclaims this
Expectation, *Surely they will fear me, and receive
Instruction.* And the Point wherein we are now instructed is this: 'What! Shall I be so vain as to be
'*dissatisfied* because I do not *understand* what is done
'by the glorious GOD in the Works of His *Providence!*'
*O my Soul, hast thou not known, hast thou not heard
concerning the everlasting God, the Lord, the Creator of
the Ends of the Earth, that there is no searching of His
Understanding?*

And then, secondly, the CHRIST of God must not
be forgotten, who is *the Lord of all. I am not ashamed
of the Gospel of CHRIST,* of which I will *affirm constantly,*
that if the *Philosopher* do not call it in, he *paganizes,*
and leaves the finest and brightest Part of his Work
unfinished. Let *Colerus*[1] persuade us if he can, that
in the Time of *John Frederick* the Elector of *Saxony*
there was dug up a *Stone,* on which there was a Representation of our *crucified Saviour;* but I cannot forbear
saying, there is not a *Stone* any where which would
not look *black* upon me, and *speak* my Condemnation,
if my *Philosophy* should be so *vain* as to make me lay
aside my Thoughts of my *enthroned Saviour.* Let

[1] Johann Jacob Coler, 16th century German theologian and writer.

Lambecius,[1] if he please, employ his Learning upon the Name of our Saviour CHRIST, found in Letters naturally engraven at the bottom of a large *Agate-Cup,* which is to be seen among the Emperor's Curiosities; I have never drank in that *Cup,* however I can more easily believe it than I can the *Crucifixus ex Radice Crambres enatus,*[2] or the *Imago Virginis cum Filiolo, in Minerâ Ferri expressa,*[3] and several more such things, which the Publishers of the *German Ephemerides*[4] have mingled with their better Entertainments: but I will assert, that a glorious CHRIST is more to be considered in the *Works of Nature* than the *Philosopher* is generally aware of; and my *CHRISTIAN Philosopher* has not fully done his Part, till He who is *the First-born of every Creature* be come into Consideration with him. *Alsted* mentions a *Siclus Judæo-Christianus,*[5] which had on one side the Name *JESUS,* with the Face of our *Saviour,* and on the other the Words that signify *the King Messiah comes with Peace, and God becomes a Man*; and *Leusden*[6] says he had a couple of these *Coins* in his possession. I have nothing to say on the behalf of the *Zeal* in those *Christianized Jews,* who probably were the Authors of these *Coins,* a *Zeal* that *boil'd* into so needless an Expression of an Homage, that indeed

---

[1] Peter Lambeck, 1628–80, German historian.

[2] "The crucifix springing from a cabbage root." Mather misprints "crambres" for "crambes."

[3] "Image of the Virgin and Child moulded in iron ore."

[4] The "German Ephemerides" was as cientific periodical in Germany, *Miscellanea Curiosa sive Ephemeridum Medico-Physicarum Germanicarum,* etc. Cotton Mather refers to articles in the volume for 1670.

[5] "A Jewish-Christian shekel (coin)."

[6] Johann Leusden, 1624–1699, Dutch scholar, and friend of Cotton Mather's father.

cannot be too much expressed in the *instituted ways* of
it to a Redeemer, whose *Kingdom is not of this World:*
but this I will say, *all the Creatures in this World are
part of His Kingdom*; there are no *Creatures* but what are
His *Medals*, on every one of them the Name of JESUS
is to be found inscribed. Celebrate, O *Danhaver*,[1]
thy *Granatilla*, the *Peruvian Plant*, on which a strong
Imagination finds a Representation of the *Instruments*
employed in the *Sufferings* of our Saviour, and especially the *bloody Sweat* of His Agonies; were the Representation as really and lively made as has been imagined,
I would subscribe to the Epigram upon it, which
concludes:

> *Flos hic ità formâ vincit omnes Flosculos,*
> *Ut totus optet esse Spectator Oculus.*[2]

But I will, with the Exercise of the most *solid Reason*,
by every part of the World, as well as the *Vegetables*,
be led to my Saviour.

A *View of the Creation* is to be taken, with suitable
Acknowledgments of the glorious CHRIST, in whom
the *eternal Son of God* has personally united Himself to
ONE of His *Creatures*, and becomes on *his* account
propitious to *all the rest*; our *Piety* indeed will not be
Christianity if HE be left unthought upon.

This is HE, of whom we are instructed, *Col.* 1. 16, 17.
*All things were created by Him, and for Him; and He is
before all things, and by Him all things consist.* It is no
contemptible Thought wherewith *De Sabunde* has
entertained us: *Productio Mundi à Deo facta de Nihilo,
arguit aliam productionem, summam, occultam, &*

---

[1] Johann Conrad Danhawer, 1603–1666, German theologian.

[2] "This flower so surpasses all others in its form that every eye
may wish to see it."

*æternam in Deo, quæ est de sua propria Natura, in qua
producitur Deus de Deo, & per quam ostenditur summa
Trinitas in Deo.*[1] And certainly he that as a *Father*
does produce a *Son*, but as an *Artist* only produce an
House, has a Value for the *Son* which he has not for
the *House*; yea, we may say, if GOD had not first,
and from Eternity, been a *Father* to our *Saviour*, He
would never have exerted Himself as an *Artist* in that
Fabrick, which He has built *by the Might of His Power,
and for the Honour of His Majesty!*

The Great Sir *Francis Bacon* has a notable Passage
in his *Confession of Faith: I believe that God is so holy, as
that it is impossible for Him to be pleased in any Creature,
tho the Work of his own Hands, without beholding of the
same in the Face of a Mediator;* —— *without which it was
impossible for Him to have descended to any Work of
Creation, but He should have enjoyed the blessed and
individual Society of three Persons in the Godhead for
ever; but out of His eternal and infinite Goodness and
Love purposing to become a Creature, and communicate
with His Creatures, He ordained in His eternal Counsel
that one Person of the Godhead should be united to one
Nature, and to one particular of His Creatures; that so in
the Person of the Mediator the true Ladder might be
fixed, whereby God might descend to His Creatures, and
His Creatures ascend to Him.*

It was an high Flight of *Origen*,[2] who urges, that
our *High-Priest's* having *tasted of Death*, ὑπὲρ παντος,
FOR ALL, is to be extended even to the very *Stars*,

----

[1] "The creation of the world, made by God from nothing, shows
that there is another creation, high, secret, and eternal, in God, which
is of His own nature, in which God is created from God, and by which
is made plain the Trinity in God." Raymond de Sebonde, d. 1432,
was a Spanish physician, author of *Theologia Naturalis.*

[2] Alexandrian Christian writer of the 2d and 3d centuries.

which would otherwise have been *impure* in the sight of God; and thus are ALL THINGS restored to the *Kingdom* of the Father. Our Apostle *Paul* in a famous Passage to the *Colossians* [i. 19, 20.] may seem highly to favour this Flight. One says upon it, 'If this be so, 'we need not break the Glasses of *Galilæo*, the *Spots* 'may be washed out of the *Sun*, and *total Nature* 'sanctified to God that made it.'

Yea, the sacred Scriptures plainly and often invite us to a Conception, which Dr. *Goodwin* has chosen to deliver in such Terms as these: 'The *Son of God* per-'sonally and actually existing as the Son of God with 'God, afore the World or any Creature was made, *He* 'undertaking and covenanting with God to become 'a *Man*, yea, *that Man* which He hath now taken up 'into one Person with Himself, as well for *this End*, 'as for *other Ends* more glorious; God did in the Fore-'knowledge of *that*, and in the Assurance of that *Coven-*'nant* of His, proceed to the *creating* of all things which 'He hath made; and without the Intuition of *this*, or 'having *this* in His Eye, He would not have made any 'thing which He hath made.'

O CHRISTIAN, *lift up now thine Eyes, and look from the place where thou art* to all Points of the Compass, and concerning *whatever thou seest*, allow that all these things were formed *for the Sake* of that Glorious-One, who is now *God manifest in the Flesh* of our JESUS; 'tis on *His* Account that the eternal Godhead has the *Delight* in all these things, which preserves them in their Being, and grants them the *Help*, in the *obtaining* whereof they *continue to this day*.

But were they not all made *by the hand*, as well as *for the Sake* of that Glorious-ONE? They were verily so. *O my JESUS, it was that Son of God who now dwells in thee, in and by whom the Godhead exerted the Power, which could be exerted by none but an all-powerful GOD, in the creating of the World!* He is that WORD of GOD *by whom all things were made, and without whom was not any thing made that was made.*

This is not all that we have to think upon; we see an incomparable *Wisdom* of GOD in His *Creatures*; one cannot but presently infer, *What an incomprehensible Wisdom then in the Methods and Affairs of that Redemption, whereof the glorious GOD has laid the Plan in our JESUS!* Things which the *Angels desire to look into.* But, O *evangelized Mind*, go on, mount up, soar higher, think at this rate; *the infinite Wisdom which formed all these things is peculiarly seated in the Son of God*; He is that *reflexive Wisdom* of the eternal *Father*, and that *Image of the invisible God, by whom all things were created*; in *Him* there is after a peculiar manner the original *Idea* and *Archetype* of every thing that offers the infinite *Wisdom* of God to our Admiration. Wherever we see the *Wisdom* of God admirably shining before us, we are invited to such a Thought as this; *this Glory is originally to be found in thee, O our Immanuel!* 'Tis in Him *transcendently.* But then 'tis impossible to stop without adding, *How glorious, how wondrous, how lovely art thou, O our Saviour!*

Nor may we lay aside a grateful Sense of this, that as the *Son* of God is *the Upholder of all Things in all Worlds*, thus, that it is owing to his potent *Intercession* that the *Sin of Man* has made no more havock on this *our World.* This *our World* has been by the *Sin of Man* so perverted from the *true Ends* of it, and rendred full of such loathsome and hateful Regions, and such *Scelerata Castra*,[1] that the Revenges of God would have long since rendred

---

[1] "Wicked settlements."

it as a *fiery Oven*, if our blessed JESUS had not *interceded* for it: *O my Saviour, what would have become of me, and of all that comforts me, if thy Interposition had not preserved us!*

We will add one thing more: Tho the one GOD in His *three Subsistences* be the *Governor* as well as the *Creator* of the World, and so the *Son* of God ever had what we call the *natural Government* of the World, yet upon the *Fall* of Mankind there is a *mediatory Kingdom* that becomes expedient, that so *guilty Man*, and that which was *lost*, may be brought to God; and the singular Honour of this *mediatory Kingdom* is more *immediately* and most *agreeably* assign'd to the *Son of God*, who assumes the Man JESUS into His own Person, and has *all Power in Heaven and Earth given to Him;* all things are now commanded and ordered by the *Son of God* in the *Man upon the Throne*, and this *to the Glory of the Father*, by whom the *mediatory Kingdom* is erected, and so conferred. This *peculiar Kingdom* thus managed by the *Son of God* in our JESUS, will cease when the illustrious Ends of it are all accomplished, and *then* the *Son of God* no longer having such a *distinct Kingdom* of His own, shall return to those eternal Circumstances, wherein He shall reign with the *Father* and the *Holy Spirit*, one God, blessed for ever. In the mean time, what Creatures can we behold without being obliged to some such Doxology as this; *O Son of God, incarnate and enthroned in my JESUS, this is part of thy Dominion! What a great King art thou, and what a Name hast thou above every Name, and how vastly extended is thy Dominion! Dominion and Fear is with thee, and there is no Number of thine Armies! All the Inhabitants of the Earth, and their most puissant Emperors, are to be reputed as nothing before thee!*

But then at last I am losing myself in such Thoughts as these: *Who can tell* what *Uses* our Saviour will put all these *Creatures* to at the *Restitution of all things*, when He comes to rescue them from the *Vanity* which as yet captivates them and incumbers them; and His raised People in the *new Heavens* will make their Visits to a *new Earth*, which they shall find flourishing in *Paradisaick* Regularities? *Lord, what thou meanest in them, I know not now, but I shall know hereafter!* I go on, *Who can tell* how sweetly our Saviour may *feast* His *chosen People* in the *Future State*, with Exhibitions of all these *Creatures*, in their various *Natures*, and their curious *Beauties* to them? *Lord, I hope for an eternally progressive Knowledge, from the Lamb of God successively leading me to the Fountains of it!*

I recover out of my more *conjectural Prognostications*, with resolving what may *at present* yield to a serious Mind a *Satisfaction*, to which this World knows none superior: When in a way of *occasional Reflection* I employ the *Creatures* as my *Teachers*, I will by the *Truths* wherein those ready *Monitors* instruct me, be led to my glorious JESUS; I will consider the *Truths as they are in JESUS*, and count my *Asceticks* deficient, till I have some Thoughts of HIM and of His *Glories* awakened in me. To conclude, It is a good Passage which a little Treatise entitled, *Theologia Ruris*, or, *The Book of Nature*, breaks off withal, and I might make it my Conclusion: 'If we mind *Heaven* whilst 'we live here upon *Earth*, this *Earth* will serve to conduct 'us to *Heaven*, thro the Merits and Mediation of the '*Son of God*, who was made the *Son of Man*, and came 'thence on purpose into this lower World to convey us 'up thither.'

I will finish with a Speculation, which my most

valuable Dr. *Cheyne* has a little more largely prosecuted and cultivated.

All *intelligent compound Beings* have their whole Entertainment in these three Principles, the DESIRE, the OBJECT, and the SENSATION arising from the *Congruity* between them; this *Analogy* is preserved full and clear thro the *Spiritual World*, yea, and thro the *material* also; so *universal* and *perpetual* an *Analogy* can arise from nothing but its *Pattern* and *Archetype* in the infinite God or Maker; and could we carry it up to the Source of it, we should find the TRINITY of Persons in the eternal GODHEAD admirably exhibited to us. In the GODHEAD we may first apprehend a *Desire*, an infinitely active, ardent, powerful *Thought*, proposing of *Satisfaction;* let this represent GOD the FATHER: but it is not possible for any Object but God Himself to *satisfy Himself*, and fill His *Desire* of Happiness; therefore HE Himself *reflected* in upon Himself, and contemplating His own infinite Perfections, even the *Brightness of His Glory*, and the *express Image of His Person*, must answer this glorious Intention; and this may represent to us GOD the SON. Upon this Contemplation, wherein GOD Himself does behold, and possess, and enjoy Himself, there cannot but arise a *Love*, a *Joy*, an *Acquiescence* of God Himself within Himself, and worthy of a God; this may shadow out to us the third and the last of the Principles in this *mysterious Ternary*, that is to say, the Holy SPIRIT. Tho these *three Relations* of the Godhead in itself, when derived analogically down to Creatures, may appear but *Modifications* of a *real Subsistence*, yet in the supreme Infinitude of the Divine Nature, they must be infinitely *real* and *living* Principles. Those which are but *Relations* when transferred to *created Beings*, are glorious REALITIES in the infinite God.   And in this View of the Holy Trinity, low as it is, it is impossible the SON should be without the FATHER, or the FATHER without the SON, or both without the Holy SPIRIT; it is impossible the SON should not be necessarily and eternally begotten of the FATHER, or that the Holy SPIRIT should not necessarily and eternally proceed both from Him and from the SON. Thus from what occurs throughout the whole Creation, *Reason* forms an imperfect Idea of this incomprehensible Mystery.

But it is time to stop here, and indeed how can we go any further!

FINIS

"POLITICAL FABLES."

I. THE NEW SETTLEMENT OF THE BIRDS IN NEW ENGLAND.

The birds had maintained good order among themselves for several years, under the shelter of charters by Jupiter granted to several flocks among them: but heaven, to chastise many faults too observable in its birds, left them to be deprived of their ancient settlements. There were birds of all sorts in their several flocks; for some catched fish, some lived upon grains; the woodpeckers also made a great figure among them; some of them scraped for their living with their claws; and many supplied their nests, from beyond sea. Geese you may be sure there were good store, as there are everywhere. Moreover, when they had lost their charters, those poetical birds called harpies became really existent, and visited these flocks, not so much that they might build nests of their own, as plunder and pull down the nests of others.

2. There were many endeavours used by an eagle and a goldfinch, afterwards accompanied with two more, —no less deserving the love of all the flocks, than desirous to serve their interest,—that flew into Jupiter's palace, for the resettlement of good government among the birds. These endeavours did for awhile prosper no further than to stop the inroads of harpies or locusts; but at length Jupiter's court was willing that Jupiter's grace, which would have denied nothing for the advantage of them, whose wings had carried them a thousand leagues to serve his empire, should not be hindered from

giving them a comfortable settlement, though not
exactly in their old forms.

3. Upon this there grew a difference of opinion between some that were concerned for the welfare of the
birds. Some were of opinion, that if Jupiter would not
reinstate the birds in all their ancient circumstances,
they had better accept of just nothing at all, but let
all things be left for the harpies to commit as much
rapine as they were doing when they were ejecting
every poor bird out of his nest, that would not, at an
excessive rate, produce a patent for it; and when Canary
birds[1] domineered over all the flocks. Others were of
opinion, that the birds ought rather thankfully to
accept the offers of Jupiter; and if anything were yet
grievous, they might shortly see a fitter season to ask
further favours, especially considering that Jupiter
made them offer of such things as all the other American
birds would part with more than half the feathers on
their backs to purchase. He offered that the birds
might be everlastingly confirmed in their titles to their
nests and fields. He offered that not so much as a
twig should be plucked from any tree the birds would
roost upon, without their own consent. He offered
that the birds might constantly make their own laws,
and annually choose their own rulers. He offered that
all strange birds might be made uncapable of a seat
in their council.[2] He offered that it should be made
impossible for any to disturb the birds in singing of
their songs to the praise of their Maker, for which they
had sought liberty in the wilderness. Finally, he offered
that the king's-fisher should have his commission to be
their governour until they had settled what good orders

[1] "Canary bird" was a slang term for rogue.
[2] "Strange birds" = non-citizens.

among them they pleased; and that he should be more concerned than ever now to defend them from the French kites that were abroad. The king's-fisher indeed was to have his negative upon the birds, but the birds were to have a negative too upon the king's-fisher; and this was a privilege beyond what was enjoyed by the birds in any of the plantations, or even in Ireland itself.

4. The birds, not being agreed in their opinion, resolved that they would refer it to reasonable creatures to advise them upon this question—which of these was to be chosen; but when the reasonable creatures heard the question, they all declared none that had any reason could make any question of it.

II. THE ELEPHANT'S CASE A LITTLE STATED.

When Jupiter had honoured the elephant with a commission to be governour over the wilderness, there were certain beasts that began to quarrel with him for accepting that commission. The chief matter of mutter among themselves was to this purpose: They had nothing to say against the elephant; he was as good as he was great; he loved his king and country better than himself, and was as universally beloved. But (they said) they feared he was but a shoeing-horn; in a year or two either Isgrim the wolf, or Bruin the bear, would succeed him. Jupiter's commissions may come into such hands as will most cruelly oppress those, whom Jupiter most graciously designs to protect.

2. The elephant understood these growlings, and assembling the malecontents, he laid these charms upon them: "My countrymen, 'tis I that have kept off the shoe, whereof ye are so afraid. I had refused the

commission for your government, if I had not seen that you had certainly come into Isgrim's or Bruin's hands upon my refusal. My desire is, that Jupiter may have the satisfaction of seeing you saved from the dangers of perishing either by division among yourselves, or by invasion from abroad, was what caused me to accept my commission. Besides, Jupiter hath now favoured you with such circumstances, that if Isgrim or Bruin themselves should come, they could not hurt you without your own consent. They might not raise one tax, or make one law, or constitute one civil office, or send one soldier out of the province, without your concurrence. And if, after all that I have done for you, not only employing of my purse, but also venturing my life to serve you, you have no better name for me than a shoeing-horn, yet I have at least obtained this for you, that you have time to shape your foot, so as, whatever shoe comes, it shall sit · easy upon you."

3. Upon this the whole forest, with grateful and cheerful hearts, gave thanks unto the elephant; and they aspired to such an exercise of reason, in this as well as in other cases, that they might not be condemned to graze under Nebuchadnezer's belly.

III. MERCURY'S NEGOTIATION.

Mercury had been long diverted from his desired employment of carrying messages between earth and heaven, by his agency in Jupiter's palace on the behalf of the sheep, for whom he was willing to do the kindness of a shepherd. It grieved his heart within him to see the beasts of prey breaking in upon the sheep, after their folds had been by the foxes broken down.

2. He laboured with an assiduous diligence to get

the sheep accommodated in all their expectations: but after long waiting and seeking to get their folds rebuilt after the old fashion, he found it necessary to comply with such directions as Jupiter, by the advice of Janus, had given for the new shaping of the folds; otherwise he saw the poor sheep had been left without any folds at all; and he could not but confess, the new modelling of the folds would more effectually defend them, in these days of common danger, from the wolves, though some inconveniences in it had caused him always to use all means for the sheep's better satisfaction.

3. When Mercury returned to the sheep, he found them strangely metamorphosed from what they were, and miserably discontented. He found that such things as the sheep would have given three quarters of the fleece on their backs to have purchased, when he first went from them, they were now scarce willing to accept of. He found that there were, (though a few,) which had the skins of sheep on them, and yet, by their claws and growls, were indeed, he knew not what. He was ready to inquire, whether no mad dogs had let fall their slaver upon the honest sheep, since he found here and there one begun to bark like them, and he feared whether these distempers might not hinder their ever being folded more.

4. Orpheus had an harp, which sometimes formerly had reduced the beasts unto a temper little short of reason, and being jealous lest the hard censures bleated out against Mercury (as if he had been the cause of their new forms now brought upon the folds) might produce ill effects, he improved his harp upon this occasion. I don't remember the rhythm of his notes, but the reason was to this purpose: "Pray, all you friends, which of Mercury's administrations is it

whereat you are so much offended? Are you angry
because he evidently ventured the ruin of his person
and family by the circumstances of his first appearance
in Saturn's palace for you? Are you angry because,
for divers years together, he did, with an industry
indefatigable to a prodigy, solicit for the restoration of
your old folds; but with a vexation like that of Sysiphus,
who was to roll a great stone up an high hill, from
whence he was presently kicked down, so that the
labour was all to begin again? Are you angry because
he has employed all the interest which God has wonderfully given him with persons of the greatest quality,
to increase the number of your powerful friends:
addressing the king and queen, the nobility, the con-
vention and the parliaments, until the resettling of
your old folds was most favourably voted for you?
Is your anger because the signal hand of heaven overruled all these endeavours? Or is your displeasure
that he hath cost you a little money to support his
negotiations? I am to tell you, that he spent two
hundred pounds of his own personal estate in your
service—never like to be repaid. He made over all his
own American estate, that he might borrow more to
serve you. At length he has obtained in boon for your
college, and in the bounty, which he lately begged of
the royal Juno, (a bounty worth more than fourteen
or sixteen hundred pounds sterling,) got more for you
than he has yet expended for your agency. Had you
not starved your own cause, you had never missed so
much as you say you have of your own expectations.
Besides, how came you to have your title to all your
lands and properties confirmed for ever? Not one of
you doth own one foot of land, but what you are now
beholden to Mercury for your being undisturbed in it.

Are you displeased because you have not a reversion of the judgment against your folds? It was none of his fault; and had such a thing happened, you had then been far more miserable than you are now like to be: for both Plymouth and the eastern provinces had been most certainly put under a commission government; so likewise had Hampshire; and if they should have a Brellin,[1] yet his government would have reached as far south as Salem itself. How finely had your flock been deprived of your trade by this, and squeezed into an atom! Nor could you have proceeded again, as formerly, upon your charter, without being quo-warrantoed. Are you displeased because he did accept of Jupiter's offers? I say he did not accept, and the way is left open for you to recover all the liberties you would have, when you see a time to move in a legal way for it. Yea, he did absolutely reject as many of the offers as he could, and procured them to be altered. The rest he did not refuse, because you had infallibly been left open to a western condition,[2] if he had gone on to protest. Moreover you yourselves had for-bidden him to refuse. Are you troubled because your liberties, whether as Christians or as Englishmen, are fully secured? Are you troubled because you have privileges above any part of the English nation what-soever, either abroad or at home? Are you troubled that your officers are to be for ever your own; so that, if you please, you may always have your judges as at the first, and the counsellors as at the beginning? Is

[1] Probably this is a misprint for Bruin, the bear, who, in the Reynard story, conspired to make himself King in place of the lion. Or, it may be a misprint for Belin, the ram, a character in the same story.

[2] "Western" is used in the not unusual sense of "declining," "nearing the end."

it your trouble that by being without your charter, you are put into a condition to do greater and better things for yourselves than the charter did contain, or could have done? Did any man living more zealously oppose those one or two things that you account undesirable, than this faithful Mercury, at whom you fret for those things? Or must very much good be frowardly thrown away, because 'tis not all? If you would have more, don't blame your Mercury that you have so much."—So sang Orpheus, and, for the better harmony of the musick, eleven more of the celestial choristers[1] joined with him in it.

5. The sound of those things caused the sheep to be a little better satisfied; but Mercury was not much concerned whether they were or no, for he looked elsewhere for all the reward of his charitable undertakings; and he knows, he that would do froward sheep a kindness must do it them against their wills; only he wished the sheep would have a care of all snakes in the grass, who did mischief by insinuating, and employed their hisses to sow discord.

IV. An additional STORY OF THE DOGS AND THE WOLVES, the Substance of which was used, an hundred and fifty Years ago, by Melancthon,[2] to unite the Protestants.

The wolves and the dogs were going to meet each other in a battle, upon a certain old quarrel that was between them; and the wolves, that they might know the strength of the dogs aforehand, sent forth a scout.

2. The scout returned, and informed the wolves that the dogs were more numerous than they. Neverthe-

[1] See Introduction, Section V.
[2] Philipp Melancthon, the great German reformer.

less, he bid them not be discouraged; for the dogs were not only divided into three or four several bodies, which had little disposition to help one another, but also they were very quarrelsome among themselves. One party was for having the army formed one way, and another party another. Some were not satisfied in their commanders; and the commanders themselves had their emulations. Nor did they want those among them, that accounted it more necessary to lie down where they were, and hunt and kill flees, than march forth to subdue wolves abroad. In short, there was little among them but snapping and snarling at one another; And therefore, said he, monsieurs,[1] let's have at them: we shall easily play the wolf upon them that have played the dog upon one another.

3. This is a story so old, that, as the good man said, I hope it is not true.

[1] This word identifies the wolves as the French.

COTTON MATHER'S LETTER TO DR. WOODWARD ABOUT "AN HORRID SNOW"

10d. X m. 1717.
[December 10, 1717]

Sr

Tho' we are gott so far onward at the Beginning of another Winter, yett we have not forgott the Last: which at the Latter End whereof, we were Entertained & overwhelmed with a *Snow*, which was attended with some Things that were uncommon enough, to afford matter for a letter from us. The *Winter* was not so bad as that wherein *Tacitus* tells us that *Corbulo* made his Expedition against the *Parthians*. Nor like that which proved so fatal to the Beasts & Birds, in the Days of the Emperour *Justinian* [nor?] that wherein the very Fishes were killed under the Freezing Sea, when *Phocas* did as much to the men whom Tyrants treat like the Fishes of the Sea.[1] But the Conclusion of our *Winter* was hard enough, & was too formidable to be easily forgotten: and of a peece with what you had in *Europe*, a year before. The *Snow* was the Chief Thing that made it so. For tho' rarely does a *Winter* pass us, wherein we may not say with *Pliny*, *Ingens Hyeme Nivis apud nos copia*;[2] yett the Last *Winter* brought with it a *Snow* that Excelled them all. A *Snow* tis true, not equal to that which once fell and Lay Twenty Cubits high, about the Beginning of

[1] Corbulo, Roman general in the first century; Phocas was a tyrannical emperor of Constantinople from 602 to 610.

[2] "A great supply of snow with us in winter."

October, in the parts about the *Euxine Sea*. Nor to that, which the *French Annals* tell us, kept falling for twenty Nine weeks together. Nor to several mentioned by *Boethius*, wherein vast Numbers of people, and of Cattel, perished; Nor to those that *Strabo* finds upon *Caucasus* and *Rhodiginus* in *Armenia*.[1] But yett such an one, and attended with such Circumstances, as may deserve to be Remembred.

On the Twentieth of the Last *February*, there came on a *Snow*, which being added unto what had covered the ground a few Days before, made a Thicker Mantle for our Mother[2] than what was usual: And the Storm with it, was for the following Day so violent, as to make all communication between the Neighbours every where to cease. People for some Hours could not pass from one side of a Street unto another, and the poor Women, who happened at this critical time to fall into Travail, were putt into Hardships which anon produced many odd Stories for us. But on the Twenty-fourth Day of the Month comes *Pelion* upon Ossa. Another *Snow* came on, which almost buried the Memory of the former: With a Storm so furious, that Heaven laid an Interdict on the Religious Assemblies throughout the countrey on this Lords-day, the like whereunto had never been seen before. The Indians near an hundred years old, affirm, that their Fathers never told them of any thing that equall'd it. Vast Numbers of Cattel were destroy'd in this Calamity; Whereof some that were of the Stronger Sort, were found standing Dead on their Legs, as if they had been alive, many weeks after, when the Snow melted away. And others had

[1] Strabo, geographer of the first century B.C.; Luigi Rhodiginus was an Italian philologist and savant, who lived from 1450–1525.

[2] "Mother Earth."

their Eyes glazed over with Ice at such a rate, that being not far from the Sea, they went out of their way, and drowned them there.

One Gentleman, on whose Farms, there were now Lost above eleven hundred *Sheep*, which with other cattel were Interred (Shall I Say, or Inniv'd) in the Snow; writes me That there were Two *Sheep* very singularly circumstanced. For no Less than Eight & Twenty Days after the Storm, the people pulling out the Ruines of above an hundred Sheep, out of a Snow-bank, which Lay sixteen foot high drifted over them, there were Two found alive, which had been there all this time, & kept themselves alive by Eating the Wool of their Dead Companions. When they were taken out, they shed their own Fleeces, but soon gott into good Case again.

Sheep were not the only creatures, that Lived unaccountably for whole weeks without their usual Sustenance, entirely buried in the *Snow-drifts*. The *Swine* had a share with the *Sheep* in Strange Survivals. A man had a couple of Young *Hogs*, which he gave over for Dead; But on the twenty-seventh day after their Burial, they made their way out of a *Snow-bank*, at the bottom of which they had found a Little Tansy to feed upon.

The *Poultry* as unaccountably survived as these. *Hens* were found alive, after *Seven Days; Turkeys* were found alive, after *five & Twenty Days;* Buried in the Snow, and at a Distance from the Ground; and altogether destitute of any thing to feed them.

The Number of Creatures, that kept a *Rigid Fast*, shutt up in *Snow*, for several weeks together, & were found Alive after all, have yielded surprizing stories to us.

The Wild Creatures of the Woods, (the *Outgoings of the Evening*) made their Descent as well as they could in this Time of Scarcity for them, towards the Sea-side. A vast multitude of Deer for the Same Cause taking the Same Course, & the Deep Snow Spoiling them of their only Defence: which is, *To Run*, they became such a prey to those Devourers, that it is thought, not one in Twenty Escaped.

But here again occurr'd a Curiosity.

These carniverous Sharpers, and especially the *Foxes*, would make their *Nocturnal Visits*, to the Pens, where the people had their *Sheep* defended from them. The poor Ewes big with young were so terrified with the frequent Approaches of the *Foxes*, & the Terror had such Impression on them, that most of the *Lambs* brought forth in the Spring following, were of Monsieur *Reinard's* complexion, when the Dams were all either *White* or *Black*.

It was remarkable, that immediately after the Fall of the Snow, an infinite multitude of *Sparrows*, made their Appearance; but then after a short continuance all disappeared.

It is incredible, how much Damage was done to the *Orchards;* For the Snow freezing to a Crust, as high as the Boughs of the Trees, anon Splitt them to peeces. The Cattle also, walking on the Crusted Snow, a dozen foot from the Ground, so fed upon the Trees as very much to damnify them.

The Ocean was in a prodigious Ferment, and after it was over, Vast Heaps of Little Shells were driven ashore, where they were never seen before. Mighty Shoals of Porpoises, also kept a Play-day in the Disturbed waves of our Harbours.

The odd Accidents befalling many poor people, whose

Cottages were totally covered with the Snow, & not the very tops of their Chimneys to be seen, would afford a Story; But there not being any Relacion to philosophy in them, I forbear them. And now, *I am Satis Terris Nivis*.[1] —And here is enough of my Winter-tale. If it serve to no other purpose, yett it will give me an opportunity to tell you, That Nine months ago, I did a thousand times wish myself with you in *Gresham-Colledge*, which is never so horribly Snow'd upon. But instead of so great a satisfaction, all I can attain to, is the pleasure of talking with you in this Epistolary way, and subscribing myself,

Syr, Yours with an Affection that knows no Winter

[Cotton Mather]

Dr Woodward.

[1] "Now enough of snow on earth."
[2] Woodward lived at Gresham College, where he was professor of physic.